ARISTOTLE ON POLITICAL COMMUNITY

Aristotle's claims that "man is a political animal" and that political community "exists for the sake of living well" have frequently been celebrated by thinkers of divergent political persuasions. The details of his political philosophy, however, have often been regarded as outmoded, contradictory, or pernicious. This book takes on the major problems that arise in attempting to understand how the central pieces of Aristotle's political thought fit together: can a conception of politics that seems fundamentally inclusive and egalitarian be reconciled with a vision of justice that seems uncompromisingly hierarchical and authoritarian? Riesbeck argues that Aristotle's ideas about the distinctive nature and value of political community, political authority, and political participation are coherent and consistent with his aristocratic standards of justice. The result is a theory that, while not free of problems, remains a potentially fruitful resource for contemporary thinking about the persistent problems of political life.

DAVID J. RIESBECK earned his PhD from the Joint Classics and Philosophy Graduate Program in Ancient Philosophy at the University of Texas at Austin. He has taught at the University of Texas, Dartmouth College, and Rice University. His articles and reviews have appeared in *Ancient Philosophy*, *Apeiron*, *Bryn Mawr Classical Review*, *Classical Quarterly*, *Phoenix*, and *Reason Papers*.

ARISTOTLE ON
POLITICAL COMMUNITY

DAVID J. RIESBECK

Rice University, Houston

CAMBRIDGE
UNIVERSITY PRESS

CAMBRIDGE
UNIVERSITY PRESS

University Printing House, Cambridge CB2 8BS, United Kingdom

Cambridge University Press is part of the University of Cambridge.

It furthers the University's mission by disseminating knowledge in the pursuit of education, learning, and research at the highest international levels of excellence.

www.cambridge.org
Information on this title: www.cambridge.org/9781107107021

© David J. Riesbeck 2016

First published 2016

Printed in the United States of America by Sheridan Books, Inc.

A catalog record for this publication is available from the British Library.

Library of Congress Cataloging-in-Publication Data
Names: Riesbeck, David J., 1980– author.
Title: Aristotle on political community / David J. Riesbeck,
Rice University, Houston.
Description: Cambridge, United Kingdom : Cambridge University Press, 2016. |
Includes bibliographical references and index.
Identifiers: LCCN 2016008993 | ISBN 9781107107021 (hardback)
Subjects: LCSH: Aristotle – Political and social views. |
Aristotle. Politics. | Kings and rulers.
Classification: LCC JC71.A7 R54 2016 | DDC 320.01/1–dc23
LC record available at https://lccn.loc.gov/2016008993

ISBN 978-1-107-10702-1 Hardback

For Richard Riesbeck and Judith Blasch

ἔστι δ' ἡ μὲν πρὸς γονεῖς φιλία τέκνοις, καὶ ἀνθρώποις πρὸς
θεούς, ὡς πρὸς ἀγαθὸν καὶ ὑπερέχον· εὖ γὰρ πεποιήκασι τὰ
μέγιστα· τοῦ γὰρ εἶναι καὶ τραφῆναι αἴτιοι, καὶ γενομένοις
τοῦ παιδευθῆναι.

Nicomachean Ethics VIII.12 1162a4–7

Contents

Acknowledgments

This book began its life as a doctoral dissertation completed at the University of Texas at Austin in 2012. I remain grateful to the members of my dissertation committee for their guidance and feedback: Stephen White, Michael Gagarin, Donald Morrison, Paula Perlman, and Paul Woodruff. Stephen White and Donald Morrison have remained generous, patient, and insightful critics as I have worked to transform the dissertation into a book. In addition to the time that they have spent reading and discussing my work, I owe each a special debt: to Steve I owe most of whatever skill I have developed in reading ancient philosophical texts closely and writing about them carefully, and to Don I owe a great deal of inspiration and encouragement of the sort that arises only from friendly but persistent philosophical disagreement. Though both will no doubt wish that I had taken their advice more often, I could not have written this book without it.

Several other friends and colleagues provided helpful written comments on portions of the manuscript at various stages of revision: Marquis Berrey, Joe Bullock, Margaret Graver, Jerry Green, Dhananjay Jagannathan, and the anonymous readers for Cambridge University Press. I am especially grateful to Joe Bullock, who read the entire manuscript at a late stage and offered an astounding number of invaluable suggestions on topics ranging from punctuation to the details of my central arguments. Though any errors that remain are my own, I am certain that I would have been guilty of many more without his help.

I have also profited from discussion and correspondence on the topics of this book with a number of scholars both senior and junior: Audrey Anton, David Armstrong, Elizabeth Asmis, Robert Bolton, Eric Brown, Daniela Cammack, David Chan, Pramit Chaudhuri, Giuseppe Cumella, Howard Curzer, Javier Echeñique, Eugene Garver, Owen Goldin, Edward Halper, Kazutaka Inamura, Irfan Khawaja, Mariska Leunissen, Thornton Lockwood, Alexander Mourelatos, Martha Nussbaum, Michael Pakaluk,

James Patterson, Christopher Raymond, C. D. C. Reeve, Jeremy Reid, John Ryan, Luis Salas, Lea Aurelia Schröder, and Michael Sevel. In some cases even a brief conversation has planted seeds that have sprouted in the pages that follow, while in others extended dialogue has helped me to refine my arguments and to address questions that I might otherwise have overlooked.

Much of the work on this book was undertaken while I was a member, first, of the Department of Classics at Dartmouth College and then of the Department of Classical Studies at Rice University. I am grateful to my colleagues in both departments for their support and for the opportunity to join them in teaching truly outstanding students.

I owe a debt of a more personal order to Jennifer Cummings, who endured me with grace and dexterity from my introduction to the Greek alphabet to the completion of my dissertation and well beyond. Were it not for her distaste for Aristotle, this book might have been dedicated to her. Instead it is dedicated to my father, Richard Riesbeck, who makes it all happen, and my mother, Judith Blasch, who keeps it all going.

Portions of Chapter 4 appeared in a modified form in "Aristotle on the Politics of Marriage: 'Marital Rule' in the *Politics*", *Classical Quarterly* 65.1, 134–52. I am grateful to the Classical Association for permission to reprint that material here.

Abbreviations

Works by or Attributed to Aristotle

AP	*Athenaion Politeia* (Athenian Constitution)
Catg.	*Categoriae* (Categories)
DA	*De Anima* (On the Soul)
EE	*Ethica Eudemia* (Eudemian Ethics)
EN	*Ethica Nicomachea* (Nicomachean Ethics)
GA	*De Generatione Animalium* (Generation of Animals)
GC	*De Generatione et Corruptione* (Generation and Corruption)
HA	*Historia Animalium* (History of Animals)
Met.	*Metaphysica* (Metaphysics)
Metr.	*Meteorologica* (Meteorology)
Phys.	*Physica* (Physics)
Poet.	*De Arte Poetica* (Poetics)
Pol.	*Politica* (Politics)
Rhet.	*Rhetorica* (Rhetoric)
Sens.	*De Sensu et Sensibilibus* (Sense and Sensibilia)
Top.	*Topica* (Topics)

Works by Plato

Ap.	*Apologia* (Apology)
Charm.	*Charmides*
Euthyd.	*Euthydemus*
Lys.	*Lysis*
Plt.	*Politicus* (Statesman)
Prot.	*Protagoras*

xi

Other Works

Dreizehnter	Dreizehnter, A. (ed.). 1970. *Aristoteles' Politik*. Munich
Hdt.	Herodotus, *Histories*
LSJ	Liddell, H. G., Scott, R., and Jones, H. S. 1996. *A Greek-English Lexicon*. Oxford
Ross	Ross, W. D. (ed.). 1957. *Aristotelis Politica*. Oxford
Smyth	Smyth, H.W. 1956. *Greek Grammar*. rev. G.M. Messing. Cambridge, MA
Susemihl	Susemihl, F. (ed.). 1894. *Aristotelis Politica*. Leipzig
Thucy.	Thucydides, *History of the Peloponnesian War*
Mem.	Xenophon, *Memorabilia*

Introduction: Community and Exclusion

The outstanding contribution of Aristotle's *Politics* to subsequent Western political thought is its distinctive conception of political community. This conception is distinctive in several ways. It is, first, distinctively Aristotle's. The opening chapter of the work's first book announces its disagreement with its predecessors, and though it declines to give names, the alternative view that Aristotle labors against is prominent in Plato, pervasive in Xenophon, and plausible enough on its face. That view is that the sort of authority or "rule" exercised in political communities is the same in kind as that exercised in any other human community. Aristotle insists to the contrary on the heterogeneity of various forms of authority, and he correlates these forms with corresponding kinds of community. The association of citizens cooperating together for the sake of their common good is to be contrasted with the relationships characteristic of a household, a village, and alternative varieties of complex social organization. Political community is marked off from all of these by its mode of authority, one that distinguishes the relations between citizens from those between masters and slaves, fathers and children, or husbands and wives. Citizens cooperate on a basis of fundamental equality, and the authority they exercise over one another is characteristically shared. Citizens reach collective decisions about their common affairs through shared deliberation, and they alternate in occupying positions of special responsibility and privilege. To be a citizen is to share in ruling as well as being ruled, and to rule one's fellow citizens is, accordingly, to shape and direct the actions of others who also shape and direct one's own, whether concurrently or by turns. Whereas a master rules his slaves for the sake of his own benefit, political rule is exercised for the sake of those subject to it. On Aristotle's view, politics differs from mastery, from parenting, and from marriage in key part through the intensely mutual and reciprocal character of this relationship. So this conception of political community is not just distinctively Aristotle's; it is a conception of a distinctive kind of community with a correspondingly distinctive variety of ruling and being ruled.

Political community stands apart from other varieties of cooperative human association in another, equally fundamental way. While all other communities aim at some more limited goal for their members, political communities aim at nothing short of the good life as a whole for their citizens. The peculiarly broad scope of this goal and the role it plays in guiding and limiting the pursuit of other, subordinate ends help to explain the characteristic shape of life in the city or polis, the only form of community that Aristotle takes to pursue this end in an organized and genuinely common fashion.[1] Likewise, the city's goal generates a set of normative requirements for its achievement, and these requirements in turn yield a framework for assessing real and hypothetical political arrangements in terms of their impact on the common good. Aristotle's concept of the political is a densely interwoven structure of value and fact, a feature that is nowhere so clear as in his famous dictum that "the human being is by nature a political animal" (*Pol.* 1.2.1253a7–18, 3.6.1278b15–30, cf. *EE* 7.10.1242a19–28, *EN* 8.12.1162a16–19, 9.9.1169b16–22).[2] This slogan encapsulates not only the idea that distinctively political communities emerge from the unimpeded development of human beings' natural capacities, but the closely related thought that the emergence of these communities is a necessary condition for the full development and integral expression of those capacities. The city is natural and human beings are political animals because it is only in and through political community that rational animals can flourish in a fully human way. Aristotelian political community therefore has both a distinctive nature and a peculiar value.

This conception of the political has been one of Aristotle's chief legacies to his intellectual heirs, and it continues to be a valuable resource for thinking about politics. Though it has had considerably less contemporary influence than the leading ideas of the *Nicomachean Ethics*, it nonetheless

---

[1] Modern historians have tended to agree that the ancient Greek polis was a distinctive, though not necessarily unique, form of social and political organization. They have disagreed about its precise character. The traditional translation "city-state" presents the polis as a centralized, politically autonomous unit formed around an urban settlement. Some more recent scholars have preferred the term "citizen-state," emphasizing the role that active membership in the community played in the institutions and ideology of the polis. Still others have argued that the polis was not a state, but either a fusion of a centralized state and a broader "civil society" or in fact a stateless society. For different views, compare Hansen 2002 with Berent 2004; Hansen 2006a; Vlassopoulos 2007; Cartledge 2009: 11–24. In part to avoid these disputes, I will either leave polis untranslated or use the English "city" as a neutral stand-in.

[2] All translations are my own unless otherwise noted.

commends itself especially to thinkers dissatisfied with dominant modern paradigms of political thought and action. To some, Aristotle has seemed to offer an alternative, if not exactly an antidote, to an emaciated vision of politics as a limited and strictly instrumental affair with the purely negative aim of protecting individual rights or minimizing social conflict. By contrast, the *Politics* lays its emphasis on the substantive goods that people share and the forms of cooperation in which they can obtain and enjoy them. Where the general drift of modern political thought has been to view individuals either as fundamentally asocial atoms or as the instrumental parts of a collective organism, Aristotle presents us with profoundly social individuals who become who they are by participation in forms of community directed toward their mutual good. In place of an identification of politics with the exercise of state power and its associated forms of bureaucratic management, Aristotelian political community provides a model for thinking about politics in terms of participation in structures of common deliberation within, beneath, or even wholly apart from the state.[3] However wide of the mark any particular contemporary appropriation of Aristotle may be, perhaps the plainest indication of the continuing power of the *Politics* to provoke and inspire is the sheer diversity of projects and perspectives to which it makes a significant contribution, as thinkers deeply at odds with one another on practical and theoretical matters nonetheless draw explicitly upon Aristotelian resources.[4] Though Aristotle has sometimes been taken as representative

[3] The term "state" is used in a confusing variety of ways by scholars working in different disciplines. I here follow many contemporary legal and political philosophers in using the term in a relatively narrow sense given currency by Max Weber: a state is "a human community that (successfully) claims the *monopoly of the legitimate use of physical force* within a given territory" (Weber 1946: 78). In this sense, the state and its associated institutions are distinguished from the much broader realm of civil society, which is characterized by notionally voluntary associations.

[4] Aristotle's *Politics* played an important, if not quite a central, role in the thought of Hannah Arendt and Leo Strauss, who, for all their differences, both turned to ancient Greek texts as a source for an understanding of politics that ran counter to what they perceived as the pitfalls of modernity: see esp. Arendt 1958; Strauss 1953, 1964. Aristotle's political thought has been a source of inspiration for the so-called communitarian critique of liberalism mounted in different ways by Alasdair MacIntyre, Michael Sandel, and Charles Taylor, though all three have rejected the "communitarian" label and draw on Aristotelian ideas in markedly different ways (in, e.g., MacIntyre 1984 and 1998; Taylor 1985; Sandel 1998). Of the three, MacIntyre associates himself most closely with Aristotle and the Aristotelian tradition: for overviews of his thought, see Murphy 2003 and D'Andrea 2006; for a history of the Aristotelian tradition that makes MacIntyre its *telos*, see Knight 2007. Thinkers less radical than MacIntyre have also stressed the application of Aristotelian ideas to nonstate communities: Simpson 1994; Young 2005; Morrell 2012. Other thinkers have drawn on Aristotle for theoretical insights taken to apply within the framework of liberal or social democratic states: Salkever 1990; Murphy 1993; Nussbaum 1990b, 2006; van Staveren 2001. Aristotle also plays an important role in one strand of recent libertarianism: Long 1996, 2005; Rasmussen and Den Uyl

of a more widely shared Greek vision of politics, he nonetheless remains its most articulate and outstanding spokesman.[5]

Despite the persistence of interest in Aristotelian political thought, the *Politics* as a whole has attracted less admiration. For many, the appeal of Aristotle's core conception of political community has been undercut by its association with a set of exclusionary and, some would say, reactionary commitments regarding slaves, women, laborers, and foreigners.[6] Aristotle defends the view that some human beings, and perhaps even most non-Greeks, are "slaves by nature"; he endorses the exclusion of women from politics and their subordination to their husbands on grounds of psychological deficiency; he advocates withholding citizenship from laborers and craftsmen; and he distinguishes sharply between the privileges and entitlements of citizens and those of mere resident aliens. Especially when coupled with the apparently limitless authority that Aristotle allows the community to exercise over individuals, these exclusions cast a dark shadow over his core conception of political community as the association of free and equal citizens sharing in ruling and being ruled.

Many of Aristotle's admirers have downplayed these exclusionary policies, dismissing them as mistaken judgments only contingently connected to the core of his political thought.[7] Admittedly, there is a strong case to be made that Aristotle's concept of political community depends for its content on contrasts between freedom and slavery, the city and the household, and citizen and foreigner.[8] Nonetheless, it is clear enough that these

2005. Tessitore 2002 and Goodman and Talisse 2007 collect essays from a variety of perspectives seeking to apply Aristotelian insights to contemporary political questions.

[5] For variants of the view that the Greeks invented politics in the sense of institutionalized public decision making preceded by collective deliberation and debate, see Meier 1980; Finley 1983: ch. 3; Gagarin 1986: 144–6; Cartledge 2009: 11–24. For a detailed synopsis of various notions of "politics" adopted by students of ancient Greece and Rome, see Hammer 2009. As I will make clear in the chapters that follow, Aristotle's conception of political community is too closely bound up with other aspects of his philosophy to make the *Politics* an unproblematic source for a generically "Greek" or "classical" idea of politics.

[6] For especially strong indictments of Aristotle on this score see, from a generally hostile perspective, Wood and Wood 1978 and, from within a self-styled Aristotelian point of view, Knight 2007.

[7] Nussbaum 1998 defends Aristotle's method against the charge that it is incapable of challenging ideologically entrenched beliefs, taking Aristotle's theories about women in both the *Politics* and the biological writings as flawed even by his own standards. So too MacIntyre 2006b: 156: "Aristotle's statement of his own positions is of course at some points in need of greater or less revision and at others – in, for example, his treatment of women, productive workers, and slavery – requires outright rejection. But the fruitful correction of these inadequacies and mistakes turned out to be best achieved by a better understanding of Aristotelian theory and practice."

[8] Aristotle would, of course, not be unique in this respect: for a forceful statement of the view that the ideology of freedom and citizenship central to the Athenian democracy depended on the tangible exclusion of slaves, women, and foreigners, see Wood 1996 in response to Hansen 1996b. It is incontrovertible that the concept of freedom essentially involves a contrast to that of slavery, but

conceptual contrasts need not be deployed in quite the way that Aristotle deployed them: a proponent of a fundamentally Aristotelian conception of politics can adopt a more cosmopolitan outlook and can affirm the dignity of labor, the equality of the sexes, and the categorical injustice of slavery.[9] So these problems with the *Politics* can perhaps be laid aside as unfortunate errors peripheral to its central insights.

Yet there are other indications that a more general tendency toward exclusion emerges from some of the core commitments of Aristotle's political thought. One central element of that thought is Aristotle's theory of justice in the distribution of political authority. This theory is designed to address one of the fundamental questions of politics: who gets to rule when, over what, and in what way? Various answers to this question are consistent with Aristotle's core conception of political community, but that conception clearly demands some answer or other. Aristotle's own approach to the question is not so much to answer it as to provide a framework for answering it in specific circumstances and for assessing the justice of particular distributions of authority and claims to inclusion or exclusion. This framework is his aristocratic or, as we might more naturally put it, merit-based conception of justice. He contrasts this conception with what he calls the democratic and oligarchic conceptions. All three agree that a just distribution assigns equal shares to equal parties and unequal shares to unequal parties. They disagree about the relevant criteria of equality. For oligarchs, the criterion is wealth, and wealthier citizens ought to have more political power. For democrats, by contrast, what is relevant is freedom, and since all free citizens are equally free, each ought to have an equal share (*Pol.* 3.9.1280a7–25, *EN* 5.3.1131a25–9).[10] Aristotle rejects both of these alternatives in favor of the eminently plausible view

while Wood and others are right to stress the role that actual social relations played in shaping the application of the concept in Athenian culture, Hansen correctly rejects the suggestion that the ancient concept is inapplicable to contexts in which there are no actual slaves.
9 For a neo-Aristotelian theory of the value and political significance of labor, see Murphy 1993. For discussions of the relationship between Aristotle and contemporary feminist theory, see Bar On 1994 and Freeland 1998, and for two rather different pieces of feminist theory that draw on Aristotle, see Nussbaum 2000 and Witt 2011. Contemporary philosophers rarely bother to argue against slavery, but Aristotle was already invoked in arguments against slavery in the New World by Francisco de Vitoria in his *De Indis* of 1539, on which see Pagden and Lawrance 1991, and by Bartolomé de Las Casas in his dispute with Juan Ginés de Sepúlveda in 1550, on which see Hanke 1994.
10 The *EN* passage includes "good birth" alongside freedom, wealth, and virtue, but neither there nor in the *Politics* does Aristotle take it seriously as a genuinely distinct criterion. He elsewhere understands "good birth" as "old wealth and virtue" (*Pol.* 4.8.1294a21–2). Hence he may disregard it as either a mixed or a redundant criterion. The main thrust of Aristotle's theory of distributive justice makes it clear that whether someone's wealth and virtue are inherited is irrelevant.

that authority ought to be assigned to those able to exercise it best. For Aristotle, the relevant criterion is neither freedom nor wealth, but the ability to contribute to the common good (*Pol.* 3.9.1280b39–1281a2, 12.1282b14–1283a22).[11]

Because the just distribution of authority in politics depends on the actual distribution of the citizens' ability to contribute to the common good, no single pattern of distribution is unconditionally just. Justice will demand different distributions in different circumstances. The context sensitivity of Aristotle's theory of justice leads him to a broad schematic division of constitutions or regimes – what he, following Greek convention, calls *politeiai* but perhaps less conventionally defines as arrangements of authority in political communities (3.6.1278b8–10, 4.3.1290a7–13). This schema categorizes constitutions by reference to two variables: the number of people who rule and whether those rulers exercise their authority in the interests of the common good or, conversely, subject the interests of others to their own. The constitutions whose rulers seek their own good at the expense of their fellow citizens are "deviations" (παρεκβάσεις) from their "correct" (ὀρθαί) counterparts, and those rulers may be many, few, or one. Hence kingship is the correct form of monarchy, while its far more common deviation is tyranny; oligarchy is the corrupt deviation of rule by the few, the correct form of which Aristotle calls aristocracy; and democracy he divides from the correct form of rule by the many, which he somewhat confusingly calls *politeia* but is often translated as "polity" in order distinguish it from the more general category (3.7.1279a22–b10). All three correct constitutions are just, but none will be suited to every community in every circumstance. If a minority of citizens is better able than the majority to promote the common good, then rule by the many will in fact be an unjust deviation, and hence, strictly speaking, not a polity at all.[12] Likewise, even an outstandingly excellent individual human being will be a tyrant rather than a king unless he is better able to rule than all of his fellow citizens.

Tidy as this scheme may be, it seems to lead to some problems for Aristotle and to reveal a deeper exclusionary tendency in his thought. Many readers have noticed an apparently inescapable contradiction

---

[11] Aristotle's argument in *Pol.* 3.9 and discussion of justice throughout the *Politics* presuppose the theory of *EN* 5, which Aristotle himself cites at *Pol.* 3.9.1280a18. My account owes much to Keyt 1991b and Miller 1995: ch. 3. For a more introductory treatment, see Roberts 2000.

[12] I discuss the relation between failing to promote the common good and ruling in one's own interest more fully in Chapter 5.

between the theory of constitutions and Aristotle's account of citizenship. By that account, a citizen is someone who shares in ruling as well as being ruled (3.1 1275b18–21). Rulers and citizens are therefore coextensive classes; a person with no share of rule is simply not a citizen. Consequently, the distinction between correct and deviant constitutions threatens to collapse. A large group of citizens might break down into smaller groups who each pursue their own interests at the expense of their fellows, and in this way rule by the many admits of unjust deviation from its correct form. Yet in other cases the distinction fails to apply. Because the few who rule in an oligarchy are themselves coextensive with the citizen body, to pursue their own interests is to pursue the common good of the citizens. The tyrant, aiming at his own benefit, thereby promotes the good of the citizen body, of which he happens to be the sole member. There is abundant evidence that Aristotle does not accept this implication: He pretty clearly believes that tyrants and oligarchs commit injustices against the people whom they exclude from power.

A prominent and now standard response to this problem is to conclude accordingly that Aristotle works with a broader notion of citizenship than his explicit definition allows, one that encompasses all of a city's free, native inhabitants. These are the people whose common good the rulers of a deviant constitution subvert.[13]

This response does little to dispel the suspicion that Aristotle's theory of justice tends toward exclusion of many individuals from full citizenship, and hence from full participation in political community. Even if the theory operates with an implicit notion of "second-class citizens" who do not share in rule, Aristotle's relegation of people to that status appears to deprive them of the opportunity to take any sort of active role in shaping the communally binding decisions that guide and constrain their shared lives with others.[14] Second-class citizens may benefit from the decisions made on their behalf, but they are nonetheless excluded from participating in the formation of those decisions. This sort of exclusion sits uneasily

---

[13] This problem was already apparent in the case of monarchy to Newman 1887–1902.i: 230. The now widely accepted solution was proposed independently by Cooper 1990 and Keyt 1993, both of whom recognize that the problem extends to aristocracy and oligarchy. Cooper and Keyt's solution was in some ways anticipated by Newman (see, e.g., Newman 1887–1902.i: 229, 324, 569–70). It is endorsed in the influential accounts of Miller 1995: 212; Roberts 2000 and 2009; and Kraut 2002: 385–6. Different interpretations pointing in a similar direction have been proposed, e.g., by Johnson 1984 and Nichols 1992, and the standard view has been challenged by Morrison 1999 and Biondi Khan 2005. I argue against all these interpretations and in favor of an alternative in Chapter 4.

[14] The phrase "second-class citizens" is from Keyt 1993.

with Aristotle's core conception of political community in at least two ways. First, it seems to deprive people of a good that Aristotle takes to be a crucial aspect of human well-being. If politics is supposed to be peculiarly valuable because it is in and through participation in political community that human beings flourish as rational animals, it would be a surprise if justice turns out to demand that large numbers of otherwise able and willing individuals be excluded from this participation, and in the name of their own common good, at that. Second, this tendency toward exclusion seems to be likewise a tendency toward an attenuation or even an outright dissolution of the political. If political community is supposed to be fundamentally a matter of shared rule, it would be a surprise if justice calls for dramatic limitations of mutuality and reciprocity in the exercise of authority.

Both of these problems are easiest to see in the case of monarchy, where they emerge in their purest and most severe forms. Aristotelian monarchy, it seems, is supposed to be a form of political community in which one person rules and everyone else is only ruled.[15] But if so, then kingship, the allegedly just variation of one-man rule, evidently denies to everyone but the king the participation in citizenship that was, we thought, essential to a fully good human life. If kingship deprives all but one person of a necessary condition for living well, then it is incompatible with justice and indistinguishable from tyranny. More paradoxically, monarchy seems to be inherently unpolitical. If political rule is necessarily shared and reciprocal, then a system in which only one person rules cannot be political in the first place: however suitable monarchy may be in other kinds of community, political monarchy is conceptually incoherent and hence impossible. Call the first of these problems the *normative problem* and the second the *conceptual problem*. In part because the conceptual problem seems most troublesome when taken together with the assumptions that yield the normative problem, these two difficulties have not always been clearly distinguished. Their conflation has contributed, in turn, to the widespread treatment of the so-called paradox of monarchy as an isolated anomaly in

---

[15] The claim that a king or a tyrant is the only person who meets Aristotle's definition of citizenship (*Pol.* 3.1 1275b18–21) in a monarchical constitution is sufficiently widespread to be called the standard view: see, e.g., Johnson 1984: 86; Vander Waerdt 1985: 249; Cooper 1990: 228; Newell 1991: 207; Keyt 1993: 140–1; Yack 1993: 85; Miller 1995: 148, 235; Blomqvist 1998: 23; Miller 1998: 502; Ober 1998: 318; Morrison 1999: 145; Roberts 2000: 357; Biondi Khan 2005: 13; Collins 2006: 134. Newman 1887–1902.i: 288–9 considers this view but does not unequivocally adopt it. A rare exception to this view is Kraut 2002: 411, followed by Rosler 2005: 179–81 (though Rosler confusingly combines this view with a version of the Cooper-Keyt distinction between first- and second-class citizens).

Aristotle's thought.[16] But in fact the problems of monarchy are simply the most visible manifestation of fundamental tensions in Aristotle's thought.

The normative problem arises as straightforwardly for aristocracy as it does for monarchy. Where oligarchy distributes political office in proportion to wealth, aristocracy grants authority to the virtuous. In virtually all circumstances, however, the virtuous are guaranteed to be relatively few. Aristocracy will therefore exclude the majority from rule, and so will deprive them of the benefits of political participation. The conceptual problem, by contrast, might seem to pose no difficulties for aristocracy, since the aristocratic few remain a plurality and so can share their rule with each other and exercise genuinely political authority over one another. Their relationship to the excluded many, however, will not involve mutual and reciprocal rule, and so will not be political at all. The virtuous will rule, and the rest will simply be ruled. Though the aristocrats might constitute a small political community among themselves, the others will not be parts of that community so long as they are not citizens. The idea of an aristocratic political community does not involve sheer incoherence as the idea of a monarchic political community does, but to concentrate authority in the hands of a few is to move toward the outright dissolution of political community that monarchy entails. So the conceptual problem is as troublesome for aristocracy as the normative problem is; in both ways, aristocracy seems to embody an attenuation of the political as such. These problems are not restricted to monarchy; they are the upshot of Aristotle's application of the merit-based conception of justice to his core conception of political community.

These problems are inescapable on many standard interpretations of the main lines of Aristotle's political philosophy. The argument of this book, however, is that Aristotle is silent about the problems not because he failed to recognize them or was happy to accept them, but because his theories of political community, authority, and justice rightly understood do not generate them. The following chapters aim to construct an interpretation of Aristotle's view of the nature and value of political community that is consistent with his defense of kingship. To be sure, his theories of political community, citizenship, justice, and constitutions as frequently

---

[16] The language of "paradox" appears in discussions of the problem by Miller 1995: 243 ("paradox of kingship") and Miller 1998 ("paradox of monarchy"). Mayhew 2009: 538 concludes that the problems with Aristotle's account of kingship are irresolvable, but goes on almost immediately to affirm that they "should not detract from the fact that with its connection to the rule of law, distributive justice based on worth, and the sharing of rule among citizens, Aristotle's conception of *political* rule is one of the more admirable features of his political philosophy."

interpreted are incoherent as a whole in just the way I have described. The most prominent strategies for resolving the difficulties fail in whole or in part to the extent that they retain certain traditionally prevalent views of Aristotelian politics. I argue that these views can be refuted, resisted, or rendered implausible on independent grounds in favor of alternative readings that avoid the problems and yield a more unified and coherent picture of Aristotle's political thought. Kingship serves as a kind of test case: provided that Aristotle, as I interpret him, can coherently endorse kingship in some conceivable circumstances, then a fortiori his theories of justice and authority are not hopelessly at odds with his core conception of political community.

In one way, then, this book is an extended attempt to solve a long-standing interpretive puzzle in the *Politics*. I have adopted this strategy because I believe that identifying problems in Aristotle's views and exploring the resources he has to resolve them is an effective and illuminating way to study his thought. My overarching goal is to understand what Aristotle thinks it is to rule and be ruled in a distinctively political way and what role it is supposed to play in a good human life. The defense of kingship in the *Politics* raises severe difficulties for traditional interpretations of his answers to these questions. My project here is to examine these questions to see whether Aristotle's answers admit of an interpretation on which they cohere with his account of monarchy. One feature of the interpretation that I develop is that kingship turns out to be more inclusive and political in Aristotle's sense than many have supposed, and its prominence in book 3 of the *Politics* becomes more intelligible. Yet I take the account of kingship as significant primarily for the light it sheds on Aristotle's conception of political community and the place of authority and hierarchy within it. Accordingly, though consistency with kingship is an essential criterion of success for my interpretation, I focus most of my attention not on monarchy per se, but on more fundamental concepts of Aristotle's political thought.

To begin with, Chapter 1 looks more closely at the defense of kingship in *Politics* 3 in order to illustrate more fully how the normative and conceptual problems arise and that they do not admit of simple solutions. A detailed summary of the argument of 3.14–17 clarifies the sometimes obscure dialectical trajectory of those chapters and situates them in the context of the book's broader concerns. I focus on the puzzles that the argument generates for any attempt to make sense of it against the background of what I have been calling Aristotle's core conception of political community, but I do not attempt to solve those puzzles directly. Instead,

I consider some prominent and intuitively plausible solutions and argue that they are all at best inconclusive. The two most promising strategies for addressing the problems posed by monarchy are to deny one or the other of two theses central to the core conception: either political participation is not an intrinsic good necessary for living a good life or political rule is not necessarily shared and reciprocal. Each of these strategies faces powerful objections. I argue instead that the objections have not been satisfactorily met, and that an adequate treatment of the issues therefore requires a more thorough reconsideration of the core conception. The following four chapters turn to that task before the final chapter returns to the defense of kingship with the goal of applying a more nuanced understanding of the core conception to the resolution of the normative and conceptual problems of monarchy.

Because the *Politics* treats political communities as one among many kinds of community, Chapter 2, "Community, Friendship, and Justice," begins by examining Aristotle's more general notion of community. Aristotle's term, κοινωνία, is sometimes translated as "association" as well as "community," but its connection with the adjective κοινός, "common," helps to elucidate its characteristic emphasis on what people share. Though the notion is taken for granted and developed in the *Politics*, its broader features are most fully elaborated in books 8 and 9 of the *Nicomachean Ethics*, where it is treated as a component of the theory of friendship. One of Aristotle's most important claims there is that friendship, justice, and community are coextensive. This chapter considers several different ways of construing this coextensiveness and argues in favor of a strong conceptual connection between community as the cooperative sharing of goods, friendship as the active disposition to wish goods to another, and justice as the common good or proportionately equal mutual benefit of the participants in a community. On this view, two primary features distinguish every genuinely distinctive kind of community. First, the participants in different sorts of community cooperate to pursue different sorts of goals. Second, the participants bring different sorts of resources, abilities, or capacities to bear on the pursuit of their common objectives. The nature of the good that these participants seek and the relevant similarities and differences among the participants jointly give rise to internal standards of justice and fairness characteristic of that form of community.

Chapter 3 sets out to understand what makes political communities distinctive. The framework established by the coextensiveness of community, justice, and friendship should lead us to expect that Aristotle's argument for the distinctive character of political community will focus above all on

identifying the distinctive good at which political communities aim and
the relevant characteristics of the people who participate in those communities. These features, in turn, will help to explain the specific form that
interpersonal standards of justice and fairness take in political communities. This argumentative structure is in fact especially prominent in the
first three books of the *Politics*, books that have often been seen as lacking
any overarching unity. The first part of Chapter 3 argues that these books,
taken in tandem with some of the systematic pronouncements that form
the background to book 7's construction of the ideal constitution, present a conception of political community that gives pride of place to the
nature of its aims and the character of its participants in distinguishing it
from other forms of community. Following Aristotle's strategy in books
1 and 2, I lay special stress on the differences between the city and the
household, with its subcommunities of husband and wife, of father and
child, and of master and slave. Drawing also on books 3 and 7, I aim to
explain how political communities differ from other forms of social life,
from the market to the military alliance, and how cities differ from nonpolitical societies. The short answer is that the city aims at the good life,
and its participants are naturally free adult males who share in exercising
rule in the community.

Completing this account of political community's distinctive nature
requires a fuller treatment of what it is to rule in a political way. Chapter 4
therefore attempts to reconstruct Aristotle's general concept of ruling and
of how ruling and being ruled politically differ from the varieties of rule
characteristic of the household. Supplementing the *Politics* with material drawn from the *Nicomachean Ethics* and elsewhere in the Aristotelian
corpus, I argue that rule is paradigmatically a matter of one agent initiating the action of another by issuing an order or command to act in
accordance with a decision made by the ruling agent. This account of rule
allows for distinctions between varieties of rule grounded in differences
between the ruler's aims and between the types of mutuality and reciprocity that mark the interaction of ruler and ruled. In this way, Aristotle's
characterizations of the varieties of ruling and being ruled – despotic,
paternal, marital, and political – become clearer, and we are put in a better
position to understand the value of citizenship. The final sections of the
chapter attempt to show that Aristotle considers citizenship, or "political
activity" as such, valuable strictly as a means: though politics may be a
medium for the expression of practical virtue, it is not choiceworthy for
its own sake, and cities do not exist for the sake of enabling individuals to
rule as a good in itself. Nonetheless, I suggest that Aristotle regards it as a

prima facie requirement of justice that all free adult males be permitted a share in ruling as well as being ruled. Though politics is not intrinsically valuable, Aristotle's view of the nature and value of political community favors inclusion and tells against exclusive arrangements.

Since there is seemingly abundant evidence that Aristotle is nothing like the egalitarian that he would have to be if he were to believe that granting a share in rule to all free adult males is a requirement of justice, Chapter 5 follows up that suggestion with a careful examination of the intersections among the concepts of citizenship, constitutions, and political justice. I argue that Aristotle's theory of correct and deviant constitutions is in fact consistent with, and even requires, the principle that all naturally free adult male permanent inhabitants of a city should be granted a share in rule. The principle is an application of the broader injunction against ruling free people despotically, treating them *as though* they were slaves, though not necessarily enslaving them. Political exclusion is unjust whenever it flouts this requirement. This claim seems implausible when coupled with prominent interpretations of Aristotle's account of citizenship and of the theory of correct and deviant constitutions. It is, accordingly, significant that these interpretations are widely thought to yield serious difficulties for the coherence of Aristotle's political philosophy quite independently of questions about whether he accepts the principle of justice that I attribute to him. Where others have argued that Aristotle's formal definition of citizenship must be supplemented or revised in order to render his theory of constitutions coherent, I argue, to the contrary, that the official account of citizenship lacks the implications that many have found in it. Most crucially, I show that the definition does not entail that the citizen body and the ruling class are coextensive. The predominant view in existing scholarship on the *Politics* sees sharing in rule as an all-or-nothing affair. By contrast, my discussion of political rule in Chapter 4 enables us to appreciate how Aristotle's descriptions of real and hypothetical constitutions suppose that sharing in rule admits of degrees. On this understanding of citizenship, aristocracy and monarchy can be correct constitutions without violating the principle that free adult male inhabitants should share in rule. These constitutional arrangements are best understood not as limiting citizenship to one or a few individuals, but as granting them the most authoritative positions without wholly depriving others of a share in rule.

This account of citizenship and authority points toward a straightforward resolution of the conceptual and normative problems of monarchy. Put simply, if the king is not the only citizen, then an Aristotelian kingship is no less a political community composed of a plurality of citizens than an Aristotelian polity would be. The arguments of Chapter 5 show that Aristotle can, *in principle*, recognize a correct and just form of monarchy alongside the deviance and injustice of tyranny. To show that there is conceptual space for kingship in Aristotle's theory does not, however, show that the kind of kingship he envisions occupies that space. Several features of Aristotle's defense of kingship cast doubt on the idea that it does: his extended comparison of kingship to the rule of a household seems to commit him to a conflation of the household and the city much like the one for which he takes Plato to task; his description of the "total king" as ruling "simply and not in part" (*Pol.* 3.17.1288a28–9) apparently denies to kingship one of the essential features of distinctively political rule and community; his characterization of the king as not subject to the rule of law evidently denies another. Even the invocation of the so-called summation argument in defense of total kingship seems to acknowledge that kingship could not be a form of political community, since it might seem that only a superhuman demigod could meet the conditions laid down by that principle, and no such person could enter into a relationship of fundamental equality such as political community is supposed to be.

Chapter 6 takes up each of these problems in turn and argues that all of them are misconceived. Aristotle's king is not a superhuman whose presence justifies a suspension of the political, but an exceptional human being whose presence justifies extraordinary ways of doing politics. After meeting these objections, the book concludes with a consideration of the theoretical aims of Aristotle's defense of kingship. One of these aims is to serve a critical function, providing a standard by which both to reject unqualified candidates for monarchy and to guide efforts toward the reform of tyrannies. More fundamentally, I explain the prominence of kingship in *Politics* 3 as part of a more extended critical response to Plato's ideal of a philosopher-king whose status as a ruler is a function of, if not identical to, his knowledge of "the kingly art." Like the ideal ruler of Plato's *Statesman*, Aristotle's king is a theoretically possible but practically improbable ideal who serves as a standard for critiquing existing arrangements and rejecting would-be monarchs. Unlike Plato, however, Aristotle insists even at the level of ideal theory that rulership is not simply a matter of knowledge and authoritative command. Aristotelian political rule is not most fundamentally the exercise and application of theoretical or technical expertise, but an inherently reciprocal mode of authority exercised via the nonscientific and nontechnical processes of practical deliberation and judgment. Aristotle's defense of kingship highlights the way in which the specifically practical nature of politics allows not only for the possibility, but especially for the excellence, of collective deliberation and judgment.

In recent years, the study of Aristotle's *Politics*, and of Greek political thought more generally, has become increasingly interdisciplinary and marked by a plurality of methodologies.[17] In most respects, my own approach follows that of mainstream analytic historians of philosophy. I seek to understand the conceptual structure of Aristotle's thought in terms of the reasons and arguments that he does, can, or should give in support of his claims. Like most other analytic historians of philosophy, I proceed on the basis of the principle of charity, a strong but defeasible presumption of consistency and coherence, and I privilege rational explanations of real and apparent theoretical problems and mistakes over appeals to psychological, sociological, or more broadly ideological factors. Perhaps unlike a majority of analytic historians of philosophy, however, I operate with a heightened sense of Aristotle's alterity and of the distance between his thought and contemporary Anglo-American academic philosophy. Consequently, I am less interested in situating Aristotle's thought in twenty-first-century debates or in considering how he might respond to objections raised from within competing theories than in understanding how his thought fits together within the horizon provided by the ancient Greek polis and its characteristic culture. This is not because I believe that Aristotle's thought is somehow radically incommensurable with our own, but because understanding it adequately requires sensitivity to the cultural background in which it developed. Though I do not devote much space to discussions of contextual matters, my historical orientation will be evident in the relatively ample treatments of such culturally contingent features of Aristotle's theory as his views of slavery, the household, labor, metics, foreigners, and distinctions between Greeks and non-Greeks.[18]

Fred Miller, developing David Charles's threefold distinction among classical scholarship, philosophical scholarship, and neo-Aristotelian philosophy, describes classical scholarship as aiming "to state the problems as Aristotle understood them and to explicate concepts and to fill out or

---

[17] For much of the previous half-century, by contrast, comparative disciplinary insularity was the norm, with historians, philosophers, and political theorists rarely engaging seriously with one another's work. Though methodological and other divisions persist, fruitful interaction among different approaches is becoming more common: see Balot 2006, 2009.

[18] Thus while I appreciate much of the theoretical work done by Quentin Skinner and J. G. A. Pocock in defending "contextualist" methods in the history of political thought, my own approach does not attribute the same kind or degree of importance to context in determining the meaning of a text. For an illuminating critique and alternative to the views represented in Pocock 1989 and Skinner 2002a, see Bevir 1994, 1997, 1999.

extend arguments using notions and techniques that would have been familiar to him"; the goal of philosophical scholarship or "reconstruction," by contrast, is "to try to understand the text not only on its own terms but also by applying external concepts, theories, and techniques."[19] Much contemporary Aristotelian scholarship seems to me to blur the boundary between philosophical reconstruction and neo-Aristotelian philosophy, the effort to develop recognizably Aristotelian philosophical theories without claims of fidelity to Aristotle's texts. I am all for neo-Aristotelian theorizing, but it is not what I do in this book. I hope, instead, to blur the boundary between philosophical reconstruction and classical scholarship. I defend Aristotle against various objections, but I make no effort to intervene on his behalf in any contemporary or perennial philosophical disputes. As I see it, one of the greatest challenges and rewards of studying the history of philosophy, and of intellectual history more generally, lies in negotiating the relationship between the concepts that we seek to interpret and those that we bring with us to the task of interpretation. Success yields the enrichment of our own conceptual schemes as well as our understanding of others. This book attempts simply to develop a more adequate interpretation of the *Politics* and, ideally, to send readers back to Aristotle's texts with an enhanced comprehension of the ideas those texts develop. Though I hope that neo-Aristotelian philosophers will find the book fruitful for their own projects, it is written in the conviction that Aristotle's political thought is a potentially valuable resource not only for those already inclined to take a broadly Aristotelian view of things, but for anyone who has a serious interest in what it might mean to be a political animal.

---

[19] Miller 1995: 22, drawing on Charles 1984.

CHAPTER I

Paradoxes of Monarchy

1. Aristotle's Defense of Kingship

In *Politics* 3, after discussing the nature of citizenship and the appropriate criteria for the distribution of political office, Aristotle turns to consider whether those criteria tell in favor of kingship:

> For we say that this is one of the correct constitutions. But we ought to inquire into whether it is beneficial for a city and a region, if it is going to be managed well, to be ruled by a king, or if, on the contrary, some other sort of constitution is more beneficial, or if kingship is beneficial for some but not beneficial for others. (*Pol.* 3.14.1284b26–40)

The initial question of chapter 14 is, then, under what conditions, if any, kingship would benefit a city. This question does not at all mark an abrupt shift from what precedes. Aristotle has just finished arguing that "the multitude" (τὸ πλῆθος) of citizens should be "the authoritative element" (τὸ κύριον) in a city unless there is some smaller group or even a single individual so excellent as to be able to manage the city's affairs better than the others could.[1] If there were such a person, he would be "like a god among human beings." It would be unjust to exclude him from the city, and likewise ridiculous to suppose that he should take turns ruling and being ruled along with all the others. The only reasonable course of action would be to obey him willingly (3.13.1284a3–17, b27–34, cf. 17.1288a28–29). Such preeminently virtuous people are, to say the least,

---

[1] I translate κύριον and its forms with the English "authoritative" and related terms. Like "sovereignty," "authority" is a potentially misleading translation insofar as both terms bear important, if at times imprecise, technical meanings in contemporary political philosophy (cf. Ober 1996c, Rosler 2005). Simpson 1997 prefers "controlling," which avoids confusion with technical meanings of "authoritative" and "sovereign" but introduces ambiguities of its own. I will use "authority" and related terms throughout with the caveat that I do not intend it in its narrow technical sense, but in the looser sense in which we say that someone has authority over X when he is "in charge of" X. I discuss the relationship of Aristotle's κύριον and ἀρχή to the technical sense of "authority" in Chapter 3.2.

exceedingly rare. Aristotle's invocation of them therefore strengthens the case for the rule of the multitude by showing what it takes to defeat it. Yet the argument explicitly maintains that, in the appropriate circumstances, the standards of distributive justice require the concentration of power in a single individual. In shifting his attention to kingship, Aristotle is considering whether that implication of the account he has offered so far is ultimately defensible.

Until putting it in question in chapter 14, Aristotle has assumed throughout book 3 that monarchy can come in good forms as well as bad. He has therefore given kingship a place in his classification of constitutions as one of the "correct" constitutions. A constitution (πολιτεία) is an arrangement of those who inhabit the city (3.1.1274b38), or, more strictly, an arrangement of the city's political offices, and especially of the office or institutional body that is authoritative over everything (3.6.1278b8–10). Constitutions may be divided into two broad kinds: Those that are organized with a view to the common good of the rulers and the ruled are "correct" (ὀρθαί), while those that aim only at the good of the rulers are corrupt "deviations" (παρεκβάσεις) from the correct varieties (3.6.1279a17–21). Deviant constitutions, because they subordinate the good of the ruled to the interests of the rulers, subvert the natural and appropriate norms of rule over people who are naturally free. Unlike supposedly natural slaves, naturally free people possess robust capacities for rational deliberation and agency, and it is a fundamental principle of justice that such people should not be subjected to forms of rule that render them the mere instruments of others. Natural slaves, by contrast, lack the capacity for full deliberative agency, and so can, on Aristotle's view, justly be treated as mere instruments of their masters.[2] The form of rule appropriate to natural slaves is "despotic rule" (δεσποτεία, δεσποτική); "political rule" (πολιτική), by contrast, is the form of rule appropriate to naturally free people (3.6.1278b30–1279a13, cf. 1.5–7). Deviant constitutions are deviant precisely because they are despotic where they should be political, and hence deviate from the correct, properly political, forms. The correct constitutions and their corresponding deviations can be distinguished, at least initially, by the number of people who hold the most

---

[2] Aristotle's theory of slavery is the subject of a vast secondary literature and is a frequent source of embarrassment to his admirers; I discuss it in more detail in Chapter 3. Kraut 2002: 277–305 provides a general overview of the issues, concluding, I think rightly, that in part because "Aristotle's framework for thinking about this subject was internally consistent and even contained a limited amount of explanatory power" (278), its failure remains philosophically instructive.

authoritative positions: Democracy is the deviation of polity (πολιτεία), both of which are characterized by the inclusion of a majority of citizens; oligarchy represents the deviant rule of the few whose correct form is aristocracy; and tyranny is the despotic and deviant form of monarchy, while the correct form is kingship (3.7.1279a22–b10).[3]

This distinction between political and despotic rule and its application to constitutions as correspondingly correct or deviant provides the conceptual framework for the question that opens 3.14. Aristotle has already concluded that justice properly speaking requires the distribution of political office to be proportionate to the merit of the people to whom the offices are distributed (3.9.1280a11–13, cf. *EN* 5.3.1131a10–b24).[4] Merit in this context is to be assessed by reference to the parties' abilities to contribute to the city (*Pol.* 3.9.1281a4–8), and "justice and political virtue" make an incommensurably greater contribution than either freedom or wealth (3.12.1282b15–1283a22).[5] This view opposes two prominent alternative conceptions of distributive justice. The democratic conception insists on strictly equal distribution among all free, adult, male members of the community: Since they are all equally free, they should all share power equally. The oligarchic conception maintains, to the contrary, that inequalities in wealth justify proportionately unequal distributions of power (3.9.1280a7–9, 22–5, cf. *EN* 5.3.1131a25–9). Aristotle's point against both parties is that the relevant standard of merit should be neither wealth nor freedom per se, but contribution to the good of the city (*Pol.* 3.9.1281a4–10). Freedom and wealth enable such contribution, and so are not wholly irrelevant. It is virtue, however, that makes people willing and able to contribute in the most important ways. Aristotle's merit-based conception of justice therefore privileges political virtue. Because it maintains that political office should be in the hands of those best able to exercise it, we might also call it the aristocratic conception (cf. *EN* 5.3.1131a29).

On its face, this conception of justice might seem to lead directly to a narrow concentration of power in the hands of the few most outstanding individuals in the community. The matter becomes more complex,

---

[3] From another perspective, Aristotle is willing to classify even correct constitutions as deviant relative to the form of constitution that is best without qualification. For more thorough treatments of Aristotle's theory of constitutions, cf. Fortenbaugh 1991, Keyt 1991b, Mulgan 1991, and Miller 1995. I return to these issues in Chapter 5.

[4] A fuller account of Aristotle's argument in *Pol.* 3.9–13 and of his theory of distributive justice requires detailed reference to *EN* 5 (= *EE* 4), which Aristotle himself cites at 1280a18. I draw here on Keyt 1991b and Miller 1995: ch. 3. For a more introductory treatment, cf. Roberts 2000.

[5] With Ross and against Dreizehnter, I read πολιτικῆς at 1283a20 rather than πολεμικῆς.

however, when Aristotle expands the scope of justice to include the merit-based claims that can be made on behalf of groups as well as individuals. In what is sometimes called "the summation argument," he defends the political participation of ordinary people of no extraordinary virtue:

> For it is possible for the many, none of whom is an excellent [σπουδαῖος] man, nevertheless to be better, when they have come together, than those [few best men], not as individuals but all taken together, just as feasts that are brought together are better than those that have been furnished at a single person's expense. And although they are many, it is possible for each to have a portion of excellence and of practical wisdom, and just as the multitude can, when they have come together, become like a single human being with many feet and hands and senses, so too [they can become like a single human being] with regard to traits of character and their thought. That is why the many are better judges of the works of culture [μουσική] and of poets; for different people judge different parts, but all of them [collectively] judge all of them. (*Pol.* 3.11.1281a42–b10)

The traditional label for this argument is misleading because the idea of "summation" suggests that what is at issue are merely quantitative considerations.[6] Yet just as a communal feast is likely to be enriched by the contribution not only of more but of a greater variety of foods, so too the work of politics is likely to be improved by the inclusion of a variety of perspectives on matters of collective concern. The common good is, like a tragic drama, complex, and though a few individuals may succeed in cultivating a refined sensitivity to the whole and all of its parts, those of us with less comprehensive critical insight may nonetheless form better judgments collectively than anyone could on his own (3.11.1281b7–10).[7]

---

[6] On the summation argument, I am indebted to especially to Keyt 1991b; see too Waldron 1995 and Ober 1998.

[7] Cammack 2013a and Lane 2013 challenge the now-standard view that Aristotle's summation argument depends on an appeal to diverse qualitative considerations, arguing instead that the argument is strictly quantitative and aggregative. Though their interpretations differ in detail, both emphasize (i) that Aristotle's analogy of a collective feast does not explicitly cite the superior quality or qualitative variety of the feast, and (ii) that the logic of Aristotle's argument is aggregative, applying as much to claims to rule on the basis of wealth as to claims based on virtue. Neither of these points makes a persuasive case against the standard interpretation. First, it scarcely follows from (i) that Aristotle does not have the qualitative superiority of the feast and the diversity of individual contributions in mind when describing the collective feast as better, or, more pressingly, when applying the analogy to collective rule. More fundamentally, neither Cammack nor Lane shows that (ii) is inconsistent with basing judgments of the relative superiority in virtue on the qualitative superiority afforded by the diversity of individual contributions. The logic of Aristotle's argument does indeed depend, as Lane insists, on claims that X possesses "more" of some relevant feature than Y, so that the argument succeeds even when the relevant feature can be compared in purely quantitative terms (as with wealth). But when the relevant feature is virtue, such comparisons must be at least partially

The summation argument shows that the aristocratic conception of justice must take account of the merit-based claims that can be made on behalf of groups as well as individuals. An individual's ability to contribute to the common good cannot be evaluated by reference to his personal virtues alone. Rather, the relevant excellences of any group to which he might contribute must be set against the individual abilities of the city's most outstanding citizens. In most circumstances, the citizen body's collective virtue will surpass that of any individual or small group of individuals. The principle behind the summation argument therefore provides a powerful basis for endorsing the rule of the multitude.

Aristotle qualifies his endorsement of rule by the multitude in at least two ways. First, he admits the possibility that some groups might be composed of people so corrupt that they could not effectively come together to govern the city well. Some people, he says with some exaggeration, are practically indistinguishable from wild animals or slaves (3.11.1281b18–20, 1282a15–17). It is unclear precisely how corrupt and slavish the people need to be in order to fail the test provided by the summation argument. Aristotle leaves little doubt, however, that the claims of the multitude might in fact be defeated. If a community includes a group or even a single individual whose excellence surpasses that of all the others combined, it will be just for that group or individual to rule. Anyone who possessed such superiority over the rest of the city would be treated unjustly if he were compelled to share power equally with the others (3.13.1284a3–11).

---

qualitative, and the most plausible way in which individuals who are not outstanding for their virtue can collectively exceed outstanding individuals is by the diversity of their individual contributions, as Aristotle's claim that "each can have some part of virtue and practical wisdom" (3.11.1281b4) and his analogy to collective judgment in poetic competitions, where "one judges one part, another another, and all of them the whole" (3.11.1281b7–10), suggest. Lane 2013: 259–60 acknowledges that these passages are problematic for her interpretation and attempts to read them in strictly quantitative terms, but does not persuasively explain away their appeals to qualitatively diverse contributions. Cammack shows convincingly that we should not follow Waldron 1995 in reading the argument in narrowly epistemic terms, as though the only significant individual contributions come in the form of knowledge rather than other forms of virtue, but this salutary point does not show that the relevant virtues are not inextricably tied up with what makes for excellent deliberation and judgment, as her account acknowledges when she writes of "the aggregation *not* of knowledge but of moral *and intellectual* capacities such as courage, justice, moderation, and *good sense*" (Cammack 2013a: 185, emphasis added). Nor does her insightful discussion of the ways in which the superior virtue of the multitude *does* derive from the quantity of people involved entail that their collective superiority does not depend crucially on the qualitative diversity of their individual contributions (as her reading of the analogy to collective poetic judgments appears to acknowledge, as when she suggests that "what distinguishes a good single man from a mass of people is that the good man comprises *in himself* all the parts of *aretē* that, in the mass, *are found scattered about*"; Cammack 2013a: 191). I discuss the summation argument and the complex dialectical trajectory of 3.11–13 more fully in Chapters 5 and 6.

Second, the presence of such outstanding individuals in the city yields a distinct condition in which the summation argument would fail to justify the rule of the multitude: In this case, the claim of the many ordinary citizens is not defeated by their corruption or depravity, but by the vastly superior excellence of one or a few citizens. The multitude envisioned in this second case does not consist of individuals comparable to slaves or wild animals. Rather, they are fully capable of managing the city's affairs collectively in the absence of any sufficiently outstanding individuals, but they cannot do it nearly so well as the outstandingly virtuous minority. That minority's ability to rule the city better than the collective multitude is the central criterion of the degree of superiority necessary to justify the rule of that minority.[8]

It is important to see that these two conditions in which the summation argument fails are genuinely distinct. It might seem otherwise, since both conditions depend on the comparative ability of one or a few people to govern the city more excellently than the multitude. Moreover, both cases require that the multitude be deficient in virtue. If the citizens on the whole were extremely virtuous, then surely no subset of them could emerge sufficiently superior to merit special consideration. Despite these similarities, distinguishing the two cases brings out an important feature of Aristotle's view: The failure of the summation argument to tell in favor of the multitude in any given circumstance does not depend exclusively on the outstanding vices of a majority or on the achievement of moral perfection by a minority. The case for rule by the multitude rests instead on a comparative claim that their ability to manage the city collectively is not surpassed by the ability of one or a few citizens. Thus the summation principle posits a single criterion for inclusion or exclusion, but that criterion can be met in two distinct sorts of conditions. In the first, only those who are not at all capable of managing the city's affairs well are justly excluded; the second apparently licenses the exclusion even of people who are well suited for political participation.[9]

---

[8] As Keyt 1991b notes, the argument seems to require that the minority be able to manage the city's affairs more excellently than any other group, *even a group that includes them*. The summation argument thus sets the bar quite high. I discuss this question in Chapter 6.4.

[9] Though the possibility that some groups might fail to meet the criteria of the summation argument is sometimes dismissed as an expression of aristocratic ideology (e.g., Ober 1998: 321), Kraut 2002: 405 seems right to conclude that "we should not take Aristotle to be saying that *whenever* defective individuals come together as a group, they make good collective decisions. He is making a far more cautious claim: When certain kinds of person come together – namely those whose deficiencies are not great – they can make decisions that promote their common good." Mayhew 2009: 537 rightly emphasizes that Aristotle does not suppose that the summation argument excludes only people who are simply incapable of ruling themselves politically.

The considerations invoked by the summation argument guide us in assessing which of the three correct constitutional types would be just in any given circumstance: Where the many meet the criterion set by the principle of summation, we get polity; where it fails because of the relative superiority of a few, we get aristocracy; and where a single individual's excellence surpasses that of the rest of the city combined, then the distributively just constitutional arrangement will be kingship. Aristotle's openness to aristocracy and kingship shows that he regards the collective merit-based claims of the multitude as in principle defeasible. Though the principle of summation dulls the edge of what might otherwise be the sharply exclusionary implications of the aristocratic conception of justice, this same principle would, in the appropriate circumstances, tell in favor of the claims of a minority and thereby justify rule by the few or the one best man. Doubts about this implication of the argument might apply to aristocracy no less than to kingship, but the latter raises special problems of its own and presents the common difficulties in their starkest form. A defense of kingship in the face of these worries is, a fortiori, a defense of aristocracy as well.

As Aristotle frames it, the primary question is whether kingship would benefit a city. This question is, however, another way of asking whether kingship is a correct constitution. Correct constitutions are those that aim at the common good (3.6.1279a16–20), a phrase that might equally well be translated as "the common benefit" or "the common advantage" (τὸ κοινῇ συμφέρον). The connection between the common good and justice is so tight that Aristotle is willing to say that justice *is* the common good (3.12.1282b17–18). If kingship were never beneficial, or if some other constitutional arrangement were always and everywhere more beneficial, then it could not be a correct constitution.[10] When Aristotle asks whether kingship "is beneficial to some but not beneficial to others" (3.13.1284b40), the "some" and the "others" he is asking about are distinct cities, not distinct groups of citizens within a single city.[11] All constitutional types benefit at least some groups in some respects, and so it would hardly be worth asking whether kingship benefits some citizens but not others. Deviant constitutions are deviant primarily because they are directed to the benefit

[10] I take it that the correctness of a constitution is primarily a feature of a kind or type: Thus it is consistent to hold that being conducive to the common good is a necessary condition of being a correct constitution *and* that monarchy is not, in some (perhaps many or even most) circumstances, conducive to the common good.

[11] This much should be clear from 1284b38–9, where the antecedents of the indefinite τισὶ μὲν…τισὶ δὲ are πόλει καὶ χώρᾳ.

of some members of the community at the expense of others. So Aristotle
proceeds to consider a series of objections to the claim that kingship promotes the common good. He supposes that answering these objections will
establish that kingship is a correct constitution.

Understanding the question in this way helps to make the trajectory of
the arguments that follow more intelligible. Aristotle first distinguishes five
kinds of kingship. The first is the sort found in Sparta, where the king has
authority only over military and religious affairs. This form of kingship,
however, differs from a generalship only in the term of its office and in the
addition of a religious role. It may also be hereditary or elected, while gen-
eralships are typically elected. Thus Aristotle calls it "generalship for life"
(3.14.1285a3–16, 26–8). The second form, "barbarian kingship," grants more
power to the king and differs from tyranny in only a few ways. Though it is
despotic because the king holds unrivaled power and does not rule for the
common good, it is only partially tyrannical because the king rules according
to law (κατὰ νόμον) over willing subjects.[12] Such kingships are also typically
hereditary (3.14.1285a16–29). Barbarian kingship closely resembles the third
form, found instead among Greeks, the αἰσυμνητεία, sometimes translated
as "dictatorship."[13] The αἰσυμνητεία is distinguished from barbarian kingship
only by being elected rather than hereditary, and may in fact be for a limited
term rather than for life. The αἰσυμνητεία and barbarian kingship are both
forms of despotic rule according to law, combining features of tyranny with
characteristics of kingship (3.14.1285a29–b1). Aristotle therefore calls them
"despotic" (δεσποτικαί), "tyrannical" (τυραννικαί), and "kingly" or "royal"
(βασιλικαί), carefully distinguishing them from pure cases of tyranny or
kingship (3.14.1285b2–3).[14] In this respect, they differ from the fourth kind

[12] One of the points at issue in the chapters on kingship is just what is and is not entailed by the rule
of law. Roughly, however, an official rules κατὰ νόμον when there is a set of rules and institutional
procedures that limit and constrain that official's exercise of authority; the alternative is for an official to be free to rule according to his own will, κατὰ τὴν αὐτοῦ βούλησιν (3.16.1287a1). Aristotle's
argument complicates the relationship between these alternatives. I discuss the issue more fully in
Chapter 6.3. "Law" and "laws" here – Aristotle uses the two expressions interchangeably – are to
be taken in the broad sense that encompasses what we might prefer to call customs or conventions
as well as formal written laws (Aristotle distinguishes these at 3.16.1287b5–8); on the use of νόμος
generally, Ostwald 1969 remains instructive.
[13] For this translation, see Simpson 1997.
[14] It is not always appreciated that these forms of monarchy are not pure tyrannies or pure kingships;
thus Robinson 1962: 52, though prepared to describe these as "at once kingships and tyrannies," is
troubled by their reappearance in 4.10.1295a11–14 "as forms of tyranny." Robinson wrongly claims
that "nothing is said about the question whether the ruler rules for his own or for the public
advantage"; in fact, part of what Aristotle means to tell us in describing these forms of monarchy
as "tyrannical" is that they do not aim at the common good. I discuss this point in greater detail in
Chapter 6.1 and 6.3.

of kingship, this one associated with the kings of heroic times. As a form of hereditary rule according to law over willing subjects, heroic kingship initially seems to differ little from the Spartan kingship. Heroic kings, however, surpassed the Spartan kings in the extent of their authority. In addition to military affairs and sacrifices, such kings served as judges and generally "ruled continuously over the affairs of the city, the country, and beyond the borders" (3.14.1285b13–14). Heroic kingship, then, was more than generalship for life. The two forms of kingship are alike, however, in lacking the elements of tyranny found in barbarian kingship and αἰσυμνητεία.

All four kinds of kingship discussed so far share two crucial features: First, they are all forms of rule over willing subjects, and hence not pure tyrannies; second, they are all forms of rule according to law. The fifth, and ultimately most important, form of kingship resembles the others in the first respect but diverges from them in the second. Aristotle initially distinguishes it from the others by the range of the king's authority: It is the form of kingship that exists "when a single person has authority (κύριος ὢν) over all the common affairs" (3.14.1285b29–30). He labels it, accordingly, "total kingship" (παμβασιλεία, 3.15.1285b36).[15] We might suppose, then, that total kingship simply takes heroic kingship one step further by giving more power to the king. In one sense, this supposition is correct. It is important to see, however, that the extension of authority in total kingship is such that the king is no longer subject to the law. Though this point is initially not made fully explicit, it is implicit in the idea of having authority over "all the common affairs," and it quickly becomes explicit: The first problem with total kingship that Aristotle considers is "whether it is more beneficial to be ruled by the best man than by the best laws" (3.16.1286a7–9), and he later explains that total kingship is the form in which "the king rules everything in accordance with his own will," in contrast to ruling according to law (3.16.1287a1–10).

At this point, we can more fully appreciate the importance of understanding the question raised at the beginning of 3.14 as a question about whether kingship is a correct constitution. After distinguishing the five kinds of kingship, Aristotle claims that his inquiry into kingship reduces to questions about the Spartan kingship and total kingship. But these two

---

[15] I follow Simpson 1997 in translating παμβασιλεία as "total kingship." This seems preferable to "absolute kingship" (as in Lord 2013), which might unnecessarily suggest that the term itself implies the exclusion of everyone but the king from participation in "rule" or that the king's authority is entirely unconditional. "Total kingship," by contrast, has vagueness on its side: Since it is unclear what the term does and does not imply, it is less likely to bias the reader's judgment on one of the central questions I hope to address.

questions are quite distinct. The Spartan form and total kingship occupy the two extreme poles of kingship as measured by the extent of the king's authority; the total king has the most authority, the Spartan king the least. More fundamentally, however, the Spartan kingship is not a kind of constitution, but merely an unusual form of office. Any kind of constitution, even a democratic one, could conceivably institute the office of generalship for life. It is worth asking whether or not cities would benefit from such an office, whether it is hereditary or filled on some other basis. That question, however, has more to do with laws than with constitutions, and it is kingship as constitutional form that interests Aristotle here (3.15.1285b33–1286a9, cf. 16.1287a3–6).

Though the other kinds of kingship do appear to be something like constitutions, there is good reason to focus the inquiry on total kingship.[16] The tyrannical features of barbarian kingship and αἰσυμνητεία pose obvious problems. Heroic kingship, on the other hand, is not tyrannical, but it remains a mitigated form of total kingship because of the constraints placed on the king's authority. To the extent that any king's authority is limited, the arrangement becomes less a distinct constitutional form and more like one particular office within a constitution.[17] An inquiry into correct and mistaken constitutional varieties would therefore do well to focus more on total kingship than the less complete forms. This focus will bring into view the most distinctive features of kingship as a constitution and will have implications for understanding the less complete forms of kingship to the extent that they approach the status of constitutions rather than mere offices.

The distinction between kinds of kingship therefore serves to clarify the subject of the inquiry. Aristotle then proceeds, as he puts it, "to run over the inherent difficulties" (3.15.1286a7). He begins with a dispute, echoing Plato's *Statesman*, about whether it is best for a city to be ruled by the best man or by the best laws. The case for rule by the best man depends on the shortcomings of law. Legal prescriptions are necessarily

---

[16] The status of barbarian kingship and αἰσυμνητεία as constitutions is unclear, but Aristotle seems to imply that they are not distinct constitutional forms when he describes them as "in accordance with law" (3.14.1285a18–19, 32–3), since he later explicitly denies that a kingship in accordance with law is a form of constitution (3.16.1287a3–4). Since he readily admits the existence of "mixed" constitutional varieties, presumably Aristotle need not be troubled if these categories are not mutually exclusive and admit of degrees of approximation to the paradigm case of total kingship.

[17] cf. 1287a6–8, where Epidamnos and Opus are said to have an office (ἀρχή) in which a single person has authority over the management of affairs (τῆς διοικήσεως). Presumably this office holds something like sole executive authority, though not sole authority over policy making; this would explain why Aristotle considers it more powerful than the Spartan kingship but, like it, insufficient to qualify either city as kingships. I owe this observation to Dhananjay Jagannathan.

framed in universal, or at least quite general, terms. Decision and judgment, however, are about particular cases, and practical life is sufficiently complex that no antecedently formulated set of general rules could yield a determinate set of correct judgments and decisions for every case. Being ruled by law is like practicing medicine in accordance with strict written rules; the best man would, like a good physician, be more responsive to the requirements of particular circumstances than any written rules could be (3.15.1286a9–15). Against these considerations, Aristotle adduces several powerful objections raised by the opponents of kingship. Laws, unlike human beings, cannot be corrupted by irrational desires and emotions (3.15.1286a17–20, 16.1287a28–32). Continuing the analogy with medicine, prescriptions generated by written rules would in fact be preferable to the prescriptions of an untrustworthy physician (3.16.1287a32–41). Even the best individual is more easily corrupted than the multitude taken together (3.15.1286a31–5); sick physicians often consult other physicians because they recognize that they are unreliable judges in their own cases (3.16.1287a41–b3). The multitude or an aristocracy could, in any case, compensate for the shortcomings of law no less well than a king (3.15.1286a36–b7, 16.1287a23–8). The exigencies and limitations of practice would compel the king to appoint corulers, and so to share his rule after all (3.16.1287b8–32). Yet it is unjust for one person to rule permanently over his equals, as these others must be if they are to be the king's corulers (3.16.1287a10–18, b32–5).

This dialectical exchange seems to point toward decisive defeat for kingship, but when Aristotle turns to adjudicate the dispute, he focuses on one particular objection:

> It is not even in accordance with nature for one person from all the citizens to have control or authority [κύριον εἶναι] over everything when the city is composed of similar people. For according to nature, justice and merit are necessarily the same for people who are similar by nature. And so if it is harmful even for those who are unequal in their bodies to have equal food or clothing, then it must be so with the honors of office, as well. And so the same goes for those who are equal receiving what is unequal. Therefore it is just for people to rule no more than they are ruled, and therefore for them to rule by turns in the same way. (3.16.1287a10–18)

Aristotle's response to this objection concedes its force in most circumstances, but insists on the conditional justice of kingship:

> But perhaps these things are so in the case of some people, but not in the case of others.... From what has been said, it is apparent that among people who are similar and equal it is neither beneficial nor just for one person

to have control or authority [κύριον εἶναι] over everything, neither if there
are no laws and he is himself a law, nor if there are laws, nor if he and the
laws are good, nor if he and the laws are not good, and not even if he is
greater in virtue, unless he is so in a certain way. What that way is needs to
be stated. (3.17.1287b36–1288a6)

The upshot of the previous objection is that if the members of a given
community are similar and equal, kingship will be neither just nor beneficial. Aristotle not only agrees with this objection, but takes it to render
much of the previous argument about kingship otiose. Kingship's proponents attempted to justify it in light of the shortcomings of law, but justice
requires at least proportionate equality, and justice is an integral part of
the common good. The deficiencies of law cannot legitimate setting aside
the requirements of justice, even in a community that has no established
laws. Correcting the law's deficiencies, whether through new legislation
or through case-by-case judgments, does not require a king, but can, as
the opponents of kingship insisted, be achieved through more cooperative
arrangements. Whether the city should have a king depends not on the
condition of its laws, but on considerations of justice. Even the most excellent man in a city with no laws does not ipso facto deserve to be king. Only
a man who is superior in "a certain way" would justly rule as king:

> Whenever there happens to emerge either a whole family[18] or even a single
> individual from among the others who is so outstanding that his virtue
> exceeds that of all the others, then it is just for this family to have the king-
> ship and to have authority [κύριον] over everything, and for this one man
> to be king. (3.17.1288a15–19)

The treatment of kingship culminates, then, in a return to the summation
principle already invoked in 3.13.

Yet the dialectic of the intervening chapters is not merely redundant;
nor are its arguments irrelevant. Rather, they clear the way for a focused
justification of total kingship on strict grounds of distributive justice.
After distinguishing various forms of kingship and showing that only
total kingship qualifies as a distinct form of constitution in its own right,
we learn that the advantages and disadvantages of rule by law supply no

---

[18] It might seem odd that Aristotle should include consideration of a family here when his focus has
been on individuals, and he has raised doubts about whether a worthy king's sons would be likely
to turn out as worthy as their father (3.15.1286b22–7). But because kingship is traditionally associated with heredity, a monarchy in which authority is inherited is a distinct possibility, but one that
must be assessed by the same criterion; the individual members of the family who stand to inherit
the kingship must possess the same superlative excellence as their father. Given Aristotle's emphasis
on the role of habituation and education in the development of virtue, there is no reason to suppose that he is here thinking of a kind of natural ethical inheritance that bypasses them.

decisive reasons in favor of rule by one man. By implication, however, neither do the arguments posed by kingship's opponents in favor of law tell decisively against the king. When it resurfaces on the other side of this unresolved dialectical exchange, the justification of kingship by appeal to the king's superiority appears in a new light. Not only are the distinguishing characteristics of kingship as a constitution now more apparent, but the conditions that the supremely virtuous individual must meet have come more plainly into view. The individual's superiority does not justify kingship in spite of the problems raised by kingship's opponents. On the contrary, it is one of the criteria of the would-be king's genuine superiority that his rule can overcome those problems.[19]

If any given individual's monarchic rule could not overcome the problems, that would be grounds for denying that he possesses the requisite degree of superiority over all the other citizens.[20] Earlier discussion has already made clear that not every kind of superiority is relevant to the distribution of political office, but only superiority in those goods or aspects of excellence that contribute to managing the city well (3.12.1282b18–1283a23). Yet most of the objections to kingship in 3.15–16 challenge a king's ability to govern well or to do better than some alternative. It seems clear, then, that the discussion of kingship's potential disadvantages serves in part to specify the content of the would-be king's superior excellence. In effect, the chapters on kingship defend the argument in its favor sketched in 3.13 by clarifying the character of kingship and the conditions for its justification. From the vague claim that an individual of sufficiently superior virtue would justly be made king, we arrive at a fuller characterization of what his rule would amount to and of what that superior excellence involves: A king would not be merely an especially powerful official, but would have authority even over the laws, and only someone who could rule in a way that would surmount the difficulties posed by the opponents of kingship meets the standards set by the summation argument.

Such, in outline, is Aristotle's defense of total kingship's claim to be a correct constitution. Yet even if we grant him his premises and concede

---

[19] This point is not always appreciated, but cf. Kraut 2002: 414, whose defense of this reading differs in detail from my own but is consistent with it.

[20] Some potential problems with kingship could result not from any deficiency on the king's part, but from incidental circumstantial features. It is also unclear which of the objections and responses in 3.14–17 Aristotle would endorse in any serious way, and which he includes simply because they are or could be put forward by supporters or detractors of kingship. No particular answer to those questions has any decisive bearing on the basic point that I defend here, namely, that the discussion of kingship's potential disadvantages serves in part to specify the content of the would-be king's superiority. Not *all* of the problems raised in 3.15–16 need be relevant in this way.

the basic moves of his argument, we might doubt whether he has said enough to vindicate monarchy. Though the discussion does something to fill in the content of the king's alleged superiority, it remains altogether vague in detail. Just how excellent would a person have to be to qualify for total kingship? Is relative superiority really enough, or would he also require an almost superhuman excellence to avoid becoming a tyrant or otherwise abusing his position? We might doubt whether such superiority is possible even in principle, and even so, whether it is so unlikely as to be of merely theoretical interest. Even if such an excellent person were available, would it really be best for him to have control over everything rather than merely to hold some extremely privileged position that nonetheless falls short of unconditional authority? Should even such a person be free from the constraints of law? Would the rest of the citizens be willing to be the king's subjects, and if so, would the practical intelligence and virtue of character necessary for them to recognize and embrace the justice and benefit of the king's rule undermine his claim to superiority? The importance of these questions seems obvious, and yet Aristotle does little to address them. That failure may be enough to cast doubt on the idea that kingship of the sort he imagines could ever be acceptable.

These are significant problems, but they pale in comparison to the charges of fundamental incoherence that have been leveled at the treatment of kingship in the *Politics*. Some have preferred the language of paradox to the language of contradiction, though commentators have not always agreed about what exactly the paradox is or whether it can be resolved. Before we can address the more specific questions that the defense of kingship raises, we must assess the objection that kingship is fundamentally incompatible with political community as Aristotle conceives it. Most, however, have underestimated the extent to which the "paradox of monarchy" is a manifestation of deeper tensions in Aristotle's thought. Far from an isolated anomaly, the apparent incoherence of Aristotle's defense of kingship has severe implications for many of the central and most celebrated ideas of the *Politics*. For that reason, a more adequate understanding of the problems of monarchy calls for a reconsideration of just what Aristotle thinks political community is and exactly why it is valuable to human beings.

2.   Normative and Conceptual Problems of Monarchy

Aristotle's account of monarchy has long been widely regarded as one of the least healthy parts of his political philosophy. Diagnoses, prognoses, and recommended remedies have varied, but most treatments cluster around one or both of two problems. The first, which I call the *normative problem*, is that Aristotle seems committed by his core conception of political community and his theory of justice to denying that a monarchy could be a *good* political community. The second, which I call the *conceptual problem*, is that Aristotle seems committed for similar reasons to denying that monarchy could be a *political* community at all. Scholars have not often distinguished these problems, in part because the normative implications of the conceptual problem are what seem to give it its bite. Nonetheless, the problems are indeed distinct; they arise from different aspects of Aristotle's broader theory, and they pose challenges to different Aristotelian theses.

One central feature of the core conception of political community is the unique value it attributes to political community. When Aristotle writes that "the human being is by nature a political animal" (*Pol.* 1.2.1253a7–18, 3.6.1278b15–30, cf. *EE* 7.10.1242a19–28, *EN* 8.12.1162a16–19, 9.9.1169b16–22) and that the city exists "by nature," he evidently means that human beings can flourish in ways appropriate to our nature only in the context of political community. He is willing to compare the relationship between individual human beings and the city to that between the parts of a body and the body as a whole: Just as a hand or a foot cannot engage in the activities essential to its being a hand or a foot unless it is a properly functioning part of a whole living body, so too individual human beings cannot live well in isolation from cities (*Pol.* 1.2.1253a20–9). Anyone who is by nature rather than by some unfortunate accident unable to share in political community or who is fully self-sufficient without it is, in some sense, not a human being; he is, rather, either lower or higher than humanity, "either a beast or a god" (1.2.1253a29, cf. 1.2.1253a3–4). In the absence of the city, human beings lack the means and opportunity to develop and exercise the virtues that enable them to engage successfully in the sorts of activity that contribute to and constitute *eudaimonia*, the happiness, well-being, or flourishing of human beings as such.[21] To live well,

---

[21] Though I will sometimes use the transliterated *eudaimonia,* I will also use "happiness," "well-being," "flourishing," "living well," and similar phrases in its place. Though in some uses these terms have importantly different meanings, on Aristotle's view as I understand it, they all either have an identical reference or are mutually entailing. On some alternative readings (e.g., Richardson Lear 2004, Cooper 2004b), *eudaimonia* strictly refers only to the highest good, the component in the happy or flourishing life of well-being that gives that life its structure and is responsible for *making* it a good and flourishing life. Even if this is the considered view toward which Aristotle moves throughout the course of the *EN*, he gives us sufficient grounds for using these terms as rough equivalents when he says, in *EN* 1.5.1095a18–20, that both "the many" and "the refined" suppose that "living well and doing well are the same thing as *being eudaimōn* [τῷ εὐδαιμονεῖν]."

human beings need not only to live with others, but to live with others in specifically political forms of community. Prepolitical forms, such as the household and the village, as well as larger forms of organization that rival or exceed the city in size fail, for different reasons, to enable human beings to flourish as fully as they might.

Aristotle plainly maintains that the city is necessary for human flourishing and that the goal of politics is to provide the enabling conditions for its citizens' well-being. Many readers, however, have quite plausibly found a much tighter connection between politics and the good life in Aristotle's practical writings. On one prominent view, political communities do not merely sustain a framework of cooperation that promotes the citizens' happiness. Rather, the city benefits its citizens directly by enabling them to engage in the specifically political activities of citizenship. Citizenship, conceived as active participation in cooperative deliberation about shared goods (3.1.1275b18–21), is intrinsically valuable and an important constitutive part of a good life.[22] Proponents of this view sometimes see it as implicit in the claim that human beings can flourish only as parts of a city, especially since Aristotle goes on to clarify that a city's parts, strictly speaking, are its citizens (3.1.1274b32–41, 3.5.1278a3, 4.4.1291a24–8, 7.4.1326a16–21, 7.8.1328a33–5).[23] Others have found it in the claim that practical wisdom, the central intellectual virtue that the *Nicomachean Ethics* makes indispensable for the possession of all the virtues of character, is the virtue of rulers and not of the ruled (*EN* 6.13.1144b1–1145a5, *Pol.* 3.4.1277a12–25).[24] Aristotle seems to endorse the intrinsic value of political activity most explicitly when he devotes two chapters of the *Politics* to defending "the political and practical way of life" against objections and misunderstandings (*Pol.* 7.2–3.1324a5–1325b32). The *Nicomachean Ethics* likewise gives an important, if ambiguous, place to "the political life" (*EN* 10.7–8.1177a12–1179a32).[25]

---

[22] The most plausible defense of this view that I know is Irwin 1990 (cf. more exhaustively, Irwin 1988: chs. 16–21), but it is pervasive. Some (variously) prominent, influential, and recent examples: Kelsen 1937: 176, 184–6 (though he denies that this is Aristotle's real view); Arendt 1958; Robinson 1962: 14–15; Strauss 1964; Vander Waerdt 1985; Nussbaum 1986: 345; Cooper 1990, 2010; Kahn 1990; Adkins 1991; Newell 1991; Reeve 1998: lxii; Schofield 1999b: 104–5, 2000: 319; Kraut 2002: 252, 257; Frede 2005: 172–9; Collins 2006: 130; Halper 2007; Garver 2011: 154–5, 186, 205; Cherry 2012; Brown 2013; Trott 2013: 83–104.

[23] Brown 2013.

[24] Adkins 1991, Newell 1991, Frede 2005.

[25] These chapters of the *EN* are the subject of a vast literature concerning the relation of the political life to the theoretical life and to *eudaimonia*, much of which involves debates about the structure of *eudaimonia* itself (cf. Ackrill 1980, Keyt 1983, Irwin 1985, Kraut 1989, Broadie 1991, White 1992,

If political participation is an intrinsically valuable form of activity essential to a good life, then any argument in favor of kingship would seem to be a nonstarter. The idea that the king himself is the only genuine citizen in a kingship is sufficiently widespread to be called the standard view.[26] The view rests on the conjunction of two apparently straightforward claims: A citizen is someone who is entitled to participate in rule (*Pol.* 3.1.1275b18–21), and kingship is a constitution in which only one person rules (3.6.1279a32–4). If so, then kingship inevitably deprives everyone except the king of the crucial good of political activity. If political activity is necessary for living well, then kingship assures that only the king has the opportunity to flourish. The core conception of political community therefore seems to guarantee that Aristotle's defense of kingship fails.

Yet this conclusion does not show simply that Aristotle has failed to justify kingship. It also has deeper implications that generate conflict between two major elements of his theory of politics, his theory of justice and his claim that political rule is distinctive in kind. If kingship necessarily deprives everyone except the king of the opportunity to live a good life, then the distinction between kingship and tyranny as correct and deviant forms of monarchy collapses. That distinction, as we have seen, is an application of the broader distinction between political and despotic forms of rule. Political rule aims at the good of the ruled or at a good common to ruler and ruled, whereas despotic rule aims at the ruler's interests at the expense of the ruled; correct constitutions are those characterized by genuinely political rule, while those that take up features of despotic rule are deviant. But if kingship necessarily harms its subjects by depriving them of a crucial component of a good human life,

---

Richardson Lear 2004, Dahl 2011). Though on some interpretations, Aristotle holds there that the best life would be a life of theoretical contemplation unobstructed by political activity, 10.8.1178a9 claims that the practical life of political engagement is happy "in a secondary way" [δευτέρως]. However we should understand that claim, the only position that would be strictly incompatible with attributing any intrinsic value to political activity is what Keyt 1983 calls "strict intellectualism," an interpretation on which only theoretical contemplation possesses intrinsic value and everything else is a mere instrumental means to it. That view seems impossible to reconcile with Aristotle's treatment of "finality" in *EN* 1.7 and with the tenor of Aristotle's ethical and political works as a whole. It is also not typically held, though Lord 1982 and Vander Waerdt 1985, both following up some suggestions in Strauss 1964, come close. I address some of the relevant issues in Chapter 4.

[26] Johnson 1984: 86; Vander Waerdt 1985: 249; Cooper 1990: 228; Newell 1991: 207; Hansen 1993; Keyt 1993: 140; Yack 1993: 85; Miller 1995: 148, 235; Blomqvist 1998: 23; J. Miller 1998: 502; Ober 1998: 318; Morrison 1999: 145; Roberts 2000: 357; Biondi Khan 2005: 13; Collins 2006: 134. Others are ambiguous on this point: Polansky 1991: 341; Nagle 2006: 113–5; Garver 2011: 102; and Garsten 2013: 334. Newman 1887–1902.i: 288–9 considers the view but does not unequivocally adopt it.

it could hardly be said to be directed to their good, and so could only be a despotic form of rule and therefore a deviant constitution. In itself, this problem may pose no insurmountable challenges to Aristotle's political theory, since he could simply accept that the distinction between correct and deviant constitutions does not apply in the case of monarchy.[27] This concession would rob the theory of constitutions of its neat symmetry, but that may be a small price to pay for avoiding theoretical incoherence and substantive injustice.

If the normative problem extended only this far, the only "paradox" would be that Aristotle did not notice his own flagrant contradiction. But in fact the difficulties penetrate all the way to the theory of justice in the distribution of political rule. The problem is well put by Terence Irwin, who holds that Aristotle endorses the intrinsic value of political activity but appeals inconsistently to two incompatible criteria for participating in political rule.[28] By the "absolute criterion," all naturally free adult males should share in rule because citizenship is essential to their well-being and they possess the capacity for it. By this standard, anyone with the capacity for political rule should, in justice, be permitted to participate.[29] But Aristotle also appeals to "the relative criterion," whereby "any great disparity of virtue justifies a departure from the norm of shared rule."[30] These two criteria are in obvious tension, and yet, as Irwin maintains, the absolute criterion is clearly more fundamental. It underlies the distinction between political and despotic rule and supports Aristotle's claim that it is unjust to treat naturally free people as slaves. If we ask why the king of outstandingly superior virtue would be unjust if he treated his subjects as slaves, the answer will appeal to the absolute criterion: Naturally free people have capacities that slaves do not, and their possession of those capacities renders their enslavement harmful to them and unjust of their masters. In the same way, the absolute criterion undermines any claim to political exclusion based on the relative criterion.[31] No theory can coherently combine the two criteria without abandoning the component of the absolute criterion that regards political participation as essential to human well-being.

---

[27] Mayhew 2009: 537 suggests that this concession would be sufficient to save Aristotle's theory.
[28] Irwin 1990.
[29] The absolute criterion of course does not preclude withholding citizenship from certain classes of criminals, members of other political communities, etc. I discuss the case of resident aliens ("metics") in Chapter 5.
[30] Irwin 1990: 95–6.
[31] Irwin 1990: 96–7.

Yet the relative criterion is at the heart of Aristotle's meritocratic conception of justice. He invokes it to justify aristocracy as well as kingship, and even his defense of polity depends on the claim that the multitude will often be better able to rule than any smaller group. If Irwin is right, the absolute criterion makes all considerations of relative political ability fundamentally irrelevant. Aristotle might have consistently held that special political virtues qualify a person to hold positions of special authority, but not that they entitle him to rule to the exclusion of others. So even where application of the meritocratic theory of justice generates distributions of authority consistent with the absolute criterion, the theory itself baldly contradicts the core conception of political community. The normative problem that emerges from Aristotle's defense of kingship is thus not an isolated feature of his theory of monarchy, but simply the most visible manifestation of pervasive incoherence in the *Politics*.[32]

Perhaps the most prominent response to this problem has been to deny that Aristotle regards political participation as necessary for living well. This move is not so ad hoc as it might first appear. Though the intrinsic value of citizenship is a famously Aristotelian thesis, there are independent reasons for thinking that it is not Aristotle's own. The final book of the *Nicomachean Ethics* not only defends an apolitical way of life devoted to theoretical contemplation as the best life, but maintains that it is plain to see that private people who avoid politics (ἰδιῶται) can act no less well, or even better, than people with great power (*EN* 10.8.1179a3–9).[33] The theory of the good life as practical activity in accordance with virtue seems to require the framework of political community, but not participation in specifically political activities of shared deliberation and judgment.[34] Politics might even be an obstacle to a more flourishing life of intellectual cultivation; kingship, in that case, would free citizens to devote themselves to contemplation.[35]

---

[32] Irwin does not draw such pessimistic conclusions even from his strong indictment of the theory. Presumably he would advise Aristotle to abandon anything like the relative criterion altogether, which would bring his politics much closer to the egalitarianism characteristic of contemporary political theory, whether liberal, communitarian, or social democratic. Yet if our interest is in assessing the *Politics* as it stands, Irwin's argument should seem devastating. However much of the wreckage may be salvageable for reuse in fashioning an egalitarian neo-Aristotelian theory, Irwin's critique, if successful, shatters Aristotle's political philosophy on its own terms. It is one thing to reject Aristotle's theory on the basis of views he did not accept; it is another to show that it is fundamentally at odds with itself.

[33] So Miller 1995: 238.

[34] Mulgan 1990.

[35] Vander Waerdt 1985, developing suggestions by Lord 1982: 196–202.

Furthermore, many of the passages cited to illustrate the necessity of political participation for the exercise of the virtues seem better understood as claiming, instead, that good political participation requires the virtues: "The ruler must have complete ethical virtue" (*Pol.* 1.13.1260a17–18); "the excellent ruler is good and practically wise" (3.4.1277a14–15); "practical wisdom is the only virtue peculiar to a ruler" (3.4.1277b25–6); "the education and the habits that make a man excellent are nearly the same as those that make him a political or kingly man" (3.18.1288b1–2).[36] So too, the claims most often taken to express the crucial role of active citizenship in the good life seem consistent with the view that the polis provides the necessary and enabling conditions of well-being rather than a distinctly political variety of action that partially constitutes well-being: "The human being is a political animal" because we need the polis to flourish, and "the city exists for the sake of living well" because part of what it is to be a specifically political community is to aim at providing the necessary and enabling conditions of the good life for the community's members.[37]

I will argue in Chapter 4 that this solution to the normative problem is partially correct: Political participation is not an intrinsic good in the way its celebrants often suppose, and active citizenship is not strictly necessary for living a good life. In advance of more detailed argument, however, the strengths of this strategy for resolving the normative problem are less noteworthy than its weaknesses. Suppose we grant that a good life is not impossible for someone who, like Aristotle himself, in no way participates in the governance of the city he inhabits. Nonetheless, just such shared and reciprocal governance is, according to Aristotle, to a large extent the feature that makes a community distinctively political. If shared rule were only incidentally connected to the good life for the sake of which the city exists, then Aristotle's emphasis on it would be misplaced and his insistence that political rule differs from other varieties of rule by being shared and reciprocal would be untenable. He would be well advised to limit his characterization of distinctly political community to the goal of promoting the good life as a whole for all of its members. Even if such communities would frequently be characterized by shared, reciprocal rule, they

---

[36] So Miller 1995: 238. The translations are his. He also cites 4.7.1293b5–7, 7.9.1329a20–1, and 7.14.1333a11–12. For appeals to these and similar passages to support the alleged necessity of ruling for the exercise of virtue, see, e.g., Vander Waerdt 1985, Kahn 1990, Adkins 1991, Newell 1991, Frede 2005, Garver 2011: 101.

[37] Salkever 1990: 70–8.

would not *necessarily* be so characterized, and hence would not be political *because* they are so characterized.[38]

Moreover, Aristotle draws a tight connection between sharing in rule and being a direct beneficiary of the political community: To be a part or member of a community is to have a share of the common good at which the community aims (7.8.1328a21–35), the members of a political community are its citizens (3.1.1274b32–41), and citizens are those entitled to share in rule (3.1.1275b18–21).[39] If people excluded from rule can nonetheless be full and direct beneficiaries of the city's activities, then Aristotle should either revise his definition of citizenship or expand his account of membership well beyond the citizen body. Instead, he shows no awareness of the problem, suggesting that he regards citizens as the sole direct beneficiaries because he regards citizenship as a central aspect of the benefit. If citizenship is not somehow crucial for the achievement of the good life, then much of Aristotle's theory of politics makes considerably less sense. So attempting to solve the normative problem by denying that citizenship is intrinsically valuable threatens to deprive Aristotle's claims about the value of political community of much of their motivation and coherence.

These criticisms further suggest a distinct, though related, difficulty. Even if Aristotle does not regard citizenship as an important means to or part of the good life and so avoids the normative problem, he will still face the conceptual problem. Kingship, that is, will be an inherently nonpolitical form of rule and community even if it does not thereby deprive the king's subjects of the means and opportunity to live good lives. Even if the supremely virtuous king leads his subjects to fully flourishing lives, he will not rule them politically if he always rules and is never ruled while they are always ruled and never rule. Even if a king and his subjects could form an ideally happy community, it could apparently not be a political one. Many commentators have emphasized this problem for Aristotle's defense

---

[38] Aristotle argues similarly when he claims that oligarchy is rule by the wealthy and not rule by the few; it just so happens that the wealthy are always few and the poor many, but a constitution would be oligarchic even if it were ruled by a rich majority (*Pol.* 3.8.1279b20–1280a6). So even if oligarchies are *necessarily* ruled by the few, the number of the rulers is still incidental to their oligarchic character; the counterfactual is taken to show that the constitution would retain its fundamental character even if, *per impossibile*, the wealthy were in the majority. If, however, it is perfectly possible for a political community to exist without shared and reciprocal rule, then the argument against taking that kind of rule as part of what makes a community political would be even stronger.

[39] Irwin 1990 rightly stresses the role in Aristotle's arguments of the assumption that citizens benefit from participation. I offer an alternative account of the value of citizenship in Chapter 4.

of kingship.[40] Few, however, have distinguished it from the normative problem, and so have raised at least partially normative objections to it. It is worth seeing, however, that the conceptual problem is distinct from the normative problem and that the defense of kingship has awkward implications for Aristotle's theory of politics even if, for the sake of argument, we suppose that the subjects of a genuine king would be supremely and unobjectionably happy.

W. L. Newman outlined the basic shape of the conceptual problem already in 1887:

> To one form, indeed, of the best State of Aristotle the foregoing account of the State does not apply. In the Absolute Kingship, the highest but also the least realizable of its forms, many of its usual features seem to disappear. The State in this form seems to fall into two sections, the Absolute King, and those he rules, one of which, the Absolute King, is not part of the State at all (3.13 1284a8). Is he then outside the State, and is the State constituted by his subjects alone? Or is he rather to be regarded as himself the State? But then the State will apparently cease to be a κοινωνία, for there will be only one κοινωνός. And on that hypothesis, what becomes of the principle that the State consists of persons differing in kind? Or of the principle that it is an aggregate of individuals? If, on the other hand, the State is composed of the Absolute King and his subjects, what is his or their relation to it, if he is not a part of the State? Aristotle's admission of the Absolute Kingship as a possible form of the State seems altogether to conflict with his general account of the State.[41]

The fundamental problem is that kingship is supposed to be a kind of constitution, constitutions are supposed to be arrangements of cities, and a city is supposed to be a political community – a specific kind of community constituted by cooperative interaction among a plurality of naturally free males who share in ruling and being ruled. If in a kingship, only one person rules and all the others are merely ruled – if, in other words, only the king is a citizen – then it seems that kingship thoroughly dissolves political community as such, and consequently could not be a kind of constitution at all. This problem has normative implications insofar as political community is supposed to be necessary for human beings to live well, but the core of the issue is basically conceptual: Aristotle wants to

---

[40] For especially clear statements, see Newman 1887–1902.i: 288–9; Newell 1991; Nichols 1992: 74; Yack 1993: 86. Garver 2011: 102 maintains that "Aristotle is inconclusive about whether rule by the man of outstanding virtue can be political rule." Scholars who focus on what I call the normative problem frequently stress kingship's apparent failure to qualify as a form of political rule, but emphasize the injustice of such an arrangement rather than the more basic conceptual problem.
[41] Newman 1887–1902.i: 288–9.

classify as a form of political community what turns out to lack features that he elsewhere treats as essential to political community.

Newman's worry was that total kingship is, by its nature, not a kind of community at all. His suspicions arise from some passages claiming that the king should not be considered a part of the city (3.13.1284a5–8, 17.1288a26–8). From one perspective, this is exactly the sort of thing that Aristotle should say: If political community necessarily consists of a plurality of people who share in rule, and kingship involves no such thing, then whatever kind of community exists between the king and his subjects, it is not political community, and so the king should not be considered a part of a political community. But if that is what Aristotle means to say when he denies that the king is a part of the city, that should merely compound our perplexity about why he persists in treating kingship as though it were a form of political community.

Even if we understand the denial that the king is a part of the city as an admission that kingship is not a form of political community, it is too quick to conclude that it would not be any form of community at all. On the contrary, several passages suggest that it is the sort of community we find in the household: Total kingship is "arranged in the manner of household management," and just as household management is a kind of kingship over a household, so too is kingship a kind of household management of a polis (3.14.1285b29–33). The initial characterization of the differences between the household and the city in book 1 associates monarchy and kingship with the household rather than the city: "Household management is [a form of] monarchy, since every household is ruled monarchically, but political rule is rule over people who are free and equal" (1.7.1255b16–20); a man rules over his children in the manner of a king (1.12.1259a37–b1, b10–12).

It is clear enough in these contexts that the household and the city are different kinds of community and that ruling and being ruled accordingly take on different forms in each. The explanation and justification of these differences appeal to disparities between the different parties' capacities for deliberative rationality. Whereas natural slaves altogether lack the capacity for self-directed rational agency, children have yet to develop it sufficiently, and though women can develop it, it cannot achieve the authority in their psychological economy that it can in the case of men (1.11.1259a38–b4, 1.13.1260a12–17).[42] In each case, the specific character of the naturally free

---

[42] I return to Aristotle's account of these relationships and their supposed psychological bases in Chapter 3.

adult male's superiority entails that his authority is appropriately exercised in different ways. Yet all of these relationships of rule within the household stand in contrast to the sort that distinguishes political community. Political rule resembles the rule over women and children insofar as it is rule over free people and therefore aims at the good of the ruled. But the form of rule characteristic of political community differs from those of the household because political community is a relationship among people who are roughly equal in their basic capacities for deliberative rationality. Yet even when Aristotle initially draws these distinctions among kinds of community, he associates monarchic rule with the household in contrast to the city. More specifically, it is a man's rule over his children that he compares to the rule of a king. Taken together, these claims seem to amount to a plain acknowledgment that kingship and political community are mutually exclusive.

As with the normative problem, at first sight the conceptual problem may seem peculiar to monarchy. After all, it is only kingship that Aristotle compares to the rule of a household, and other constitutional forms include a plurality of citizens. They therefore meet the criteria for being political communities. Once again, however, monarchy merely presents the most severe symptoms of the problem. If monarchy completely dissolves political relationships and instead sets a paternal authority figure over something like an extended household, then aristocracy limits genuine political community to relations among the ruling few. If the few rule over people who do not also somehow share in rule, then they do not rule them politically, and whatever kind of community they have with the ruled, it is not a political one. This conclusion would make an awkward fit at best with the normative dimensions of Aristotle's account of politics for the reasons already discussed. The strictly conceptual problem, however, is not that Aristotle seems to suppose that this sort of restriction of the realm of the political would be harmful and unjust, but that he seems not to think of the aristocracy as reducing the size of the city or as transforming the mode of rule that the rulers exercise over the ruled. If we suppose that the relationship remains political because the rulers aim at promoting the well-being of the ruled, then we collapse the distinction between political rule and household rule on which Aristotle lays so much stress. Polity, aristocracy, and kingship would therefore constitute a spectrum of decreasingly political arrangements of rule over free adult men. Yet, while Aristotle is occasionally willing to echo Plato in asserting that a corrupt or deviant polis is not truly a polis, the conceptual problem seems to show that he is committed to saying the same thing about supposedly *correct* constitutions.

This attenuation of the political across the correct constitutions sheds light on a more widely recognized problem for the theory of constitutions in the *Politics*. As I noted when discussing the normative problem, the distinction between correct and deviant constitutions seems to be unavailable in the case of monarchy: A corrupt regime aims at the good of the rulers rather than the common good of the citizen body, yet in a monarchy the king *is* the citizen body. Once again, this problem reappears in less extreme form in the case of aristocracy and oligarchy. When the ruling body is made up of more than one person, then it will be possible for some of its members to seek their own interests at the expense of the common good. So a distinction between correct and deviant forms of rule by the few remains applicable. But Aristotle pretty clearly does not conceive of oligarchies as corrupt and unjust only when the oligarchs fail to seek the common good of their fellow oligarchs. Rather, oligarchies are unjust because they fail to seek the common good of the larger group constituted by the oligarchs and the multitude of people they exclude from ruling. The distinction that remains available to Aristotle in the case of rule by the few therefore fails to apply to the whole range of cases that he rightly wants it to cover.

Aristotle's definition of citizenship often takes the blame for this problem. Because he defines citizenship in terms of ruling, he evidently makes the ruling class and the citizen body coextensive. Distinguishing correct and deviant constitutions in terms of their promotion of the common good of the citizens therefore limits constitutional deviance to faction within the ruling class. Since Aristotle apparently does not accept that implication, the most prominent response to the problem has been to suppose that he implicitly works with a more expansive notion of citizenship that extends to people who do not share in rule. These "second-class citizens" cannot hold positions of authority but nonetheless count as members of the community and therefore are included in the group whose common good is the goal of a correct constitution.[43] But the distinction between the city and the household, with their correspondingly distinct varieties of rule, raises difficulties for this solution. On these terms, people who in no way share in rule but are merely ruled do not have properly political relationships to the people who rule them, and hence cannot be even "second-class" members of the political community. The city might have ample reason to seek the good of these nonmembers, but their good

---

[43] For variants of this approach, Cooper 1990, Keyt 1993, Morrison 1999, Biondi Khan 2005. The term "second-class citizen" is Keyt's.

cannot be a nonderivative part of the city's common good. To suppose otherwise would be to conflate political and paternal rule and to abandon the claim that the former is essential to political community.

The price of accepting the standard solution to the apparent collapse of the distinction between correct and deviant constitutions is to reject a central component of the core conception of political community. Yet that very conception seems to entail that constitutional deviance is strictly a matter of how corulers treat one another and never a matter of how they treat those whom they exclude from rule. This problem is worth taking seriously in part for its worrisome normative implications, but the conceptual problem remains even if we suppose that those who are excluded from correct constitutions are never made the victims of injustice and live perfectly happy lives. Aristotle plainly supposes that a constitution may be deviant by virtue of excluding from citizenship people whom it ought to include. If his account of deviance is limited to relations between citizens, then it apparently cannot allow for this possibility. So even if we suppose that correct constitutions will include everyone whom they ought to and treat everyone else impeccably, the theory will still lack an important element that Aristotle rightly expects it to have. Even if it yields all the right answers, it will not recognize all the right reasons. So the problem lies in the conceptual structure of Aristotle's theory, not simply in the normative conclusions it supports.

The collapse of the correct/deviant distinction is therefore an aspect of the conceptual problem of monarchy as well as the normative problem. None of these problems is uniquely applicable to monarchy; they simply show up there in their strongest forms. It is therefore a mistake to dismiss them as peripheral to Aristotle's main concerns. Not only do the problems arise for aristocracy and any other exclusionary political arrangements, but they arise from the attempt to combine the two central components of the core conception of political community with a theory of justice and constitutions. To see whether these problems can be resolved, then, it is not enough to look to the defense of kingship in book 3. It will instead be instructive to reexamine the central tenets of Aristotle's account of the nature and value of political community with an eye to whether they make the normative and conceptual problems of monarchy inevitable or, conversely, contain the resources to alleviate or even avoid the problems altogether. For the most part, I will argue that, when properly understood, Aristotle's theory does not generate these problems.

Before turning to my argument, however, I want briefly to address an alternative interpretive strategy, primarily in order to justify largely

ignoring it in the rest of the book. This alternative is that of so-called
esoteric interpretation, an approach cultivated prominently, though not
exclusively, by Leo Strauss and his followers.[44] The common feature of
esoteric interpretations, both Straussian and otherwise, is to see tensions
and contradictions in a philosophical text not as mistakes or flaws, but as
purposeful intimations of deeper truths intended to be appreciated only
by readers careful enough to spot the problems. Theorists influenced by
Strauss often approach the *Politics* this way, but the defense of kingship
has seemed so amenable to esoteric treatment that even scholars hostile or
indifferent to Strauss have defended it. Motivations sometimes cited for
this kind of writing on Aristotle's part include the desire to avoid offend-
ing his Macedonian patrons by explicitly condemning monarchy and the
need to conceal his covert support for Macedon and their variety of hereditary kingship.[45] However plausible one finds such biographical specula-
tions, esoteric interpretations face a simple but fundamental objection.
For any sort of esoteric interpretation to be warranted, two conditions
must be met: First, it must be clear that the arguments or the positions in
question actually are contradictory, incoherent, or seriously problematic;
second, it should be implausible that the author could simply have failed
to see the problems. The first condition requires us to make a considerable effort to determine whether the text can be read in some way that
dispels the appearance of contradiction. The second condition requires us
to show that the contradictions are sufficiently apparent that the author
probably did not make them unintentionally.[46] These are large demands,
and though no esoteric interpretation that I have encountered has come

---

[44] Nichols 1992 presents perhaps the most fully developed esoteric reading of the defense of kingship
I know. For other Straussian readings, cf. Lord 1982, Lindsay 1991, Newell 1991, Bates 2003, Collins
2006, Pangle 2013. Strauss 1964 includes a chapter on the *Politics*, but does not treat it, like Plato's
Republic, as an esoteric writing that conceals its true teachings beneath a surface of explicit claims
whose problematic and contradictory features are left to careful readers to uncover.

[45] Kelsen 1937 takes the *Politics* to be an ideological defense of hereditary monarchy against democracy. Kahn 1990 suggests that Aristotle in fact rejected monarchy but wanted to avoid giving
offense. Miller 1998 argues that Aristotle was an "agent" of Macedon. Ober 1998 does not explain
the defense of kingship as part of a pro-Macedonian agenda, but encourages such speculation with
his similar suggestion that Aristotle envisioned the "best constitution" of *Pol.* 7–8 as being imple-
mented in a colonization project opened up by Alexander's conquest of Asia. Strauss 1952 located
the motivation for esoteric writing in the threat of persecution: When a political philosopher's
teachings are opposed to the fundamental beliefs of his community, he must conceal them in order
to avoid the community's oppression. It seems worth noting that the *Politics*, like the *Republic*,
seems to have something to alienate everyone of any ideological persuasion; neither book reads like
something written in order to avoid giving offense.

[46] These conditions were formulated clearly already by Klosko 1986 in a discussion of Plato; the persistence of esoteric readings of Aristotle suggests that they bear repeating.

close to meeting them, it will be sufficient to leave the question open and to proceed to consider various attempts to resolve or explain the puzzling features of Aristotle's argument in the *Politics*.

To do that, my first step will be to explore Aristotle's general theory of community and its relationship to friendship and justice. Only then will we be in a position to understand his account of distinctively political community, citizenship, and constitutions in preparation for returning to the problems of monarchy.

CHAPTER 2

Community, Friendship, and Justice

Chapter 1 has shown that Aristotle's defense of kingship in the *Politics* raises two related but distinct problems when set in the framework of his core conception of political community: Monarchy seems to be inherently unjust (the *normative problem*) and inherently unpolitical (the *conceptual problem*). Worse, these problems are not peculiar to monarchy, but arise in some form for any political arrangement that excludes a significant number of would-be citizens from political participation. The problems of monarchy therefore seem to be merely symptomatic of the fundamental inconsistency of Aristotle's theory of justice with his vision of politics. Coming to grips with these problems requires a reexamination of the core conception of political community. Two questions stand out as especially salient: What *is* political community, and what is its *value*? Neither of these questions can receive a satisfactory response without some answer to a third: What is the genus "community" of which political community is apparently only a single species? Yet Aristotle's conception of community can only be understood adequately in light of his theories of friendship and justice.

This chapter attempts to show the connections among community, friendship, and justice as a framework for understanding what makes political communities distinct from other forms of cooperative human interaction. I first survey Aristotle's use of the language of community and argue that community exists wherever people cooperate with a view to their mutual benefit. This broad and flexible notion of community finds expression in Aristotle's claim that community, justice, and friendship are coextensive, and the remainder of the chapter aims to understand that coextensiveness. I begin that task by laying out an interpretation of Aristotle's theory of the nature and varieties of friendship, with an emphasis on "advantage friendships" in which the friends value their relationship only instrumentally. I distinguish these relations both from "complete friendships" in which the friends value one another for their own sake and from the manipulative and exploitative relations that Aristotle agrees are not forms of genuine friendship or community. The upshot of this discussion is that Aristotelian community and friendship exist between people with separate but shared interests. This conception of friendship and community enables us to understand how both can be coextensive with justice, and the remainder of the chapter argues in favor of a strong interpretation of that coextensiveness on which the cooperative pursuit of shared goals generates standards of justice internal to the community constituted by that cooperative pursuit. Hence different sorts of people cooperating with a view to different sorts of goods will be rationally constrained to recognize different requirements of justice. With this framework in place, Chapter 3 will turn to consider how the nature of the goals and of the members of political community distinguishes it from other varieties of community, and especially the household.

1. The Idea of Community

Politics 1 begins by identifying the polis as a distinct kind of community. Like every community, the polis is established for the sake of some good. Its most immediately distinctive features, however, are its scope and authority: The political community embraces or includes various subpolitical associations and aims at a good that controls and limits those associations in their pursuit of their characteristic aims (*Pol.* 1.1.1252a1–7). Yet the polis differs from the communities that it embraces not merely by its place at the top of a hierarchy of authority. Hierarchical superiority alone would be consistent with the view that the forms of rule exercised by masters, heads of households, statesmen, and kings differ only quantitatively.[1] Aristotle rejects that view. There are, of course, quantitative differences. The household manager rules over more people than the slave master but fewer than the king or statesman; the statesman's rule is shared with others while the king's is reserved to him alone. Simply pointing to the numbers, however, fails to account for more fundamental differences of kind

---

[1] Saunders 1995 and Simpson 1998 read the οὖν in μὲν οὖν at 1252a7 inferentially, thereby supposing that Aristotle presents the differences in kind between political rule and other kinds of rule as a logical consequence of the superior scope and authority of the polis. But that inference is false; one community might be more inclusive and authoritative than another without involving a different *kind* of rule or authority. There is, however, no need to suppose that Aristotle thinks otherwise, since μὲν οὖν is often merely transitional with no suggestion of inference: e.g., *Pol.* 5.1.1301a19, the position of which at the opening of a new book shows that it is not there inferential (see too Denniston 1950: 470–3).

(1.1.1252a7–16). Aristotle attributes the strictly quantitative distinction to certain unnamed predecessors, and though he initially announces his disagreement without argument, the remainder of book 1 defends it and aims to illustrate the specific differences among the polis, the household, and the relationships that constitute the household.[2] Beyond the divergence in the number of rulers and ruled lie more basic variations in their characteristic modes of rule and authority.

The attention that Aristotle devotes to these points and their emphatic position at the beginning of the *Politics* suggest that he considers them to be among his more important insights.[3] Yet for all the emphasis on their differences, the polis, the household, and the relationships that make a household are all of them kinds of the more general class "community." Nor are they the only sorts of community that Aristotle explicitly recognizes. Given his insistence on the distinctness of the political as one among many forms of human community, we might reasonably hope to better appreciate that distinctiveness in light of the features that belong to all communities as such. Aristotle nowhere provides a focused or systematic analysis of the genus as he does with its various species. Nonetheless, it is possible to piece together a view of community in general from various comments in the *Politics* and from its role in the theories of friendship in the *Nicomachean* and *Eudemian Ethics*.[4]

Aristotle's word for "community" is κοινωνία. Already I have alternated between "community" and "association" in translating it, and not merely for the sake of variety. Each English word carries connotations in its

---

[2] Commentators routinely point to Plato, *Statesman* 258e–9d and Xenophon *Memorabilia* 3.4 as sources for the view that Aristotle opposes. Saunders 1995 reads the opening chapter as presupposing a detailed knowledge of the *Statesman*, but as Simpson 1997 notes, the underlying assumption seems likely to have been widespread. I discuss some aspects of the relationship between the *Politics* and the *Statesman* in Chapter 6.

[3] Though the naturalness of the polis and slavery have tended to dominate discussion of book 1, the book as a whole is devoted to defending its initial thesis that the forms of community and rule differ in kind. For appreciation of this point, see Schofield 1990, who emphasizes distinctions in kinds of rule, and Deslauriers 2006, who focuses on the related distinctions between kinds of people. Cf. Newell 1991, Simpson 1998.

[4] For this strategy, compare Newman 1887–1902.i.41–3, Finley 1970, and Yack 1993: ch. 1. I draw throughout on the *EE* despite the disputed problems about its authorship, relative date, and consistency with the *EN*, on which see Rowe 1971, Kenny 1992, Woods 1992, and, more briefly, Bobonich 2006. Most recent scholars take the *EN* as the primary companion to the *Politics*, though Kraut 2002 argues that the *EE*, but not the *EN*, predates the *Politics*. Though I have no firm view on the chronological relationship of the three works, I take the *EN* to be consistent with the *Politics* in substance, though not always in terminology. I avoid the thorny problems surrounding the *EE* by appealing to its account only where I believe it to be either consistent with the *EN* or to illuminate the latter by its differences.

ordinary use that are foreign to the Greek. To the suggestion of tight-knit bonds of emotional warmth sometimes conjured up by "community," "association" responds with its distinct intimation of abstract formality and procedural aloofness. "Partnership" fares little better. Though its uses are too varied to lend it a distinct connotation, phrases like "political partnership" inspire images of behind-the-scenes handshakes and carefully planned press conferences. The Latin *societas* might serve, but the English "society" would not, since it tends to denote groups formed around special interests when it does not refer to collections of individuals conceived on the model of a corporate agent. The solution, as with most important words in the Greek philosophical vocabulary, is to lay aside whatever connotations of the English translation do not also suggest themselves in the author's actual use of the terms.[5] Yet no translation is entirely innocuous, and though I will sometimes shift between "community" and "association," my marked preference will be for "community." Why?

Perhaps the most literal translation of κοινωνία would be "commonality," a sharing of something in common.[6] It is etymologically connected to the adjective κοινός, which means "common," and to the verb κοινωνεῖν, which can mean "to share something in common" or "to have a share of something." "Community" preserves that formal and semantic link, while "association," by contrast, lacks the clear connection between the sharing and what is shared. "Community" is not perfect; notably, it fails to serve even as a component of a sensible translation of many uses of the verb, which is sometimes best translated "to associate." The linguistic features that favor "community" are therefore not independently decisive, and the ultimate justification for my choice is interpretive. "Community," in my judgment, is less misleading and more illuminating – more illuminating because it focuses attention on what people share in common when they associate rather than the mere fact of their association; less misleading because the impersonality and formality of "association" are even less characteristic of Aristotelian κοινωνία per se than the intimacy and solidarity often suggested by "community."[7] The best way to justify these claims is to get on with the task of interpreting Aristotle's scattered characterizations

[5] Kraut 2002: 354–5 takes a similar view.
[6] For discussions about translating κοινωνία, leading to opposite verdicts, Yack 1993: ch. 1 and Pakaluk 1998: III.
[7] On this point, Yack 1993: ch. 1 helpfully distinguishes Aristotelian community from "communion," in which members identify themselves with a collective will or interest. Aristotle conceives of community "in terms of what people share rather than in terms of collective identities" (30). Cf. Nussbaum 1980, Nichols 1992: 153–80.

of κοινωνία. Let these remarks about translation stand as a preface and a disclaimer of what I do *not* intend to convey with the term "community."

A brief survey of Aristotle's use of the word and its related forms underscores the centrality of sharing things in common to the idea of κοινωνία.[8] He applies the term to a wide range of relationships formed around a variety of shared goods. Thus he can specify communities by grammatical objects as diverse as food and land (*Pol.* 7.8.1328a25–8); wives, children, and possessions (2.1.1261a4–8); commodities (*EN* 8.14.1163a31); goods (*EE* 7.12.1245a19–20); words and actions (*EN* 2.7.1108a11, 4.8.1128b5–6); and a way of life (5.6.1134a26).[9] They can also be distinguished by their grammatical subjects, from husbands and wives (*EE* 7.10.1242a31–5) and fathers and sons (*EN* 8.10.1160b24, *EE* 7.9.1241b38–40, 7.10.1242a31–5) to farmers and doctors (*EN* 5.5.1133a16–18) and members of phratries, religious revelers, and business associates (*EE* 7.9.1241b24–6). The noun can also refer to more permanent communities of distinct kinds, not only the city (*Pol.* 1.1.1252a6–7, 1252b27–8), but also the household (1.2.1252b12–14) and villages (1.2.1252b15–16). Though the verbal form sometimes appears in contexts that do not imply cooperative sharing with others (e.g., "contemplation" at *EE* 1.4.1215b11–14, "pleasures" at *EE* 3.2.1231a28), its most characteristic use parallels the use of the noun (e.g., *Pol.* 2.1.1260b37–9).[10]

We can get a sense of what it is to share goods in common from a passage in *Politics* 7.8: "There must be some single thing that is common (κοινόν) and the same for those who share in community, whether they share it equally or unequally; this is, for instance, either food or a quantity of land or some other of these sorts of things" (7.8.1328a25–28). Aristotle conceives of a community as a kind of whole composed of parts, and to be a part of a community is to share something in common with others. Any whole composed of parts will require that certain conditions be

---

[8] I will frequently use the expression "sharing in common" when describing κοινωνίαι and what their members do together. This preference comes as an attempt to preserve the semantic link to "community" and to keep the distinctiveness of the Aristotelian concept more clearly in focus than the deceptively familiar "sharing" might allow.

[9] Aristotle's examples show that it is a mistake to suppose, with Cooper 2010: 231, 242, that communities must be established for the sake of *activities*. Cooper is therefore likewise mistaken to maintain that a community's ends, whether they are activities or not, must be achieved *in* the activity that constitutes the community and not merely produced by that activity. These two assumptions are foundational for Cooper's general account of Aristotelian community and political community specifically. See my further comments on exchange communities.

[10] The "noncommunal" uses of the verb, as we might call them, are closely related to the "communal" use. They seem to describe either obtaining a part of something rather than all of it (hence, "to have a share of") or sharing a capacity for something (such as pleasures in the passage cited previously) with others, or both.

met in order to exist. Being a necessary condition for the existence of a whole, however, is not sufficient for being a part of it (7.8.1328a21–25). With many complex wholes, it is a relatively straightforward matter to determine what is only a necessary condition of its existence and what is a part of it. The existence of the sun and the penetration of its rays to the surface of the planet, for instance, are necessary conditions for the existence of a plant. But neither the sun nor its light is a part of the plant. With communities, the question is more difficult.

What, then, is to count as sharing a good in common with others? Aristotle here provides an argument from analogy to distinguish sharing in some good from standing in a merely instrumental relationship to it and to the community formed around it. He takes as his example the relationship between a craftsman or his instruments and their product, here a house builder and a house (7.8.1328a28–33). The house builder, his craft, and his instruments stand in a purely instrumental relationship to the house that they produce, and they therefore do not share anything in common with it. In light of the connection between sharing goods in common and being a part of a community, we should read this as a claim about parthood: To deny that there is anything common to them is to deny that either is a part of the other or that they jointly make up the parts of any single thing. This way of putting the point may be obscure, but its truth is intuitively apparent. A house builder and his instruments are not parts of the house that they build; they just build it. By analogy, anyone who only produces a good that is shared in common does not thereby count as sharing in it, however necessary his activity may be for its existence.[11]

This passage has been misunderstood by commentators who have taken it primarily as an explanation of why slaves do not count as parts of the city.[12] To be sure, the context seems to point in that direction. The chapter's initial distinction between parts of a whole and necessary conditions for its existence is the first step in an argument that proceeds to exclude property, animate as well as inanimate, from proper membership in the city. In fact, however, Aristotle's point here is quite general and does not primarily concern the relationship between masters and slaves or between

[11] Aristotle's conception of parts in the *Politics* is notoriously obscure and apparently contradictory. One potential problem with the argument here is that distinguishing merely instrumental relationships from functional roles belonging to parts seems to require appeal to a pretheoretical intuition about what counts as a part; if so, the argument threatens to become circular. On parts and wholes in the *Politics*, see Mayhew 1997 and Chapter 6.4.

[12] Newman 1887–1902:i.41–3, iii ad loc.; Kraut 1997 ad loc.; Simpson 1998 ad loc.

individual people of any specific sort. The instrumentality he has in mind is not first and foremost a relationship between two people, but between a person or an activity and some material or subject matter that is shared among others. To take Aristotle's conveniently simple example of food, being a member of a community formed around food is a matter of having a share of the food. Someone might devote the bulk of his efforts to growing, preserving, and even distributing the food, but he will fall short of being a member of the community if he does not receive a share of it himself. Admittedly, this claim has implications for the relationship between individuals: Those who do receive a share of the food stand in a different relationship to one another than they do to the laborer who merely produces it. Yet while such a laborer might be a slave, he need not be. Even a free person who stands in this sort of relationship to some shared good falls short of sharing in it.

More to the point, if the argument is supposed to illustrate the relationship between a slave and his master, then it fails by Aristotle's own account. For he elsewhere connects the instrumentality of the slave's relationship to his master with the slave's being a part of the master, while the argument here treats instrumentality as precluding parthood (1.4.1253b27–1254a13). In fact, he elsewhere denies that master and slave as such form a genuine community precisely because the slave is, in effect, a part of his master and therefore does not have any good distinct from his master's (*EN* 8.11.1161a32–b5, *EE* 7.9.1241b17–24).[13] In that case, however, the slave stands to his master as an instrument to a craftsman. In contrast, the instrumentality discussed in *Politics* 7.8 receives illumination by analogy with a craftsman's relationship to his product. To read this passage as primarily concerned with the relationship between master and slave would therefore force us to conclude that Aristotle envisioned the master as the passively receptive product of the actively productive slave. These contradictions vanish once we appreciate that the relationships here contrasted are not between individuals, but between individuals and some good shared in common. Moreover, the disanalogy with slavery shows that there are at least two ways in which someone could fail to share goods in common with another: either through being insufficiently distinct

[13] Some, such as Schofield 1999e, have held that Aristotle's account of slavery is incompatible with the accounts in the ethical works. I argue against this view later, but my point here would be unaffected even if Schofield's thesis were true: For as I go on to show, even in the *Politics* itself, the slave's status as an instrument is tied to his being a part of the master.

from him, as the slave is from his master, or by standing in some merely instrumental relationship to those goods.

2.   Community, Distribution, and Exchange

Community, then, is a matter of sharing some good in common, whether equally or unequally, and producing or sustaining that good is insufficient for sharing in it. The same emphasis on sharing goods recurs throughout Aristotle's discussions of community. He begins his consideration of actual and theoretical candidates for well-ordered constitutions in book II of the *Politics* by distinguishing political arrangements in terms of how much the citizens share. Formally, there are three possibilities: they might share everything, or nothing, or some things but not others. The second possibility, however, is not really a possibility, since "a constitution is a kind of community" (*Pol.* 2.1.1260b37–1261a1), and there would be no community if there were not people sharing something in common. Minimally, they must share the place, since "one city has one place and the citizens share one city" (2.1 1260b41–1261a1). Among other things that the citizens might share in various ways are spouses and children, land, food, property more generally, and activities such as judging legal cases, deliberation and decision on matters of common concern, and particular offices. From these examples we can see the range and the variety of what can be shared as well as the importance, in Aristotle's view, of what is shared and how it is shared to determining the general character of a community.

The examples in 7.8 had the virtue of simplicity: Both food and land are material goods that can be physically divided, and sharing in them is a straightforward matter of receiving some amount of the material. Such would be the case with property more generally. Sharing in activities is a more complex matter, but one that we can still understand on the model of distribution and to which it is not difficult to apply Aristotle's dictum that for those who share in it there must be "some one thing that is common and the same" (7.8.1328a25–28). Those who share in the activity of judging legal disputes do not thereby receive some definite amount of material goods, but they do participate in the same activity. Whether they jointly contribute to a single case of adjudication or serve in the same capacity on separate occasions, they can be said to share in the activity and, conceivably, to share in it equally or unequally. Though juries might most often weigh each juror's verdict equally, a deliberative assembly need not assign equal weight to everyone's vote or give each participant the same ability to shape the discussion.[14] Similarly, people might share unequally in an activity by having greater or lesser parts to play in carrying it out. Aristotle's ease in accommodating these examples illustrates the applicability of the distributive model that is most at home in contexts of material goods to the somewhat different context of shared activities.[15]

That model might begin to seem strained when we turn to the apparently more tenuous varieties of human interaction that Aristotle classes as kinds of community. At the opposite extreme from the hypothetical political community in which everyone shares everything stand economic transactions that he labels "exchange communities" (*EN* 5.5.1132b31–2). Whether we have in mind the unmediated barter of shoes for a house (5.5.1133a5–8) or the more complex exchange of commodities for currency (5.5.1133a18–24), these transactions seem to lack the one feature that the other passages so far considered made central to community: "the one thing that is common and the same." Partners to an economic exchange, that is, apparently do not have equal or unequal shares of any single common thing, whether a material good or a common activity. The very rationale of their interaction seems not to be to share anything, but to trade. Yet Aristotle refers to these relationships as a kind of community, and he gives them a central place in his discussion of reciprocal justice, making the striking claim that "the city is held together by proportionate reciprocity" (5.5.1132b33–4).

Besides intimating the importance of exchange communities to the political community as a whole, Aristotle's handling of these relationships reflects his acute awareness of the differences between these sorts of interaction and the communities of sharing that we have seen so far. Exchange communities involve a form of justice distinct from the distributive and corrective forms discussed in *EN* 5.3–4. Reciprocal justice differs most obviously from corrective justice in not presupposing that one of the parties to the exchange has made an unjust gain.[16] Its distinction

---

[14] Aristotle considers weighted voting of this sort at *Pol.* 6.3.1318a27–b1; for discussion, Keyt 1999: 205–6 and Kraut 2002: 457–60.

[15] Hence Cooper 2010: 243 is at best misleading when he suggests that what is genuinely common in Aristotle's sense cannot be divided among the participants in the community: Activities and material goods can be divided among a community's members in a variety of ways.

[16] Polansky 2014b: 161 argues that correction is of secondary importance to what is misleadingly translated as "corrective justice": "Aristotle's concern is with the just in transactions and not merely with correcting them when they go wrong, as usually supposed.... *Diorthōtikon* should translate as that which sets things right rather than be restricted to correction *after* an unjust transaction, or if kept as 'corrective,' Aristotle should be understood to employ this available particular name for

from distributive justice, however, is less clear and has been the subject of scholarly dispute.[17] Without attempting to resolve those disputes or to supply an answer to the vexed question of exactly how proportionate reciprocity fits into Aristotle's theory of justice, we can see that it is marked off from distributive justice by not involving the distribution of a common subject matter such as honor, money, or property. Whether or not Aristotle intended reciprocal justice to play some wider or deeper role in his account, his introduction of it in a treatment of exchange communities shows that he was sensitive to one basic difference between such communities and the sorts we have seen so far: Partners in communities of exchange do not share an equal or unequal distribution of some common stock or activity.

Yet Aristotle persists in describing these interactions as communities. He might have simply called them "exchanges" and refrained from treating exchange as a kind of community, but he does not. So either he is inconsistent or communities need not involve sharing in a particular distribution of some common asset.[18] If he is not inconsistent, however, there must be some sense in which partners to an exchange do share something, or some way in which their interaction is analogous to the sorts of sharing that he elsewhere associates with communities. In light of Aristotle's implicit acknowledgment that communities of exchange are unlike communities formed around distributed goods, it is attractive to suppose that what exchange partners share is precisely the mutually beneficial,

something wider." Against this claim, we might observe that the discussion of *EN* 5.4 focuses firmly on cases in which one party to a transaction has been harmed or suffered loss, and that the chapter's emphasis on the work of judges in rectification fits with this emphasis. But while the truth of Polansky's claim would complicate the relationship between corrective and reciprocal justice, it would not be inconsistent with the conclusions I draw here about community.

[17] For an overview, see Miller 1995: ch. 3 and Roberts 2000. Yack 1993: ch. 4 and Meikle 1995: ch. 7 view reciprocal justice as more fundamental than distributive or corrective and do not take it to be limited to commercial exchange. Cf. Irwin 1988: ch. 20, Mayhew 1997: 334 n 25, Kraut 2002: 98–177. Polansky 2014b: 163–5 suggests that reciprocal justice applies to transactions rather than distributions (and hence is distinct from distributive justice) but only to transactions in which merit and motivation are relevant (and hence is distinct from "the just in transactions"), but his ultimate view of these relationships is obscure.

[18] Cooper 2010: 231 implicitly denies that exchange communities are communities – because in exchange we find individuals "each acting on their own merely in some coordinated way so as to produce some 'common' product." He is more explicit in 1990: 229, where he rejects what he calls "the joint-stock company model." But Cooper's position depends on the claims that the goal of an Aristotelian community must be a shared activity and that this goal must be achieved *in* the activity that constitutes the community, not merely produced by it. Since, as I have argued, both of these claims are mistaken, Cooper provides no reason to conclude that exchange communities are not genuine communities.

cooperative activity of exchange. After all, to describe the benefit as mutual is already to point to its source in a shared, common activity.

This hypothesis might seem implausible if we suppose that a mere isolated swap of goods constitutes an exchange community; such a relationship could seem too temporary and limited to establish a community of any kind. We might suppose instead, then, that Aristotle identifies exchange communities with more extended relationships that emerge from a recurring pattern of exchanges over time.[19] Repeated interaction requires coordination and establishes a sort of relationship of which it would be true to say that the partners share an activity in common. Yet this hypothesis not only fails to find explicit confirmation, but seems ruled out by the character of Aristotle's analysis. Justice in exchange is a matter of the proportionate equalization of goods that differ in kind; an exchange is just when the goods exchanged are proportionately equal (*EN* 5.5.1133a16–b18). Notwithstanding the difficulties of understanding how Aristotle conceives the commensuration of goods that differ in kind – and there are reasons to suspect that he was not himself satisfied with this analysis[20] – the more important point is that this sort of justice, however exactly it works, presupposes a community of exchange; it is, in Aristotle's terms, only to partners in such an exchange community that justice of this sort applies.[21] But since fair exchange of goods clearly does not presuppose an established diachronic relationship between the same two partners – how many times will a shoemaker exchange shoes for a house?, we might

---

[19] Cooper 2010: 231 takes this sort of view when he stipulates that communities are constituted by activities "performed regularly and on a continuing basis."

[20] Aristotle's attempt to explain the commensuration of objects of different kinds is a major theme of Meikle 1995, who says that Aristotle "had his reasons for thinking an ultimate reconciliation to be beyond anybody's capacities, because it followed from his analysis that it was logically impossible" (20). What is logically impossible, on Meikle's view, is not that qualitatively incommensurable objects could be commensurated by coinage, but that this commensuration could reflect any real equivalence of value in the commensurated objects. Meikle himself considers this a virtue of Aristotle's analysis, since he regards it as an insight that exchange value is not reducible to or a simple function of use value. Polansky 2014b: 165–7 rightly objects that Meikle exaggerates Aristotle's interest in determining how prices are set, and hence overstates the significance of this point for the analysis of reciprocal justice, but Meikle's interpretation of *EN* 5.5 remains among the most illuminating available.

[21] What is unclear is whether or not "communities of exchange" exist only in cases of "commercial exchange," i.e., exchange of commodities, or also include exchanges of less tangible forms of assistance; at the limit, Aristotle might see "exchange" wherever there is reciprocity, whether positive or negative (cf. Meikle 1995: 141). "Commercial" is an unsatisfactory choice of words in either case, since Aristotle's concept of exchange is intended to cover simple cases in which no money is involved, and "commerce" often suggests an activity aimed at making money itself. My point here is that, whatever kinds of interaction Aristotle classifies as exchanges, he sees communities of exchange as the necessary context for the applicability of reciprocal justice.

ask – it follows that no such recurring pattern of interaction is necessary for the existence of community between partners to an exchange.

We might suppose instead that the partners to an exchange are members of a community because they are fellow citizens and hence share in a broader common good even when they do not exchange goods with one another on a regular basis; Aristotle suggests as much when he describes weavers and shoemakers exchanging goods in "political friendship" (9.1.1163a32–5).[22] But Aristotle rightly does not restrict exchange communities or justice in exchange to relations among fellow citizens. On the contrary, he emphatically distinguishes political community from a prepolitical community of "exchange and alliance" in which people associate merely to trade goods and prevent injustice against one another (*Pol.* 3.9.1280b22–3, 29–31). Aristotle thinks that many and perhaps most human beings fail to live in political communities, but he does not suppose that they fail to exchange goods or to recognize standards of fairness in their exchanges.[23] So it seems that he does in fact regard a one-off exchange between a weaver and a shoemaker as a kind of community.

Tenuous as such a relationship might seem, Aristotle is on solid ground when he takes it to be a kind of community. Partners to an exchange cooperate for the sake of a common, mutually beneficial goal. An exchange benefits each of the parties to the extent that they acquire something useful for themselves through it. The exchange itself is therefore a common benefit. Moreover, each partner recognizes that the other will be willing to exchange only on condition that he acquires something valuable in return, and so seeks to provide that benefit to the other. The exchange is therefore a common goal, as well. Exchange partners coordinate their activity in pursuit of a goal that each regards as a source of benefit; in other words, they aim at a common good.[24] To be sure, they do not regard

---

[22] Hence Curzer 2012: 252 note 10.

[23] It has occasionally been denied that Aristotle believes that human beings can or do exist in pre- or nonpolitical societies: Kullmann 1991, Trott 2013: 46–7. But Aristotle is in fact quite clear about this point: *Pol.* 2.2.1261a27–9 and 7.4.1326b2–5 both acknowledge the existence of nonpolitical "nations" (ἔθνη), as the term is often translated. I discuss this point more fully in Chapter 3.

[24] Curzer 2012: 252–3 denies that exchange relations – "the relationship of businessman to customer" – are a form of Aristotelian friendship, and so, by implication, denies that an exchange community is a form of community. He concedes that exchange partners benefit from their coordinated cooperation, but insists that they do not aim at a genuinely common goal. But when I choose to buy apples from the local orchard, and the orchard owner chooses to sell them to me, we both choose the same thing – the exchange – and so aim at a common goal. We may have no *further* common goals, but neither do the parties to relationships that are uncontroversially utility friendships; see my further discussion of friendship later in this chapter.

exchange as good for its own sake, but only for the sake of the goods they acquire by means of it. So, too, traders often seek to maximize their gains while minimizing their losses, and hence seek to benefit at their partners' expense. But the same is true of other kinds of relationships that Aristotle uncontroversially classifies as communities, and so these considerations present no reason to deny that commodity exchange is a kind of community. These communities of exchange illustrate that Aristotelian community exists wherever people cooperate with a view to their mutual benefit.

We can gain a considerably richer understanding of Aristotelian community once we appreciate its role in Aristotle's theory of friendship. Because community, as cooperative interaction aimed at some common good, is the correlate and context of friendship, the kinds of the former are isomorphic to those of the latter. This feature of Aristotle's theory is sufficient to account for why he does not supply an independent account of community as such; his account of friendship just is in part an account of community. Much has been written about Aristotle's theory of friendship, which raises many questions that are only indirectly relevant to understanding political community. A broad view of the theory, however, will clarify the framework in which Aristotle thinks about politics as a distinct kind of cooperative interaction with a distinctive value.

3. Community and Friendship

The clearest expression of a tight connection between friendship and community appears at the beginning of *EN* 8.9:

> It seems, as was said in the beginning, that friendship and justice concern the same things and exist among the same people. For in every community there is a kind of justice and a kind of friendship as well. People use the term "friends," at any rate, to address their fellow travelers and their fellow soldiers, and likewise those in the other communities as well. And to the very same extent that they share something in common [κοινωνοῦσιν], there is friendship, because there is also justice. Indeed the proverb "the things of friends are common" is rightly said, for friendship exists in community. (*EN* 8.9.1159b25–32)

Aristotle repeats the same point a few chapters later, when, summarizing the conclusion of the preceding arguments, he says that "every friendship exists in community" (*EN* 8.12.1161b11). The implication is that friendship and community are correlative: When we find one, we

will find the other. More strikingly, the two have an equally close relationship to justice, suggesting that in fact the three are coextensive phenomena and that each implies the other two.[25] To allay any initial doubts
that Aristotle could mean quite what he seems to say, it is worth noting that
the *Eudemian Ethics* appears to bind friendship, community, and justice even
more closely together:

> It is thought both that justice is a kind of equality and that friendship exists
> in equality, unless it is said to no purpose that "friendship is equality." All
> the constitutions, too, are a form of justice; for there is [in them] com-
> munity, and every common thing is established through justice, so that
> there are as many forms of justice and community as of friendship. (*EE* 7.9
> 1241b11–16)

And, a little later:

> To inquire how one should relate to a friend is to inquire about a sort of
> justice; for in fact, quite generally all justice is in relation to a friend, since
> justice exists among particular people who also share something in com-
> mon [τισι καὶ κοινωνοῖς], and a friend is a person who shares something
> in common [κοινωνός], one sort sharing in family, another in a way of life.
> (7.10.1242a19–22)

It turns out, however, that a number of difficulties arise in understanding what sort of relationship Aristotle envisions in these passages among
community, friendship, and justice. A variety of interpretations might
be compatible with the strict letter of the texts, each yielding incompatible answers to the crucial question of whether Aristotle really means to
say that community and friendship – not to mention justice – are always
found together. Before considering a few broad alternatives and the case
in favor of each of them, it is important to get a clear view of some central
features of Aristotle's theory of friendship. Understanding friendship will
not only enable us to assess rival interpretations of Aristotle's claims about
its relationship to community. It is also crucial for grasping Aristotle's
view of the range of different positive attitudes that individuals may have
toward fellow participants in different kinds of community. A proper
appreciation of those attitudes will, in turn, help us to address questions
about the value of political community and what, if anything, is distinctive or characteristic of the way that citizens relate to one another as such.

It is a scholarly commonplace that the terms φιλία and φίλος have a
much different range in Greek than their English counterparts "friend"

---

[25] I take the term "coextensive" from Pakaluk 1998: 111.

and "friendship." Though usage is not consistent across the authors of the Classical period, in general the terms apply both to relationships more distant and less often marked by emotional ties – at the limit, to military and political allies in addition to fellow citizens or members of a region within a polis – and to relations of family or more extended kinship.[26] The broader application of these terms goes some way toward explaining why Aristotle's account of friendship takes the expansive shape that it does, encompassing so much more than the close, affectively toned relationships between two individuals to which our "friendship" is often restricted.[27]

Far from merely reflecting ordinary Greek usage and thought, however, Aristotle's theory of friendship is in part an attempt to bring some systematic order to bear on the sometimes confused and inconsistent beliefs of "the many and the wise" about what friendship is, who counts as a friend to whom, and why. Aristotle's methodological commitment to preserving and explaining ordinary beliefs and reputable opinions while resolving the inconsistencies and puzzles they raise precludes some theoretical possibilities and makes others difficult to resist.[28] In particular, it leads him to eschew elegant but simplifying accounts of friendship in order to avoid obscuring the heterogeneity of cooperative human interaction that is one source of conflicting views on the subject. Not everyone has

---

[26] For φιλία in Greek usage, cf. Whitlock-Blundell 1989: ch. 1, Stern-Gillet 1995, Konstan 1997. These works offer accounts of φιλία that are at variance on a number of important points. Comparison brings out a special problem with interpreting the many texts in which φιλία or φίλος is applied to relations that English speakers today would not describe, at least in the first instance, as "friendship": When should a use of the terms be understood as we understand someone who talks about her friendship with her mother or describes his political allies as his friends? This problem is about the sense and the connotations of the word, not about its extension or the conditions of its correct application. It is probably a mistake to expect to be able to construct a relatively simple unified account of Greek uses of the term. Aristotle, however, is not in the business of lexicography or ordinary-language conceptual analysis; his aim is to analyze φιλία and its kinds, not what people say about φιλία and its kinds.

[27] O'Connor 1990, in an insightful and undeservedly neglected discussion, distinguishes Aristotelian friendship as partnership, focused on shared activity and common action, from a modern Western ideal of friendship as intimacy, which identifies personal insight and concern as the core of friendship and privileges "being together" over "doing something together." Though this analysis perhaps calls for elaboration and refinement, it offers a suggestive diagnosis of some of the difficulties that modern interpreters have had with Aristotle's theory of friendship.

[28] My understanding of Aristotle's method in ethics and other areas of philosophy roughly follows Barnes 1980, Irwin 1981, Nussbaum 1986, and White 1992; cf. Kraut 2006b for a different view. Irwin 1988 addresses the question across the Aristotelian corpus and supplies a useful corrective to Nussbaum's account by stressing Aristotle's metaphysical realism. My claims here do not depend on any particular resolution of the most important disputes among these interpretations of Aristotle's method, such as the differences or similarities of his method in ethics with his philosophical method more generally and the role, if any, of substantive metaphysical theses in ethics. Most recent discussions of these questions are indebted to Owen 1961.

been or will be convinced that Aristotle has liberated himself from the impulse toward excessive schematization in the interest of theoretical economy. Nonetheless, its insistence on capturing the varieties of friendship and community is one of the most important features of Aristotle's theory, especially as it forms one major part of the ethical background to the *Politics*.

4. The Varieties of Friendship

One of Aristotle's most decisive moves is to divide up friendship into three broad classes. The distinction of kinds corresponds to a difference in the basis of the friendship and the reasons that the friends have for associating together. Generally speaking, one might have friendly affection for a person or any other thing either because it is useful, because it is pleasant, or because it is good (*EN* 8.2.1155b18–21, *EE* 7.2.1236a10–14). This sort of affection, however, is necessary but insufficient for friendship. While one can have friendly affection of a sort for inanimate things, friendship requires that the affection be reciprocated and that each of the parties be aware of the reciprocation; only then are they rightly called "friends" (*EN* 8.2.1155b27–31, 1156a2–5; *EE* 7.2.1236a14–15). The "friendly affection" (φίλησις) in question is not merely some sort of passive affective response or a vaguely emotional proattitude, but essentially involves a cognitively informed desire for the other person's good, what Aristotle describes as "wishing goods for one another" (*EN* 8.2.1155b28–31, 1156a3–5).[29] Though this sort of friendly affection can arise as a more or less spontaneous emotional response, once a friendship has been formed each of the friends possesses a fairly settled disposition toward the other not only to wish for his good, but to choose it and, where possible and appropriate, to act to promote or preserve it (8.5.1157b28–31).[30]

The division of friendship into three kinds, however, is not merely a distinction in the ways in which people might come to wish goods for each other. Rather, each kind of friendship also embodies a different way of

[29] On "wish" (βούλησις) as "rational desire," see *EN* 3.2.1111b10–30, 3.4.1113a15–b2, and Cooper 1999b.
[30] Though *EN* 8.5.1157b28–31 is primarily concerned with friendships based on goodness between people of good character, the point applies, with qualification, to friends of other varieties. The qualification concerns the extent to which the disposition can be taken as settled; not only can people of unstable character engage in friendships based on pleasure or advantage, but those kinds of friendship are liable to dissolution as a result of changes in circumstance, and not only of changes in character. This point does not count against taking a settled disposition of φιλία toward another as a criterion of friendships of each kind, because even in friendships based on goodness there can be and are many imperfect instances of the general type.

wishing for the friend's good: "People who are friends to one another wish goods to each other in the way in which they are friends" (8.2.1156a9–10). Those who are friends on the basis of utility do not love their friends in themselves, but only insofar as they obtain some good from them. Those who are friends on the basis of pleasure, similarly, do not love their friends on the grounds that they have some good qualities that belong to them intrinsically. Rather, they value the pleasure that they gain from interacting with their friends. In friendships of these kinds, what the friends primarily value about one another is that they each provide the other with some pleasure or instrumental benefit. It turns out, accordingly, that what they value in each other are their friends' incidental features rather than the characteristics that belong to their friends "in themselves," as particular people of a certain sort of character.

In friendships based on goodness, by contrast, what friends value about each other are the traits that make them the sort of people they are, those dispositions of character and intellect that make a human being good of his kind and are, as it were, central to his practical identity as an embodied rational agent. The affection and friendship that friends of this sort have for one another are not limited to an impersonal admiration for each other's excellent qualities – this would amount only to what Aristotle calls "goodwill" (εὔνοια, 8.2.1155b32–56a5, 9.5.1166b30–67a21). On the contrary, one effect of such friendship is that the friends' interests become fused, so that each becomes in himself a good for the other (8.5.1157b34–35). A friend of this kind is, in Aristotle's famous phrase, "another self" to his friend (9.4.1166a31–32, 9.9.1169b6–7, 1170b6–7; cf. 8.12.1161b27–29). Because of these differences in the ways that friends can value each other – the ways in which they "wish goods" and "love" or "are friends to" one another (βούλεσθαι τἀγαθά, φιλεῖν) – Aristotle insists that the relationships themselves are different in kind, and he classes friendships of pleasure and utility as forms of friendship "incidentally." The relationships are incidentally friendships because what the friends value about each other are only incidental features of who and what they are (8.3.1156a14–19).

The distance among these three forms of friendship comes to appear even greater if we follow Aristotle in conceiving of friendship based on goodness in light of its fullest possible manifestation. His characterizations of each kind of friendship are more often paradigmatic than exhaustive, but this feature comes to the fore with friendships based on goodness because the paradigm turns out to be the friendship of fully virtuous individuals. Only completely virtuous people are without qualification and in themselves good of their kind and therefore not only such as to benefit but also such as to value one another in their own right. The rest of us will, to the extent that we are not virtuous people, either fail to become the objects of other people's friendly affection in our own right or, if we do, will do so only because our friends have made a false judgment of our character, either taking us to be a different sort of people than we really are or believing certain sorts of people and traits of character to be good when they are, in fact, bad and harmful.[31] In part because of the important role of friendship in human well-being and of the role of wishing *goods* – not merely *apparent* goods – to one another in friendship, the friendship of people who mistakenly believe each other to be good cannot serve as the paradigm of friendship. It does not follow, as Aristotle sometimes appears to suggest, that only the fully virtuous can have friendships of this kind at all. It merely follows that all such instances of this kind of friendship will be imperfect of their kind.[32]

There are a number of attractions to analyzing friendship based on goodness by focusing on its fullest manifestation as a paradigm or central case, and any number of reasons why Aristotle might have chosen to do so. It is at least potentially fruitful, when dealing with a complex and variable phenomenon, to direct one's attention first to the central cases that most fully display all of the subject's most distinguishing features, and to understand other cases by reference to those. Rather than dismissing the instances that do not exhibit all of the characteristics of the paradigm on the grounds that they thereby fail to be genuine instances of the phenomenon, we may hope to gain a clearer view of the nonparadigm cases precisely by understanding them as nonparadigmatic but nonetheless genuine cases.[33] Just such a central-case analysis is what Aristotle offers in his

---

[31] The major exception to this pattern is the relationship between parents and children. Children can be the objects of their parents' intrinsic concern without having first developed any definite traits of character because children begin their existence as physical and metaphysical parts of their parents and continue to be so for an indefinite period. I discuss the "parthood" of children to their parents briefly in Chapter 2.5.

[32] For this distinction between complete friendship and perfect instances of it, see Price 1989: 104 note 3, who, however, persists in using "perfect" where I will use "complete." As he notes, neither translation is fully satisfactory. For the same point that not all genuine instances of complete friendship are perfect, cf. Cooper 1980: 306–7: Complete friendships can "be based on the conception of the other person as morally good (in some respect, in some degree), even though the person does not have, and is not thought to have, a perfectly virtuous character." See too Belfiore 2001 on family relationships as imperfect instances of complete friendship. Stern-Gillet 1995 is ambiguous on this point.

[33] See Finnis 1980: 9–11 on central case analyses of "law"; Finnis's account, which draws in roughly equal portions on Aristotle and Weber, shows that Aristotle's strategy is less unusual than it might appear.

characterizations of the "complete friendship of men who are good and similar in virtue" (8.3.1156b7–8).

The paradigmatic structure of Aristotle's account of this kind of friendship is also integral to his handling of the division of friendship into kinds. His principal motivation for that division is, as we have seen, that the varieties of positive reciprocity among human beings exhibit differences sufficiently great to preclude their being classed as minor divergences among particular instances of a single type. The differences are so great, in fact, that one might easily be inclined to deny that friendships of pleasure and friendships of advantage are really friendships at all. In a way, Aristotle does just this: Unlike the friendship of the virtuous, these friendships are friendships only incidentally. Yet this claim is not a way of denying that these relations are friendships, but a way of saying *how* they are friendships. Notably, however, it is a way that goes a great bit further in recognizing their differences than simply treating them as differences in kind. To stop there would be to miss one of the most important aspects of these kinds as Aristotle sees them, namely, that they do not stand to one another as the species of a single genus. Rather, friendship based on goodness enjoys a kind of conceptual priority over the other two that no species of a genus has over other species.

These differences emerge early in Aristotle's account. Pleasure and advantage friendships are only incidentally friendships; complete friendship based on goodness is uniquely friendship "without qualification" (8.3.1156a16, 1156b9–11; 8.4.1157b4–5). Complete friendship is treated as friendship in the primary and chief sense; the others are friendships only because and insofar as they resemble complete friendship in various respects (8.4.1157a30–2, 1157b4–5). The nonprimary forms are therefore friendships to a lesser degree, and features that are characteristic of complete friendship vary among the other forms by degrees (8.3.1156b23–4, 8.5.1157b25, 1157b36–1158a1); friendship based on pleasure resembles friendship more than friendship grounded on advantage (8.6.1158a18); both are more like friendship than the mixed forms in which one friend associates with the other for pleasure, the other for profit (8.6.1158a18–20; cf. 8.4.1157a7–14, 9.1.1163b32–64a22). Yet none of this is true of the species of a single genus. Hawks, crows, and grackles, for instance, are all equally species of bird. None is a bird only incidentally; none is a bird in some primary sense, the rest being secondary; none is a bird because and insofar as it resembles one primary species of bird.[34]

---

[34] Admittedly, Aristotle's conception of the relationship between species and genera does, on some accounts, give an important place to difference in degree (see esp. Lennox 1987). Rather than

To say this much, however, is to leave much unsaid about exactly how the forms differ and how each resembles complete friendship. The story I have told so far denies that the three kinds differ by instantiating some single set of properties that vary only in degree. The division among the kinds, as we have seen, follows the distinction among their objects, and "those who are friends wish goods to one another in the way in which they are friends" (8.3.1156a9–10). We should expect, accordingly, that the reciprocal and mutually acknowledged wishing of goods at the center of each kind of friendship will not differ among the forms solely by exhibiting more or less of the very same features it shares with the others. How, then, does it differ across kinds?

This question runs up against an important controversy in the interpretation of Aristotelian friendship among those who affirm and those who deny that each of the three forms essentially involves wishing goods to another for his own sake as opposed to one's own. Differently put, there is disagreement about whether friendship of all kinds must be "disinterested" if it is to count as friendship.[35] The relevance of this disagreement for understanding Aristotle's theory of political community should be obvious: When we ask what kind of community a political community is, one of the things we want to know is whether it is a kind of community in which all of the members have a disinterested concern for one another or, by contrast, one in which the participants regard their relationships with one another as of merely instrumental value.

---

differing from one another by the possession of some additional set of distinct properties, the various species of a genus possess the features that characterize that genus, but possess each to different degrees; so all of our species of bird have beaks, feathers, and wings, but their beaks, feathers, and wings will differ in size, shape, and other quantifiable respects. They do not differ, however, in being more or less birds, or in being more or less beaked, feathered, or winged. The features that distinguish the kinds of friendship, in contrast, do not differ in degree alone; each kind counts as friendship to a greater or lesser degree by virtue of resembling the complete variety, but the resemblance is not a matter of possessing a lesser degree of the very same properties. The very need for an appeal to resemblance to unify the kinds presupposes that they are not related as species to a genus and that the concept of degree functions differently in the account of friendship and in the classification of animal species. Thus, even if Aristotle's treatment of species and genera in the biology differs from standard modern accounts – so that Lennox, for instance, rightly prefers to translate Aristotle's terms as "kind" (γένος) and "form" or "form of a kind" (εἶδος) – his treatment of the kinds of friendship differs even from his treatment of biological kinds.

35 The most influential proponent of the "disinterested" view is Cooper 1980, which combines portions of 1977a and 1977b. For a similar view applied to Aristotle and Classical Greek thought in general, see Konstan 1997: ch. 2. For objections and alternatives, cf. Alpern 1983, Irwin 1988: ch. 18, Price 1989, Stern-Gillet 1995, and Pakaluk 1998.

Rather than argue against alternative views in detail, I will set out what I take to be strong reasons in favor of the view that only complete friendship is "disinterested" in essentially involving reciprocal and mutually acknowledged wishing of goods among friends for the sake of each other. I will also try to indicate why, despite the apparently "interested" character of the other friendships, they are not inherently suspect on ethical grounds or deserving of disparagement as little more than pale reflections of the complete friendship of virtuous men.[36] These considerations will help to make clear just what is and is not at stake when we consider how friendship and community are related to justice and how political community fits into the conceptual framework that they form.

Aristotle's characterization of the friendships of advantage and of pleasure is filled with indications that they are not disinterested. The initial description of these friendships as incidental suggests as much: "It is not insofar as he is who he is that the person loved as a friend is loved, but only insofar as they supply some good or some pleasure" (8.3.1156a17–19). The friendships last only so long as the friends remain useful or pleasant to each other (8.3.1156a19–24). Those who are friends because of advantage cease to be friends as soon as they cease to be advantageous, *because* they are friends, not of each other, but of the benefit that they receive from one another (8.4.1157a14–16). Friendships based on advantage are peculiarly liable to complaints and quarrels because, unlike friendships grounded in excellence, where each friend is eager to benefit the other for the sake of his friend, advantage friends associate for the sake of a distinct benefit. Consequently, the motivation and goals of the relationship leave room for dispute when one party believes that he has received less than he should. Friendships of pleasure, by contrast, do not give rise to many complaints because when one person stops being pleasant to the other, that other simply loses his grounds for associating with his erstwhile friend; so long as it is open to one not to associate with the other, he has no motivation to complain or to quarrel (8.13.1162b5–21).[37] These distinctions would

---

[36] In this respect, my view is similar to that of Alpern 1983: 304, who argues "that the inferior friendships do not involve disinterestedness, but that these relationships nonetheless can be seen to exhibit cooperation, trust, commitment, and other virtues of interpersonal relationships." Despite much that has been written on friendship in the intervening years, Alpern's article remains particularly helpful for its careful philological argument and its clarity in laying out interpretive and philosophical alternatives.

[37] This claim requires at least two important qualifications. First, we should not understand Aristotle as holding that advantage friendships are characteristically conflict-ridden; rather, his point is that such friendships are distinctively susceptible to conflict in ways that the other kinds are not, because each friend's aims in associating with the other make it possible for that other to fail to reciprocate adequately without thereby dissolving the friend's reasons for interest in reciprocation

seem out of place if each sort of friendship essentially involved a noninstrumental interest on the part of each friend in the good of the other.

Further indication that Aristotle restricts this sort of interest to friendships of the complete variety – though not only to perfect instances of its kind – is that when he turns to discuss it in light of his initial division and description of the other kinds, he treats the fact that friends of this kind wish each other goods for their sake as an important factor in the completeness of complete friendship: "Those who wish good things to their friends for their sake are most of all friends" (8.3.1156b7–11). Similarly, *EN* 9.5 apparently denies that goodwill (εὔνοια) – a kind of disinterested well wishing that falls short of friendship and friendly affection – is a part of the friendships of pleasure and advantage (9.5.1167a10–14).[38]

The main philosophical motivation for seeking noninstrumental concern for the friend as essential to every sort of friendship is, I take it, a worry that relationships that lack it hardly deserve to be called friendships. Notwithstanding the doctrine of partial resemblance by degrees, excising the for-the-sake-of-the-other condition from any sort of friendship may

---

(cf. Kraut 2002: 467 for a different view). Second, we should not imagine that Aristotle thinks all instances of complete friendship are immune to conflict. Conflict within friendships of the complete variety is the result of ethical failures on the part of one or both friends, and so is possible within imperfect instances of the kind, but their imperfections are, on his account, precisely ways in which they fail to resemble friendship. Thus, while Aristotle does not explicitly make the first qualification about conflict in friendships of advantage, his explanation of why bad people cannot be friends does supply the material for the second qualification when we allow that people can fail to be virtuous to various degrees and in various respects. Whether it is fair or wise of Aristotle to characterize complete friendship by reference to its fullest manifestation but to treat flawed instances of the other kinds without any special qualification is a different question.

[38] Interpretation of this passage is vexed. The text says that "goodwill does not arise in these cases," but ἐπὶ τούτοις might also be translated as "for these things" or "on these terms," where "these" refers to pleasure and benefit. It might, then, be read as a more limited denial that goodwill develops spontaneously for people whom we regard as potentially useful or pleasant but with whom we have not entered into any sort of active friendship. But the lines that follow (a14–18) deny that one has genuine goodwill toward another when it is returned in gratitude for benefits received or when one wishes goods to another in the hope that he will reciprocate. Furthermore, *EN* 8.2.1155b34–1156a1 apparently asserts that a person *can* have goodwill for another whom he does not know on the grounds that he is a useful or beneficial person. Taken together, these passages suggest that we can have goodwill toward others whom we judge to be good, pleasant, or useful, but that goodwill is not a constituent of friendships based on pleasure or advantage. This point is readily intelligible if we understand εὔνοια as a sort of benevolence unaccompanied by any further motives – even, as the text suggests, the motive of justice. It is difficult to see how an attitude to those whom we "have not seen" but regard as useful could be disinterested in this way, but only the inherent disinterestedness of εὔνοια makes sense of the argument. *EE* 7.7.1241a2–10 makes the same point. It may help to observe that both the *EN* and the *EE* passages appear to use the word "friend" in a restricted way to refer only to friends of the primary or complete variety. For discussion of these passages, see Alpern 1983: 309, Price 1989: 152–4, with comments on Cooper 1977a and 1980; for a concise treatment of the *EN* argument, see Pakaluk 1998: 179.

leave what is left looking more like mutual manipulation than anything resembling friendship.[39] This intuition is not based simply on mistaking a narrow modern conception of friendship for Greek or Aristotelian φιλία; it is more firmly grounded in a textually plausible sense that φιλία and φιλεῖν must involve some genuine affection and concern that, however limited and circumscribed by the utility or pleasure that provide the rationale for the relationship, they are inconsistent with the sort of selfishness that treats others as mere suppliers of our own independent interests. If I regard your interests as worth my consideration only insofar as they contribute instrumentally to my own, then you are not so much my friend as my tool. Aristotle himself hardly seems to treat merely manipulative interests in others as sufficient for friendship. As the most eloquent and persuasive proponent of this view puts it, "Aristotle seems to feel, as we do, that the expectation, at least, of interest in the other person's good for his own sake was part of what the word itself conveyed."[40]

Philosophical intuitions, however, are unreliable interpretive guides. The key textual support for this reading comes from passages in which Aristotle seems to make the for-the-sake-of-the-other condition necessary for anything to count as friendship. His discussion of friendship in the *Rhetoric* apparently does so (*Rhet.* 2.4.1380b36–1381a1), but that work's different aims justify doubts about whether its treatment of common ideas is intended to advance very far beyond pretheoretical conceptions of them.[41] Far more striking is the explanation, in *EN* 8.2, of why we cannot be friends with inanimate things:

> Although there are three things on account of which people have friendly affection [φιλοῦσιν], it is not called friendship in the case of friendly affection for inanimate things. For there is no reciprocal affection, and there is no wishing of those things' good[42] (since it would presumably be ridiculous

---

[39] Vlastos 1973c gives an influential and eloquent statement of the alleged poverty of Aristotle's (and Plato's) understanding of love and friendship. More bluntly, Joachim 1951: 247 has it that people in friendships of advantage "exploit" one another, while Adkins 1963: 38–9, following Stewart 1892, describes all three kinds of friendships as "entirely" and "equally selfish." Though the influence of Cooper's interpretation has displaced these assessments from their former position as the *opinio communis*, one burden of any alternative to Cooper's view is to explain why we should not return to the old view if Aristotelian friendships are not inherently disinterested.

[40] Cooper 1980: 316. Cf. his comments about the apparent "self-centeredness" of Aristotelian friendship understood as not disinterested; Cooper calls the alternative that he rejects "an extremely harsh view ... a depressing result" (305–6).

[41] Irwin 1996 considers the vexed issue of the relationship between Aristotle's claims in the *Rhetoric* and the ethical works.

[42] Following the ἐκείνων of the mss. rather than Bywater's ἐκείνῳ; I take it that ἀγαθοῦ is an objective genitive, ἐκείνων a possessive dependent on it.

to wish good things for one's wine; but if someone does so, he wants it to
be preserved in order that he himself might have it). But people say that
one ought to wish goods to one's friend for *his* sake. (*EN* 8.2.1155b27–31)

It is instructive to contrast this argument with the parallel passage in the
Eudemian Ethics. There, the reciprocity of friendly affection is apparently
sufficient to mark the difference between friendship and affection for
inanimate things (*EE* 7.2.1236a10–15).[43] Here, however, genuine friendship with another person transcends mere friendly affection of the sort
we have for nonliving things by involving a rational desire for the good of
the other person that is, if not impossible, at least ridiculous in the case of
inanimate things. The chief distinguishing feature of that desire is, apparently, that it is directed at the good of the other for the other's sake, while
any desire we might have for the good of a nonliving object is ultimately
a desire for our own good. So unless Aristotle means to retract this point
later on, consistency should demand that he treat noninstrumental concern for the other as essential to every kind of friendship.

As others have noted, however, matters are not so simple.[44] The position
of this argument in Aristotle's treatment of the kinds of friendship should
caution us against uncritically taking it as his considered view. In fact,
when this argument appears he has not yet distinguished the kinds from
each other and declared the friendships of advantage and of pleasure to
be friendships incidentally. The argument introduces the for-the-sake-of-
the-other condition as a widely held opinion and does not unambiguously assert it as true. It is therefore quite possible that Aristotle means
to reject it, to accept it only in one of several possible senses in which it
could be true, or to restrict its unequivocal application to friendships of
the complete kind. That is exactly what seems to happen when he turns
to complete friendship: "Those who wish goods to their friends for their
sake are friends most of all" (*EN* 8.3.1156b9–10). If friends of every kind
wished goods to their friends for their friends' sake, then no specific variety of friendship could be distinguished by that feature. The appeal to
noninstrumental concern for the other in 8.2 therefore hardly clinches the
argument that such concern must be essential to any form of friendship.

Yet if Aristotle does retract his apparent endorsement of the
for-the-sake-of-the-other condition in the case of the friendships of

---

[43] No doubt reciprocity alone changes the character of the relationship significantly, and so alters the
expression of friendly affection. The point is simply that the *EE* sees no need to add that qualification, even though its substantive view may ultimately be identical to that of the *EN*.

[44] See especially Alpern 1983, Price 1989, Pakaluk 1998.

pleasure and of advantage, that seems to threaten the distinction between friendship among people and friendly affection for nonliving things. Friends of these sorts will turn out to wish goods to each other only in the tenuous and ridiculous way that people wish good for their wine. This conclusion would justify the charge that these forms of friendship are "self-centered" and at least potentially manipulative. More puzzlingly, though, it would require such a strong qualification of the initial argument that we should be surprised not to find a more explicit recognition of it in a chapter dedicated to qualifying the various ways in which friendships of each kind count as friendships. The role that noninstrumental concern for the other plays in distinguishing complete friendship shows that Aristotle qualifies his endorsement of the for-the-sake-of-the-other condition in some way or other, but a near-obliteration of the distinction between friendship and wishing good things for one's wine seems tantamount to a rejection. If it is not, then we need to be able to say how Aristotle's view qualifies the condition without reducing the other kinds of friendship to a more complicated variety of our concern for our possessions. The solution to this difficulty lies, I think, in the gradual transformation of the for-the-sake-of-the-other condition from a vague, pretheoretical notion into a more precise and rigidly specified requirement. At its introduction, it takes its content from its contrast with our typical attitude toward our favorite possessions, and in that sense it applies to each of the forms of friendship. Aristotle's elaboration of those forms, however, brings to light a narrower but more robust sense in which friends can wish goods for the sake of each other, and it is that sense that is restricted to friendships based on goodness of character.

5. Wishing for the Good of the Friend

We can begin by looking more closely at the structure of the argument that friendly affection for inanimate things falls short of friendship. The common opinion that a friend wishes goods to his friend for his friend's sake serves to qualify the initial claim that we do not wish goods to nonliving objects. At first sight, the qualification may appear simply to exclude wishing goods to another for merely instrumental reasons. Taken that way, however, the qualification would in fact be a correction to the initial claim. The initial assertion is that when we have friendly affection for an inanimate thing, we do not wish good for it. To wish good for our wine would be ridiculous; if we choose to regard our interest in the wine as wishing for its good, we must note that what we wish is for the wine to be preserved so that we can have it. This way of framing the thought suggests that Aristotle is at least reluctant to consider this sort of interest in something as a genuine case of wishing for its good. But to wish good to something for instrumental reasons is, in fact, to wish good to it. Aristotle's treatment of instrumental goods, at least, insists on recognizing them as goods in a way and not withholding the attribution of goodness to them on grounds of their instrumental value and dependence on the value of intrinsic goods (*EN* 1.6.1096b10–14, cf. 1.7.1097a25–8). So if the requirement that one wish goods to a friend for his sake is intended here to mark the distinction between wishing his good for instrumental reasons and wishing his good noninstrumentally, then we must take Aristotle to be correcting a piece of hyperbole on his part that he elsewhere regards as an obstacle to gaining a clear view on the nature of goods. The clumsiness of Aristotle's expression on this reading should encourage us to ask whether he might mean what he says, namely, that our interest in the preservation of our wine or other inanimate things does not really amount to wishing for its good.

One thought is that we cannot wish good to the wine because, strictly speaking, only living things can be said to have a good at all.[45] But the sense in which the wine cannot be benefited or harmed is at least initially obscure, and Aristotle does at least once describe inanimate things as receiving benefit (8.11.1161a35–b2).[46] Moreover, he gives us the material to appreciate the main sense in which they can. We want our wine to be preserved so that we can have it. Presumably, to have it is to drink it, and so the preservation that interests us includes the preservation of whatever qualities make for good drinking (potency, flavor, etc.). Any change in the wine that would ruin it for drinking would count as bad for the wine; whatever preserves or protects its good features counts as good for it.

Perhaps, then, cases like these are excluded because what we want, at least eventually, is to consume the wine and so to destroy it.[47] Certainly any relationship in which we preserve someone only in order to destroy him for our own benefit should not count as a friendship. So we might think that the example serves to set a condition on wishing goods for something, requiring that we want it to be preserved indefinitely, not only for a limited period before we consume it. This suggestion, however, is too weak. Aristotle denies that we wish goods to any nonliving thing, not only

[45] Pakaluk 1998: 60.
[46] The referents of πάντα ταῦτα at 1161b1 are slaves, bodies, and *instruments*.
[47] Pakaluk 1998: 60.

to those we intend to consume. Typically, at any rate, we do not intend to destroy our houses for our own benefit, and yet they are no more alive than wine. Furthermore, simply failing to intend the destruction of something we value seems to fall too far short of any plausible sense of "wishing good to another for his sake." That phrase may not distinguish instrumental and intrinsic concern for another, but it is plainly supposed to stand as a gloss or qualification on the kind of concern that friends have for one another but that we can only have for inanimate things by making ourselves ridiculous. Not wishing for someone's destruction is surely necessary, but hardly sufficient.

We can get a better handle on the issue if we ask why wishing good for one's wine is supposed to be ridiculous. Presumably Aristotle is not here disparaging people who take care that their wine does not spoil. It seems no more likely that he regards enjoying the pleasures of wine for their own sake as especially worthy of disdain, since the appropriate enjoyment of it, as of other pleasures, is characteristic of the virtue of temperance (σωφροσύνη, 3.11.1119a11–20). Aristotle's formulation of the point suggests that the ordinary interest that people have in their wine is not aptly described as a wish for its good. Whatever such a wish would involve, it would go beyond wanting to preserve it so as to drink it. So what is it about the ordinary, nonridiculous interest people have in their wine that makes it fall short of wishing goods to it in anything but a tenuous sense? We have seen that it is not that there is no sense in which we do not want good things for the wine or that our interest in consuming it means that what we want is ultimately what is bad for it. In that respect, wine is a poor example to illustrate a point equally applicable to all nonliving things. It would be an especially good example, however, if the feature that distinguishes this sort of concern from our concern for friends is that the inanimate things, unlike our friends, do not have any value independent of our interest in them and their contribution to our good. In that case, the same aspect of our interest in wine that makes it seem a poor candidate as a paradigm of an inanimate object of friendly affection turns out to make it an especially appropriate example. Though our interest in inanimate objects often does not include an intention to consume them, those whose value to us does entail their destruction illustrate most vividly that all such things have no value independent of their contributions to our interests. It is not that we can give no sense to the idea of wanting good things for them; it is that we can give no sense to their having any good that is not entirely a function of our own.

This understanding of Aristotle's point ties together his claim that wishing goods for our wine would be ridiculous and his invocation of the idea that friends wish good for their friends' sake. To wish good for our wine would, if possible at all, be to treat the wine as though it were somehow a being with interests independent of one's own. Whatever forms that affection might take, it is easy to imagine some ridiculous ones. More importantly, to wish goods for someone for his sake can be understood not as excluding a merely instrumental motivation for one's concern for him, but as requiring that we wish what is genuinely good for him as a distinct human being with independent interests. This is, crucially, not the same as having a noninstrumental concern for a person, at least if noninstrumental concern requires that we take an interest in another person's good just for his sake, making his good an end that we value in itself and thus as a part of our own good. We are not left with the alternatives of either treating the good of others and our relationships with them as constitutive components of our own or regarding them and their interests as mere appendages to our own. Even in those relationships that we enter into and maintain for their instrumental value, we may wish good to others as people whose interests extend widely beyond their ability to serve ours. To do so, however, does not render our motivations or the value of the relationship noninstrumental. Our reasons for associating with and wishing goods to those others continue to be a function of their instrumental value to us.[48] But wishing goods to others as subjects with independent interests precludes the manipulative or "instrumentalizing" attitudes and actions that might follow from regarding others in the way that we regard our possessions.

The double duty that the metaphor of instruments does in our discourse is, no doubt, one reason why it can seem so difficult to carve out some conceptual space between disinterested benevolence and the self-centered manipulation of others. On the one hand, we employ the metaphor to name an important sort of value that can be had by actions, objects, events, and conditions when they contribute to procuring or preserving

---

[48] Because I understand the instrumental benefits that the friends take away from their interaction as supplying the *reason* for their relationship and for their mutual wishing of goods to one another, my view differs nontrivially from Cooper's and those like it, which distinguish the instrumental benefit as the *grounds* of friendship from its goals or aims, where the grounds are understood as playing a psychological-causal role in generating a concern that is disinterested insofar as the good of the friend is taken as (the source of) an independently sufficient reason to take some action to promote or preserve that good. On this point, cf. Cooper 1977a: 621–2 with the remarks in Alpern 1983: 305.

other things that we value for their own sake. On the other, we reach for the metaphor in various ways when we want to denounce the subjection of one person's interests to another's. The two uses are connected insofar as the inherently negative connotations of "instrumentalization" flow from the thought that such subjection involves treating others as though they were of merely instrumental value.[49] Yet we might doubt that the objectionable features of "instrumentalization" are best explained as the effects of appreciating the instrumental value of others, and so suspect that the metaphor does irreducibly different work in each case.[50]

However our own moral discourse functions, it is instructive to note that Aristotle generally avoids the metaphor of instruments when talking about friendship. He cites tools as an illustration of things that we choose for the sake of something else, and hence as what we could describe as having instrumental value (1.7.1097a25–6), and he characterizes the class of such goods as "useful in the manner of tools" (χρήσιμα ... ὀργανικῶς, 1.9.1099b28). The only explicit comparison of friends to instruments that appears in the *Nicomachean Ethics* joins friends, wealth, and political power as external goods that enable an agent to perform many of his actions, just as tools do (1.8.1099a34–b2). Notably, however, such passages fall far short of modeling the relationship between friends of any sort on the relation between a craftsman and his tools. That relationship does provide Aristotle with a model, but it is a model for a master's relation to his slave, and it serves to explain why that relationship is not one of friendship (8.11.1161a30–b8). So while certain aspects of friendship allow for the application of the metaphor, for one person to relate to another as a craftsman to his tools would be to treat him as a slave.

The contrast between slaves and friends further supports the idea that friendship essentially involves a recognition of the other as a separate subject with independent interests. We have already seen that Aristotle denies community between masters and slaves on the grounds that they are not

---

[49] Similar ambiguities plague the language of "objectification." Nussbaum 1995a insightfully unpacks that language and analyzes a variety of phenomena that fall under the term, including "instrumentalization." Though her focus is on sexual objectification, many of the problematic features that she identifies are common to other forms of injustice. Her account perhaps understates the extent to which what makes the actions and attitudes she describes objectionable is insufficiently explained in terms of a distinction between instrumental and intrinsic value or concern or related distinctions between an "object" and a "subject," a "person," and a "thing."

[50] Many craftspeople lavish far more care and attention on their instruments than we find in even mildly harmful instances of "instrumentalization" between persons, and an appreciation of another's beneficial traits frequently (ordinarily?) gives rise to respect and gratitude rather than wanton abuse.

sufficiently separate. As a part of his master, the slave has no independent good that is not a part of or somehow a function of the good of his master. The same consideration leads Aristotle to deny that there is any friendship between them, as well, and likewise that there is any justice (8.11.1161a32–b5, *EE* 7.9.1241b17–24). In this regard, slaves are compared not only to instruments, but to nonliving things more generally (*EN* 8.11.1161b2). These comparisons are rooted in the nature of both slaves and instruments as parts or possessions of their masters and owners. The absence of friendship and justice does not, however, express or justify any indifference on the part of masters, craftsmen, and owners of property; "all these things are benefited by those who make use of them" (8.11.1161a35–b1). Rather, their interest in their possessions is not sufficiently distinguishable from their interest in themselves to count as friendship, and there is no justice between them because the possessions do not have any distinct good. As the *Eudemian Ethics* has it:

> There is no community of these things [i.e., of body and soul, craftsman and tool, master and slave]. For they are not two. Instead, the former is one, and the latter is a part of that one and not one itself.[51] Nor is the good divisible to each of them. Rather, the good of both belongs to the one for whose sake it is. (*EE* 7.9.1241b20–3)

At first sight, these denials that friendship, justice, or community exist between masters and slaves appear to fly in the face of Aristotle's defense of natural slavery in the first book of the *Politics*. Following his initial characterization of the relationship between a master and a slave as one of possession and parthood, he argues that for a natural slave – someone who, because he lacks the capacity for fully developed rational agency, is naturally suited to belong to another and not to himself (*Pol.* 1.4.1254a14–17, 1.5.1254b20–4)[52] – this relationship is just and beneficial (1.5 1254b17–19, 1255a1–3). Earlier, he had even referred to the relationship between master and slave, along with that between husband and wife, as one of the "two communities" from which a household comes into existence (1.2.1252b9–10). So it appears that there are justice, community, and even some kind of friendship between master and slave. This apparent

---

[51] Alternatively: "For they are not two, but one of them is a single thing, and the other belongs to [lit., 'is of'] the single thing but is not a single thing." οὐ γὰρ δύ' ἐστίν, ἀλλὰ τὸ μὲν ἕν, τὸ δὲ τοῦ ἑνός οὐδ' ἕν.

[52] With these descriptions of the natural slave, cf. the definition of a free person in the *Metaphysics*: "One who exists for his own sake and not for the sake of someone else" (*Met.* 1.2.982b26–7).

contradiction with the arguments of both *Ethics* is just one of many problems that commentators have found with the *Politics*' defense of slavery. Yet in this respect, at least, the three works are more consistent than their terminological discrepancies suggest, and in fact draw the same distinction between the master-slave relationship and others.

As Thornton Lockwood has argued, the shared benefit that the *Politics* finds in natural slavery differs from the common benefit between friends who share in community with one another.[53] What the *Politics* asserts is that the natural slave and his master share "the same benefit" (ταὐτὸ συμφέρει, 1.2.1252a30–4, 1.6.1255b9–15, 3.6.1278b33–6), and the explication and defense of this claim show that sharing "the same benefit" differs from sharing a "common benefit" (τὸ κοινῇ συμφέρον, 3.6.1278b21–2, 3.12.1282b16–18).[54] Master and slave share the *same* benefit, according to Aristotle, precisely because the slave is a part of his master. Two things have the same benefit if one is a part of the other or their good is otherwise indistinguishable: "For the same thing is beneficial to the part and to the whole, and to body and soul, and the slave is a sort of part of the master, a kind of animate but separated part of his body, as it were" (1.6.1255b9–12).

If there is a conceptual difficulty here, it is with the thought of one person's being a part of another, not with the idea that two things share the same benefit when they stand in the appropriate sort of relation to one another. Aristotle's examples of part and whole and body and soul are illustrative. Though a doctor who heals a patient's eyes does not thereby benefit the same man's legs, he does thereby benefit his patient as a whole. Body does not stand to soul as part to whole, but just as the part's benefit is itself a benefit to the whole, so too the benefits that a body receives are ipso facto benefits for the soul. Whether Aristotle has in mind the hylomorphic theory of the soul as the actualization of an organized body (*DA* 2.1.412a27–8) or a more Platonic conception of the body as the soul's instrument, his point is the same, since he understands tools as belonging to their users, and nothing could count as a benefit to a tool that would

---

[53] Lockwood 2007. I am indebted to this article for bringing this distinction to my attention. Though my own account of it differs from Lockwood's at various points that I have noted later, the space I devote to criticism should not be allowed to obscure my fundamental agreement with his article.

[54] The translations are Lockwood's. It should be admitted that his English glosses make the distinction more intuitive than Aristotle's Greek. For ταὐτὸ συμφέρει, we might have translated "the same thing is beneficial," which makes for a much less apparent contrast with phrases like "the common benefit," for which the *Politics* often has τὸ κοινὸν συμφέρον as well as τὸ κοινῇ συμφέρον; cf. *Pol.* 3.7.1279a32–b10.

not in itself be a benefit to its user.[55] Far from contradicting the two *Ethics,* this argument could in fact be effectively glossed by the passage quoted previously from the *Eudemian*: Master and slave are not two; rather, the master is one, and the slave is a part of him and not himself one.

So it turns out that the same feature of the relationship between masters and slaves grounds the assertion in the *Politics* that the relationship is beneficial to the slave and the denial in both *Ethics* that the relationship is one of friendship, community, or justice. Though there is a real terminological inconsistency here, it does not translate into a substantial difference in Aristotle's view.[56] If one thing or person is a part or possession of another, the two share the same benefit, but the good of the former is too bound up with and dependent on the good of the latter to count as a distinct good.

This principle is not restricted to slaves, instruments, and possessions, but also applies to children before they have reached a stage in their development at which they are separate from their parents. Thus Aristotle

---

[55] It is difficult to estimate the extent to which Aristotle's references to the soul in both *Ethics* and the *Politics* presuppose at least a general familiarity with the psychological theories that he develops in the *De Anima*. *EN* 1.13.1102a23–26 holds that political science must inquire into the soul, but need not and should not do so with the same precision that we rightly demand of a separate theoretical inquiry. The consistency of the psychology that follows in the *EN* with the theories of the *De Anima* has been subject to dispute; see Miller 2002. In light of these problems, it is worth noting that Aristotle's point about body and soul sharing the same good does not depend on a hylomorphic conception of their relationship.

[56] Lockwood 2007 understates the discrepancies in terminology; for instance, he claims that "the *Politics* never contradicts the *Ethics* concerning whether or not the master and slave exist together in a κοινωνία" (211, cf. 212). But I have already pointed to *Pol.* 1.2.1252b9–10, in which the referent of "two communities" can only be those between husband and wife and between master and slave. The language may support the contention of Schofield 1999e that *Politics* 1 was written before the accounts of friendship in either the *EN* or the *EE*. Even so, Lockwood's article considerably weakens Schofield's case by showing that the accounts are substantively identical; the strongest claim justified by the discrepancies would be that Aristotle came to recognize, after writing *Politics* 1, that on his own account of the relationship between master and slave, the two do not share in community, justice, or friendship in a strict sense any more than soul and body or craftsman and instrument. But the consistent distinction between "the same benefit" and "the common benefit" shows that there is no real change of view. Note, too, that even in *EN* 5.6.1134b9–13 (discussed later), a single sentence denies the possibility of injustice in the relationship between master and slave and yet persists in referring to "despotic justice." The context of the passage suggests a clear motive: Though in one sense there is no "despotic justice," there is a normative dimension to the relationship, and since one of the aims of the passage is to illustrate similarities and differences in the normative aspects of various relationships, the term serves to highlight the similarity (cf. the distinction at 1134a32–4 between "injustice" (ἀδικία) and "doing an injustice" (τὸ ἀδικεῖν)). I can see no reason why the same consideration could not explain Aristotle's talk of justice, community, and friendship between master and slave in *Politics* 1, where he is focused primarily on illuminating what he takes to be analogies and disanalogies in the relations of the household and between those relations and those of citizens.

argues that, since there is no injustice toward oneself, and property and children before a certain age are parts of oneself, there is likewise no injustice toward them (*EN* 5.6.1134b9–13). Notably, however, Aristotle distinguishes children from property despite their sharing the features relevant to his argument. His reason is that children can be expected to develop into separate subjects in a way that slaves and nonliving property will not. This separation, in fact, is crucial to the development of community and friendship between parents and children; "parents love children as themselves, for the children that come from them are, as it were, other selves because they have been separated" (8.12.1161b27–29). Before they become sufficiently separate, they are effectively parts of their parents and therefore there is no justice, community, or friendship between them; but they do, if all goes well, develop into separate rational agents, and the potentiality for that development plays a fundamental role in determining how their parents should treat them.[57]

As noteworthy as the contrast between children and property, however, is that it is a contrast between children and *property* rather than children and tools. This contrast is in keeping with the analysis of slavery in the *Politics*, where being a possession involves more than merely being an instrument. A possession or piece of property is also an instrument, and many tools are no doubt the property of their users. Property, however, has the further distinction of sharing the characteristics of a part: Both parts and pieces of property belong entirely to their owners

---

[57] This point is controversial. Lockwood 2007: 218 denies that being a part of their parents precludes children from sharing in a common benefit, and therefore in community, friendship, and justice, with their parents. Accordingly, he interprets Aristotle's talk of the friendship and community of parents and children to imply that these already obtain before the children are separated, since the children will become separate and the treatment they receive from their parents is guided by that *telos*. But 1162a27–29, in conjunction with 5.6.1134b10–12, suggest that separation is a necessary condition of genuine friendship and community between parents and children. Resistance to this conclusion might be motivated in part by an assumption that separation involves a kind of independence that we normally associate with complete maturity. But Aristotle's word in both passages is τέκνον, a word for very young children, which suggests that children may attain the level of separateness that he has in mind at a rather early age, perhaps as early as they can return their parents' affection in a distinctively rational way that transcends more or less instinctive and pleasure-driven attachments to their caregivers. Another source of resistance comes from Aristotle's claim at 8.12.1161b8 that parents have affection for (στέργουσι) children "on the grounds that [the children] are something of their own"; since Aristotle sometimes uses the plain genitive to express the sort of parthood relation that he attributes to natural slaves and their masters, his use of it here can be read in the same way. Yet in *EN* 5.6, when Aristotle wants to be clear that parthood is what he has in mind, he makes it explicit with the word μέρος. Though the difference between my own view and Lockwood's may be merely one of nuance, it seems most consistent, both conceptually and textually, to see separateness as a necessary condition of friendship and community. For Aristotle's understanding of friendship between parents and children, cf. Tress 1997, Belfiore 2001.

(*Pol.* 1.4.1254a8–13). Yet an instrument need not be either a piece of property or a part: A look-out man on a ship, to take Aristotle's example, is an instrument of the ship's captain (1.4.1253b27–30). Yet the captain does not own the look-out man, either as property or as a part of himself. There is nothing inherently "instrumentalizing" about a ship captain's instrumental use of his look-out man as such. The instrumentality that Aristotle envisions here is innocuous, however, only because the look-out man is not a possession or part of the captain. "Captain" and "look-out man" name roles that people play; the instrumental subordination essential to these roles as such does not extend to every aspect of the relationship between the people who perform those roles. The master-slave relationship, by contrast, is totalizing in a way that instrumentally subordinated roles as such are not. A slave does not merely play an instrumental role in serving his master's interests; rather, he is by his very nature an instrument for his master's action, and hence is a possession and, in a sense, a part of him. Unlike being a master, being a slave is not just a role that the slave sometimes plays or a wholly contingent relationship in which he stands to another person, but mediates every aspect of his life: "The master is only a master of the slave, but does not belong to him; the slave, however, is not only a slave of a master, but belongs to him entirely" (1.4.1254a11–13).

So the relationships in which Aristotle explicitly describes one party as the instrument of another are not, just as such, inherently "instrumentalizing." But the unobjectionable sort of instrumentality appears restricted to the subordination of roles within complex cooperative activities. When the instrumentality extends beyond limited roles to the total relationship between people, the subordinate agent becomes a slave; when Aristotle discusses friendship, he uses the metaphor of instruments only rarely to describe one aspect of the relationship. The upshot is that Aristotle's conception of cooperative human relationships eludes accurate description in terms of a simple distinction between intrinsic and instrumental forms of interest in others. Rather, he recognizes at least three distinct kinds of relationship that would ordinarily fall on the "instrumental" side of the distinction: specialized roles involving subordination of tasks and authority, the full-blown instrumentality of a possession or a part, and friendships that do not involve intrinsic concern for the good of the other. The differences among these relationships are at least as important as their similarities. For understanding friendship and community, the most salient point is that friends, though comparable to tools in some limited respects, are never said to be tools as the look-out man is said to be a tool. Surely this is because the captain's interest in the look-out man as such does not extend beyond the latter's being in good condition to perform the function for which the captain needs him, just as a carpenter and his tools. This is the kind of interest that Aristotle takes to be insufficient for friendship.

These considerations about instruments, possessions, slaves, and inanimate things strongly suggest that Aristotle's aim in *EN* 8.2 is to contrast our interest in these things with the wishing of goods that he takes to be essential to friendship. If genuinely wishing goods to another presupposes that friends regard one another as distinct agents with independent interests, then even friendships based on the friends' instrumental value to one another will differ in important ways from mutually self-interested attempts to treat each other as mere tools, let alone as property. To wish goods to another as an agent with independent interests precludes any subjection of his interests to one's own, since such subjection would not genuinely be to his benefit.

If it is clear how such friendships transcend our relationships with tools and possessions, it may now seem obscure how they differ from disinterested affection at all, and how this understanding of wishing goods to another "for his sake" could conceivably be weaker than any other sense distinct enough to characterize complete friendship to the exclusion of the friendships of pleasure or advantage. But Aristotle's description of the two incomplete varieties of friendship gradually reveals that, in a strict sense, friends of these kinds do not have affection for or wish goods to one another in themselves (καθ' αὑτούς, *EN* 8.3.1156a11) or because they are people of a certain sort of character (τῷ ποιούς τινας εἶναι, 8.3.1156a12–13). What makes these friendships "incidental" is that the friends value one another and want goods for each other *as* people who are pleasant or advantageous for them. Pleasure and advantage, as the objects of friendship, supply the motivation and goal of each friend's association with the other, but also circumscribe the forms in which they wish each other goods. I associate with some friends because they provide me with distinct benefits, with others because the interaction itself is a source of pleasure. Likewise, what I aim to provide to them in return is, accordingly, pleasant interaction or distinct benefits.

To value and benefit others in these ways, however, is not to value or benefit them in their own right or as people of a certain sort of character. To do the latter is to value and benefit them "in themselves" in two related ways: It is to value them and seek their good as one of my ends, and it is to value *them* rather than their incidental features or contingent relations to me (8.3.1156b7–11, 8.5.1157b31–4). Once Aristotle has shown how incomplete friendships are "incidental" as well as "interested," he can claim that only a friend who values another "for himself" wishes good to his friend for that friend's sake.[58] The shift in the significance of the expression does not lead to a retraction of his earlier claim, but to a refinement. It also succeeds in showing how the kinds of friendship do not differ merely in the degree to which they manifest properties of the same type. We do not come to value another for his own sake simply by valuing his beneficial and pleasant characteristics to a greater extent; nor do we seek his good as one of our own ends by seeking to be even more beneficial or pleasant to him, or to be so more often or in a wider variety of contexts. Friends who value each other in and for themselves are friends to a higher degree than friends of pleasure or advantage, but not simply because their affection and benevolence exceed those others' in quantity. As Aristotle puts it, "even things that differ in kind admit of the more and less" (8.1.1155b14–15).

6.   The Coextensiveness of Community, Justice, and Friendship

The foregoing discussion of friendship and its forms has made two especially important points for understanding its relation to community. First, friendship and community exist wherever people cooperate with a view to their mutual benefit, and are not limited to relationships in which the participants value one another for their own sake. Yet, second, even the most temporary and self-interested manifestations of friendship and community differ from merely exploitative relations, because each of the participants acknowledges that the others have a separate interest in cooperating and are not merely the tools of others. These claims lay the groundwork for an approach to the intriguing proposition that "in every community there is a kind of justice and a kind of friendship, as well" (*EN* 8.9.1159b26–7). This assertion and the later claim that "every friendship exists in community" (8.12.1161b11) seem to declare the coextensiveness of community, friendship, and justice: Where we find one, we will find the others. But coextensiveness seems problematic for a variety of conceptual and textual reasons, and these claims admit of several different

---

[58] Thus while Cooper 1977a rightly distinguished between these two ideas and their related expressions (ἐκείνων ἔνεκα, "for their sake" vs. δι᾽ αὑτούς, "for themselves," "because of themselves" or καθ᾽ αὑτούς, "in themselves," "per se"), Aristotle in fact argues that the two go together. Alpern 1983: 308–9 is helpful on this point, which can be obscured by the superficial similarities between the English expressions "for his sake," "for himself," and "in himself."

interpretations. Some scholars have read these chapters as a discussion of friendships in communities or associations, understanding them as a sub-class of friendship and thereby implicitly denying that community and friendship are coextensive.[59]

Even if we accept their coextensiveness, however, it is open to at least two broad alternative interpretations. Roughly, the connections among community, justice, and friendship might be *causal* or *conceptual*. On the causal interpretation, each of the three terms picks out a separate phenomenon that can occur independently, but Aristotle holds that the sharing of goods in common tends to lead people to develop standards and expectations of justice as well as bonds of friendship. On the conceptual reading, each of the three entails the other, and all of them are best conceived as aspects of a single phenomenon. In their strong forms, both of these interpretations face serious problems, and an adequate interpretation will need to embrace elements of each. To pose them as alternatives is, therefore, ultimately misconceived. It is helpful, however, to see the initial attractions of each approach as well as the problems that they generate and that a satisfactory account should avoid.[60]

The causal interpretation has some intuitive appeal. Whether or not it requires a community as the context for every instance of friendship and justice, it does not entail the apparently implausible claim that participants in any community are ipso facto friends or that they necessarily adhere to standards of justice. Aristotle takes friendship to be a more or less settled disposition to wish goods to another, but it seems unreasonable to deny that a group of people could share goods in common without having any such dispositions. As for justice, Aristotle himself suggests that it can come apart from friendship when he says that "if people are friends, they have no need of justice, but if they are just, they need friendship on top of that" (8.1.1155a26–7) and later claims that "equality does not appear

---

[59] Pakaluk 1998: 107–11. The view is a long-established one: Burnet 1900 on 1159a25. It cannot gain support from the idea that a community necessarily involves more than two people, since there are communities of husband and wife and father and son. Close personal relationships between two people who are not members of the same family (what Aristotle describes as ἑταιρικὴ φιλία) furnish some of Aristotle's examples in the very passage that defends the coextensiveness of friendship and community.

[60] To my knowledge, no scholar has explicitly formulated an interpretation in these terms, and most combine elements of both. But some accounts are couched in language that suggests a more causal conception of the relationship: Stern-Gillet 1995: 154, for instance, writes that friendship "evolves" within communities and "generates" obligations of particular justice. Cf. Yack 1993: 34, who has it that "participants in every kind of social group ... develop some form of both friendship and justice." Cf. Konstan 1997: 70–2. Others sometimes present the relationship in terms that suggest a conceptual connection: Pakaluk 1998: 106–11, Lockwood 2003, 2007.

to be the same thing in matters of justice and in friendship" (8.7.1158b20–30). So friendship, at least, seems separable from justice and community.

Moreover, there seems to be no reason why a community could not exist without a great extent of justice among its members; a perfectly unjust community might be impossible, but injustice is surely something that occurs within communities. Such, at least, seems to be a presupposition of Aristotle's discussion of corrective justice and of a great deal of the *Politics*. If, however, Aristotle is primarily interested in the causal relationships among the three, then what he says is compatible with these sorts of separation among community, justice, and friendship. To say that there are a kind of friendship and a kind of justice in every community is to say that sharing goods in common tends to produce bonds of friendship and adherence to standards of justice, not that the latter must be present already wherever people share goods.

Against the causal interpretation, we might observe that Aristotle's treatment of the issue seems to draw much tighter conceptual connections among community, friendship, and justice. Friendship and justice both seem to presuppose community necessarily, and the language of the text does not suggest that their relationship is a contingent causal one between distinct phenomena. When Aristotle says that "there is friendship to the very extent that people share in community" (8.9.1159b29–30), he seems to mean that the two vary together in degree. They also apparently vary together in kind: The friendships of parents to children (8.10.1160b24–5), husband and wife (8.10.1160b32–3), brothers (8.10.1161a3–6), and companions (8.12.1161b12–13) all figure in the discussion as instances and types of community.

The relationship between friendship and justice is no less tightly drawn: There is no friendship between masters and slaves because they do not share anything in common, and the same reason supplies the grounds for the denial of any justice between them (8.11.1161a32–b6). Already in the treatment of justice in *EN* 5, Aristotle explicitly sets each of the three forms of justice in the context of community. Distributive justice concerns the distribution of things "to those who share in [τοῖς κοινωνοῦσι] the constitution" (5.2.1130b31–2), reciprocal justice obtains in "exchange communities" (5.5 1132b31–3), and exchanges are also the context for corrective justice (5.4.1131b25–1132a1). Aristotle apparently identifies justice "without qualification" with political justice, the justice between people "who share in a way of life in common with a view to self-sufficiency" (5.6.1134a24–7).[61] The bulk of 8.10–12 is devoted to an analysis of the forms

---

[61] For this identification, see Yack 1993: 134, Zingano 2013: 203–5.

that justice and friendship take in different sorts of community, especially in familial and political relationships. Rather than making causal generalizations, Aristotle's aim seems to be to show that community is the context in which friendship and justice obtain and that the latter two are integral components of the former.

Despite these considerations in favor of a conceptual interpretation, however, treating friendship, justice, and community as three aspects of a single phenomenon threatens to leave unaddressed the very problems that motivated the causal reading. If the causal interpretation drives the three too far apart, a conceptual reading runs the risk of binding them too tightly together. The challenge for any interpretation of these claims is to account for the close connections that Aristotle sees among friendship, justice, and community without effacing the distinctions among them that he also apparently recognizes. To this end, it is worth giving careful attention to the structure of the argument that opens *EN* 8.9.[62]

7. Community and Justice

In support of his claim that a kind of justice and friendship exists in every community, Aristotle initially appeals to the common use of the term "friends" among companions in a wide range of communities. His choice of sailing expeditions and military campaigns as examples shows that the term's application in ordinary speech extends to communities that are temporarily formed for fairly limited purposes and is not restricted to more permanent forms of association. Ordinary usage, however, is only a guide, and so Aristotle follows this observation with a more formal argument. "There is friendship to the very extent that people share things in common; for there is also justice" (*EN* 8.9.1159b29–31). The argument is compressed and underdeveloped, but important. The existence of friendship in every community is explained by the existence of justice.[63] Without elaboration, the thought seems obscure and implausible. Two questions arise: Why does Aristotle think that there is justice in every community, and how does friendship follow from justice?

The justice that Aristotle finds in every community is τὸ δίκαιον. Its difference from δικαιοσύνη can be obscured by the common practice of translating both terms with the word "justice."[64] Δικαιοσύνη, however,

---

[62] For the basic shape of the interpretation that follows, I am indebted to Pakaluk 1998.
[63] Cf. Stern-Gillet 1995: 154, which claims that it is friendship that "generates" obligations of justice.
[64] It is to avoid this obscurity that Polansky 2014b consistently translates τὸ δίκαιον as "the just" and reserves "justice" for δικαιοσύνη. I have not adopted that practice here in part out of stylistic

generally names the virtue of justice possessed by individuals, while τὸ δίκαιον refers to the principles or standards of justice that a person with the virtue of justice reliably observes, as well as to instances of just action.[65] The first implication of this point is that Aristotle is not here maintaining that communities only exist where their members possess the virtue of justice. Possessing the virtue requires not only adherence to the standards of justice, but appropriately motivated adherence: A just person does what is just at least in part because it is just (2.4.1105a28–33). Yet we also need not suppose that he is making a high level of adherence to the principles a condition on the very existence of a community, as though a community exists so long as its members act appropriately, regardless of how they are motivated.

The best indication of what Aristotle is here asserting comes from a passage in which he denies it. Just as there is no friendship between master and slave or in relation to inanimate things, likewise there is no justice; indeed, there is no friendship *because* there is no justice (8.11.1161a32–b3). The point is not that masters fail to observe the principles of justice that should govern their treatment of slaves, but that, strictly speaking, no such principles obtain.[66] So when Aristotle claims that there is justice in every community, we should understand him to be asserting that there are principles of justice that apply whenever people share goods in common. A group of people sharing goods in common does not cease to be a community simply because its members frequently fail to treat one another justly.

This understanding of Aristotle's thought receives confirmation in the passage that follows. Of the ways in which communities differ, one of the most salient is in the amount of goods that they share. At the

---

considerations and in part in the hope that, once the distinction has been marked, it should be clear in any given context how I am using "justice."

[65] The ambiguity in translation is matched, and justified at least to some extent, by a similar ambiguity in English "justice." It is a point of dispute among philosophers whether justice as a trait of persons is explanatorily prior or posterior to justice as a set of principles or standards governing the interaction between persons. Interpreters of Aristotle likewise disagree about his own view on this question, and my account of the meaning of these two terms is not intended to stake out a position in that debate. For subtly opposed viewpoints and a brief survey of the issue in twentieth century political philosophy, cf. Miller 1995: ch. 3 and Yack 1993: ch. 4. Williams 1980 reads Aristotle as attempting to treat the virtue of justice as prior to its principles and takes a negative view of that strategy's success. For the opposite view, cf. O'Connor 1991. My own view is that Aristotle's account of the virtue of justice gives explanatory priority to the principles of justice, but nothing in my argument here is intended to depend on that point.

[66] "Strictly speaking" is an important qualification, since Aristotle argues at length in *Pol.* 1.4–6 that slavery is just when the enslaved person is a natural slave. See my previous discussion.

limit, brothers and companions share everything; others share more or less of a limited range of goods.[67] But standards of justice and injustice vary together with these communities. What counts as just in relations between parents and children differs from what counts in relations between brothers, and yet a different set of standards obtains among fellow citizens. Injustice, too, increases with the extent of the relationship. It is worse to steal from a friend than from a fellow citizen, to refuse assistance to a brother than to a nonrelative, or to strike one's father than anyone else (8.9.1160a1–8). Though Aristotle initially presents this covariation in quantitative terms, subsequent discussion confirms that justice differs in form along with the nature of the parties and their relation to one another. This point is already implicit in the distinctions between brothers and companions; though they both share "everything" in common, justice takes different forms in each relationship.

The following chapters of *EN* 8 analyze relationships within the household and the polis, distinguishing the forms that friendship and justice take with reference to the degree and kind of equality between the participants (8.10–13) as well as the extent of their sharing and the character of the goods that they share. One prominent feature of this analysis is an extended analogy between the relationships of the household and the forms of political constitution. Aristotle's willingness to describe some forms that familial relations can take as analogous to the deviant constitutional forms (8.10.1160b35–61a9) further suggests that the justice he finds in every community need not be, strictly speaking, correct. While their deviance implies that they fail to adhere to some set of standards that would be correct, they might also display "a kind of justice" insofar as they exhibit some pattern of distribution of harms, benefits, privileges, and burdens. In any case, when Aristotle claims to find "a kind of justice" in every community, he is not insisting that the only real communities are, in fact, unqualifiedly just communities.

Why, though, should Aristotle think that standards of justice obtain in every community? The claim could be strictly prescriptive: Whenever people cooperate together, they should observe certain standards of justice. The standards that they should observe might then be justified by considerations independent of the character of that specific sort of community or indeed of community more generally. Yet there are at least two reasons to suspect that Aristotle does not intend merely to recommend

---

[67] Aristotle surely exaggerates when he says that brothers and companions share "everything," for they do not, at least characteristically, share houses, wives, children, etc.

some set of standards whose normative force derives from considerations external to the nature of community in general and the specific forms that community can take. First, as we have just seen, the proposition that there is a kind of justice in every community seems to apply to cases in which even the standards of justice themselves are nonideal. Second, even where Aristotle apparently focuses his attention on justice as the set of ideal norms applicable to a specific sort of relationship – those between brothers, or between husband and wife, or between companions, for instance – his discussion suggests that the nature of those relationships generates the norms. This is not to say that for any given form of cooperative association there are no normative considerations that are prior to that form of community and constrain the shape that it can legitimately take. Rather, it is to suggest that the substantive content of justice depends on and is determined by the character of the communities that these standards of justice govern. How could this be?

If we start from the idea of a community as a group of distinct agents sharing some goods in common, we can see how the acceptance of some standards of fairness could be a necessary feature or condition of any community. To stay with the relatively simple examples of communities of distribution or exchange: If people are to persist in voluntarily exchanging goods with one another or in contributing to the production and maintenance of some common stock, there must be at least some general agreement about what is to count as a fair exchange or distribution. Without some such standard of assessment, exchanges and distributions are likely to be unpredictable and arbitrary, and the communities thereby liable to dissolution. If people cannot generally regard themselves as receiving a fair return or distribution of goods, then they will lose their motivation for exchanging goods or contributing to their maintenance and production. Even where the nature of the case prevents these people from voluntarily dissociating themselves from others, if they cannot expect to receive fair treatment from those others, then they will at least be extremely reluctant to share goods in common with them, and may attempt to benefit at their expense. To this extent, their interaction with others ceases to be cooperative. On the minimal assumption that sharing goods in common involves cooperative behavior rather than strictly zero-sum competition, then the existence of a community will necessarily require some generally accepted standards of justice.

It is not that community, understood in this way, precludes all forms of competition. Many forms of competition, even zero-sum competition, are possible only because they are embedded in a broader framework of cooperation. To take an example that would have been familiar to Aristotle's audience, consider athletic competitions such as the funeral games for Patroclus in *Iliad* 23. The value of success in the competition depends upon cooperation in observing the rules of the game. The competitors may not manage to avoid acting unfairly, and may still value victory even when it is unfairly achieved. But the competition itself could not even occur if the participants did not cooperate; in fact the competition itself is a special kind of cooperation. So, too, the participants in any community might seek to cheat each other or to gain unfairly at one another's expense without thereby ceasing to cooperate at all. In this sense, the alternatives to cooperation are mutual indifference or outright hostility; as Aristotle puts it, "with their enemies people do not wish to share even a road" (*Pol.* 4.11.1295b24–5). It is, accordingly, neither arbitrary nor mere moralizing to maintain that every community necessarily involves the general recognition of some standards of fairness.

Such reflections on the psychology of cooperation support Aristotle's contention that there is a kind of justice in every community. But do they reflect Aristotle's own thought? The point can be reformulated in terms of practical reason, that is, as a claim about what agents have reasons to do. We know that "every craft and every inquiry, and likewise every action and decision seem to aim at some good" (*EN* 1.1.1094a1–2). So too we see that "every community is established for the sake of some good, since everyone does everything for the sake of what they think to be good" (*Pol.* 1.1.1252a2–3). It follows that the reasons that any agent has for participating in some community are grounded in some benefit that he can achieve through that participation. But if the aim of participating in any community is to achieve some good, then every agent who participates in a community will also have reasons to value fairness in the distribution and exchange of goods in that community. How so?

In the first instance, each of the participants will have decisive reason to prefer that he receive benefits at least roughly equal to what he contributes or exchanges. If participation in a community entails giving up more than one gains, then it will be harmful rather than beneficial, and since no one can rationally choose to harm himself (*EN* 5.6.1134b11–12), participating in the community on those terms will be irrational. Though he might still receive goods from the association that he would otherwise lack, the net loss that his participation entails gives him reasons not to participate. Since many communities are formed for the sake of goods that every human being requires in order to live even a tolerably decent life, participation in them will not be rationally optional. What reason demands is not disengagement, but that the agent seek at least a roughly equal benefit in return for his efforts.

Crucially, however, the good that each agent can achieve for himself through participating in any sort of community depends on the cooperation of other agents, and all agents have the same kind of reasons to seek an equal return for themselves. Each individual agent therefore has reason to value both the goods that he can achieve through participation *and* the cooperation of the other participants. But since the rationality of those others' cooperation depends on *their* receiving at least an equal benefit in return, then all the participants have reason to value fairness in distribution and exchange. Only fairness can guarantee that each member of the community will continue to have sufficient reason to cooperate with the others. Each participant therefore has strong reasons to value fair treatment for himself and to treat the other participants fairly.[68]

A considerable advantage of interpreting the connection between community and standards of justice in terms of what agents have reason to do is that it can account for the descriptive as well as the normative dimensions of that relationship.[69] Ordinary talk about reasons involves a systematic ambiguity between normative and explanatory reasons. Explanatory reasons are those considerations – beliefs, desires, judgments, aims, or whatever – that explain why agents act in the ways that they do. Normative reasons, by contrast, are those considerations that justify one course of action or another, whether or not the agents to whom they apply act for those reasons.[70] Aristotle does not explicitly formulate such a distinction, but he recognizes that agents can act for one set of reasons when they should act for another. So much is assumed, at any rate, when he appeals to the agent's motivations to distinguish merely performing a virtuous action or an act in accordance with a virtue from acting virtuously in the fullest sense (2.4.1105a28–b9); the same applies to performing vicious actions and acting viciously (5.6.1134a17–23; 5.8.1135a15–1136a9). The foregoing considerations about the practical rationality of participation

---

[68] Kraut 2013 and Morrison 2013, for all their disagreements, agree in connecting the common good and justice through practical reasons in roughly the way I have here. Curzer 2012: 275–92 gives a similar account.

[69] For discussions of the simultaneously descriptive, explanatory, and normative character of key concepts in Aristotelian ethics and politics, see Salkever 1990, Yack 1993, Murphy 2002.

[70] The nature and tenability of this distinction are controversial. Its most basic form, however, is no more ambitious than the assertion that an agent can act for reasons other than the ones he should and that we can, in principle at least, say what each of these is. I show here that Aristotle recognizes that much; my appeal to this distinction here is not intended to attribute to him any more robust conception of it.

in community, however, can be stated in terms of both normative and explanatory reasons. On Aristotle's account, practical agents always act with a view to some good; the exercise of practical agency necessarily involves pursuing ends conceived as worth pursuing under some description.[71] Virtuous practical agents act correctly in pursuing the ends that they should pursue in the ways that they should pursue them, while various deficiencies of practical agency lead people to pursue ends that they should not pursue, to pursue appropriate ends in inappropriate ways, or even to pursue inappropriate ends in ineffective ways. This view of practical agency and the various ways in which it can succeed or fail provides a framework for explaining not only why people do in fact develop standards of justice to govern their cooperative interactions in community, but why those standards take the broad shape that they do in specific sorts of community. Put simply, different conceptions of the goods to be achieved in community lead to different norms. But since Aristotle's objective account of well-being entails that what agents have most reason to do is not ultimately determined by their beliefs or attitudes, he can also maintain that some standards of fairness are correct.

Determining the correct standards of justice even in outline is obviously an enormous task, and one that occupies much of the *Politics*. Aristotle leaves little room for doubt, however, about how that inquiry must proceed. Standards of justice are simply those standards that, when followed by a community's members, promote and protect their common good (*EN* 5.1.1129b14–19). To ask what the correct standards of justice are, therefore, is to ask what set of standards best promotes and protects the common good of a community.[72] Aristotle connects justice to the common good in this way most explicitly in discussions of political community. His account suggests, however, that the formal role of justice remains constant across all forms of community. Aristotle's approach to practical

---

[71] Thus Aristotle endorses the Guise of the Good thesis, as it is often called these days. There is disagreement about whether he extends the Guise of the Good thesis to all voluntary acts, including those that proceed from nonrational motivations such as desire for pleasure or avoidance of pain, since, by Aristotle's own lights, nonrational desires do not depend on an agent's beliefs about what is good. Hence some (e.g., Irwin 1988: 330–3, 604–5 note 25) restrict the Guise of the Good thesis to voluntary acts undertaken with a view to some goal conceived of as good. Others (e.g., Moss 2010, Pearson 2012: 62–87) argue, I think persuasively, that desires aimed at the pleasant are directed at what appears good to the agent without depending on any *conceptualization* of their objects as good.

[72] For discussions of justice and the common good broadly consistent with mine, see Irwin 1988: ch. 20, Miller 1995: ch. 3, Roberts 2000, Kraut 2002: 98–177 and 2013, Curzer 2012: 275–92, and Morrison 2013.

reason allows us to see how every community necessarily requires some standards of fairness to govern the interactions between its members and that these standards must be such that the members can regard themselves as, on the whole, benefiting from their participation in the community rather than being harmed. This formal role of justice in relation to the rationale for cooperation in communities provides a framework both for explaining the variety of principles and standards that different communities recognize and for determining which standards are correct.[73]

There is much more to be said about how the character of specific forms of community shapes the accepted standards and normative requirements of justice between their participants. In particular, I have said nothing about how the character of the people involved affects the relevant standards of fairness. I will have more to say about this in Chapter 3, when I consider how political community differs from other forms of community. For now, it should be enough to remark that Aristotle's insistent focus on equality as a defining element of both justice and friendship coheres well with the account I have given so far and provides his principal means of differentiating the form and content of justice in various sorts of community. For it is primarily in relationships among people who are unequal in important respects that it becomes difficult to determine what justice requires. I have helped myself to the examples of relatively simple communities of exchange and distribution. But most forms of community – whether a simple commercial exchange or the relationship between a father and his sons – depend on proportional equality in one way or another. A more detailed account would be required to show how proportionality can be rationally determined in various cases and how proportionate equality in communities contributes to the common good of their members. Supposing, however, that Aristotle's claim to find a kind of justice in every community now has some definite sense and has

---

[73] It might be objected that this interpretation makes Aristotle seem to be a contractualist by emphasizing mutual benefit in its account of the nature and formal structure of justice. Though Aristotelian and contractualist theories of justice have traditionally been contrasted, Ober 1996b treats Aristotle as a "quasi-contractualist" on the grounds that his theory of politics stresses mutual benefit, and Schofield 1999b presents a view of Aristotelian political community in contractualist terms. Yet Aristotle gives no fundamental role to *agreement* in explaining why some set of proposed standards of justice is correct or mistaken by nature rather than by convention; agreements or procedures to generate agreement are, in fact, subject to critique by appeal to the correct standards, and correct standards are ones that promote and preserve numerically or proportionally equal mutual benefit among the participants in a community. Agreement is not fundamental for Aristotle, because he embraces an objective theory of the good; contractualism, by contrast, characteristically gives a fundamental explanatory role to agreement precisely because it begins from subjectivism about the good. Aristotle's theory is therefore not contractualist.

gained some plausibility, it remains to ask, how does the existence of justice explain the existence of friendship?

8. Justice and Friendship

By now the answer to this question should be more apparent. Friendship exists wherever there is a reciprocal and mutually acknowledged wishing of goods among separate individuals. But to the extent that people cooperate in sharing goods in common, and therefore accept some standards of fairness in their interactions, they thereby wish goods to each other. For acting in accordance with standards of justice inherently involves treating others equally, whether numerically or proportionately, and to treat others equally is to benefit them, and hence to wish goods to them.[74]

This link between justice and friendship does not entail that any instance of conflict, ill will, or injustice between people ipso facto dissolves the community between them. For it no more severs the friendship between them. When Aristotle describes friendships of advantage as especially liable to give rise to disputes and complaints, he treats that conflict as an episode in a relationship structured by mutual expectations of reciprocal benefit. Such conflict can lead to the dissolution of the friendship, but parties engaged in a dispute have not dissolved their friendship, however likely they are to do so as a result of their dispute. For Aristotle *contrasts* this sort of conflict with what typically happens when people who associate with one another for the sake of pleasure cease to enjoy interacting with each other: They cease to be friends.

If the alternatives to cooperation are mutual indifference and outright hostility, the sort of disputes that Aristotle has in mind should be thought of as cooperative. After all, arguing with an associate who has treated me unfairly is not an act of enmity; the point of complaining to him about his treatment of me is to lead him to acknowledge his failure and to make amends for it, not to harm him. The basically cooperative character of many such disputes is no less apparent when the disputants have recourse to some third party; submitting the dispute to the judgment of an arbiter or a more formal legal institution is at least as cooperative as competing

---

[74] One might object that I can treat someone equally even if I would prefer that he suffer harm. This objection, however, wrongly supposes that if I wish goods to someone, I must wish them for his own sake and not solely for the sake of something else. But because I can in fact wish goods to someone only as a means to something else, wishing goods to someone is compatible with preferring that he suffer harm. Wishing goods to someone is incompatible only with complete hostility, as I go on to argue. I thank Joe Bullock for pressing me on this point.

for prizes in athletic contests. Of course, this sort of conflict involves at least a temporary interruption of the reciprocal well wishing that makes for friendship. But the genesis of these disputes within friendships and their orientation toward resolution mark them as components of defective friendships rather than instances of enmity. Enemies aim to harm one another; friends seek justice from each other.

How, then, could Aristotle say that "if people are friends, they have no need of justice, but if they are just, they need friendship on top of that" (*EN* 8.1.1155a26–7) or that "equality does not appear to be the same thing in matters of justice and in friendship" (8.7.1158b29–30)? Both of these statements seem straightforwardly incompatible with the coextensiveness of community, justice, and friendship as I have interpreted it. Both can, however, be explained by appeal to Aristotle's treatment of kinds of friendship in terms of resemblance to the paradigmatic and complete form.

The first claim is easier to explain. It appears in the first chapter of Aristotle's account of friendship, and therefore prior to any of his developed theoretical distinctions among the kinds of friendship and their relationship to justice. We should, accordingly, not be surprised if these later points entail that he can accept the claim only with some qualification. A suitably qualified sense of the thought emerges if we take the reference to friendship here to be restricted to what the later chapters classify as complete friendship. In that case, the view that "people who are just need friendship on top of that" could mean one of at least two things, either of which would be acceptable to Aristotle. It might mean, first, that people who possess the virtue of justice but do not engage in any shared interaction with others will thereby fail to live good lives.[75] Though this point might seem too obvious, its purpose in the chapter is to support the claim that friendship is necessary (8.1.1155a4–5, 28–9); the necessity of many goods is fairly obvious, but philosophical discussions frequently need to belabor the obvious. Still, this reading may seem too weak, because being just apparently requires interacting justly with others. But there is a stronger reading: Being just even in an active sense is insufficient for a good life; for that, we need not simply to interact with others on fair terms, but to have friends whom we value for their own sake. Friendship, as the passage goes on to say, is not only necessary but also noble or fine (καλόν, 8.1.1155a29). As Aristotle goes on to argue in book 9, even the blessedly happy and self-sufficient need friends of this kind. We

---

75 Pakaluk 1998: 112.

could be just without having any "other selves," but we could not flourish without them.

"If they are friends, they have no need of justice." Expressed in isolation from any developed theoretical taxonomy of friendship, the idea seems to be that friends do not need justice, because they are already disposed to benefit one another. In light of the coextensiveness of friendship with community and justice, Aristotle must reject this way of putting the point. But the substance of the thought is just that friends who value each other for themselves do not need to look to some external standards of fairness in order to constrain their pursuit of the good they aim to achieve through the friendship. It is not that their actions violate standards of fairness, but that they do not need to worry about fairness per se. Their attitudes toward one another already suppose that they will aim at fairness in their treatment of each other, because they will aim at each other's good directly. They will not need justice, not in the sense that they can dispense with it, but in that it is already contained and presupposed in their friendship. It is worth noting that the word here translated as "need" (δεῖ) can also mean "lack."[76]

The same sense that friendship in its fullest and most paradigmatic forms transcends mere justice accounts for the more puzzling claim about equality in friendship and in "matters of justice." Though this statement also appears before the arguments for the coextensiveness of friendship and justice, it is not so easily explained in terms of that doctrine. We might note that equality only "appears" (φαίνεται) to be different in these cases, but this seems not to be a mere appearance. The difference, as Aristotle expresses it, is that "in matters of justice, equality in accordance with worth is primary, and equality in accordance with quantity is secondary; but in friendship it is equality in accordance with quantity that is primary, and that in accordance with merit is secondary" (8.7.1158b30–3). Equality based on worth corresponds to proportionate equality; equality based on quantity corresponds to numeric or arithmetic equality. Proportionate equality is necessary in one way in distributive justice when the parties to the distribution are of unequal merit, and in another way in the reciprocal justice of exchange when the goods to be exchanged differ in kind. These two sorts of equality play different roles in justice and in friendship.

---

[76] Pakaluk 1998: 112 describes this interpretation as implausible. But why? It is no less plausible than the thought that friendship is "immune to slander and stable," but that is what Aristotle says about complete friendship at 8.6.1158b8–9. The implausibility stems from supposing that the claim is intended to cover every instance of friendship, but it is just that supposition that we should reject.

In Pakaluk's analysis of this passage, we are to understand the difference in terms of which kind of equality serves as the ideal.[77] In matters of justice, it is proportionate equality based on worth that is ideal, and arithmetic equality is acceptable, when it is, as a second-best approximation. In some contexts of distribution, for instance (Pakaluk's example is the distribution of military honors), we will gladly accept a numerically equal distribution of goods even when we recognize that some parties to the distribution deserve a greater share, because distributing precisely according to merit would be too difficult, too time-consuming, or in some other way impractical. In friendships, by contrast, numerical equality is the ideal. Yet strict equality is impossible in some friendships because one party is too far superior to the other and the inferior is incapable of reciprocating equally; Aristotle's example is the friendship of a father and his son. In these cases, proportionate equality is accepted as an approximation to numeric equality. Unlike the proportionate equality that people aim for in matters of justice, friends embrace proportionate equality as a way of approximating strict equality. This interpretation makes for a real difference between justice and friendship. As Pakaluk puts it, "the tendency of justice is to magnify differences among persons, in so far as it aims to allot goods in such a way as to express most exactly the differences in the worth of the persons involved; but the tendency of friendship, rather, is to close differences and equalize, since its aim is some kind of strict reciprocation or equality."[78]

Pakaluk does not address the implications of his interpretation for the coextensiveness of justice and friendship, but his strong statement of the differences between them might seem to conflict with it. Yet here too the appearance of contradiction dissipates when we take the reference of friendship as most fully applicable to its primary or complete form. Friendships characterized by the superiority of one friend to the other need not be friendships of this kind. Yet Aristotle's focus in this passage is on just such cases. Parents love their children, once they have become sufficiently separate, as other selves (8.12.1161b27–29). The friendship of husbands and wives is at least possibly based on excellence (8.12.1162a24–27). Aristotle also cites the relationship between rulers and ruled as characterized by superiority, but he quickly distinguishes them from familial relationships and does not mention them again in his discussion (8.7.1158b11–17). His treatment of equality in friendships between unequals applies to all such

---

[77] Pakaluk 1998: 94–6.
[78] Pakaluk 1998: 96.

friendships, whatever their kind, but the sort of concern for another in himself that typifies complete friendship supplies the best explanation for the priority of strict equality as an ideal. Valuing another person's good for his own sake rather than for the pleasure or benefit that he provides leads away from a concern even with preserving the disparities between oneself and one's friend, let alone with ensuring that those disparities be reflected in the proportion of affection and benevolence. Equal reciprocity maintains an important role insofar as friends will seek to avoid being benefited by their friends to a markedly greater extent than they benefit them in return. But for friends who love each other for themselves, there is no rationale to aim at proportionate equality in its own right. It becomes the standard only when the inequality between the friends is too great.

Admittedly, friendships of other kinds might aim primarily at strict numerical equality. Friendships for pleasure, at least, do not characteristically seem to seek to proportion the pleasure in accord with the relative worth of the friends. Friendships of advantage could also seek a strict equality. But many, if not most, friendships formed for advantage will involve the exchange of goods differing in kind. In these cases, aiming at numeric equality is impossible, since things differing in kind can only be commensurated proportionally. Yet the friends in these cases do not accept proportionate equality as an approximation of numeric equality. The equality sought in exchange relations is not a matter of proportioning the benefits to the merit of the friends, but of proportioning the value of the goods exchanged.[79] Proportionality is therefore as central to equality in these friendships as it is in distributive justice.

Furthermore, Aristotle's account of the coextensiveness of friendship, justice, and community yields a plain sense in which friendship exists between the participants in a community formed for the sake of procuring some instrumental goods to its members. Yet distributive justice proportioned in accord with the members' contributions would play a central role in any such community and would not be only a second-best alternative to strict equality. Rather than taking this as evidence for inconsistency in Aristotle's views, we should see it as part of his characterization of friendship by reference to its paradigmatic form. To the extent that any friendship approximates complete friendship, it will take strict equality

---

[79] For a sustained defense of this somewhat controversial claim, see Meikle 1995. My point here would be unaffected, and perhaps even strengthened, if we were to suppose that justice in exchange should proportion goods to reflect the proportional merit of the parties, since the focus on proportionality is in neither case accepted as an approximation of numeric equality.

as its ideal. Friendships that fail to share this feature do not fail to be friendships any more than friendships in which the friends do not "spend their days together" or "enjoy one another's company," the very things that Aristotle says are "most characteristic of friendship" (8.6.1158a8–10).

I have given this issue sustained attention not only to show that it poses no serious problems for Aristotle's account, but also to illustrate the complexities of community, justice, and friendship as Aristotle sees them. The shapes that friendships take in any community will, along with justice, be as various as the goods that people share in common and the ways in which they share them. Some of these friendships may seem too tenuous to merit the title, but as Aristotle says of the friendships of pleasure and advantage, "they seem both to be and not to be friendships on account of their similarity and dissimilarity to the same thing" (8.6.1158b5–6). If the forms of friendship and justice vary together with community in form, content, and degree, then we should expect the standards of justice and the patterns of positive reciprocity to depend on the character of the goods that people share together and on the character of the people who share them. With this framework in place, I now turn to specifically political forms of community and ask, Who shares what, and how do these facts explain and constrain the relevant and legitimate forms of justice and friendship in the polis?

CHAPTER 3

From the Household to the City

The *Politics* begins by asserting the distinctiveness of political community. Failure to appreciate what distinguishes political communities from other kinds of community has, Aristotle thinks, led his predecessors to neglect the heterogeneity of rule and authority. For Plato and those who agree with him, the household manager, the slave master, the statesman, and the king differ from one another only incidentally. The household manager rules over more people than the slave master, the statesman and the king rule over still more people; the statesman shares his rule with others; the king rules alone. Yet each one rules others, and in this respect they do not differ. Aristotle rejects this view out of hand as a conflation of distinctive forms of rule (*Pol.* 1.1.1252a7–16). In defense of this rejection, he considers the origin and composition of political communities out of smaller communities. By showing that these communities differ in kind from each other and from the city, he hopes to establish that each one characteristically displays a correspondingly different form of rule (1.1.1252a17–23).

In the previous chapter, I reconstructed the outlines of Aristotle's theory of community from his scattered and unsystematic discussions in the *Nicomachean* and *Eudemian Ethics* as well as the *Politics*. On the view developed there, two primary features distinguish every genuinely distinctive kind of community. First, the participants in different sorts of community cooperate to pursue different sorts of goals. Second, the participants themselves bring different sorts of resources, abilities, or capacities to bear on the pursuit of their common objectives. The nature of the good that these participants seek and the relevant similarities and differences among the participants jointly give rise to internal standards of justice and fairness characteristic of that form of community. This conceptual framework should lead us to expect that Aristotle's argument for the distinctive character of political community will focus above all on identifying the distinctive good at which political communities aim

97

and the relevant characteristics of the people who participate in these communities. These features, in turn, will help to explain the specific form that interpersonal standards of justice and fairness take in political communities.

When we turn to the *Politics* itself, we find that its argument meets these expectations. Book 1 is the most explicitly and systematically concerned to establish and explain the difference between political communities and the less complex and comprehensive communities from which they emerge. The book pursues this aim primarily through a contrast between the city and the household, and it is here that Aristotle most fully elaborates his conception of the distinctively political. Book 2, though ostensibly dedicated to a critique of real and hypothetical candidates for the title of well-ordered constitutions, derives much of its critical force from its claims about the nature of political community as such. Book 3 expands these earlier claims in the process of examining citizenship and the principles of justice in the distribution of authority. Here Aristotle spells out more completely what it is to participate in political community as such and how the city's distinctive aims set it apart not only from the household, but from other forms of social life, from the market to the military alliance. Taken in tandem with some of the systematic pronouncements that form the background to book 7's elaboration of the ideal constitution, these books present a conception of political community that gives pride of place to the nature of its aims and the character of its participants in distinguishing it from other kinds of cooperative activity.[1] In short, the polis aims at the good life, and its participants are naturally free male adults who share in exercising rule in the community.

To say only this much leaves too much unsaid. Yet it is enough to suggest that the nature and value of political community are inextricable; we cannot hope to understand one without the other. Understanding each, in turn, will allow us to understand and explain the principles of political justice, both those that cities rationally ought to recognize and those that they in fact do. Only then will we be able to return to the problems of kingship, namely, whether kingship can possibly be just and whether it can be a genuinely political form of community.

---

[1] Books 4–6 are concerned with specific kinds of constitutions in their own right, and hence focus on what distinguishes different political communities from one another rather than on their shared political character. Book 8, though a continuation of 7, is devoted to education in the best constitution and accordingly has less to say about politics more generally. I draw on these books selectively in what follows and turn to books 4–6 more directly in Chapter 5.

1. The Household as a Community

In his effort to substantiate the distinctiveness of political community, Aristotle adopts an analytic method in search of the smallest parts out of which a city comes to be and is constituted (*Pol.* 1.1.1252a18–23). These parts themselves are communities, each different from one another and from the city. In one way, the smallest community is the household. Yet the household itself consists in a plurality of relationships of different kinds. At its most basic, the household is composed of the communities of husband and wife and master and slave (1.2.1252b9–10). Aristotle marks the distinctive character of each of these communities in two ways. First, he distinguishes their defining aims: Husband and wife come together "for the sake of generation," while master and slave come together "on account of preservation" (1.2.1252a26–31). Second, he underscores this difference with the insistence that "by nature, the female and the slave are distinct" (1.2.1252b1). His point is not that women should not be slaves, nor even that some women should not be slaves.[2] Rather, it is that the properties in virtue of which some person or animal is female and those in virtue of which someone is a slave are different and do not stand in any direct causal or explanatory relationship.[3] To be female is to possess the organically embodied capacity to play a specific role in biological reproduction; to be a slave is to lack the capacities for deliberative rationality that enable one to live and guide one's actions successfully on the basis of reflective rational decisions. Of course, some particular women might also lack this capacity, and therefore be what Aristotle considers "slaves by nature." Aristotle apparently believes that all or most barbarian women, as well as men, are like this (1.2.1252b5–7).[4] Yet it is only incidentally that such

---

[2] This seems to be the interpretation of Saunders 1995: 64, though he is ambiguous on this point. Simpson 1998: 18–19 recognizes that some women are, on Aristotle's view, slaves by nature. Yet Simpson's reading of the claim that female and slave are distinct seems inconsistent with that possibility, since he sees it as resting on the purported impossibility of a natural entity's having more than one function (for a less developed expression of the same view, see Newman 1887–1902.ii: 108). Simpson's reading may yet be consistent, however, once we appreciate that the claim that nature makes "one thing for one thing" (1.2.1252b1–3) is not a claim that a complex organic entity cannot have more than one function, but that each of its distinguishable natural features must have a single unified function; otherwise Aristotle would violate his own principle when he attributes different functions to the human being as such and to the human being's bodily organs and associated psychic capacities for growth, nutrition, locomotion, and perception (*EN* 1.7.1097b30–1098a18).

[3] The generality and abstractness of Aristotle's point here are apparent in his use of the neuter substantives "the female" (τὸ θῆλυ) and "that which is a slave" (τὸ δοῦλον) rather than "the woman" (ἡ γυνή) and "the [masculine or feminine] slave" (ὁ δοῦλος, ἡ δούλη): 1.2.1252b1–7. These are claims about people's features, properties, or (in)capacities, not about those people as such.

[4] For an argument to the contrary, see Ward 2002. Though she convincingly argues that Aristotle takes being non-Greek to be neither necessary nor sufficient for being a natural slave, she seems to

women are also natural slaves; that is, they are not natural slaves in virtue of being women.

So, while this distinction entails that women are not necessarily natural slaves, it has a more immediate relevance to Aristotle's argument about communities. In the community of husband and wife, the male and the female relate to each other precisely as male and female; as such, their common aim is the procreation of children. Master and slave, by contrast, work together for their common preservation. Neither master nor slave may require the other in order to survive, but both increase the likelihood and ease of survival through their coordinated activity.[5] These two relationships are distinct because the common ends that the participants pursue are distinct. Both kinds of relationship also involve a division of roles grounded in the different capacities that each partner possesses. Nature determines what kinds of relationship a particular person can enter into, but the distinctive character of that relationship is fundamentally determined by its end.

The household is formed primarily from these two relationships and is directed at their ends of procreation and preservation. The aim of the household as such is just the composite of the goals of these two communities. Yet the household is not an aggregate of two independent relationships that happen to be brought together for the sake of convenience. In fact, the aims of the household are prior to and determinative of the goals of those relationships, as we can see when we consider that households aim at preservation even when they have no slaves, as Aristotle explicitly notes (1.2.1252b12). Preservation and generation are both ends that individuals seek by nature, prior to any rational decision (1.2.1252a28–30). The two are, in fact, closely linked, since Aristotle sees reproduction as a way

---

underestimate Aristotle's assumption of the great prevalence of natural slaves in non-Greek populations; cf. Kraut 2002: 277–305.

[5] Because the aims of these communities are procreation and preservation, it is tempting to read Aristotle's description of their members as "those who are not able to exist without one another" (1.2.1252a26) as a claim that masters require slaves in order to survive, or at least that slaves will perish without their masters (so, e.g., Reeve 2009: 514–15). This is patently false, and Aristotle acknowledges the existence of households without slaves and of natural slaves without masters in the very same passage (1252b6–7, 12). He probably means instead that the members of each pair cannot fully actualize their respective capacities without one another. This is clear enough in the case of male and female; insofar as these are reproductive roles, they require one another. As for master and slave, Aristotle claims that natural slaves benefit from slavery because their masters' rational guidance (ideally) keeps them out of trouble and enables them to participate in virtue to a limited extent (1.13.1260b3–7), and the best constitution's reliance on slave labor reflects Aristotle's view that free people require the support of slaves in order to attain the level of self-sufficiency required for living well (7.9.1328b–1329a26).

in which all living things seek to preserve themselves in another, as it were (cf. *DA* 2.4.415a26–b7). The household, whether it includes slaves as in its "complete" form (*Pol.* 1.3.1253b4) or makes use of domesticated animals alone, is the most fundamental way in which human beings seek these ends.[6]

Success in achieving these ends expands the composition of the household with new members and the new relationship of parent and child.[7] In one way, children just are the aim of the relationship between husband and wife. Generation, however, is only the beginning. Successful reproduction gives rise to new demands of sustenance and education for the child, and while providing their children with these goods is an aim of both husband and wife, the children themselves become members of the household as participants in the distinctive relationship between parent and child.[8] Like the other subcommunities constitutive of the household, the parent-child relationship has features that set it apart from the others. In this case, the child's own good is the end that supplies the rationale for the relationship. "Rationale," of course, is an awkward word in this context, since children do not choose to enter into the relationship, and even adults, on Aristotle's view, have prerational motives for producing and raising children. Yet it is their common pursuit of the child's good that typifies the parent-child relationship as a distinctive sort of community and friendship. Perhaps uniquely among Aristotelian friendships, the community of parent and child can take as its focus the good of one of its members, because the child himself is a good for his parents, part of his parents' good, and even initially, in some more than merely physical

---

[6] For the distinction between "complete" and "incomplete" households, see Saunders 1995: 72 and, more fully, Nagle 2006.

[7] Cooper 2010: 236 treats the community of parent and child as an extension of the community of husband and wife, and hence regards the household as constituted by only two communities rather than three. But conflating the husband-wife and parent-child communities not only ignores the textual evidence for Aristotle's distinction of them, but, most importantly, obscures the differences in these relationships, as this chapter shows. Cooper also ignores the community of brothers, for which see note 13.

[8] Aristotle's interest is overwhelmingly in the *father*, and not in the mother; he even describes the characteristic form of rule as *paternal* (πατρική, *Pol.* 1.12.1259a38) rather than parental. Given his hierarchical conception of the relationship between husband and wife, however, we need not infer that he intends his account to exclude the mother, as though she has no relationship to her children or some entirely separate one. Rather, on Aristotle's view, we must understand her relationship to her children by reference to the father's, but not vice versa. It should go without saying that I do not regard this view as normatively or explanatorily satisfactory, even as an account of the relationship between Greek or Athenian mothers and children in Aristotle's own day. I do, however, believe that it licenses an interpretation of Aristotle's claims as claims about the relationship between parents and children, and not merely between fathers and children (or sons; see later discussion).

sense, a part of his parents (*EN* 8.12.1161b18–33, 1162a4–9).[9] In any other context, a relationship devoted to the good of only one of its participants could only be a form of slavery, and hence unjust and unworthy of anyone other than a "slave by nature." It is, in fact, precisely this feature of the master-slave relationship that leads Aristotle to deny that it amounts to a genuine community or friendship in even the qualified sense that applies to friendships of pleasure and advantage (8.11.1161a32–b4).[10] The slave, however, stands to his master as a tool to its user; the child, by contrast, is to his parents "another self."

The three forms of community that constitute the household differ, then, in their characteristic and proper aims. The community of parent and child, like the other two communities, is characterized by a division of roles grounded in its participants' different capacities. In this case, the salient disparity lies in the degree to which the parent and the child have developed those capacities. Like his parents, the child possesses the capacity for rational deliberation and action but unlike them has not yet developed it (*Pol.* 1.13.1260a13–14). In aiming at the child's good, the parents seek above all else to foster the development of that capacity in addition to meeting the other needs whose satisfaction is a necessary condition for it. As the child matures, he gradually moves from a state of complete dependence on his parents to a position in which he will, in effect, take their place, caring for them in their old age and eventually producing children of his own.[11] The child's reciprocity toward his parents does not belie the centrality of his own good in the structure of the parent-child relationship. On the contrary, Aristotle describes the deference and care that children owe their parents as a debt of gratitude for their own existence, sustenance, and education (*EN* 8.12.1162a4–7, cf. 8.7.1158b11–28).

Though this account of the community of parent and child can be pieced together from various passages in the *Politics* and *Nicomachean*

---

[9] For more on the relationship between parents and children, see Chapters 2.2 and 3.2, Tress 1997, Belfiore 2001.

[10] On the apparent discrepancies between the accounts of the master-slave relationship in the *Politics* and the *Nicomachean Ethics*, and reasons to think that the two accounts are consistent after all, see Chapter 2.2.

[11] As with his focus on fathers, Aristotle's attention is, unsurprisingly, focused on *male* children. In this case, the differences seem more resistant to neat unification, because Aristotle expects such different outcomes for sons and daughters; the different roles of mothers and fathers in rearing children can more plausibly be viewed as different aspects of the same kind of activity and the same kind of relationship. Though his account could no doubt be expanded to make explicit the differences he expects in the treatment and development of daughters and sons, I have followed him here for the sake of simplicity.

Ethics, Aristotle has little to say about children in the opening chapters of the former. This silence is primarily a product of his aims. What the opening chapters give us is not a theory or analysis of the household, but an account of the emergence of political community from the household and the village that grows out of the household.[12] Aristotle's interest in the household is, at this stage, in the household as a whole rather than its parts. Though its parts are the three communities that we have seen so far, the features that distinguish them from one another are less significant for Aristotle's argument than the unity that they constitute.[13] For all their differences, all three are aspects or elements of the pursuit of preservation and reproduction, and this is the complex but unified end of the household. A more complete understanding of the household as a form of community would demand greater attention to its complex structure, such as we find in later chapters of book 1 (*Pol.* 1.13.1259b18–1260b7, 3.6.1278b32–1279a2, cf. *EN* 8.11–12.1161a10–1162a33).[14] To illustrate the distinctive character of political community, however, the first step is to establish the distinctness of its aims from those of the smaller communities to which it owes its origin. The first of these communities is the household, "the community

---

[12] Trott 2013: 46–7 argues, drawing on Kullmann 1991, that Aristotle's analysis of the household and the village is not intended as a historical account and that Aristotle does not believe that human beings have ever existed in a pre- or nonpolitical condition; Brown 2013 is likewise skeptical. Yet Aristotle plainly attributes some sort of historical veracity to his account of scattered villages when he writes that "that was how people lived in ancient times" (*Pol.* 1.2.1252b24), and other passages appear to embrace a cyclical view of history not unlike the one laid out in Plato's *Laws* (676a–82e), with the periodic destruction and reemergence of civilization: *Pol.* 2.8.1269a4–8, 7.10.1329b25–30; *Metr.* 1.14.351b7–27; *Met.* 12.8.1074b1–15. Furthermore, Aristotle recognizes a variety of peoples who live in forms of social organization that he calls "nations" (ἔθνη), and he makes clear that nothing that is a polis is also an *ethnos* (*Pol.* 2.2.1261a27–29, 7.4.1326b2–5; on the *ethnos* in Aristotle's thought, see Depew 1995 and Ward 2002). The thesis that human beings are naturally political does not entail that we are "always already" in the polis, as Trott puts it.

[13] The *EN* includes the relationship between brothers in its discussion of the communities of the household (8.12.1161b30–1162a5, see also Lockwood 2003). The account of the household in *Pol.* 1, however, ignores it, presumably because it is not marked by its own characteristic form of rule and authority, as the other three relationships are, and so supplies us with less comparative insight into the specifically political variety of community and rule.

[14] It is worth noting, however, that even in the later chapters Aristotle's interest is never in the household per se, but only in the ways in which the household and its distinctive forms of community and authority illuminate political community by their similarities and differences. An inquiry into the household as such would be out of place in a work devoted to "the things of the polis"; it was, perhaps, an appreciation of this difference that led the author of the pseudo-Aristotelian *Oikonomika* to try his hand at developing a fuller Aristotelian account of the household (see Zoepffel 2006). In this regard, we might compare Aristotle's discussion of the household in the *Politics* to his treatment of psychology in the *Nicomachean Ethics* (*EN* 1.13.1102a18–26).

established in accordance with nature for the needs of every day" (*Pol.* 1.2.1252b12–14).[15]

2. The Village as a Community

Successful households produce a plurality of offspring, and hence give rise to other households. Once formed, the members of these new households do not cease to interact with their families or keep their distance from one another, but come to form a larger, more complex community, the village (κώμη, *Pol.* 1.2.1252b16). Aristotle says frustratingly little about the village, and he virtually ignores it after his analysis reaches the city. His introductory comments, however, make clear that he conceives it as a new and different kind of community that does not merely extend the features of the household across a wider geographical space. On the one hand, the village transcends the household by serving a higher end; it is a community composed of multiple households "for the sake of more than daily need" (1.2.1252b15–16).[16] On the other hand, though the relationships between households and the characteristic mode of authority in villages owe much to their origin in the household, they do not simply reproduce it.

As "offshoots" or "colonies" (ἀποικίαι) of the household (οἰκία), the village and the households that make it up are bound by ties of kinship (1.2.1252b16–18). In many cases, mature adult males will head their own households well before their fathers have died. Through their sons' continued respect and gratitude, these older men maintain at least a de facto authority and influence on them. More generally, the respect for seniority and the habit of deferring to a single authoritative figure are extended into the relationships among households, leading to the general recognition of some single individual as preeminent. This preeminence of the eldest male in the prepolitical village is the historical origin of kingship.[17] To be sure, the sort of proto-kingship exemplified in villages falls short of the monarchic constitutional arrangements that Aristotle finds among

---

[15] For this translation, see Newman 1887–1902.ii: 112. The idea of need is to be supplied from the preposition εἰς expressing purpose or object (LSJ s.v. εἰς A.V.2).

[16] For χρῆσις as "need," see again Newman 1887–1902.ii: 112 and LSJ s.v. χράω (B) C.2. The more regular sense of "use" comes to the same thing in this context; in contrast to the community established "for every day," the more complex community formed "for the sake of nondaily use" is the one formed for employments and activities that transcend daily needs.

[17] Keyt 1999: 144 observes that the *Politics* offers three different accounts of the origin of kingship: the preservation of the patriarchal structure of the household, as here; gratitude for outstanding beneficence (3.15.1286b8–13); and the protection of elites from the people (5.10.1310b9–12). But these are not obviously exclusive alternatives.

fully political communities. Yet the latter are genetically dependent on the former. Cities were first ruled by kings, Aristotle thinks, as are the prepolitical nations (ἔθνη) of his day, because they had their origins in villages ruled by the eldest in the manner of a king (1.2.1252b19–22).[18]

The differences between these kinds of "kingship," however, are as broad and deep as the differences between the village and the city. Above all else, the monarchic authority found in the village would be less formal and more limited in scope in comparison with that of a city's king. For the village itself is marked by a comparatively low level of integration and formality. Aristotle describes the situation as he envisions it with an allusion to Homer's depiction of the Cyclopes in *Odyssey* 9: "That is what Homer says: 'Each man laid down sacred right for children and wives'; for they were scattered, and that is how people lived in ancient times" (1.2.1252b22–24).[19] Though the inhabitants of a village recognize one of their elder members as a leading authority in their common dealings, Aristotle apparently imagines those common dealings as rather limited.[20]

Nonetheless, the households of a village do amount to a community, and hence interact among themselves in pursuit of an end distinct from the multigenerational preservation and reproduction that typify the

---

[18] Thus Reeve 2009: 515 is mistaken to suggest that Aristotle offers no explanation for his claim that primitive villages were ruled monarchically rather than politically. Saunders 1995: 66–7 observes that Aristotle's model of the village assumes that the households will all be related by blood or marriage. No doubt it is this (admittedly unrealistic) assumption that allows Aristotle to infer monarchic rule with such little argument. Saunders's citation of Plato's *Laws* 680e–1d shows that Aristotle had some reason to question this assumption.

[19] The referent of "that" is unclear, and many commentators have been inclined to read the description of the Cyclopes as applying only to the household. Newman 1887–1902.ii: 116–18 notes that this is an unnatural reading of the Greek, since it ignores the intervening clause about the village, but he goes on to discuss the Homeric quotation as though it were relevant solely to the household. Simpson 1998: 20 rightly takes the quotation as illustrating the monarchic character of rule in households and villages alike.

[20] The reference to the Cyclopes raises complicated puzzles to the extent that we try to make sense of it in light of the details of Homer's depiction of them. It is instructive to recall, however, that Homer's Polyphemus is not a typical Cyclops in the degree of his antisociality; the other Cyclopes readily respond to his call for assistance, and the picture of their minimal society seems consistent with what Aristotle describes in another context as a prepolitical community of "exchange and alliance," where people associate and even have laws against injustice in exchange (3.9.1280b17–23, cf. *Od.* 9.105–15, 399–406). For an interesting interpretation of how the Cyclopes bear on Aristotle's conception of human beings as political animals, see Depew 1995. Depew reads "scattered" at 1252b23 in light of the classification of animals as "political," "gregarious," "solitary," and "scattered" in the *HA* and argues, against Cooper 1990 and others, that the "scattered" category must involve geographical dispersion. Since this passage cites the Cyclopes to characterize prepolitical village life, and prepolitical village life, as I will argue, involves a fair amount of interaction among households, I doubt whether the use of the term "scattered" here is fruitfully connected with its technical usage in the biological works.

household as such. Understanding the village therefore requires understanding this end. Yet Aristotle describes it only as "more than daily need" (1.2.1252b15–16). If we take the idea of an isolated household seriously for analytic purposes, the daily needs of a small group devoted to its members' survival and the procreation of children should be limited. The household will meet these needs if it succeeds in obtaining adequate food and shelter each day to preserve its members. To seek more than daily need is therefore to seek more than what is strictly necessary in order for a household to preserve itself across several generations. This is, admittedly, unsurprising, since a village can come to exist and persist only if households are able to persist. The persistence of a household is, however, not a goal that can be reached once and for all; its members must pursue it continuously if they are to survive. Yet once they have attained a level of success sufficient to generate the population of a village, meeting those basic daily needs becomes easier as cooperation and support from other households reduce the time and effort necessary for any individual household to keep its members alive. The less that individual households need to struggle simply to survive, the more opportunity they will have to turn their attention toward relative ease, comfort, and even pleasure. This kind of progression seems to be a plausible enough candidate for the content of "more than daily need." We can see more clearly that it is what Aristotle has in mind, however, when we turn to his view of the eventual emergence of political community out of villages advancing toward "self-sufficiency."

Villages, once they exist, evidently begin to interact with one another. Aristotle has even less to say about this interaction than about the village itself. Yet he plainly envisions the city developing out of several villages: "The community formed from several villages, when it is complete, is a city, possessing at that point the limit of practically every self-sufficiency; though it comes to be for the sake of living, it exists for the sake of living well" (1.2.1252b27–30). Separate villages, each made up of a collection of households linked through ties of kinship, cooperate over time in some unspecified ways. Their cooperation, in turn, leads them further toward self-sufficiency. Once attained, this self-sufficiency somehow brings about a transformation of the community formed by these villages. Where they previously cooperated only in the pursuit of "living," the community that they eventually form aims at a higher good, "living well." To appreciate Aristotle's account of the city, as well as his conception of prepolitical but supradomestic social life, we need to get clear on what he means by "self-sufficiency" and on how he intends to distinguish "living" and "living well."

3.   Self-Sufficiency and Living Well

In English, the term "self-sufficiency" tends to suggest independence from others. We can, for instance, say that a person lacks self-sufficiency to the extent that he is unable to provide for himself without assistance from other people. A man who can neither cook nor manage his finances, but depends on his wife to feed him and to organize the household budget, is, other things being equal, less self-sufficient than someone who is capable of these things but happens not to do them because he lives with an eager accountant-chef. Similarly, a community is less self-sufficient to the extent that it depends on resources supplied by others. A state that must purchase its fuel from foreign companies or governments depends on those others for its ability to operate; a self-sustaining rural community that produces all the power it needs via windmills is, by contrast, more self-sufficient in that respect because it does not depend on outsiders to meet its power needs. Some of Aristotle's readers have supposed that he has just this conception of independence and self-reliance in mind when he speaks of self-sufficiency.[21] On this view, an individual will be maximally self-sufficient when he does not rely on others to meet his needs and achieve his ends, and a city will be maximally self-sufficient when it is able to supply all of its resources from within without depending on trade.

Aristotle appears to reject precisely this interpretation of self-sufficiency early in the *Nicomachean Ethics*, where he says, "By 'self-sufficient' I mean not [self-sufficient] for an individual alone living a solitary life, but for parents and children and a wife and, in general, friends and fellow citizens, since the human being is political by nature" (*EN* 1.7.1097b8–11). One might suppose, however, that this qualification simply acknowledges that there are limits to how self-sufficient a human being can be; because we are political by nature, we cannot achieve complete independence

---

[21] Chappell 2009 criticizes Aristotle's view of the city's self-sufficiency on the assumption that independence is what is at issue. Ober 1998: 295 defines αὐτάρκεια as "the ability of a corporate whole to secure and defend its material needs without having to enter into any relationship with an outside entity that would compromise its independence." Compare his gloss of αὐτάρκεια as "an ability to defend against aggression and a sufficiency of material goods" in Ober 1996b: 168. For a useful corrective, compare Meikle 1995: 44–5. Meikle acknowledges that the word carries the sense of "independence" in some Greek texts and even in some passages of Aristotle, but argues persuasively that as it appears in important passages in the *Politics*, it "primarily means having enough, and only secondarily, if at all, independence of others." Mayhew 1995 provides a more sustained analysis of the term as it appears in the *Politics*, insightfully setting it alongside uses in earlier Greek texts and affirming Meikle's main point. Though I criticize aspects of Mayhew's view in Chapter 3.5, I am in substantial agreement with most of his claims.

from others, and so we must not demand maximal self-sufficiency. Yet Aristotle's appeal to self-sufficiency at this stage in his argument about the structure of the human good suggests a rather different point and a different idea of what it is for something to be self-sufficient. He concludes that "what is self-sufficient is that which, taken by itself, makes life choiceworthy and lacking in nothing" (1.7.1097b14–15), and the subject that he describes as self-sufficient in this passage is not an individual human agent, but "the complete good" (1.7.1097b7–8) and *eudaimonia* (1.7.1097b15–16).

The complete good of human flourishing is self-sufficient because, considered on its own, it lacks nothing that would, if added, make it more worth choosing.[22] Living together with others, and even depending on them in various ways, does not set a limit on the degree of self-sufficiency to which human beings can realistically aspire. Rather, it is part of the content of a self-sufficient life, one that lacks nothing that could make it more choiceworthy. A life that is self-sufficient in this sense may in fact require a high degree of independence, autonomy, and self-reliance; if we rely too extensively on others, we may become too vulnerable to contingencies, insufficiently able to make our own decisions, or excessively deferential and subservient to others. A self-sufficient life would also impose limits on just how independent a person could realistically expect to be; if we refuse to depend on others in any way, our lives will lack much that would make them richer, more valuable, and more worth choosing.[23] Yet different views about the kinds and degrees of interdependence and autonomy that the good life requires or allows will not be different views about how self-sufficient such a life should be. They will be, instead, disagreements

---

[22] cf. Pakaluk 2005: 72, who argues that the self-sufficiency criterion in *EN* 1.7 favors a conception of *eudaimonia* as constituted by a single specific kind of activity, since "the more self-sufficient an activity, the less it would become combined with or require other activities or goods, and the more it alone would satisfy us"; a more inclusive conception of *eudaimonia* would threaten to make us more dependent, but "rest and further dependence are the core ideas" of self-sufficiency. This view, however, faces several difficulties accounting for Aristotle's claim that what is self-sufficient makes life "lacking in nothing" (*EN* 1.7.1097b14–15); it also sits uneasily with the earlier instruction not to understand self-sufficiency in terms of independence (1.7.1097b8–11) and generates a problematic interpretation of the nonaggregatability condition in 1097b16–20. A fully satisfactory treatment of this passage would need to address the thorny problems surrounding the interpretation of *eudaimonia*. For further discussion of these issues see Lawrence 1997 and Cooper 2004b. I agree with Brown 2013 that *EN* 1–9 endorse what he calls "political self-sufficiency" in contrast to "solitary self-sufficiency," and I find the same conception of self-sufficiency at work in the *Politics*. I do not consider Brown's further claim that *EN* 10 shifts to embrace solitary self-sufficiency as a criterion of *eudaimonia*.

[23] For in-depth considerations of the role of external goods and luck in Aristotle's ethics, see Nussbaum 1986 and White 1992.

about what makes for a self-sufficient life. For Aristotle, a self-sufficient life is one that lacks nothing that would make it more worthy of choice, not one that depends on nothing outside of itself.

Aristotle's invocation of self-sufficiency in his account of the city's emergence from the village likewise does not intuitively suggest the idea of independence. If the progression from scattered villages to the city is a progression toward self-sufficiency, it hardly seems to lead to a decreased dependence on others. On the contrary, the individual households and the villages they compose would all become *more* dependent on one another once they had joined to make up a single city. The villages do not become a city by decreasing their dependence on one another, but through an intensification and expansion of their interaction. Aristotle sees this development as a movement toward self-sufficiency. Since it is plainly not a movement toward greater independence, it is implausible to interpret self-sufficiency in terms of independence. Yet the transition from the village to the city does make possible a way of life in which human beings can pursue and to some extent achieve more of the goods that together make life "choiceworthy and lacking in nothing." This much, at least, becomes clear from the tight connection that Aristotle draws between the city and living well. In Aristotle's view, the city plays an indispensable role in making human flourishing possible, and his claim that human beings need to live in political communities in order to live well is at the center of one of his most famous and controversial theses, that the city exists "by nature."

For Aristotle, the city's naturalness is not a matter of its coming into being spontaneously or by necessity, apart from deliberate choice or rational action. Nor is it a matter of the city's being a natural entity with its own internal principle of change and development.[24] Nor, again, does the

---

[24] Both of these claims are somewhat controversial, and a full defense of them is beyond the scope of this book. My interpretation of the naturalness of the city primarily follows Miller 1995, which has come to gain wide favor, despite some disagreements of detail (for expressions of agreement, see Annas 1996, Simpson 1998, Kraut 2002, Rosler 2005, each with varying degrees of qualification). Similar views, though disagreeing on points of detail, are defended in Everson 1988, Salkever 1990, Kullmann 1991, Chan 1992, Yack 1993, Nederman 1994, Depew 1995, Cherry and Goerner 2006, Cherry 2012, Brown 2013, Leunissen (forthcoming). For a forceful statement of the opposing view that Aristotle does consider the city to be a natural organism that comes into being without the aid of rational agency, see Keyt 1991a, which stimulated and provoked much of the recent discussion of the naturalness of the city. Keyt raises a series of devastating objections to the coherence and plausibility of the thesis so interpreted; his objections are to the point, but they count against his interpretation supposing we adopt even a weak version of the principle of charity. Since, as Miller and others have shown, there are textually plausible alternative interpretations of what it is for something to be "by nature" and for the city to be "prior" to the household and to individual human beings, and since these alternatives entail neither that the city is a natural organism nor

city exist by nature primarily because human beings have some innate impulse, desire, or tendency to form political communities.[25] The first two claims are false; Aristotle does not believe that cities come into being apart from the deliberate exercise of rational agency or that the city is a kind of natural organism over and above the human beings who constitute it. The third claim, though true, does not explain the naturalness of the city, but is in fact explained by it. The more fundamental point, in Aristotle's view, is that human beings must live together in political communities if they are to develop and exercise their essential capacities as rational animals. These capacities for practical agency and rational thought are, for Aristotle, what make human beings the kind of beings that we are, and the development and exercise of these capacities are the development and exercise of our nature.

Human beings have a nature because we have an internal principle of motion and rest (*Phys.* 2.1.192b9–22); that is, we are complex but unified wholes that change and act in a variety of ways of our own accord and not simply because we are changed by others. The specific nature that we have is the nature of rational animals, which is to say that the kinds of self-initiated change and activity that we engage in include not only nutrition, growth, locomotion, perception, and imagination, but rational thought and reflectively chosen goal-directed action informed by reasons (*EN* 1.7.1097b22–1098a18, *DA* 2.3.414a29–415a13). To have a human nature is to have the capacities for these kinds of activity. But capacities can be exercised well or badly, and the good of any being with a specific

---

that it exists independently of rational agency, we should prefer these alternatives if, as Miller et al. argue, they do not lead to the problems of the organic interpretation; cf. Keyt 1996 for a response to Miller. Johnson 2005 interprets the teleological dimensions of Aristotle's account of the city as committing him to the view that the city is a natural organism; Reeve 2009 argues that the city must have a "standard nature" in just the way that organisms do, but does not defend this claim at length. Trott 2013 develops a similar view that she calls the "internal principle of change interpretation," but her arguments do not successfully show that the city has a nature of its own in the strong sense that organisms do, and her criticisms of Miller et al. miss the mark. None of these defenders of the organic interpretation successfully addresses what is perhaps the most serious objection to it, raised by Mayhew 1997: Aristotle typically denies that substances can be composed of other substances (*Met.* 7.13.1039a3–4, 14.1041a4–5), and yet clearly believes that individual human beings are substances. Perhaps the single best succinct, introductory discussion of the naturalness of the polis is Miller 2000.

[25] It is sometimes supposed that when Aristotle claims that human beings are political animals by nature and, later, that we have a natural impulse for political community, his principal claim is that human beings have an innate, conscious drive to engage in specifically political activities of citizenship just as such; see, e.g., Ober 1996b: 163. For a persuasive rebuttal of this view, see Salkever 1990: 73. For an excellent account of the relationship between an animal's natural impulses or tendencies and its characteristic way of life, see Depew 1995.

nature consists in the harmoniously integrated exercise of its basic essential capacities. Different kinds of nonrational animals pursue and achieve their ends in a variety of different ways; though the well-being of each kind consists in the full and well-integrated exercise of its capacities for nutrition, growth, reproduction, and perception, different kinds of animals embody these capacities in widely divergent ways and seek to exercise them in varied ways of life.[26] Rational animals, of course, exercise the same kinds of capacities as their nonrational counterparts. We differ, however, not only in our possession of an additional capacity for rational agency, but in the characteristic subordination of our subrational capacities to our reasoning. Thus we eat and procreate, as dogs and sheep do, but eating and procreation take on a very different shape in human life largely because these activities become embedded and integrated within broader patterns and more extended practical projects. In this way, rational agency is both distinct from and inclusive of the subrational capacities that human beings share with nonrational animals and even plants. Excellent rational agency, then, will be a matter not only of *thinking* well, but of successfully guiding the exercise of our various capacities, from nutrition to theoretical contemplation, in the light of reflective deliberation about how we can most fully actualize those capacities.[27]

When Aristotle says that the city exists by nature, he means most fundamentally that it is only in the context of a distinctively political form

---

[26] For the well-being and ways of life of nonrational animals, see Depew 1995, Johnson 2005.

[27] This paragraph compresses several points of considerable complexity, both interpretive and philosophical, that have been ably elaborated by others. In addition to the argument in *Pol.* 1.2 that the city exists by nature, my account relies on a reading of the famous "function argument" of *EN* 1.7 and draws on the broad claims of Aristotle's physics, psychology, and biology. My understanding of the relationship between nature and normativity in Aristotle owes most to Wilkes 1980, Whiting 1988, Gomez-Lobo 1989, White 1992: 139–57, and especially Miller 1995: 27–66. For some attempts to minimize the role of nature and metaphysical commitments in Aristotle's ethics more generally, see Nussbaum 1986, 1995b and Rosler 2005. For helpful discussions of the function argument, see Lawrence 2001, 2006. Much discussion of Aristotle's views is driven (sometimes tacitly) by a desire to avoid making him guilty of the alleged "naturalistic fallacy." Though even a cursory treatment of this issue is impossible here, I do not regard naturalism about value as a fallacy and do not believe that Aristotle anywhere attempts to derive normative conclusions from purely non-normative premises (for concise introductions to and critiques of the fact-value distinction, see Geach 1956, Martin 2004). Contemporary defenses of views similar to Aristotle's come in different flavors: For a traditional view that commits itself to an essentialist and nonreductively teleological theory of human nature, see Rasmussen 1999, Rasmussen and Den Uyl 2005. For less metaphysically ambitious accounts, cf. Quinn 1993, Sher 1997, MacIntyre 1998, Foot 2001, Thompson 2008. For a sophisticated defense of a teleological account of human well-being as good human functioning, without traditionally Aristotelian commitments to essentialism or nonreductive natural teleology, see Murphy 2001. For accounts less Aristotelian in spirit and inspiration but ultimately quite similar in structure, see Boyd 1988, Brink 1989.

of community that human beings can adequately develop and exercise their essential capacities for rational agency. Humans do have a natural impulse and tendency to form political communities when external circumstances or developmental disorders do not obstruct that development. This tendency, however, is explained by the role that a political way of life plays in the development and exercise of human nature, not the other way around. By analogy, animals have a natural impulse to eat food because eating is necessary for their preservation. Though it is also true that animals are preserved because they eat, Aristotle's explanatory framework for natural beings – that is, beings with a specific nature, a dynamic, internal principle of self-initiated change – gives priority to the formal and final aspects of an animal and its behavior. In organisms, at any rate, what a being is (formal) and what it specifically does (final) are, in a sense, identical: Its form is specified by its essential capacities, and the actualization of those capacities is its function and goal. Behavioral tendencies or psychological impulses are to be explained by reference to these capacities and their actualization.[28] This explanatory priority of form and function has a further implication that may sound counterintuitive in a modern, non-Aristotelian idiom: It allows Aristotle to describe behaviors, activities, institutions, and the like, as "natural," "by nature," or "according to nature" even when they are not innate, unconscious, spontaneous, widely shared, or developed independently of rational deliberation. For an activity or behavior to be natural is, first and foremost, for it to be conducive to or expressive of the nature of the being in question. Accordingly, even an innate impulse could conceivably be contrary to nature if its expression hinders or obstructs the development or exercise of the animal's fundamental capacities.[29] In arguing for the naturalness of the city, Aristotle maintains just the opposite: The city is an indispensable condition for the actualization of human nature.

---

[28] For an illuminating discussion of the explanatory priority of form and end, see Johnson 2005. Depew 1995 illustrates the application of this explanatory principle to the explanation of animal ways of life. Frede 1992 gives an insightful and concise account of formal explanation in Aristotle.

[29] Aristotle and ancient Greek thought more generally were by no means immune to the troublesome ambiguities of "nature" and "natural"; in *EN* 2.1, for example, Aristotle claims that the virtues do not arise in human beings "by nature," where he means innately, spontaneously, without habituation; he similarly contrasts nature, habit, and reason as causes in *Pol.* 7.13.1332a38 and 7.15.1334b6. But he also distinguishes the two different kinds of "business" or "moneymaking" that he identifies in *Pol.* 1.9 by saying that one is "by nature" and the other is "not by nature," where that difference depends on whether the agent aims at obtaining things that are useful for living well or simply at making more money without limit (I discuss this distinction briefly in Chapter 3.6). "Nature," we must admit, is said in many ways. For Aristotle's own awareness of the homonymy of "nature," see *Phys.* 2.1.192b35–193a1. On "nature" in Aristotle more generally, see Lennox 2001b and 2001c.

A crucial step in Aristotle's argument for the naturalness of the city is his claim that individual human beings are not self-sufficient in isolation from political community: "For if each is not self-sufficient when separated, he will be like other parts in relation to the whole" (*Pol.* 1.2.1253a26–9). Once again, this appeal to self-sufficiency does not suggest the idea of independence. On the contrary, the passage implies that participation in political community makes individuals self-sufficient. The formulation is, admittedly, not strictly inconsistent with the claim that parts as such are never self-sufficient. If that were Aristotle's point, however, this would be an awkward way to put it. For anything that is essentially a part necessarily depends on other parts to be what it is, and so is inherently dependent on something else (1.2.1253a20–5). Why, then, if "not self-sufficient" meant "dependent," would Aristotle add the qualification that something is like a part if it is not self-sufficient *when it is separated*? When he describes the individual human being as a part of the city, he is not implying that humans who do not live in cities cannot survive. His point is, rather, that when we are separated from political communities we cannot fully exercise the essential capacities in virtue of which we are the kind of beings we are. In this context, then, self-sufficiency is not contrasted with interdependence. The specific sort of interdependence that characterizes life in political communities is, rather, the way in which human beings achieve self-sufficiency.

Aristotle tends to describe the community, rather than the individual, as the subject of self-sufficiency. Thus he says, for instance, that "a household is more self-sufficient than an individual, and a city more than a household, and a city tends to exist just at that moment when the community of the multitude becomes self-sufficient" (2.2.1261b11–13). Yet this formulation is just what we should expect if human beings become self-sufficient through participation in political communities; for I do not achieve self-sufficiency insofar as I am an individual, but insofar as I cooperate with others in a form of community that enables me to live well. A city's self-sufficiency, too, should be understood in terms of what it provides to the people who constitute it rather than its independence or freedom from reliance on external resources. As Aristotle stresses in a different context, the city, in an important sense, just is the multitude of people who form it: The city is "composed of the first multitude sufficiently great to be self-sufficient for life in accordance with political community" (7.4.1326b7–9), "not any chance multitude, but one that is self-sufficient for life" (7.8.1328b16–19). Just as "it is impossible for a whole city to flourish unless all or most or some of its parts are in possession of happiness"

(2.5.1264b17–19), so too we should think that the city is self-sufficient because all or most or some of its parts are able to fulfill their needs.[30]

We are now in a position to resolve the ambiguities in Aristotle's description of self-sufficiency as "having all things and lacking nothing" (7.5.1326b29–30). The scope of "everything" and "nothing" is delimited by the needs and requirements of our nature as rational animals. We achieve self-sufficiency when we are in a position to pursue and achieve the goods that would jointly make life "choiceworthy and lacking in nothing" (*EN* 1.7.1097b15).[31] The internal connection between self-sufficiency and living well, in turn, illuminates Aristotle's claim that the city, in achieving self-sufficiency, exists for the sake of living well. Yet several puzzles remain. What does Aristotle mean when he says that the city comes to be for the sake of living, but exists for the sake of living well? How exactly does the city differ from the prepolitical forms of cooperative interaction within and between villages? What is it about the city that makes it possible for human beings to flourish? What is the relationship between the good life and the characteristic features of political community that seems to distinguish it from other forms of association? What does living well have to do with characteristically political forms of rule, authority, and justice?

4.   Law, Justice, and Self-Sufficiency

In his argument for the naturalness of political community, Aristotle closely associates its value with the institutions of law and justice: "For just as a human being is the best of animals when perfected and complete [τελεωθείς], so too when separated from law and justice he is the worst of all" (*Pol.* 1.2.1253a31–3). In book 7, the institutional judgment of justice

---

[30] Miller 1995: 50–3 offers a slightly different interpretation of the argument, supplying as a tacit premise the proposition that "the part as such is not self-sufficient." On my reading, the part *as such* can be self-sufficient; it cannot be self-sufficient when it ceases to function *as a part:* An eye is self-sufficient when it lacks nothing necessary for it to see. Miller's analysis of the argument is otherwise insightful, but it does not go far enough in rejecting the assumption that the self-sufficiency that Aristotle has in mind is a matter of independence, as though an eye could be self-sufficient only if it did not depend on any other parts of the animal or any external conditions in order to see.

[31] One ambiguity my account does not resolve is just how expansive or inclusive a good *eudaimonia* must be in order for a flourishing life to be lacking in nothing. On the one hand, it cannot include every intrinsically good thing, since no single life could combine them all. On the other hand, it cannot be limited simply to what would make a life worth living at all, since a life might lack important goods and yet still be better than not living at all. Richardson Lear 2004: 47–71 presents challenges for inclusivist interpretations of self-sufficiency, but the discussion in White 1992: 3–21 remains persuasive.

and advantage appears in a list of necessary functions or "works" (ἔργα) without which a community cannot be self-sufficient: "Most necessary of all is judgment about what is advantageous and just in their relations to one another" (7.8.1328b13–15). The emergence or self-conscious creation of legal institutions is, then, a crucial moment in the development of the city out of a collection of villages. Several considerations suggest that it is, in fact, the decisive shift that transforms those villages into a city.

First, consider the other functions in Aristotle's list from book 7: food, crafts, weapons, money and commodities, and "care for the divine" (7.8.1328b5–13). Some of these resources, and coordinated activity connected with them, plainly exist already in the isolated village if not in the household. No human being could survive without food, and the development and stability of villages surely depend on some relatively reliable means of procuring it. At least some crafts, likewise, must develop within the village; if nothing else, human beings must build shelters, make clothing, and construct rudimentary tools. Aristotle clearly supposes that religious ritual and myth were a part of prepolitical life when he appeals to the monarchical structure of the household and the village to explain the traditional belief that the gods are ruled by a king (1.2.1252b24–7). Though organized warfare may need to wait for the emergence of more complex communities, there is no need to suppose that prepolitical villages possessed no weapons, especially if they engage in any amount of hunting.[32] Commodities and wealth suggest trade and exchange. It may be tempting to suppose that commercial exchange develops only with the institutions of the city, but there are reasons to think otherwise. First, though Aristotle sensibly denies that the members of a single household exchange goods with one another, exchange does indeed come about "when the community is composed of more people" (1.9.1257a19–21). This community is not explicitly identified with the village, but it seems apparent that various households within a village would engage in exchange. Aristotle recognizes a premonetary form of exchange among "the barbarian nations"

---

[32] It is apparent that Aristotle does not believe that warfare is a strictly political phenomenon, since he denies that the "nations" (ἔθνη) live in political communities and yet is fully aware that these people engage in war, sometimes even highly organized wars. Generally, Aristotle appears to believe that cities are less violent and warlike than complex but nonpolitical communities. Because the relationship between the prepolitical village communities and the nonpolitical but complex *ethnos* is unclear, however, it is difficult to determine whether he supposes that the former were especially belligerent. For an interesting argument that the *ethnos* is not "a necessary stage of social development leading to the polis so much as an alternate, less differentiated path of development, in which villages remain loosely tied through patriarchy and hereditary kingship," see Depew 1995: 173. Ostwald 2009b surveys Aristotle's pronouncements on warfare.

(1.9.1257a24–8, cf. *EN* 5.5.1133a5–26), whose communities are not political. Second, even if exchange between households connected through kinship took the form of generalized reciprocity rather than the more strict reciprocity of nonmonetary exchange, a more formal exchange of goods is the most obvious rationale for prepolitical interaction among villages. Finally, Aristotle explicitly denies that commercial exchange is sufficient for political community, while acknowledging that it is a necessary condition for its existence: "Though these things must exist if there is to be a city, nonetheless there is not yet a city even when all these things are present, but only when households and families form a community in living well for the sake of complete and self-sufficient living" (*Pol.* 3.9.1280b31–5).[33]

Aristotle claims that all the works or functions that he lists in book 7 are necessary for the existence of a self-sufficient political community. Yet only the last, "the most necessary," does not exist in some form in prepolitical villages. Evidently, then, a collection of villages engaging in relations of exchange becomes a city when it establishes some unified institutional means of judgment about "what is advantageous and just in their relations with one another." One reason to doubt that even this much is sufficient, however, turns out on closer examination to lend further support to this conclusion.

The passage from 3.9 cited previously insists not only that a community established for the sake of exchange falls short of being a city. It also denies that mutual agreements between people to forgo unjust treatment of one another are enough for the existence of a political community. Such agreements exist between cities, but they do not transform those cities into a single political community (3.9.1280a34–40). Nor would it be sufficient for a city if people living apart from one another were to establish laws prohibiting injustice in their exchange of goods (3.9.1280b17–23). In the sort of community that Aristotle has in mind here, different people specialize in different crafts, producing more food, shoes, or whatever than they need for themselves in order to exchange those products for other useful goods likewise produced by specialized craftsmen. The members of such a community might quickly come to see a need for some generally recognized rules to govern their commercial dealings, and hence agree to come to one another's aid in enforcing those rules against anyone who violates them. Yet such a community of "exchange and alliance," as Aristotle calls it, would not amount to a city (3.9.1280b22–3, 29–31). The

---

[33] My translation of this sentence is indebted to that of Simpson 1997.

people who come together only to exchange goods and enforce rules of fairness in that exchange do not come together or cooperate for the sake of living well. But that is just what a political community is for. The argument in book 3 is no less insistent than the argument in book 1 that we will misunderstand the city if we do not take account of this distinctive aim and properly grasp its implications. The argument appears to be that since the city exists "not merely for the sake of living, but for the sake of living well" (3.9.1280a31–2), legal institutions do not make a city.

It is important, however, to observe the limited character of the laws that Aristotle envisions in the community of "exchange and alliance." The aim of these laws is purely negative: to prohibit unjust dealings in relations of exchange. In this context, injustice is likely to be limited to the use of force or deception in place of honest agreement, probably including failure to abide by agreements or to give one's partner a fair return. Such minimal standards, if generally accepted and somehow enforced, would deserve to be called laws. Yet they hardly have the character that Aristotle attributes to law in its full-blown or focal case: "The laws speak about everything, aiming either at the common advantage for all or for the best or for those in authority or in some other such way, and so in one way we call just those things that produce and protect happiness and its parts for the political community" (*EN* 5.1.1129b14–19).[34] In the fullest sense, law and justice can only be understood in relation to the common good of a community. In the paradigmatic case, this community is the community that aims at happiness or human flourishing, the complete and self-sufficient good. Treating this robust and developed system of norms as the paradigm instance of law and justice does not commit Aristotle to denying that more limited cases are genuine instances of either. As we saw in Chapter 2, his structurally similar analysis of friendship does not prevent him from concluding that there is a kind of friendship and justice in every community. What the analysis suggests is not that the limited agreements to forgo injustice in communities of exchange do not count as laws, but that when Aristotle emphasizes the importance of legal institutions in the nature and value of political community, he does not have such a minimal conception of law and justice in mind.

---

[34] This passage has confused readers and divided interpreters. Compare the translation of Irwin 1999 ("in every matter that they deal with, the laws aim") with the comments of Kraut 2002: 113 note 23: "The laws address all matters, in that for every ethical virtue there is a law that requires action in accordance with that virtue." Part of the dispute is whether Aristotle means to say that law has a universal scope. Fortunately, I need not take sides in this debate here. For discussion, see Kraut 2002: 111–18.

This more robust system of norms surpasses narrowly focused negative prohibitions on injustice in exchange in at least two ways. First, it involves a more expansive set of mutual expectations governing the interaction among members of the community. In place of limited prohibitions on violence and deception in the community of "exchange and alliance," the city's more developed standards of law and justice come to include prohibitions on certain types of behavior not directly connected to exchange relations. So, for instance, laws against homicide, assault, theft, adultery, or the disgraceful treatment of others (ὕβρις) – to name a few offenses familiar from Athenian law that also appear in the *Politics* – proscribe actions that fall at least partly outside the scope of merely commercial exchanges. The laws of a city do not prohibit these actions only in the context of the market. Rather, the prohibitions extend to relations among members of the community in any context. Among people whose formal interactions do not extend beyond the community of "exchange and alliance," cases of these sorts of offense occurring outside the realm of exchange would be dealt with privately, if at all, by the victim or the victim's family. The emergence of the city's legal institutions is, in part, a transition from a social framework in which offenses of this kind are understood as private matters, and dealt with accordingly, to one in which these actions are understood as having a negative impact on the common good of the community. Prohibiting these offenses comes to be seen as conducive to the shared interests of the community's members. Once the public prohibition of these offenses becomes understood in this way, it also becomes possible to envision laws that are not merely proscriptive. Instead of simply forbidding certain kinds of behavior, the laws may require other sorts of actions that positively contribute to the community's good. Thus a system of laws might, for instance, institute communal meals and require that participants each contribute a determinate amount of food to the common stock. By aiming to promote the practices and arrangements that "produce and protect happiness and its parts" for the members of the community, the laws of a city become more expansive in scope and less narrowly focused than the prepolitical exchange community's prohibitions on injustice.

Second, the laws of a city also surpass the rules of the free-floating market in the extent and intensity of their institutionalization. Beyond a minimum threshold of complexity, the formulation and application of laws require some institutional framework.[35] General agreements to avoid

---

[35] I take this assumption to be implicit in Aristotle's argument. It is, however, not an especially controversial claim. By contrast, consider what Miller 1995: 17–18, 366–73 calls the "principle of

the use of force and deception and to aid one another in defense against them might emerge and persist through relatively informal and unstructured processes.³⁶ A greater number of more detailed requirements, however, demands a more formal and structured set of procedures, and these in turn must be embodied in some kind of institutional arrangement that can gain a level of authority sufficient to establish and maintain those rules. The laws need not only to be formulated and generally accepted, but also applied. For the laws to function as laws, the community needs some means of resolving disputes that arise from the real or perceived violation of those laws. So too the community will need to be able to correct injustices, where possible, by directing offenders to compensate their victims for damages or by otherwise punishing or imposing sanctions on those who violate the laws. None of this is possible without some sort of institutional framework.

Aristotle makes clear that he has just such a framework in mind when he describes the "most necessary" feature of a self-sufficient political community as discrimination (κρίσις) about what is just (*Pol.* 7.8.1328b13–15). The role of jurors (δικασταί) and legal judgment (δίκη) is so central to Aristotle's understanding of the city that he classifies "the part that administers justice" (τὸ δικάζον, τὸ δικαστικόν) as one of the three essential components of every political community (4.14.1298a3, 4.16.1300b13–1301a15). The institutional embodiment of legal judgment is necessary because even the most well-crafted laws cannot prescribe the correct and most just response to every possible particular circumstance (*EN* 5.10.1137b26–32, *Pol.* 3.11.1282b1–6). Even excellent laws that

rulership," which maintains that a community can only attain order if some individual or group exercises political rule consciously directed at securing that order. Miller cites modern theorists of "spontaneous order" from Adam Smith to F. A. Hayek and beyond to cast doubt on this assumption. Whether or not Aristotle believed in anything like spontaneously generated order, such theories do not put the assumption that I have identified in question; for the crucial assumption is not that institutions can only be generated by consciously planned, intentional acts, but that no complex system of norms can be formulated and applied in the absence of some kind of institution. An institution may come into being as an incidental result of cooperative interaction and yet still be an institution. If Aristotle accepts the principle of rulership without good reasons, this should count against his political theory. By contrast, if the assumption that complex systems of laws require institutional frameworks – socially recognized rule-governed procedures aimed at formulating and applying norms – turns out to be false, this would be a startlingly counterintuitive discovery. It is, however, not trivially true; it is easy enough to dream up some mythical creatures whose mysterious mental powers enable them to maintain a flexible and changing system of laws without ever coming together to decide how to do so.

³⁶ Like most classical Greek political theorists, Aristotle tends to see laws as the products of a lawgiver or an assembly's conscious intention. At least once, however, he explicitly acknowledges that the development or effects of some laws are not part of the lawgiver's intention: *Pol.* 2.12.1274a11–12.

admit of no exceptions, however, still need to be applied. If nothing else, the community needs judges who are not directly involved in disputes to determine whether the laws have been violated. Legal judgment can be institutionally embodied in a variety of ways; no single institutional arrangement is necessary for the existence of a city. Yet without some such arrangement for the judgment of disputes and the application of the laws, there can be no political community.

If political community requires the existence of full-blown institutions of law and justice, it is no less true that the full-blown institutions of law and justice presuppose the existence of a political community. The expansiveness, complexity, and institutionalization of law as I have described them are intelligible only in the context of a group of people who interact for the sake of common interests that extend well beyond the mutual utility of commodity exchange. This connection between law and political community is not a matter of mere stipulation. It is, rather, an empirically grounded claim: When we look at the clearest cases of what we call cities and what we call laws, we find that we cannot understand either without the other. Political communities are not the only communities that do or can have laws. But the most fully developed and complex systems of laws are the ones that we find in cities. These laws, taken together, are best understood as a set of norms directed at promoting and protecting the happiness or well-being of the political community. That is to say, it is only when we grasp that promoting and protecting the flourishing of its members are the goals of the political community that the laws we find in cities become fully intelligible. Appreciating this point, in turn, supports the contention that political communities aim at the good life rather than at some more limited and subordinate good. It also helps to explain why cities need laws; without some generally recognized and authoritative set of norms to govern the interaction among members of the community in ways that are conducive to their shared good, none of those members will be able to live well.

Aristotle underscores this connection between legal institutions and common aims when he describes the judgment that is necessary for a self-sufficient community as judgment "about what is advantageous and just in people's relations to one another" (7.8.1328b13–15). Judgments about justice go along with judgments about what is advantageous. This is not simply a claim that judgments of justice presuppose some judgments about shared advantage. Aristotle affirms the priority of the good to claims about justice; not only does he say as much in the characterization of law that I have already quoted (*EN* 5.1.1129b14–19), but he reiterates the point when he says that human beings, by virtue of their capacity for articulate rational speech, can "indicate the beneficial and the harmful, *and consequently* the just and the unjust" (*Pol.* 1.2.1253a14–15) and later identifies justice with the common good (3.12.1282b16–17). His reference to judgment of the advantageous, however, points more concretely to institutionalized practices of common deliberation. Just as judgment about what is just is embodied in "the part that administers justice," judgment about what is beneficial is embodied in "the part that deliberates" (τὸ βουλευόμενον, 4.14.1297b41–1298a9). Both of these functions are necessary for a self-sufficient community. For one thing, the deliberative element is responsible for making and changing laws (4.14.1298a5). Even less dispensable, however, is its role in decisions about what the community as a whole should do, whether it is a question of going to war, electing officials, or any other matter of common concern (4.14.1298a3–7). Even more obviously than law, common deliberation presupposes common aims, and a city cannot pursue its common aims unless it has some institutional means of collective deliberation. The deliberative and judicial functions are distinct and may be embodied in a variety of institutional arrangements. But no city could exist without some means of fulfilling both functions.

Aristotle's account of the origin of the city out of scattered villages and his list of the features that are necessary for a self-sufficient community jointly suggest that political community emerges with the development of these institutions of law, justice, and common deliberation.[37] These institutions mark a decisive change in the relations among members of disparate villages because they unify those villages and their inhabitants around a new common aim. The most profound difference between the city and the typical modes of interaction among prepolitical villages, however, lies in the nature of that aim. Where the villagers first came together to exchange useful goods, they now come to cooperate for the sake of living well. The most immediately apparent consequence of this distinctive aim is, as we have seen, the more extensive and intensive coordination of mutual interaction made possible by shared norms and common deliberation. The more significant consequence, however, is the self-sufficiency that these institutions create. With the emergence of these institutions, it becomes possible for the first time for people to turn their attention toward living well. Once these institutions are in place, the community achieves self-sufficiency in the sense that it requires nothing more in order

---

[37] Brown 2013 reaches a similar conclusion by a different route.

to make it possible to organize life around those forms of activity that people value for their own sake. In the absence of these institutions, people must devote most or all of their energies to obtaining and preserving the means for a stable, secure, and moderately comfortable existence. Once cooperation has risen to a level at which these means can be more or less reliably and easily achieved, people naturally begin to look beyond them toward intrinsically worthwhile goals.

5. Varieties of Self-Sufficiency

Aristotle says that the first city to exist is the community composed of an adequate number of people to be self-sufficient for living well (*Pol.* 7.4.1326b7–9). Consistently with the formulation of his argument for the naturalness of the city, this claim suggests that self-sufficiency is a necessary condition for political community; if a community is not self-sufficient, it is not a city. Yet this implication might seem counterintuitive. In particular, it might seem to follow that only a community that creates the conditions in which all of its members can achieve the good life as Aristotle understands it will count as a city at all. This is, in fact, how Aristotle describes the best constitution: "It is fitting for those who govern themselves best to do the best things from what is available to them, unless something happens contrary to reasonable expectation" (7.1.1323a17–19); "the best constitution is necessarily that arrangement in accordance with which anyone could do the best things and live blessedly" (7.2.1324a23–5). Yet Aristotle is clearly not committed to the view that only a community with the best constitutional arrangement is really a city. Though he is sometimes willing to say that especially deviant constitutions do not count as cities, he does not deny that correct but imperfect constitutions remain constitutions, and one motivation for his distinction between correct and mistaken constitutions is to avoid the conclusion, which Plato was willing to make in the *Laws*, that a corrupt constitution is not a constitution.[38]

---

[38] For this point, see Fortenbaugh 1991, although Fortenbaugh assimilates Aristotle's concerns too closely to those of so-called ordinary language philosophers. Though Aristotle's standard dialectical strategies lead him to avoid radically rejecting ordinary language, he evidently does not treat it as much of a constraint. His claim that a severed hand is no longer a hand, for instance, seems no less counterintuitive at first glance than Plato's denial that an unjust constitution is really a constitution. In fact, the two claims appear to rest on the same consideration: If being an X essentially involves performing a function F, then anything that cannot perform that function is not an X. Aristotle's disagreement with Plato on this point more likely reflects his insistence on distinguishing between a bad X and a non-X than a refusal to revise ordinary habits of speech. Nonetheless, Aristotle is willing to deny that some tyrannies are cities or constitutions at all.

One strategy for avoiding this problem would be to understand self-sufficiency as admitting of degrees. After all, Aristotle is happy to use the comparative when he says that the city is more self-sufficient than the household, and the household than the individual (2.2.1261b11–12). Robert Mayhew has defended a view of this kind.[39] Mayhew distinguishes between "simple self-sufficiency," which he takes to be self-sufficiency with a view to living, and "self-sufficiency with a view to living well." Simple self-sufficiency, on Mayhew's reading, is a matter of attaining a supply of necessities adequate for survival, comfort, and enough leisure to pursue the good life. Self-sufficiency with a view to living well, however, depends on the community's appropriate use of this leisure; a city structured by a mistaken conception of human flourishing will not be self-sufficient in this sense. Mayhew's view faces several difficulties, however, and appreciating them will help to formulate an alternative understanding of Aristotle's distinction among different kinds of self-sufficiency. This understanding, in turn, will further illuminate the distinctive character of Aristotelian political community.

The most serious problem with Mayhew's view is that it leads to the same unacceptable conclusion that motivated an interpretation of self-sufficiency in terms of degrees.[40] If a city can be self-sufficient for living well only when its constitutional arrangements reflect the single correct conception of the human good, then a genuine city will exist only in the best constitution; all other constitutional forms will be self-sufficient merely for living. This runs against the grain of Aristotle's characterization of self-sufficiency with a view to living well as a defining mark of the city. This characterization is explicit in the passage from book 7 cited previously (7.4.1326b7–9), but is implicit already in the invocation of self-sufficiency in the argument for the naturalness of the city (1.2.1252b27–30). These passages do not appeal to a more limited sense of self-sufficiency. Furthermore, to suppose that the self-sufficiency necessary for the existence of a city is a self-sufficiency only with a view to living would have an awkward implication: Those forms of community that Aristotle treats as prepolitical would then need to be understood as falling short of self-sufficiency for living. Yet it is clear that Aristotle supposes that prepolitical villages can exist and survive without becoming unified in a political community, and the various "nations" (ἔθνη) seem perfectly self-sufficient for living without achieving

---

[39] Mayhew 1995.
[40] Mayhew does not offer his interpretation as a resolution of this problem, but any general account of self-sufficiency in the *Politics* ought to be able to address it.

distinctively political forms of community. Though it is not implausible that cities might be more self-sufficient for living than nonpolitical communities, a mere difference of degree in this respect is insufficient to account for the difference of kind that Aristotle sees between political communities and their nonpolitical counterparts.

An important passage for Mayhew's view comes from Aristotle's discussion in book 7 of the functions necessary for a self-sufficient community, which I have already cited several times. After listing those functions, Aristotle continues:

> These are the functions that just about every city needs; for the city is not any chance multitude, but one that is self-sufficient for life, as we say, and if any of these things happens to be left out, it is impossible for this community to be simply self-sufficient. It is therefore necessary for a city to be established in accordance with these works. (7.8.1328b15–20)

On the strength of this passage, Mayhew identifies "simple self-sufficiency" with self-sufficiency for living and treats this kind of self-sufficiency as a necessary condition for the city. When we recall the items in Aristotle's list of functions, however, this reading becomes problematic. For among those functions is the judgment about justice and common advantage that has been central to my argument so far. This judgment, though most necessary for the existence of a city because its emergence transforms prepolitical villages into a political community, is by no means necessary for survival, even relatively comfortable survival. Aristotle cannot, then, be presenting these functions as necessary for self-sufficiency with a view to mere living.

Moreover, when Aristotle elsewhere describes a community that is self-sufficient for life alone, he insists that such a community is not a city: "A city composed of too few people is not self-sufficient (but the city is a self-sufficient thing), and the one composed of too many people will be self-sufficient in necessities, like the nation, but not a city" (7.4.1326b2–5). Despite the seemingly paradoxical talk of a city that is not a city, this passage asserts that a community that is self-sufficient only in necessities falls short of being a city.[41] If there was any doubt that a community too small

---

41 The formulation is not in fact paradoxical or problematic, except perhaps on the surface. One way of putting the point would be to say that, for Aristotle, in the phrase "non-self-sufficient city," the adjective "non-self-sufficient" functions logically as an *alienans*, indicating that the noun in question is not a genuine instance of its kind; compare "glass diamond," "plastic flowers," "counterfeit money." In each case, the item in question bears some sort of suitable resemblance to a genuine instance of the kind picked out by the noun, but is not in fact a genuine instance of that kind (plastic flowers are not flowers; glass diamonds are not diamonds; counterfeit money is not

to be a city could be self-sufficient for life alone, there should be no such doubts about the community that is too large; its ability to maintain its tremendous population shows that it has more than enough resources to keep people alive and suitably supplied with necessities. More noteworthy, however, is that this passage describes the city as self-sufficient without adding any qualifications. The qualification is reserved for the community that is self-sufficient only in some limited respect. This suggests that when Aristotle elsewhere appeals to self-sufficiency without adding any qualifications, he has in mind self-sufficiency with a view to living well. This suggestion can be strengthened by two further considerations: First, this is just how Aristotle does talk in at least some other contexts in which he evidently intends to link self-sufficiency with living well (1.2.1252b27–30); second, in other contexts he frequently uses the term that Mayhew translates as "simply" (ἁπλῶς) to mean "without qualification."

If self-sufficiency without qualification is the condition in which the members of a community require nothing further in order to live well, then the passage quoted from 7.8 can be read in the most straightforward way as asserting that institutions of justice and common deliberation are necessary if the members of a community are to be able to live well. Thus the problematic implication of Mayhew's reading disappears; Aristotle is not here making the bizarre claim that these institutions are necessary if people are to live at all. Yet Mayhew was led to this interpretation by the phrase "self-sufficient for life." If unqualified self-sufficiency is self-sufficiency with a view to living well, then why does Aristotle apparently identify it here with self-sufficiency for life? The answer is surely that living and living well are more closely connected than mere survival and integral human flourishing. To flourish is not to survive more fully and completely; to live well, by contrast, is indeed to live more fully and completely. A life that is self-sufficient without qualification just is self-sufficient for living well. Accordingly, when Aristotle describes the city as self-sufficient for life, he need not mean that it is self-sufficient for life alone, but that it provides everything that is necessary in order for its members to live well. Mayhew is mistaken, then, to distinguish self-sufficiency with a view to living well from self-sufficiency with a view to living and to assimilate unqualified self-sufficiency with the latter. Rather, while communities may be self-sufficient in various limited

money). In these examples, the resemblance is a matter of appearance; in the case of a city, it might be that the community *would* be a city if only it could achieve the requisite self-sufficiency. On *alienans* adjectives, see Geach 1956, Murphy 2006: 13–14.

respects, the community that is self-sufficient without qualification is the one that is self-sufficient for living well, and this is the distinctively political community.

Nonetheless, Aristotle does contrast communities and actions that aim at merely living with those that aim at living well. We are now in a position to see, however, that this is not primarily a distinction between activities directed at mere survival and those directed at flourishing.

6.　Living and Living Well

In *Pol.* 1.9, Aristotle distinguishes between two different kinds or uses of "business" or "moneymaking" (χρηματιστική).[42] One kind, which aims at the acquisition of property and commodities that are necessary or useful for living well, is natural because it arose as a way for people to fulfill their natural needs. The other kind, which aims instead at increasingly greater profit, is not natural. It neither develops as a part of human beings' pursuit of the instrumental means to living well nor in fact conduces to the fulfillment of those needs. It is, instead, the limitless pursuit of a pure means, one that does not even have the value characteristic of instruments.[43] Yet people tend not only to go in for this unnatural sort of business, but also to think that the limitless pursuit of profit is the only kind of moneymaking there is. To explain this practice and its corresponding

---

[42] Neither "business" nor "moneymaking" is an entirely satisfactory translation. We are told in 1.8 that χρηματιστική is concerned with acquiring commodities and property, whereas household management (οἰκονομική) uses them (1.8.1256a10–12). Saunders 1995 opts for "the art of acquiring goods." One might object to this, as Simpson 1998: 27–8 note 27 does, on the grounds that it loses the connection with χρήματα, which *EN* 4.1.1119b26–7 defines as "all things whose worth is measured by money." I am not so sure as Simpson seems to be, however, that ordinary uses of the English term "business" describe "precisely this general art of activity concerned with commodities and with making money through the producing or acquiring or exchanging of commodities (or even of money itself)." Yet the misleading connotations of "business" seem less worrisome than the excessive generality of "the art of acquisition." Jowett 1885's "art of getting wealth" fares better on this score, but is too cumbersome for my purposes. Simpson's choice of "business" follows Lord [1984] 2013.

[43] The value of an instrument is primarily its *use* value; though instruments may also have exchange value, their exchange value typically depends on their use value. Money, by contrast, has no use value. There is no specific kind of practical or productive activity in which we use money to achieve the end of that activity. Its only use is for exchange, and exchange is not a specific kind of practical or productive activity. Money per se is useless; by contrast, a good hammer, though of merely instrumental value, is useful by virtue of what it is. This analysis does not, of course, make Aristotle oblivious to the acquisitive power that money provides and that hammers do not. His point is, rather, that money is, as it were, two steps removed from the intrinsically valuable activities that constitute human flourishing. Structuring one's life around the pursuit of money is therefore outstandingly foolish. For these points, see *Pol.* 1.9.1257a5–b16 and Meikle 1995. As Simpson 1998: 51 shows, however, Meikle is mistaken to conclude that exchange per se is unnatural.

attitude, Aristotle appeals to a distinction between concern for living and concern for living well:

> The explanation of this disposition is that they are serious about living, but not about living well. So, since that desire is limitless, they also desire things that are productive of it without limit. Even the ones who direct themselves toward living well seek what leads to bodily pleasures. Consequently, since this too appears to depend on property, they spend all their time concerned with moneymaking, and the other kind of business has come about because of this. For, since their pleasure is in excess, they seek what produces pleasant excess. If they are not able to procure it through moneymaking, they attempt to procure it through some other cause, using each of their capacities in a way that does not accord with nature. For the work of courage is not to produce money, but boldness. Nor is producing money the task of generalship or medicine; rather, the task of the one is victory, and of the other, health. But these people make all of these into forms of moneymaking, on the grounds that this is the goal and that everything ought to conduce to the goal. (*Pol.* 1.9.1257b40–58a14)

There are two distinct attitudes that lead people to take up the unnatural sort of business, with its disordered focus on accumulating profit rather than acquiring property sufficient for fulfilling natural needs. Those whose conception of the good life gives pride of place to bodily pleasures recognize that money and wealth are conducive to these. Since their desires are excessive, they end up excessively devoted to accumulating more and more wealth. Yet these somatic hedonists, as we might call them, do at least engage in business for the sake of living well. To that extent, they resemble practitioners of the natural sort of business. Because they act with a view to some conception of the good life, they retain some sense of what their wealth is *for*; but because their desire is for an effectively limitless pleasure, their pursuit of wealth becomes practically limitless. The purer case of unnatural business, however, is not undertaken with a view to living well at all, but only with a view to living. Aristotle clearly intends to distinguish the two cases.[44] What is the difference?

---

[44] That Aristotle means to distinguish two attitudes here should be clear from 1258a2–3: ὅσοι δὲ καὶ τοῦ εὖ ζῆν ἐπιβάλλονται, which might be translated "and all those who *also* direct themselves toward living well." Given this distinction, we cannot suppose that failure to "be serious" (σπουδάζειν) about living well is a simple matter of having an incorrect conception of the good. If it were, then those who *are* "serious" about living well would have a correct conception of the good, and yet Aristotle proceeds to describe even people who are "serious" as engaging in the unnatural sort of business. Simpson 1998: 56 conflates the two attitudes. Saunders 1995: 92–4 observes the difference, but takes the first group to "mistake the means, a subsidiary end, for the real end" and construes being "serious about living" as having "an infinite desire for (mere) life, i.e. either to busy themselves with the ordinary business of living, or to live as long as possible." The first alternative is

Both groups pursue an apparently limitless profit. We should not suppose, then, that those who do so for the sake of mere living are engaged in business just to survive. Someone who seeks to obtain only as much as or a little more than he needs to keep himself alive is not aiming at limitless wealth. Rather, when a person pursues wealth only for the sake of survival, his pursuit in fact has a limit. A limit is supplied by the goal to be achieved. If a person seeks wealth solely for survival, he will seek only as much as he needs to stay alive. Put the other way around, the goal of survival is insufficient on its own to render the pursuit of excess wealth intelligible.

Moreover, pursuing the means to keep oneself alive would hardly be unnatural on Aristotle's terms. If the natural sort of business is natural because it is aimed at fulfilling natural needs, then engaging in business for the sake of survival would be as natural as any pursuit could be.[45] Achieving reliable means of survival is so basic, in fact, that it is hard to suppose that the unnatural kind of business or moneymaking as Aristotle understands it would be possible for anyone who had not already secured it. Money, Aristotle thinks, emerges only in fairly developed communities. Some barbarian nations (ἔθνη) exchange goods for goods without the use of money, a kind of exchange that is not a kind of business at all (1.9.1257a19–30).

The people who practice the unnatural sort of business solely with a view to living nonetheless accumulate a great deal of wealth, and so do not aim strictly at survival. Their counterparts, the somatic hedonists, engage in the same sort of business, but do so for the sake of living well. It is noteworthy that Aristotle does not describe the somatic hedonists as acting on the basis of limitless desire. Their desire is excessive, but it does indeed have a kind of limit supplied by their conception of the good. That conception supplies them only with a formal sort of limit, however, because the desire for bodily pleasures is effectively limitless when it is not constrained and limited by any broader or higher-level ends. By contrast, those who are serious only about living have a genuinely limitless desire. They do not pursue wealth for the sake of any specific goods for which

obscure (what exactly is "the ordinary business of living," and how could someone have an infinite desire for it?); the second, as I argue later, cannot be what Aristotle has in mind.

[45] Aristotle, of course, denies that survival is unconditionally choiceworthy: The great-souled, for instance, are willing to die in the right circumstances "on the grounds that it is not worthwhile to live at all costs" (EN 4.3.1124b23–4); more generally, "it is perhaps impossible to be compelled to do some things; one should rather die after suffering the most terrible consequences" (EN 3.1.1110a26–7; my translations here are indebted to Irwin 1999). Survival is, however, obviously among the necessary conditions of living well; even those who choose or accept a noble death have to be alive long enough to choose it.

that wealth might be useful. They focus their energies almost exclusively on acquiring more and more instrumentally valuable means without giving thought to what they would use those means *for*.

This obsession with means might seem to make their action radically unintelligible. If they do not somehow fall into the illusion that money and wealth are valuable for their own sake, then they must appreciate that the value of wealth lies in what it can get them. If they do not, in turn, have any sort of interest in any further ends, then their pursuit of wealth is not so much foolish as practically unintelligible (*EN* 1.1–2.1094a1–22, 1.7.1097a15–b6).[46] But we need not suppose that these people fail to appreciate that wealth is a means or have no interest in any further ends at all. When Aristotle says that they are not serious about living well, he need not imply that they are motivated solely by purely instrumental goods. What they lack, rather, is even the minimally coherent, reflective, and stable conception of the good that guides the somatic hedonists. If asked, they could probably run down a list of goods whose value explains the value of wealth: food, clothing, shelter; better tasting food, more refined clothing, more secure shelter; the ability to procure more food, clothing, and shelter in the case of emergencies; even entertaining friends, funding festivals, educating sons, or providing a dowry for daughters. The people who are serious only about living do not fail to see that money is a means to further ends. They simply do not focus their attention on those ends; instead, they preoccupy themselves with attaining more and more of the means. Their desire for the means becomes limitless because it is not guided and controlled by any stable, coherent conception of the ends.

It should be clear why Aristotle would deny that people with this kind of practical orientation are serious about living well. It should also be apparent why he would be reluctant to describe them as valuing money as an end in itself. For, strictly speaking, valuing money as an end in itself would not be practically intelligible.[47] Why, though, should he say that

---

[46] The opening chapters of *EN* 1, and the more elaborated argument of 1.7, seek to establish two important theses: first, that productive and practical activities must aim at some end that is valued for its own sake if their pursuit is to be intelligible; second, that there is a single supreme end for the sake of which all other ends are valued. It is only the first claim to which I am appealing here. The second claim is, understandably, much more controversial, as is the interpretation of Aristotle's argument in its favor. For helpful treatments of the argument, see Broadie 1991: 24–54; White 1992: 5–21; and Richardson Lear 2004: 8–71. For an impressive contemporary defense of one interpretation of it, see Lebar 2013: 9–61.

[47] Valuing money for its own sake could, of course, be perfectly intelligible if what one valued about it were, say, its aesthetic properties. But to value money in this way would not be to value it *as money*, but as an object of aesthetic contemplation.

they are serious about living? We can see why when we recall that acting for the sake of living is not reserved to those who suffer from the peculiar sort of practical irrationality that we have been considering. This is, in fact, how Aristotle describes the community of exchange and alliance that he imagines in *Politics* 3.9: such a community would not be a city because it would not be formed for the sake of living well, but only for the sake of living (*Pol.* 3.9.1280a25–32, cf. 1281a29–35).

We act for the sake of living when we come together to exchange goods in order to acquire possessions that are necessary or useful. We also act for the sake of living when we produce these goods for ourselves. We are not, in these cases, acting for the sake of survival alone, because we frequently seek more of these goods, or goods of a higher quality, than we would need to survive. We also seek greater security, efficiency, and comfort through exchange and craft production. Yet when we pursue these things alone we are not yet acting for the sake of living well.[48] For that, we must deliberately choose to pursue some more or less coherent set of activities that we value for their own sake and not solely or primarily for their products.

It is this deliberately chosen pursuit of intrinsically valuable ends that political community makes possible. The city, and no other form of community, is self-sufficient for living well because once distinctively political institutions of justice, law, and common deliberation are in place, the community requires nothing more to make this pursuit possible. Some cities, of course, are better than others. Cities can be inefficient, unjust, or structured around distorted conceptions of the good. Yet even imperfect and unjust cities are cities because they are complex communities whose members cooperate with a view to living well and who are able to provide everything that is needed in order to do so. The best constitution will be better able to make its citizens capable of living well than any other constitution, since it will, *ex hypothesi*, be endowed with an ample supply of external goods and will devote its attention to educating its citizens for a collective way of life that is as happy as possible (7.1.1323a14–19). Thus it might, in one sense, be more self-sufficient than cities that lack these

---

[48] Ober 1998: 303 sees that even those who seek and achieve wealth at luxury levels can count as "merely living." He overestimates the richness of this sort of living, however, when he compares it to what Charles Taylor describes as "ordinary life" in contrast to noble, heroic, philosophic, or religious ways of life devoted to a purportedly higher good and necessarily reserved for a select few (see Taylor 1989). Those who embrace the "affirmation of ordinary life" that Taylor sees as a central feature of modern thought in the West would, in fact, join Aristotle in disdaining the limitless pursuit of profit; it would disagree with Aristotle's distinction between living and living well primarily in rejecting his view of productive labor as an impediment to the latter.

features. But every city will be self-sufficient with a view to living well in the minimal sense that it will be capable of enabling some, most, or all of its members to aim at living well and not merely at living.

Aristotle says, somewhat mysteriously, that the city "comes to be for the sake of living, but exists for the sake of living well" (1.2.1252b29–30). Understanding the distinction between living and living well can dispel some of this mystery. The city emerges from a plurality of villages that first come together for the sake of exchange, its various members aiming at a more productive, efficient, and reliable means of acquiring those instrumental goods that are necessary or useful for their preservation, security, and comfort. Success in this endeavor, however, leads to a more extensive interaction among people even when they do not need anything from each other. Indeed, as political animals, human beings "desire to live together [συζῆν] no less even when they have no need of assistance from one another" (3.6.1279a20–1). As their economic success gradually frees them from the necessity of devoting themselves to acting for the sake of life alone, people will begin to associate more frequently without any further purpose of exchange or utility. In the context of this intensified social life, a distinctively political community can develop as people come to recognize the possibilities of unified cooperation for the sake of their shared interest in living well.

Aristotle says nothing about just how this transition takes place. He may have thought that there was little more to say at the level of theory about exactly how cities were formed. The Lyceum's research into existing cities and their constitutions might have convinced him that their developments were too varied to admit of any more detailed general description. But the broad contours of his account suggest that cities might develop in at least two ways. They might stem, first, from a general recognition of a need for some authoritative set of legal norms and procedures to manage the inevitable conflicts of living together. Alternatively, cities might be formed for more positively formulated aims. Neither alternative excludes the other. Even the first, however, is not incompatible with Aristotle's insistence that political community exists for the sake of living well. As we have seen, Aristotle sees the legal institutions characteristic of cities as directed toward the promotion and protection of the city's common good. Whatever the initial intentions of the people who first form these institutions and recognize their authority, once those institutions are in place, the members of the community who observe, endorse, and enforce the laws and the corresponding institutions are ipso facto cooperating for the sake of living well. Aristotle does not say enough about the process to justify any confidence that he had just this sort of development in mind. It would, however, further demystify his description of the city as coming to be for the sake of living but existing for the sake of living well. For the formation of the political community, on this view, need not be a self-conscious and deliberate project of constitutional design undertaken in the light of some explicit and substantive view of the human good. It might, instead, be the product of an effort to devise solutions to conflicts and problems that beset the prepolitical social life of economically interdependent but disunified villages.[49]

This chapter has considered Aristotle's account of the development of the city from the household and the village in the hope of illuminating the distinctive character of political community by understanding its peculiar aim of living well. Important questions remain about the relationship between this goal and the forms of activity most characteristic of politics. Yet the city is not only a distinctive kind of community, but is also characterized by a distinctively political form of rule or authority and distinctively political standards of justice. The next chapter, before turning to questions about the value of political activity, will consider how the goal of living well and the relevant features of the people who participate in political communities explain the forms of rule and norms of justice that are natural and appropriate to politics as Aristotle understands it.

---

[49] Leunissen (forthcoming) elaborates a rather different reading of the claim that the city "comes to be for the sake of living, but exists for the sake of living well." Drawing on Aristotle's biological treatises, she argues for a two-level teleological explanation of the city: On one level, human beings more or less instinctively come together in cities in order to survive; the formation of specific constitutional arrangements, however, is deliberately undertaken for the sake of living well. This two-level explanation coheres with her broader interpretation of Aristotle's natural science in terms of a distinction between "primary" and "secondary" teleology, for which see Leunissen 2010. But her application of this two-level account to the *Politics* is hard to square with the distinctiveness of the city. Insofar as her reading supposes that human beings need to live in cities to survive, it cannot explain the existence of large populations of human beings who do not live in cities. Yet if humans need the city not to survive, but to flourish, it becomes hard to see how the two levels of teleological explanation are distinct in this case.

CHAPTER 4

Rule and Justice in the Household and the City

Aristotle aims to distinguish different kinds of community along with the different standards of justice and modes of interaction characteristic of each those kinds. Yet he begins, as we have seen, by focusing on different forms of *rule*: The *Politics* commences with a declaration of his predecessors' failure to distinguish forms of rule, and he returns to this point later in book 1 as well as in books 3 and 7 to underscore the importance of appreciating the heterogeneity of rule for a proper understanding of politics (*Pol.* 1.7.1255b16–20, 3.4.1277b7, 7.2.1324b32–40, 7.3.1325a25–30, 7.14.1333a3). The different forms of rule that Aristotle identifies are, moreover, crucial aspects of each of the different forms of community that we have seen so far. Part of what it is to be a political community is to be a community in which political rule is exercised; similarly, the community of parent and child is a community characterized by distinctively paternal or parental rule.

Yet the association of different forms of rule with corresponding forms of community is not merely a descriptive thesis. On the contrary, one of the ways in which communities of various kinds become corrupt and unjust is through the application of modes of authority that are properly restricted to other kinds of community. The identification of specific forms of rule as "political," "paternal," "despotic," and so on, is therefore inelim inably normative. This normativity is not, however, merely an application of external standards that constrain the legitimate pursuit of various goals. Rather, as I argued in Chapter 2, standards of justice are *internal* to various kinds of community: The form of rule that is just in each kind of community is the form of rule that people with certain sets of capacities pursuing a certain kind of goal must exercise if each of the participants in that community is to achieve a fair and equal benefit from participating. Since Aristotle believes that rational agents ordinarily seek what they consider to be at least a fair and equal benefit in their cooperative endeavors with others, his association of specific forms of rule with specific kinds of community also has descriptive and explanatory aspects and is not merely prescriptive.[1] Thus these forms of rule are not only just or appropriate because they are best. They are also characteristic of their corresponding forms of community in the following sense: Interaction among people with certain kinds and degrees of relative capacity cooperating with a view to certain sorts of goals tends to be mediated by specific forms of rule, and even the departures from that norm are to be explained, in part, by reference to the norm.

Though these descriptive and explanatory features of Aristotle's theory of rule and community are important, my emphasis will be on the normative dimensions of his account.[2] While he makes the connection between forms of rule and the relative capacities of the participants abundantly clear, he is less explicit about how and why these forms of rule are just and beneficial. Since one major challenge that the conceptual and normative problems of monarchy pose is the apparent incompatibility of political and monarchic forms of rule, it will be especially important to get a clear view of what it is that makes political rule and specifically political standards of justice distinctive from others.

1.   Ruling

First, however, it is worth asking what Aristotle has in mind when he talks about "rule" and whether there are any common features shared by all of the forms of rule he describes. The word for rule, ἀρχή, does a great deal of work in Aristotle's thought, and even its specifically political uses are ambiguous. The most evident ambiguity is between a narrower use in which the noun refers to specific political offices or magistracies and a broader and more abstract use in which it describes any position or

---

[1] The idea is not that everyone always aims at fairness, but that the norm is internal to cooperative interaction and shapes the background against which we need to understand behavior that violates the norm. Agents with various vices tend to seek an unfair proportion of benefit for themselves, and the "greedy" or "grasping" person (πλεονέκτης) appears to seek to gain at others' expense as such: *EN* 5.1.1129a21–b11, 5.2.1130a14–b5, 1130b30–31a9. Nonetheless, the treatment of distributive justice in *Pol.* 3.9.1280a7–25 suggests that many people act on mistaken conceptions of justice but believe that their actions are just, even if their beliefs are shaped by self-serving desires that bias their judgment in their own favor (1280a13–22). Furthermore, even agents who self-consciously aim at injustice typically need to pretend to be just and operate with a view of what would constitute a fair or equal benefit. Thus even such acts are to be explained by reference to the norm of seeking fairness in co-operative interaction with others.

[2] Salkever 1990, Yack 1993, Murphy 2002, and Rosler 2005 helpfully stress the interplay between the explanatory and normative aspects and uses of Aristotle's conceptual framework in ethics and politics.

exercise of authority. Though it can sometimes be unclear which sense of the word is operative in a given passage, the relationship between the two uses is clear enough, and Aristotle even argues for it in the process of arriving at a definition of citizenship. Following his initial suggestion that "a citizen is defined by nothing else more than by sharing in judgment and ἀρχή" (*Pol.* 3.1.1275a22–3), he immediately addresses the ambiguity and defends his use of the term ἀρχή to cover both particular offices held by different individuals at different times and the "indefinite" office exercised by members of juries and assemblies:

> Of offices [τῶν ἀρχῶν], some are divided by time, so that it is, in general, impossible for the same person to hold some offices twice, or it is possible only after some defined period of time. But there is also the indefinite kind, such as the juryman or the assemblyman. Now perhaps someone would say that these sorts of people are not even rulers [ἄρχοντας] and consequently do not share in rule [ἀρχῆς]. Yet it would be ridiculous to deprive the people with the most control [τοὺς κυριωτάτους] of rule. But it should make no difference, since the argument is about a name. What is common to a juryman and an assemblyman has no name, and so it is necessary to describe both of them like this. So, for the sake of a definition, let it be "indefinite office" [ἀόριστος ἀρχή]. We posit, then, that people who share in this way are citizens. (3.1.1275a23–33)

As a first stab at a definition of citizenship, Aristotle observes that citizens are distinguished from noncitizens above all by having a share in judgment and ἀρχή. The sense of ἀρχή here is neutral between "rule" and "office," but it takes the ensuing argument to make this clear. The initial distinction between offices that are limited by time and those, such as jury service and participation in the assembly, that are not so limited makes Aristotle's meaning plain: A citizen is someone who exercises rule, but one can exercise rule only by holding some particular form of office or other. Some people, however, would balk at the idea of describing membership in the assembly or the law court as an "office," perhaps relying on ordinary Greek or Athenian usage of the term.[3] Yet it is precisely the assembly and the courts that exercise the most control in some cities, and especially in

---

[3] Newman 1887–1902.iii: 136 observes that membership in the assembly and the law court would not normally have been described as an ἀρχή. He cites Plato *Laws* 767a, where Plato makes an argument similar to Aristotle's in favor of treating jury service as an office, suggesting that he anticipated some resistance on this point. Newman also cites Aristophanes' *Wasps* 575, where Philokleon describes his service on juries as an ἀρχή. Newman does not note that this passage probably relies on the novelty of this description for its effect: Part of Philokleon's absurdity is the delight he takes in serving on juries as a way of exercising power over others.

Athens. It would, accordingly, be arbitrary and obfuscatory to deny that members of these bodies share in and exercise rule simply because ordinary language does not describe such participation as the holding of an ἀρχή or the participants as ἄρχοντες.[4]

Aristotle is by no means averse to following ordinary usage in applying the term in its narrower sense to offices assigned to perform specific, delimited tasks. Indeed, he includes such offices as one of the three parts of every constitution:

> There are, then, three parts of all the constitutions, and the excellent lawgiver should contemplate what is advantageous to each constitution with regard to these three. When these are in good condition, the constitution is necessarily in good condition, and the differences among the constitutions depend on the differences between each of these. One of these three is the part that deliberates about common things, the second is that which concerns the offices (that is, which offices should have control over which things, and what kind of selection of them there should be), and third is the part that administers justice. (4.14.1297b37–1298a3)

When he turns to the question of which assigned roles count as offices, however, he reasserts the essential connection between this narrower sense of ἀρχή as "office" and the broader sense of "rule." Not every role that is assigned to someone by election or by lot should be considered an office. After all, priesthoods can be elected or assigned by lot, as can heralds, ambassadors, and those who are responsible for financing and organizing choruses for the performance of tragedies, comedies, or dithyrambs at city-sponsored festivals (4.15.1299a14–20). Like participation in the assembly and law court, these positions would not ordinarily be described as offices. Unlike the former, however, these roles do not involve the exercise of ἀρχή in the broader sense:

> To speak without qualification, one should call "offices" most of all those to which it has been assigned to deliberate about certain things and to pass judgment and to give orders, and this last especially. For giving orders is more characteristic of rule [ἀρχικώτερον]. (4.15.1299a25–8)

The immediate aim of this argument is to distinguish offices from other functional roles that the city assigns to some individuals rather than others. Offices differ from other assigned positions because the functions of an office involve *ruling*. By showing how the narrow sense of ἀρχή

---

[4] For this interpretation of the argument, cf. Newman 1887–1902.iii:135–7 and Simpson 1998: 134–6.

depends on the broad sense, the argument offers some insight into what it is to exercise rule.

The appeal to the role of deliberation and judgment recalls the definition of citizenship that Aristotle eventually settles on: The citizen is one who is entitled or permitted to share in rule involving deliberation and judgment (3.1.1275b18–20).[5] Though this definition has often been read as referring specifically to participation in the assembly and the law court – an impression reinforced by translations such as "deliberative and judicial rule" – the argument in 4.14 shows that deliberation and judgment are features of every embodiment of political rule, including the "definite" offices or ἀρχαί in the narrow sense.[6] The latter passage also makes explicit what is otherwise left implicit in the *Politics*'s discussions of rule: Ruling involves issuing commands or orders. This point may seem obvious, and no doubt that is one reason why Aristotle does not feel any need to call regular attention to it. As we will see, however, keeping the centrality of commands in mind will help us to gain a clearer view of what is involved in political rule and how it does and does not differ from other varieties.[7]

We can gain some more insight into what it is to exercise rule by turning to the entry for ἀρχή in the so-called philosophical lexicon of *Metaphysics* 5. The concept of an ἀρχή as a "principle" is central to

---

[5] There has been some controversy over whether this passage represents Aristotle's settled view about what a citizen is and about what Aristotle intends by saying that a citizen is one who is "entitled or permitted" or who has ἐξουσία. I agree with Simpson 1998: 135, against Irwin 1990 and Schofield 1999c, that the definition at 1275b18–20 is a refinement of the definition proposed earlier at 1275a22–3. The recurrence of this formulation at 3.5.1277b34–5 seems sufficient to show that it is Aristotle's considered view. Simpson is ambiguous, however, when he writes that a citizen is "someone who is entitled" to share in rule "without actually now sharing." Provided that "entitled" is more or less synonymous with "permitted," so that citizens are those with the recognized entitlement to participate, then I share Simpson's view. The alternative, that a citizen is someone who *deserves* to participate, is excluded by Aristotle's insistence that the definitional question he is trying to answer should not be confused with the normative question of who ought to be a citizen. For interpretations that fail to heed Aristotle's advice to keep those questions distinct, see Robinson 1962: 7; Johnson 1984; Collins 2006: 128–30; Rosler 2013: 149–50.

[6] I owe this observation to an unpublished paper by Stephen White.

[7] Though, as I argue in more detail later, ruling is not simply a matter of commanding, the tight connection between rule as command, deliberation, and judgment and the definite and indefinite "offices" tells against the attempt of Garsten 2013 to identify participation in the assembly or law court as a way of *being ruled*. Garsten's claim not only runs against the grain of the classification of participation in juries or assemblies as forms of ἀρχή, but meets a decisive objection from Aristotle himself, who, as we have just seen, responds to those who "say that these sorts of people are not even rulers [ἄρχοντας] and consequently do not share in rule [ἀρχῆς]" by remarking that "it would be ridiculous to deprive the people with the most control [τοὺς κυριωτάτους] of rule" (3.1.1275a23–33). Assemblies and law courts wield considerable political power; to treat membership in them as though it were a form of being ruled rather than sharing in rule obscures that fact in addition to yielding a torturous interpretation of Aristotle's distinction between ruling and being ruled.

Aristotle's metaphysics and epistemology, and as such it bears a number of complex and related senses, most related to the basic meaning of the word as "beginning, origin, source, starting-point." The word also carries some less technical but closely related meanings; the ἀρχή of a road, for instance, is just the place where the road begins (*Met.* 5.1.1012b34). The entry in *Metaphysics* 5 distinguishes six uses of the term, the fifth of which is its use in political contexts. Aristotle inherited from ordinary Greek the use of ἀρχ- terms to describe the exercise of rule by some people over others, but the entry in the lexicon not implausibly treats this sense as related to the others:

> ἀρχή is also said of that according to whose decision things that are moved move and things that change change, as the offices in cities and dynastic powers and kingships and tyrannies are called ἀρχαί, and so are the crafts, and the most architectonic of these in particular. (*Met.* 5.1.1013a10–14)

This use of the term is not merely equivocal in relation to the others, whether the mundane (the beginning of a road) or the technical (metaphysical and epistemological principles). On the contrary, "it is common to all ἀρχαί to be the first thing from which something either is or comes to be or is known" (*Met.* 5.1.1013a17–19). The use of the term in political contexts thus picks out the exercise of rule as the initiation of collective or cooperative action. By adding that the same sense of the term applies in the realm of crafts, the passage suggests that there is nothing essentially political about rule per se.[8] Rather, rule can be exercised in any collective human enterprise, whether it is a case of action (πρᾶξις) or production (ποίησις); politics and craftsmanship simply serve as useful illustrations because ordinary language reflects the exercise of rule in these contexts with its talk of "offices" and "architectonic" craftsmen.

The most distinctive feature of this practical and productive sense of ἀρχή as "rule" is the role of decision (προαίρεσις). The involvement of decision distinguishes rule from the other senses of ἀρχή by bringing it within the scope of intentional human action, but it also distinguishes the exercise of rule from other ways in which human beings can influence one another's behavior. In the simplest case, when one person exercises rule and another is ruled, the latter implements a decision that the former has made. In other words, a person is ruled when the source of her action is

---

[8] Compare the use of the verb at *EN* 5.8.1135b25–7: A person who acts in anger does not act from forethought, "for the one acting in anger doesn't start it [ἄρχει], but the one who made him angry." Here the idea of initiation is at the fore, and the connection to "rule" virtually nonexistent.

another person's decision (cf. *EN* 3.3.1112b31–1113a9). We need not suppose that the agent who is ruled is entirely passive or that she cannot make any decisions relevant to executing the decision that the ruling agent makes. Agents can be ruled willingly or unwillingly (*Pol.* 3.14.1285a27–9, b2–3, 4.10.1295a14–23, 5.4.1304b10–17), and the difference must lie in the ruled agent's attitudes toward the ruling agent's decision and command. Though not all willing or voluntary action expresses an agent's decision, someone who is ruled *can* at least decide whether to be ruled willingly or unwillingly, if not whether to be ruled at all. The ruling agent's role in supplying the decision does not altogether exclude the ruled agent's making any decisions; what it excludes is the ruled agent's determining the content of the particular decision that directs his action in the relevant circumstance. So, for instance, if a father instructs his son to practice reading and writing, the son does not cease to be ruled simply because he first considers whether to do as he is told. So too, Socrates might decide to accept the laws of the city as unconditionally binding on the grounds that it is open to him to take up residence elsewhere or to persuade his fellow citizens to alter the laws if he finds them objectionable. But when Socrates accepts his death sentence or the son practices his letters, they are ruled because they are not the source of the decisions in accordance with which they take precisely those actions.

Rule, then, is paradigmatically a matter of one agent's initiating the action of another by issuing an order to act in accordance with a decision that the ruling agent has made.[9] It is, accordingly, apparent why Aristotle does not believe that rule is a feature of every form of community.[10] Exchange communities, the relationships between brothers and "comrades," and other varieties of friendship do not involve rule because

---

[9] Contrast my account here with that of Trott 2013: 143–52, who claims that Aristotle "appears to slip on the meaning of rule" (146), shifting between ruling in the sense of holding office and ruling in the sense of deliberating, "which citizens out of office as well as officeholders do." On my view, not all ruling involves holding office – men rule their wives, their children, and their slaves but do not hold office – but all officeholding involves ruling, and while ruling paradigmatically involves deliberation and decision and not merely command, not all deliberation, even collective deliberation, is connected to ruling.

[10] Newman 1887–1902.i: 42 observes that there is not ἀρχή in every kind of κοινωνία. Rosler 2005: 186 cites *Pol.* 1.5.1254a28–32 in support of the opposite contention, but this passage is far from decisive. Though it evidently asserts the presence of a "ruling" and a "ruled" element in every compound substance, it seems not to assert it of every κοινωνία; if it does, it is inconsistent with Aristotle's treatment of exchange communities in *EN* 5.5, as Newman shows, and, by implication, with his discussion of the friendships of brothers and companions in *EN* 8.12 (for both of which cf. Chapter 2). But we have ample reason to think that communities are not substances at all, so that the claim of *Pol.* 1.5 does not apply to them.

neither of the parties commands the other to act and neither accepts the other's commands as a source of decisions to act in one way rather than another. In other words, neither party rules or is ruled. In a community of exchange, each party agrees to exchange a certain quantity of possessions in return for what he considers a proportionately equal quantity of the other party's goods. The house builder does not order the shoemaker to give him so many shoes for a house, and the shoemaker's agreement to supply however many shoes he supplies is not an implementation of the house builder's decision. Each person, rather, reaches his own decision on the basis of his own deliberation. Considering whether to accept the house builder's offer differs from considering whether to obey a command because when the shoemaker accepts the offer he does not make the exchange *because* the house builder made the offer, but because he judges that the offer is a good one. The house builder's offer is not a decision that the shoemaker can decide to accept or reject, but a proposal that he accepts or rejects on the strength of the reasons that he recognizes in favor of one course of action or the other. So too, one friend is not ruled by another when he accepts the other's proposal that they meet at a given time to drink, train, hunt, or philosophize together. For his friend's proposal does not guide and constrain his action as a command would, and he does not accept the proposal because his friend has made it.[11] By contrast, if the son who considers whether to obey his father's command decides in favor of obedience, he does what he does because his father commands it, even if the fact that his father has issued a command is insufficient on its own to motivate the son's obedience. In other words, deliberating about whether or not to accept a command differs from deliberating about whether or not to perform the same action uncommanded. Though the son may deliberate about whether to accept or reject the command, his decision is not based solely on his evaluation of the strength of the reasons that obtain independently of his father's issuing that command.[12]

[11] Of course, friends *can* accept one another's proposals simply because their friends made them; the point is that they *need* not do so in order to interact as friends. Curzer 2012: 249–53 maintains that rule as "decision making" is a feature of every friendship, and hence of every community, but this view requires him to deny that exchange communities are genuine communities (which, as I argued in Chapter 2.1, they are). Curzer sees character friends as sharing decision making equally, but to reduce ruling to decision making obscures the difference between coming to mutual agreement via shared deliberation – whether among friends of the highest variety or mere exchange partners – and having one's actions guided and constrained by the decisions of others; it is important to remember that Aristotle distinguishes command from deliberation and describes the former as most characteristic of rule (*Pol.* 4.14.1299a25–8).

[12] If an agent does what he is commanded to do *only* because he deliberates about whether or not the action in question is worth doing on independent grounds, then Aristotle should deny that he

2. Forms of Rule in the Household

Aristotle emphatically denies that we have said enough about rule if we have said only that ruling is a matter of initiating the action of others by issuing commands to act in accordance with a particular decision. Though this account appears to apply to every form of rule, the different forms that rule can take are at least as significant as what they all have in common. The broadest and most fundamental difference is that between rule over free people and rule over slaves: Rule over slaves is exercised in the interest of the ruler, while rule over the free is exercised in the interest of the ruled or for the sake of some common good shared by both ruler and ruled (*Pol.* 1.7.1255b16–20, 3.6.1278b30–1279a2). Rule over slaves, despotic rule or mastery (δεσποτική), does not disregard the interests of the slave altogether. Rather, the master's concern with the slave's interests is entirely a function of his concern for his own (1.6.1255b9–15, 3.6.1278b34–7). As I argued in Chapter 2, the slave, as an "ensouled instrument," is in effect a part of his master. Thus, like a person's concern with the parts of his body or a craftsman's concern with his tools, the master's concern with the good of his slave is not distinct from his concern for his own good. Master and slave share not a common good or benefit, but "the same benefit." Free

---

is, strictly speaking, being ruled; if the agent would not otherwise choose to do the action, even resentfully, then the command is not the *source* of his action. Aristotle does not consider this question, but the plausibility of this sort of response should be apparent; anyone who does what he is ordered to do only because he considers the action to be the right action in the circumstances for reasons completely independent of the command would not be following an order, except in the incidental sense that what he was doing was also the same thing that someone had ordered him to do. The command itself would have, at best, an indirect causal influence on his action: It may, for instance, not have occurred to him to take that course of action before he was commanded to do it. But that would be to treat the command as a mere suggestion or proposal and not as a command. In this respect, Aristotle's concept of ἀρχή overlaps with the concept of authority employed in contemporary political philosophy and philosophy of law. Rosler 2005 provides an informative introduction to that concept of authority and the controversy over its applicability to Aristotle and pre-Roman Greek thought in general (for a less historical but accessible treatment of the concept, see Finnis 1980: 231–59; for more detail, see Raz 1986: 23–109), but his own view seems to go too far in understating the differences between Aristotle's conceptual scheme and the concepts employed by contemporary philosophers. For Rosler, it is essential that authority exclude coercion and persuasion; "where force is used, authority itself has failed … where arguments are used, authority is left in abeyance" (90–1, quoting Arendt approvingly; cf. 96). While I maintain that Aristotelian "rule" is not reducible to coercion or persuasion, I see no reason to believe that it must exclude them; the threat or use of coercive sanctions does not appear to be excluded by the exercise of ἀρχή; nor does persuasive public reasoning. Thus Aristotelian ἀρχή is not coextensive with Rosler's "authority," and since coextensiveness is a necessary condition for identity between concepts, ἀρχή cannot be identified with "authority." Note, however, that as I use the term throughout, "authority" should not be understood in the contemporary technical sense that excludes persuasion or coercion, but in a looser sense connected with socially acknowledged positions of command.

people, by contrast, are not parts of anyone else. The good of a free person is therefore separate from the good of others in the minimal sense that it is not a function of contributing to the good of another. Accordingly, rule over a free person as such must aim at the good of the ruled independently of the ruler's good, even if it aims at a common good that includes the ruler's separate good as well (3.6.1278b37–1279a2).

Rule over the free comes in several varieties that take the shape they do as a result of the relative capacities possessed by the ruled party in each case. Just as despotic rule, properly speaking, is exercised over people who lack the capacity for higher-order deliberative rationality, rule over the free varies along with differences in the level of that capacity's development among the ruled. Children, like natural slaves, are not able to engage in higher-level practical reasoning; unlike slaves, however, naturally free children will develop that ability so long as their development is not thwarted (1.13.1260a13–14, cf. 1.12.1259b1–4). Adult women, on the other hand, have developed the ability for deliberative rationality; their deliberative abilities are simply "not in control" (ἄκυρον, 1.13.1260a13). Women, as Aristotle understands them, are peculiarly liable to bouts of practical irrationality because the rational part of their soul cannot reliably achieve authority over their emotions, at least without support from their husbands' authority.[13] Naturally free adult males, by contrast, both have the developed capacity for high-level practical reasoning and can put this capacity in control of their overall psychic economy (1.13.1260a20–4). These psychological differences among children, women, and naturally free adult males lead to differences in the forms of rule that are appropriately and naturally exercised over each.

The easiest form of rule to understand is a father's rule over his children (πατρική, 1.12.1259a38). On the one hand, Aristotle's justification for this form of rule is the most straightforward and the least objectionable. On the other, parental rule most clearly illustrates the basic difference between rule over free people and rule over slaves. The justification appeals to some easily recognizable features of human developmental psychology: Children, who have not yet fully developed the capacity for independent practical reasoning, should be under the authority of their parents not only because their parents can guide the children's actions until their deliberative abilities mature, but also because parental direction

---

[13] Interpretation of the claims about women in the *Politics* is controversial. My account here follows, in broad outline, Fortenbaugh 1977 and Modrak 1993; for similar views, cf. Saunders 1995: 96–7, Simpson 1998: 66–7. I elaborate and defend the view taken here in greater detail in Riesbeck 2015.

is crucial for the proper development of those abilities. A detailed account of Aristotle's theory of moral education would take us too far afield, but its broad outlines are plausible and point in the direction of parental authority. Human excellence and well-being require a harmony between one's reasoning and one's nonrational emotional and appetitive dispositions.[14] Because the latter develop first, however, they must be trained and habituated to be receptive to reason and to desire the right sorts of ends (7.14.1333b3–6, 7.15.1334b6–28, 8.3.1338b4). In aiming at the good of the child, parental rule is ultimately directed toward fostering the child's ability to be an excellent independent rational agent.[15]

This last aspect of parental rule is, of course, the one that most distances it from despotic rule or mastery. At first sight, children and slaves seem to have much in common. Neither has the ability to engage in higher-level practical reasoning, and both of them are in some sense "parts" of another. Yet because children will not remain parts of their parents, but will develop the capacity to be independent rational agents, the mode of authority appropriate for a father to his children differs dramatically from his authority over his slaves. To treat a naturally free child as one would treat a slave would be to harm the child by impeding the development of his rational faculties, perhaps even to the extent that the child would be left in the condition of a natural slave.[16] The slave, by contrast,

---

[14] See, generally, Burnyeat 1980, Kosman 1980, Broadie 1991: 103–10, Depew 1991, Cooper 1999b.

[15] As noted in Chapter 3, Aristotle focuses his attention on *male* children, both in his brief discussions of paternal rule in *Pol.* 1 and 3 and in his more detailed discussion of education in *Pol.* 8. Though the account must apply, mutatis mutandis, to females as well as males, Aristotle's silence on the matter leaves us to speculate on just what the *mutanda* are.

[16] The interpretation of natural slavery is disputed on this point: Though many have assumed that a natural slave must, for Aristotle, be born without the first-order potentiality to develop the second-order potentiality or ability for higher-order deliberative rationality, others have plausibly argued that Aristotle believes that human development can be impeded to such an extent that even a human being born with normal first-order potentialities can become unable to develop them into second-order potentialities or abilities. This view differs from the more radically revisionary interpretations of Simpson 1998, 2001; Frank 2005; Nagle 2006; and Trott 2013, who argue in various ways that, according to Aristotle, natural slavery is a corrigible condition (Ober 1998: 345 suggests this possibility but does not embrace it). The intermediate view, suggested by Depew (unpublished, discussed in Nagle 2006: 111–12) in connection with Aristotle's sometimes baffling discussions of the psychology of non-Greek peoples, allows that a naturally free person can become a natural slave; the more radical view goes further in asserting that a natural slave can become a naturally free person. I cannot address these views here, except to say that my sympathies lie with the intermediate view and that the revisionary interpretations appear to be inconsistent with passages such as *Pol.* 8.2.1337b4–20 (cf. 7.9.1328b33–29a2), which prohibit free people from engaging in slavish activities on the grounds that those activities tend to make people slavish: Even if this passage does not suggest that performing slavish activities can make a person a slave (rather than leading to the development of dispositions that are *slavelike*), it does tell against the idea that Aristotle might believe that serving as a slave could conceivably transform a natural slave into a naturally free person. Moreover, as I argue earlier, the qualified justice of despotic rule seems to presuppose that the

cannot develop the capacity for independent rational agency. The slave is therefore not harmed by being subjected to a permanent form of rule that neither promotes that development nor leaves him free to live as he likes. On the contrary, the natural slave, precisely because he lacks the capacity for independent rational agency, is *better off* living under the permanent authority of another than he would be if he were left to his own devices. So Aristotle maintains, at least.[17] Slavery can be just only because it is beneficial to the slave, even though the slave's benefit is not the fundamental goal of the master-slave relationship. The child, however, cannot be justly subjected to any form of rule that aims fundamentally at the good of the ruler, because such a form of rule cannot fail to harm the child by undermining his proper development.

The features of a child's psychology that make him a child and neither an adult nor a slave therefore explain and justify the characteristic form of rule that his parents exercise over him. On the one hand, the community of parent and child has the child's good as its basic aim. It is therefore hardly surprising that actually aiming at that good turns out to be a necessary condition of justice in the relationship, given that the good of the participants in any community guides and constrains the shape that their relationship can justly take. On the other hand, the child's nature as an incomplete and developing rational animal in need of education and guidance gives some determinate content to the requirements of paternal rule, and the marked asymmetry in the psychological capacities of parent and child both explains and justifies a correspondingly asymmetrical relationship of authority. Though Aristotle is short on details in the *Politics* and both of the *Ethics*, one basic feature of the relationship is not in doubt: The parents rule and the children are ruled; at least so long as the children are children, the relationship does not run both ways.

Matters are not so simple in the relationship between husband and wife. Here Aristotle makes several claims that, taken together, seem to point in incompatible directions. On the one hand, the husband rules his wife, and this form of rule is a part of household management and therefore distinct from political rule (1.12.1259a37–9, cf. 1.3.1253b4–11, 3.6.1278b37–40, 1279a8–10). On the other hand, when he contrasts the

---

slave *cannot* develop into an independent rational agent: Otherwise, to treat him in ways that will not be conducive to that development could not be just because it could not be even incidentally beneficial.

[17] Aristotle seems insufficiently sensitive to the gap between the kind of authority that his argument justifies and even an idealized version of the master-slave relationship; as Kraut 2002: 295 puts it, "decision-making authority does not entail ownership rights." So too Smith 1991.

husband's rule over his wife (γαμική, 1.12.1259a39) with the father's rule over his children (πατρική, a38), he describes the husband as ruling his wife "in a political way" (πολιτικῶς, 1.12.1259b1). The difficulty that this description poses should be apparent. The husband's rule over his wife, as a part of household management, must differ somehow from the political rule exercised by citizens over one another. Yet Aristotle evidently thinks of the relationship between husband and wife as "political" in some analogous sense.

In concluding his defense of slavery, Aristotle had contrasted mastery with political rule, glossing the latter as "rule over people who are free and equal" (1.7.1255b20). We might, then, think that the husband's rule is political because his wife is his equal in some sense. The very same passage, however, contrasts political rule with household management as a whole (1.7.1255b18–19), which explicitly includes the householder's relationship to his wife and children as well as to his slaves (1.3.1253b3–12). Furthermore, Aristotle's treatment of these relationships in *EN* 8.7 groups the friendships of husband and wife along with those of parents and children as friendships "based on superiority" (*EN* 8.7.1158b11–14), and the very passage in the *Politics* that describes the husband's rule as political immediately goes on to assert that "the male is more suited to lead than the female," a claim evidently intended to explain why the husband rules (γάρ, *Pol.* 1.12.1259b1–3). If equality is at issue, then, it must be a somewhat different sort of equality from the equality of citizens. We cannot resolve this confusion by supposing that the husband and wife stand in a relationship of proportionate equality while political rulers and ruled enjoy strict numerical equality. Not only is proportionate equality important in fully-blown political relationships, but *all* forms of friendship based on superiority admit of a proportionate equalization of benefits and affection (*EN* 8.7.1158b23–9), and even the relationship between ruler and ruled is included in the list of superiority-based friendships. If Aristotle's views on this matter are not hopelessly confused, there must be some sense in which the relationship between husband and wife can resemble political rule without being identical to it.

With some help from the discussion of justice in the *Nicomachean Ethics*, we can see just how this might be. First, however, consider how the *Politics* passage continues:

> Now in the majority of instances of political rule, the ruling and the ruled element change positions. For they tend to be equal in nature and not to differ at all.[18] Nonetheless, whenever the one rules and the other is

[18] For "tend to" as a translation of βούλεται, see Saunders 1995, Reeve 1998, and Lord 2013 against Newman 1887–1902: ii and Simpson 1997. This sense of the word is not infrequent in Aristotle: See

ruled, they seek to have a difference in appearance, in forms of address, and in honors, just as Amasis, too, told the story about his footpan.[19] But the male is always disposed in this way in relation to the female. (*Pol.* 1.12.1259b4–10)

After declaring that husbands rule their wives in a "political way," Aristotle immediately draws a contrast between what usually happens in cases of full-blown political rule and what happens with husbands and wives. Political rule characteristically involves an alternation in positions of ruler and ruled. Instead of one person's holding the same office permanently, he will hold it for one period and then hand it over to someone else. This alternation reflects the underlying equality in the nature of the participants in the political community. Given that equality, the only alternative to alternation would be an unjust concentration of ruling positions in the hands of some rather than others. Yet because not everyone can hold those positions at once, alternation is necessary, and it puts the participants into a hierarchical relationship of ruler to ruled. Citizens mark these positions out by associating certain offices with special manners of dress, forms of address, and formal honors. Yet in most cases the official hands those privileges over to another when he leaves office.

This is where the relationship between the husband and wife differs most from that between citizens. When Aristotle says that "the male is always disposed in this way in relation to the female," he can not mean merely that husbands always remain distinguished from their wives by outward appearance, forms of address, and honors. He must mean, more importantly, that husband and wife do not alternate positions of authority. Rather, the husband always retains a superior position. The asymmetry inherent in this arrangement fits his description of the virtues of a

---

LSJ s.v. βούλομαι III and the examples cited there, *Pol.* 1261b12, 1293b40, 1255b3; *GA* 778a4; *Sens.* 441a3.

[19] For Amasis, see Hdt. 2.172. Simpson 1997: 30 explains the reference well: "Amasis, a king of Egypt of lowly origin, had his golden footpan made into a statue of a god, which the Egyptians then worshipped. Footpan and statue were thus the same stuff but different in outward form, and so it is also with equals when they alternate between ruling and being ruled." The example is perhaps less fitting than Aristotle may have thought, since Herodotus's Amasis does not seem to point toward any underlying equality between the footpan and the statue. In fact, the king's message may be that the statue's dignity depends on what it is, not where it came from; Aristotle's point, by contrast, is that the statue is revered only for its outward form and not for what it essentially is. Insofar as Amasis points toward the conventional character of the difference in dignity accorded to the statue and the footpan, he denies that the inequality reflects any real superiority of merit. It would be surprising for such a king to announce to his subjects that his apparent superiority rested entirely on their own decision to invest him with that superiority. Nonetheless, we need not suppose that Aristotle had any complex or subtle allusions to the Herodotean text in mind.

man as "ruling" virtues and the virtues of a woman as "assisting" virtues (1.13.1260a20–4).[20] This contrast, in turn, fits Aristotle's view of the principal psychological difference between men and women. Women, though they have the capacity for higher-level deliberation just as men do, are not able to put their deliberation firmly in control of their actions without the aid of their husbands. Though Aristotle elsewhere suggests that women and men are suited to different roles by virtue of their physiological differences (*EN* 8.12.1162a10–24), the husband's permanent position of authority is grounded not in physiology but in psychology.[21] If women are to attain the degree of well-being available to them, they must, like men, achieve a harmony of reason and emotion. But women can only achieve that harmony when under the authority of their husbands. Such, at least, appears to be Aristotle's thought.[22]

In light of this asymmetry, it begins to seem unclear why Aristotle would compare the relationship between husband and wife to political rule at all.[23] Citizens typically exchange positions of authority to reflect their underlying equality; husband and wife do not exchange positions

---

[20] I translate ὑπηρετική as "assisting," with Simpson 1997 (cf. "of an assistant" in Reeve 1998) and against "of a servant" in Saunders 1995, "serving" in Lord 2013, and the "obeying" of Lockwood 2003. Saunders's and Lord's translations obscure the difference between wives and slaves, since "servant" – despite the cultural associations that have given the word a softer set of connotations – basically means "slave." Lockwood avoids this problem, but wrongly highlights obedience rather than assistance as the distinctive characteristic of female virtue: Both Greek usage and the context show that assistance is the core idea here. Though ὑπηρέται are often slaves and typically subordinates of some kind (e.g., *Pol.* 1.4.1253b27–54a8; 3.16.1287a21; 4.15.1299a24; *Rhet.* 1.9.1366b13; *AP* 35.1, 50.2, 63.5), to assist is not inherently to be subordinate: The great-souled man eagerly assists others (*EN* 4.3.1124b18), friends assist one another (8.8.1159b5; 9.2.1164b25; *EE* 7.2.1237b19; 7.10.1243a21–24; 7.11.1244a2), and one can assist others out of either kindly benevolence or calculating self-advantage (*Rhet.* 2.7.1385a32–b7). Aristotle's only other use of the adjective suggests that one craft is "assisting" with respect to another, rather than identical to or a part of it, if it provides either material or instruments for the latter (*Pol.* 1.8.1256a5). It is perhaps worth considering whether the wife's deliberative contributions can be understood as material or instruments for the husband's rule, but Aristotle does not draw this connection, and it is unclear whether the model of productive crafts can or should be applied to the relation between the husband and wife's practical deliberations. In any case, it should be clear that describing her virtues as "assisting" is consistent with taking her deliberative contributions to be her most important form of assistance. I discuss this and related points at greater length in Riesbeck 2015.

[21] For female biology and psychology as they relate to the *Politics* in particular, see Lockwood 2003: 9–13 and Fortenbaugh 1977; for the role of male and female traits in Aristotle's biology more generally, see Matthews 1986, Mayhew 2004.

[22] Fortenbaugh 1977, Modrak 1993, and Riesbeck 2015.

[23] Simpson 1998: 62–3 underestimates the differences and treats the husband's rule over his wife as genuinely political. Yet his own account of the relationship seems inconsistent with that conclusion. Though he argues (rightly, as I will argue in Chapter 6) that alternation in positions is not necessary for political rule, fully blown political rule is incompatible with the kind of authority that a husband has over his wife. I defend this claim more fully in due course.

because they are unequal. That inequality seems sufficient to explain why the husband's rule over his wife is not simply political, but it leaves us to wonder how it is not the same kind of rule that a father exercises in relation to his children. A passage from *EN* 5 sheds some light on this question:

> The justice of a master to his slaves [τὸ δεσποτικὸν δίκαιον] and the justice of a father to his children [τὸ πατρικόν] are not the same as these [i.e., political justice and its perversion in tyranny], but similar. For there is no injustice without qualification in relation to one's own things, and a possession and a child, until it reaches a certain age and becomes separate, are, as it were, parts of oneself, and no one deliberately chooses to harm oneself. That is why there is no injustice toward oneself, and so there is not political justice or injustice either. For [political justice] exists in accordance with law and among those who are naturally suited for law, and these are people who have equality in ruling and being ruled. That is why there is justice more in relation to one's wife than in relation to one's children or possessions. (5.6.1134b8–17)

After describing political justice as existing "among those who share in a way of life [ἐπὶ κοινωνῶν βίου] with a view to self-sufficiency, who are free and equal either proportionately or arithmetically" (5.6.1134a26–8), Aristotle comes to distinguish this kind of justice and its corruption, most prominently on display in tyrannies, from the sorts of justice characteristic of the relationships of the household. As we have already seen, justice in relation to one's slaves and one's children must be qualified because slaves and children are not fully distinct from their masters and parents. Neither relationship fits the model of justice between citizens, which Aristotle takes to be the fullest and most paradigmatic variety (5.6.1134a24–6, 28–30).[24] Yet justice in the relationship between husbands and wives more closely resembles political justice because here too the participants have a kind of equality in ruling and being ruled. What this passage suggests is that a husband's rule over his wife, though not strictly a form of political rule, closely resembles it, and hence differs markedly from a father's rule over his children, because the wife shares in ruling as well as being ruled, and the respective shares of husband and wife are allotted in accordance with their proportional equality. How could this be?

---

[24] Note that Aristotle here describes the justice that obtains between people who do *not* fit the model of political justice as "justice of a sort in virtue of a similarity" (*EN* 5.6.1134a29–30). That is, his analysis of justice takes the same shape as his analysis of the kinds of friendship. For a fuller account of this resemblance relationship and its difference from analysis in terms of focal homonymy, see Zingano 2013 and 2015.

One way in which a wife might share in ruling is through her authority to issue commands to other members of the household. It would be implausible to suppose that wives would not be permitted to direct their children and slaves to act in certain ways rather than others. On the one hand, Aristotle's endorsement of the more or less traditional gendered division of labor in the household gives wives authority in their own special sphere. On the other hand, a woman's authority traditionally extended beyond the ability to direct children and slaves in their performance of tasks marked off as distinctively female. Women could issue orders to male slaves as well as female, whether their specific responsibilities were in farming or weaving. So too, a mother's authority over her children would not have been restricted to a limited range of "female" domestic tasks. A mother can command her sons to go study their letters or to stop playing dangerous games with farming tools, just as a father can. In short, there is no apparent reason to believe that a woman's authority over her children and the household's slaves did not extend to the same range of activities as the father's authority.[25]

The ability to issue commands, however, is insufficient for sharing in rule. This becomes clear when we consider that even slaves can be in a position to give orders. Not only can some slaves be put in charge of others, but slaves can give commands to their masters' young children. A slave entrusted with the task of teaching freeborn children to read and write, for instance, will direct the children to perform certain exercises in certain ways, correct them when they are mistaken, and so on. If that sort of example seems too sophisticated for a natural slave, a simpler illustration will do just as well: A slave, no less than a father or a mother, could be expected to tell children to stop playing dangerous games with farming tools, particularly if his masters had explicitly instructed him to make sure that the children stayed out of trouble.[26] The situation would be similar with siblings when one is sufficiently older than the other. Yet neither slaves nor brothers are described as ruling each other or anyone else in the household.

The likely reason why slaves and siblings do not count as sharing in or exercising rule when they issue commands to other members of the

---

[25] Xenophon's *Oeconomicus* presents a highly idealized version of the traditional gendered division of labor within the household. Pomeroy 1994 supplies a useful commentary that compares Xenophon's picture to other available evidence, though she fails to do justice to the subtleties of Aristotle's view.

[26] I take my inspiration for these examples from Plato, *Lysis* 207d–209a.

household is that their ability to give orders derives from the authority of the father. If a slave can give orders to a child when he is teaching that child to read and write, the force of those orders nonetheless depends on the father's previous instructions: He directs the slave to teach the child his letters, and he orders the child to study his letters with the slave. Similarly, when a slave tells a child to stop fooling around with dangerous tools, the child's decision to obey the slave flows from the supposition that his father would at least endorse the command if he has not already explicitly given it himself. If we imagine, by contrast, a slave ordering his master's child to perform some particularly unpleasant bit of manual labor, the child can disobey with impunity and can even disregard the command altogether if he knows that his father would never support it. It is not that slaves can in no way give commands that their masters would not support. It is, rather, that any regularly recognized authority that slaves have over their master's children depends entirely on their master's endorsement.[27] The same condition applies to siblings in their relations to one another and even to children in their relations with slaves. If the ability to issue commands to other members of the household does not suffice for slaves and children to count as sharing in rule, then it will be no more sufficient to account for how wives share in rule.

We might wonder, though, just why Aristotle should deny that examples like the ones I have given count as exercises of rule. After all, in cities as well as other complex organizations, such as armies, authority is often delegated. The assembly may decide whether to go to war, but the general decides the strategy. The general, in turn, delegates his authority to lower-level officers who command smaller segments of the army; these officers may then direct their commands to yet lower-level officers who lead even smaller groups of men into battle. Aristotle even describes armies and navies as groups in which more or less all of the members share in ruling and being ruled (*Pol.* 2.11.1273b15–17). Of course, the example of slaves and children already shows that there is more to sharing in rule than issuing commands with recognized authority. The military example, however, shows that the ability to deliver such commands does not fall short of ruling simply because the authority is delegated. Aristotle says little about how he understands military organization, but his general account of ruling suggests that the two cases differ because ruling inherently involves

---

[27] When Socrates points out to Lysis that his parents let a slave rule him, Lysis responds, "So what? He's *ours*" (*Lysis* 208c3–4). Lysis rightly sees himself as the slave's superior despite being constrained to do what the slave tells him.

making decisions. A slave might command his master's child to spend ten more minutes performing his reading exercises rather than five more, but he does not decide that the child should learn to read, or even that he should teach the child. His commands are, instead, an implementation of his master's decision that the child should learn and that the slave should teach. Delegated authority likewise involves the implementation of decisions made at higher levels. Yet in complex organizations such as armies, lower-level officials do not merely disseminate orders or determine minor details of their application. Rather, subordinate officials make decisions because they deliberate about how to achieve the objectives given by their superiors, and they exercise rule because they issue commands that direct others to implement those decisions.[28]

Decisions, as Aristotle makes clear, involve deliberation (*EN* 3.2.1112a13–17, 6.2.1139a31–b9). Since rule, in turn, involves decision, it follows that ruling involves engaging in deliberation. The role of deliberation in rule explains not only why children and slaves do not exercise it, but also why Aristotle thinks that it is good and just for them to be ruled but not to share in rule; for natural slaves lack the capacity for higher-order deliberation altogether, and children have it only in an incomplete way (*Pol.* 1.13.1260a12–14). Given their relative incapacities, children and slaves could not exercise rule well, if at all. Women, by contrast, have the same capacity for deliberative rationality that men do; their natural susceptibility to practical irrationality, however, requires their subordination to their husbands. Yet we can now see more clearly what this subordination does and does not involve, and why Aristotle compares the husband's rule over his wife to political rule while drawing attention to its nonpolitical

---

[28] How simple does means-end reasoning need to become before it ceases to count as deliberation? Aristotle gives no clear answer, though the *EN* account of deliberation and decision and the *Pol.* theory of natural slavery suggest that even fairly complex means-end reasoning can fall short of deliberation. But if slaves can be left in charge of other slaves (e.g., *Pol.* 1.7.1255b35–7), then presumably they can exercise delegated rule in a way similar to low- and middle-level military officers. This poses something of a problem for the theory of natural slavery if ruling requires forming a προαίρεσις. This is, of course, only one of the places where that theory begins to break down. It may not have seemed so problematic to Aristotle, however, because he seems to have thought of a natural slave as being able to develop and exercise virtues when properly guided by his master's reason (1.13.1260a31–b7) and so might have supposed that a slave implementing his master's προαίρεσις could, by extension, engage in means-end reasoning that issues in προαίρεσις (Deslauriers 2003 gives a similar account of the virtues of natural slaves). An alternative possibility is that exercising despotic rule does not require forming a προαίρεσις in the strict sense; after all, non-Greek natural slaves are still ruled despotically even though they all lack "the naturally ruling element" (τὸ φύσει ἄρχον, 1.2.1252b6); so natural slaves must be capable of ruling others despotically. It seems clear that these difficulties are a product of the theory of natural slavery, not the theory of ruling.

character. A wife shares in rule not simply because she can issue commands to other members of the household, but because she can participate in the deliberation that forms the decisions that initiate and govern the collective activities of the household and its members.

It is hardly surprising that women should exercise rule in this sense within the domestic sphere that Aristotle, like most ancient Greeks, thinks of as specifically "female." There is reason to suppose, however, that he has a more expansive authority in mind. First, he does not say merely that wives share in rule, but that husbands and wives both share in ruling and being ruled (*EN* 5.6.1134b13–16). Second, when he says that the husband rules his wife in "a political way," his formulation suggests that the husband's authority itself differs from his authority as a father and a master (*Pol.* 1.12.1259a39–b1). These two claims illuminate one another. Taken together, they imply that a husband's rule does not differ from a father's or a master's simply in delegating genuine authority over certain domestic spheres to his wife. Rather, a husband exercises authority over his wife in a different way because he shares that authority with his wife and allows her to participate in his own deliberations, taking her judgment and advice into account. The husband's rule is comparable to political rule because he not only rules, but is also ruled; he does not make all of the important decisions on the basis of his own deliberation alone, but engages in cooperative deliberation with his wife. The wife exercises a degree of rule over her husband because her own deliberative contributions can shape the decisions that are the source of the household's collective actions.[29] To be sure, there is little here to satisfy gender egalitarians: The wife shares in rule, but she shares in accordance with a kind of proportionate equality that leaves her permanently subordinate to her husband's authority. Yet because she shares in deliberation with her husband and can herself form decisions that are binding on other members of the household, a wife is not ruled in the same way that slaves or even children are ruled. Inegalitarian though it is, Aristotle's vision of a husband's rule assimilates it to neither domination nor paternalism.[30]

---

[29] Compare Saunders 1995: 96–7, who denies that wives rule in any sense and concludes only that, because women have capacities for rational deliberation, they "require consultation, argument, and persuasion." But this would fail to distinguish women clearly from slaves: "Those who deprive slaves of rational speech and tell us that we should merely give them orders do not speak well, for slaves need to be admonished more than children" (1.13.1260b5–7): If what Saunders has in mind is not simply that husbands must *reason with* their wives, but that they must also give their wives a genuine role in their common deliberation, then he would be mistaken to say, without qualification, that wives do not share in rule with their husbands.

[30] For a helpful treatment of justice between husbands and wives and the importance of avoiding the temptation to conflate the husband's rule with paternalistic or despotic modes of authority,

We have now seen how Aristotle's account of distinctive kinds of rule within the household fits into his framework of community, friendship, and justice. The relative capacities of husband and wife, father and child, and master and slave, each seeking the complex good of the whole household as a crucial component of his or her individual good, explain and justify certain characteristic modes of authority. For Aristotle, these modes of authority are natural in the complex sense that they reflect the natural inequalities among the participants and, when properly exercised, promote the good of each to the extent that they can achieve it. Few if any of us will be even partially satisfied with Aristotle's account because we do not believe in natural slavery and we do not believe that women are naturally susceptible to practical irrationality to any greater extent than men.[31] As a tool for understanding Aristotle's conception of political community and political rule, however, his views about just rulership in the household are illuminating; for his account of the distinctively political depends just as much on implicit contrasts with the household as it does on his explicit descriptions of the city. With these distinctions in place, then, we can turn to ask how political rule differs from household management and how it fits into the broader framework of justice and community.

3.   Political Rule

A husband rules his wife in a political way insofar as his wife shares in deliberation and therefore actively contributes to shaping the course of their common action. This suggests that what is distinctive of political community and rule is precisely this sharing and mutuality. Indeed, when

see Lockwood 2003: 8–11. Lockwood perhaps underestimates the extent of natural inequality that Aristotle finds between men and women. He suggests, for instance, that such inequality would have been due primarily to the marked difference in age between husbands and wives. Though Aristotle's view of these matters is more subtle than commentators sometimes allow (e.g., Schofield 1990), its inegalitarianism seems to me inescapable. I elaborate on these issues in Riesbeck 2015.

[31] Many educated men and women do, of course, continue to believe that women are naturally (i.e., innately) more "emotional" than men. Even if this were true, and not a mere stereotype or a fallacious inference from the discovery of neurological correlates for emotional states and dispositions to the conclusion that those traits are innate rather than acquired, it is not Aristotle's view. In that sense of "natural," Aristotle does not seem to believe that males are naturally less prone to be led by their emotions than women (cf. *EN* 1.3.1095a2–11, 1.5.1095b14–22, 2.1.1103a18–26, 4.9.1128b16–18, 6.13.1144b30–1145a1, 10.9.1180a1–5). His view hinges on women's allegedly diminished capacity for being led by their own reason (cf. *Pol.* 1.12.1259b1–3), not their supposedly innate tendencies to experience strong emotions. Thus Simpson 1998: 67 misses the mark when he appeals to "what we now speak of as the effect of hormones and the monthly cycle." Periodic susceptibility to mood disturbances hardly subverts one's ability to guide one's life by reason without being subordinated to a male.

Aristotle characterizes political rule, he stresses the reciprocity of ruling and being ruled. Just as he contrasted the husband's rule over his wife with political rule by appealing to the typical political practice of alternation in office, he likewise fastens onto this way of sharing rule in his more focused discussions of political community. A passage especially notable for its generality comes in book 2's critique of the Platonic Socrates' proposal, in the *Republic*, to unify the city as much as possible. This proposal, Aristotle objects, presupposes a mistaken view of the kind of community a city is and of the degree and variety of unity that it can sustain. Not only does a city consist of many individuals, but it requires people who "differ in kind" and are not "similar" (*Pol.* 2.2.1261a22–4) insofar as they must play different roles, hold different positions, and distribute rule unequally among those positions.[32] But because the people who make up a political community are free and equal, they must adopt a system of reciprocity in sharing authority:

> This [reciprocal equality] is necessary among people who are free and equal, too, since it is not possible for all of them to rule at the same time, but only at yearly intervals or by some other arrangement of time. In this way, it turns out that everyone rules, just as all would be shoemakers and carpenters if the shoemakers and carpenters were exchanging positions and the same people were not always one or the other. But since it is better this way for the affairs that concern the political community, too, it is clear that it is better for the same people to rule continually, if it is possible. When, however, it is not possible because all the people are equal in nature, it is then also just for all to share in rule, whether ruling is a good or a base thing. For equals to yield in turn and to be alike when they are out of office imitates this [i.e., everyone sharing in rule]. For some rule and others are ruled in turn, as though they were becoming different people. The same goes for when some people hold some offices and others hold others. From these things it is clear that the city is not by nature a unity in the way that some people say. (2.2.1261a32–b7)[33]

---

[32] Deslauriers 2013: 132 argues that these differences must be differences in virtue and not merely "differences in profession … since his claim is that the differences are necessary for a self-sufficiency that is moral as well as economic." But self-sufficiency does not require differences in virtue, and the differences Aristotle has in mind seem to include not only differences in profession, but also differentiation in the political roles required for self-sufficiency.

[33] The text of this passage is disputed, and the disputed points are not inconsequential (cf. Simpson 1997: 36 note 7, who says that "the general sense is clear"). For the δέ of the mss. at 1261b1, I am inclined to accept Susemihl's δή, though the δέ might also be read as apodotic (see Smyth 2837 and Denniston 1950: 177–85); in either event, it matters whether we read the clause, as I do, as an apodosis or as the second part of a complex protasis. The case for reading it as an apodosis is strong: If it were merely specifying a further condition, then we would need to understand Aristotle to be claiming that alternation of office and ruling and being ruled "in turn" (ἐν μέρει, κατὰ μέρος) would only successfully "imitate" (μιμεῖται) the participation of all *if* such sharing

Similarly, in 3.6, Aristotle again compares political rule to rule over children and wives, but then distinguishes political rule by the alternation and sharing of rule typical in cities: "People think it right to exercise political offices by turns, too, when the city has been established in accordance with an equality and likeness of the citizens" (3.6.1279a8–10). This way of sharing rule differs from the way that husband and wife should share, because citizens do not typically stand in permanent positions of authority over each other. The practice of alternation is a response to the citizens' underlying equality, an equality not in their acquired skills or talents, but in their nature.[34] Unlike women, naturally free adult males do not need to be unqualifiedly subordinate to others if they are to exercise their deliberative faculties well. This is not because men are invulnerable to practical irrationality or spontaneously tend toward justice and virtue. On the contrary, Aristotle is strikingly pessimistic about the prospects for the development and retention of human excellence in the absence of excellent laws and moral education (e.g. *EN* 10.9.1179b23–1180a24). The difference between free adult men and women, on Aristotle's view, is not that men do not need to be subject to rule of any sort; it is that the kind of rule that promotes their well-being and preserves justice in their relations with others requires that each of them share in a way that precludes the kind of permanent subordination of one to another found in the community of husband and wife.

Stated in this way, Aristotle's view is a strong one. It sets it down as a condition of justice among those who cooperate with a view to unqualified self-sufficiency that each participant should share in rule as well as being ruled and that no member or group of members should hold a position of unchecked superiority over the rest. This view of justice in political

---

were just; but that seems both false (alternation and shared office have the same "imitative" effect whether or not the distribution is just) and logically awkward (if the justice of shared rule were an additional condition rather than a result of the citizens' equality, in what sense would the permanent rule of the same individuals be "impossible"?). By contrast, reading the clause as an apodosis makes clear that the justice of shared rule is a consequence of the participants' equality; the point about "imitation" then shows us how cities can achieve a just distribution despite the impossibility of everyone holding the same offices simultaneously. Note, too, that Ross's γε at 1261b2 is unnecessary if we read the previous clause as an apodosis; in fact, on that reading, we should expect the δὲ that the manuscripts provide; we thereby also avoid the awkward asyndeton produced by Ross' punctuation.

34 Deslauriers 2013: 139 maintains that Aristotle endorses alternation in rule among equals as a way of imitating inequalities between ruler and ruled that she thinks are required for the "moral self-sufficiency" of the city. But *Pol.* 2.2.1261a32–b7 has nothing to say about imitating inequalities among equals. What is imitated is, rather, an arrangement in which everyone shares in rule; alternation is a way of preserving equality, not imitating inequality.

community raises several immediate problems. Not only does it seem to make the normative and conceptual paradoxes of monarchy irresolvable in principle, but it also seems to entail that only a strong form of democracy could conceivably meet the criteria of justice.[35] Yet even if the defense of kingship were irredeemably inconsistent with Aristotle's conception of justice, it is, to put it mildly, implausible that Aristotle was a democrat.[36] All of the correct constitutional arrangements, with the possible exception of polity, apparently restrict citizenship to a fraction of a territory's free adult male population.[37] Yet to be a citizen is to share in rule. If the interpretation of political rule that I have sketched is correct, then all or most of the constitutions Aristotle endorses as correct will turn out to violate his own principles of justice.

I will address these questions in the next chapter with the intention of showing that Aristotle's general theory of constitutions and justice in the distribution of political rule is in fact consistent with the view I have developed so far. First, however, it is necessary to address some more general questions about Aristotle's conception of political rule. For although it is clear enough that he regards political rule as the appropriate form of rule over free adult men, it is not equally clear whether this form of rule strictly requires that anyone subject to it must also be granted an active role in collective deliberation and judgment. Nor is it apparent why access to such a robust form of political participation should be a requirement of justice. To answer these questions, we need to know what sort of value political rule has for the people who exercise it. Understanding its value will, in turn, help us to see just how extensive political participation has to be in order to count as sharing in rule.

---

[35] Ober 1998: ch. 6 argues for this conclusion explicitly; Schofield 1999b comes close with his reading of the "rational model" of political community as "a regulative ideal," which strongly resembles Ober's "natural polis."

[36] As Nussbaum 2000 observes, the "democracy" that many of us today endorse is closer in many respects to Aristotelian polity than to Aristotelian or Athenian democracy. Some theorists might prefer to give priority to the Athenians in determining the core of the concept and argue that a politics that embodied some of the Athenian democracy's central features would be superior to contemporary liberal democracy as we know it (so Finley 1985, Ober 1996c, Woodruff 2005). Though I have some sympathies with this approach, the concept of democracy is, in our culture at least, essentially contested and so devoid of determinate content as to be of little analytic value, barring some inevitably question-begging stipulation. Thus I use the term, unless otherwise specified, to stand in for Aristotle's δημοκρατία.

[37] Aristotle sometimes suggests that polity typically restricts citizenship to men who possess sufficient wealth to own and maintain heavy arms (2.6.1265b26–9, 3.7.1279b2–4, 5.6.1306b6–9), and the best constitution does not permit citizens to be farmers or to practice crafts for a living, despite relying on a population of people who do so (7.9.1328b33–1329a26).

4. The Good of Political Rule

Despite his general characterization of political rule as shared and reciprocal, we might doubt whether such rule should be a requirement of justice in political communities as Aristotle understands them. In any community, justice is a matter of promoting and preserving the common good of the participants, a good that is achieved when each of those participants benefits in a fair and equal proportion to their own contributions and those of others. So unless exercising political rule is itself an essential component of the good for the sake of which political communities exist, there might seem to be no reason why people could not benefit from being ruled without sharing in rule themselves. Of course, one prominent traditional reading of the *Politics* sees the intrinsic value of citizenship or "political activity" as one of the work's defining theses.[38] On this view, the city exists for the sake of the flourishing of its citizens, and the distinctively political activity of participation in collective deliberation and judgment is choiceworthy for its own sake and a crucial part of a flourishing human life. Justice requires that all citizens share in rule because ruling is a central component of the good that political communities aim to promote, and so participation should ideally be as extensive and intensive as is necessary for all of the citizens to flourish fully. This conception of the value of political rule has the advantage of explaining why justice demands inclusion in a shared form of rule, but it entails that Aristotle repeatedly endorses distributions of political power that directly prevent many people from living well. In part to avoid this implication, an alternative account has sought a solution to the difficulty in a minimalist interpretation of "ruling and being ruled." On such a view, "ruling" does not require active participation in deliberation and judgment, but includes the influence that citizens have when their rulers deliberate with a view to the common good. Hence all the citizens can rule and be ruled even if only one or a few hold formal positions of authority. Neither of these interpretations is, in my view, satisfactory. I will argue against the first in this section before turning briefly to the second in the concluding portion of this chapter. Reconsidering Aristotle's claims about the value of political rule will show that although ruling necessarily involves active participation, it is not an intrinsic good, choiceworthy for its own sake.

---

[38] See the works cited in Chapter 1, note 22.

Arguments that Aristotle regards political participation as intrinsically valuable have tended to emphasize one or more of four considerations, two more abstract and two more firmly grounded in textual details. First, some of Aristotle's readers have seen his claim that political community essentially aims at the good life as already implying that political activity is of noninstrumental value. Second, and similarly, this assumption might seem necessary to account for Aristotle's apparent identification of the participants and beneficiaries of politics. More often, however, the claim seems to lie closer to the surface of the texts. Many have read the discussion of the good citizen and the good man in *Politics* 3.4 as restricting the exercise of practical wisdom to political rulers; since exercising practical wisdom is essential to living well, they conclude that the good life must include political rule. That conclusion seems most explicit in *Politics* 7.2–3, which defends the value of ruling politically in the course of sketching an account of the best way of life for human beings. These passages seem at least broadly consistent with what we find in both the *Eudemian* and *Nicomachean Ethics*, which treat "the political life" as a serious contender for the best way of life. Yet despite the importance of flourishing for politics and of politics for flourishing, none of these arguments shows that active participation in the tasks of citizenship is an intrinsic good.

To begin with, consider Aristotle's frequent claim that political community is for the sake of living well. This claim must be meant to draw a tight connection between human well-being and the activities of politics. It has long been recognized that, for Aristotle, to say that X is for the sake of Y might mean either that X causally promotes Y and therefore is choiceworthy as an instrumental means to Y, or that X is a part of Y and therefore choiceworthy as a constituent of Y.[39] On its face, then, the claim that political community is for the sake of living well does not tell us whether politics is an instrumental means or a constituent part of human flourishing. It might seem, however, that the instrumental relation is too weak and indirect to capture the essential connection between them. As Aristotle sees it, every action that we choose on the basis of rational deliberation aims at *eudaimonia;* ultimately, we choose everything either as a means to or as a constitutive part of living well.[40] If politics were merely

[39] Greenwood 1909 and Ackrill 1980 have been especially influential statements of this distinction. It has occasionally been rejected – e.g., by Kraut 1989: 13, who argues that Aristotle picks out only instrumental means with the phrase "for the sake of" – but has, I think rightly, become the standard view.

[40] It is important to note the restriction of this claim to actions chosen on the basis of deliberation; Aristotle does not suppose that every intentional action aims at *eudaimonia*. For a brief discussion

an instrumental means to achieving the good life, its relationship to living well would be no closer than that of many other instrumentally valuable crafts and activities, such as medicine or gymnastics. But Aristotle plainly thinks that politics is more closely connected to living well than medicine or gymnastics. By singling out *eudaimonia* as the end of political community, he must mean to indicate a more direct relationship between political activity and the good life. We might therefore conclude that he regards political activity as a constitutive part of living well and, if any constitutive part of well-being must be choiceworthy for its own sake, an intrinsic good.[41]

On closer inspection, however, it should be apparent that the direct and essential teleological relationship that Aristotle finds between politics and living well does not entail that political activity is even partially constitutive of the good life. We can appreciate this point by more carefully considering the for-the-sake-of relation. As Aristotle recognizes, this relation can be direct or indirect.[42] One activity or product X might be indirectly for the sake of some other product or activity Z if X is for the sake of some third product or activity Y that is itself for the sake of Z. Borrowing examples from the introductory chapter of the *Nicomachean Ethics,* we might say that bridle making is indirectly for the sake of victory in war because it is directly for the sake of horsemanship, which is chiefly exercised in war, itself for the sake of victory.[43] Aristotle never suggests that politics is for the sake of living well in this indirect sort of way. But the case of bridle making shows that a teleological relationship can be direct even when instrumental; bridle making is directly for the sake of horsemanship, but making bridles is of course no part of riding a horse. Nonetheless, the teleological relationship between bridle making and horsemanship is essential to bridle making. The activity of horsemanship both explains why anyone would want to make a bridle in the first place and determines what features a bridle needs to have in order to be well made.[44] Hence bridle

---

of Aristotle's reasons for holding this view, see Irwin 1988: 359–60 and, for a contemporary defense, Lebar and Goldberg 2012.

[41] In this paragraph I am summarizing the argument of Irwin 1990: 75. Cooper 2010 presents a similar view with explicit debts to Irwin.

[42] Aristotle does not make this distinction explicit, and his use of for-the-sake-of language typically describes a direct relation. But he implicitly acknowledges indirect teleological relations when he writes, for instance, of *eudaimonia* that "we all do everything else for the sake of this" (*EN* 1.12.1102a2–3).

[43] Aristotle's "horsemanship" is the use of horses as part of a cavalry. On other varieties of horseback riding, see the following note.

[44] These two features seem to be necessary for any Aristotelian *telos*, at least as it figures in human action. I draw here on the general treatment of for-the-sake-of relations in Richardson Lear

making is both essentially and directly for the sake of horseback riding, despite being a merely instrumental means to it. So, too, if *eudaimonia* directly explains why people engage in political activity and directly determines what political activity needs to be like in order to be successful, then it would not be inappropriate or misleading for Aristotle to claim that political community is for the sake of living well, even if politics is only an instrumental means to the good life rather than a constituent part of it. The teleological claim alone does not entail that political activity is an intrinsic good.

A second reason for supposing that Aristotle must regard political activity as an intrinsic good is that he seems to restrict membership in political community to those who benefit from it. In maintaining that the city exists for the sake of living well, he argues that if the city were solely for the sake of mere life, then groups of nonrational animals or natural slaves could be cities. There cannot be cities of natural slaves or nonrational animals, however, because both lack the capacity for *eudaimonia* and rational decision (*Pol.* 3.9.1280a31–34). But if political activity is of merely instrumental value, it might seem unreasonable to make a capacity for *eudaimonia* a necessary condition for membership in a political community. If the work of deliberation and judgment that constitutes citizenship is not part of the good that cities aim to promote, then there would seem to be little reason to restrict that work to its beneficiaries. If, on the other hand, participation in citizenship is itself a crucial component of human well-being, then the requirement that citizens have a capacity for *eudaimonia* readily makes sense. Hence we might conclude that Aristotle's argument assumes that political participation is an intrinsic good, since that assumption helps make the argument coherent where it otherwise would not be.[45]

Yet in fact there are several good reasons why Aristotle maintains that those who cannot be the beneficiaries of a community cannot be its parts. As I argued in Chapter 2, communal "parthood" or membership is, on Aristotle's view, just a matter of sharing in the good for the sake of which

2004: 11–31. For a similar account that also borrows Aristotle's own example of bridle making and horsemanship, see Meyer 2011. The example is misleading insofar as it supposes that the fundamental aim of all horseback riding is to serve as part of a cavalry. As Meyer 2011: 50 observes, however, different forms of horseback riding will have different sorts of requirements for what counts as a good bridle, and we will choose different bridles depending on the kind of horseback riding we aim to do; cavalry riding and dressage do not make the same demands on bridles. So Aristotle's example is oversimplified, but the general point about the structure of teleological relations survives the qualifications needed to account for the rich variety of equestrian pursuits.

[45] I here rehearse the argument of Irwin 1990: 76–80.

the community exists. This point applies to all communities, even those formed for the sake of instrumental goods. To recall the example from Chapter 2, being a "part" of a community formed for the sake of sharing food is just a matter of getting a share of the food; but food is not an intrinsic good. Admittedly, this criterion of communal parthood is insufficient to explain why Aristotle treats the principal beneficiaries of political communities as coextensive with those who participate in deliberation and judgment. It may therefore seem mysterious why a capacity for *eudaimonia* and rational decision should be required for participation if participation is no part of human flourishing. We can, however, dispel the mystery just as effectively and more directly without appealing to the intrinsic value of political activity. For animals and natural slaves are, in Aristotle's view, radically incapable of deliberation and judgment. It is not simply that they cannot perform these activities well – that is why women and children are excluded from politics, but neither women nor children completely lack capacities for deliberation and judgment – but that they cannot engage in them at all. If political activity is essentially a matter of sharing in deliberation and judgment with a view to promoting and preserving the well-being of oneself and one's fellows, then the capacity to conceive of such a good and to deliberate with a view to achieving it is a necessary condition for engaging in politics. Nonrational animals and natural slaves can do neither of these things, and so cannot be participants in political activity. Moreover, the one uncontroversial thing we can say about Aristotelian happiness is that it centrally involves rational activity in accordance with virtue, which in turn involves deliberation and rational decision (*EN* 1.7.1098a16–17, 2.4.1105a28–33). Hence, given that politics aims at happiness, nonrational animals and natural slaves cannot be its beneficiaries either. These claims therefore do not suggest that political participation itself is a component of human flourishing. The impossibility of a city of slaves or animals shows that cities do not aim at mere life, not that political activity is an intrinsic good.[46]

---

[46] Brown 2013 offers a different argument based on the connection between happiness and "parthood" or membership in the city. Brown reads the argument of *Pol.* 1.2.1253a18–29, which claims that the city is "prior to" human beings in the sense that human beings can only fulfill their functions well and flourish as parts of a city, as maintaining that an individual must engage in the distinctly political activities of citizenship in order to live well. But this interpretation assumes that the relevant sort of parthood or membership in a city is citizenship in the strict sense, and though Aristotle elsewhere identifies a city's parts with its citizens (3.1.1274b32–41, 3.5.1278a3, 4.4.1291a24–8, 7.4.1326a16–21, 7.8.1328a33–5), he does not do so in the priority argument. To do so would have the problematic consequence that neither metics nor women could be happy. Though the status of metics is controversial (see Chapter 5), we should be reluctant to conclude that Aristotle considered himself, as a metic, cut off from the possibility of *eudaimonia*. More decisively, Aristotle explicitly

Many readers of the *Politics*, however, have thought that Aristotle makes that assertion quite clearly several times in the work. In book 3, Aristotle turns from the question of what it is to be a citizen to consider what makes a good citizen. He asks in particular whether the virtue by which a person is a good citizen is the same virtue by which he is a good man. He first argues that the two cannot be identical in every case because different traits make a citizen excellent in different kinds of constitution, whereas the traits that make a man good are everywhere the same. Within a single constitution, too, the dissimilar tasks for which citizens can be responsible require different competences and dispositions (3.4.1276b16–1277a12). For all that, there is one sort of citizen whose virtue is identical to the virtue of a good man:

> We say, in fact, that the excellent ruler is good and practically wise [φρόνιμον], and that it is necessary for a statesman [πολιτικόν] to be prac-tically wise.[47]... But if the virtue of a good ruler and a good man are the same, yet the person who is ruled is also a citizen, then the virtue of a citi-zen would not be unqualifiedly the same as the virtue of a man, though it would in the case of a particular citizen. For the virtue of a ruler is not the same as the virtue of a citizen ... yet being able to rule and to be ruled is an object of praise, and it is thought to be the virtue of a reputable citizen to be able to rule and be ruled well. If we posit, then, that the good man's vir-tue is ruling virtue, but the virtue of a citizen is both, they would not both be praiseworthy in the same way. Now, since it is thought that the ruler and the ruled should learn different things rather than the same things, but that the citizen should know both and have a share in both, one can see what follows ... the virtue of these is different, but the good citizen must know how and be able both to be ruled and to rule, and this is the virtue of a citizen, to know the rule of free people in both ways. (3.4.1277a12–b16)

The details of this passage are murky, but the general thrust of the argu-ment should be clear enough. Though the virtue of a citizen cannot be identical to the virtue of a good man for the reasons already given, there is nonetheless one aspect of citizenship, ruling, that depends for

---

holds that women can be happy (*Pol.* 1.13.1260b8–20; 2.9.1269b13–19; cf. *Rhet.* 1.5.1361a5–11) despite being naturally unsuited for citizenship. Furthermore, even if Brown were right to take citizen-ship as the relevant sort of parthood in 1253a18–29, it would not follow that political activity is an intrinsic good or a component of happiness, but only that it is necessary for a flourishing life. But if Aristotle took the argument of *Pol.* 1.2 to establish that conclusion, it would be odd for him to begin book 7 – which explicitly refers to book 1 – by asking whether the best way of life includes political participation; I discuss the book 7 argument more fully later.

[47] I follow Newman and the manuscripts in reading πολιτικόν at 1277a15 against Ross's πολίτην οὐκ, which seems insufficiently motivated and contrary to the ensuing argument. See also the com-ments of Simpson 1997: 83, note 22.

its excellence on the same disposition by which a good man is good.[48] This disposition is practical wisdom, the virtue of practical reason that enables a person to deliberate well about what is good and advantageous for him and, by extension, for the communities of which he is a part (*EN* 6.5.1140a24–b11, cf. 6.8.1141b23–6). With his reference to the "statesman" (πολιτικός), Aristotle may have in mind not every office or position in which rule is exercised, but a citizen who takes a more comprehensive leadership role in formulating and guiding public decisions (1.13.1102a7–21, 3.3.1112b11–15, 6.5.1140b10). Since practical wisdom is distinguished from other, more narrowly circumscribed deliberative excellences by its concern with general human goods and their place in human flourishing as a whole (6.5.1140a24–8), its possession will be more important for those citizens who formulate and guide the city's most general policies than for those who hold limited offices that merely implement already fixed policies. Yet Aristotle is willing to describe people as practically wise with regard to some more restricted area whenever they "reason well with a view to some excellent end among those for which there is no craft" (6.5.1140a28–30, cf. 6.9.1142b28–31). Since even offices that govern a narrow domain frequently require deliberation, the excellent exercise of rule on any level will require at least some degree of practical wisdom (cf. *Pol.* 7.14.1333a11).[49]

Practical wisdom, then, is the virtue of every exercise of rule. Nonetheless, it is not the virtue of a citizen as such because citizens do not always or exclusively rule. They are also ruled, even when they are ruling, and being ruled well does not depend on practical wisdom. For the ruler must deliberate well and reach reasonable conclusions if he is to rule well, but the ruled do not need to do either in order to be ruled

---

[48] Inglis 2014: 272–6 argues that this claim is restricted to the virtue of a ruling citizen in the best constitution. But since all correct constitutions aim at and reliably achieve the common good to the extent possible in the circumstances, and that achievement is the work of phronesis, it seems as though the virtue of a ruling citizen should be identical to the virtue of a good man in all correct constitutions. One of Inglis's reasons for rejecting that conclusion seems to be that Aristotle does not believe that many individual citizens in a polity can become fully virtuous human beings. But they may nonetheless collectively achieve a phronesis-like success in deliberation, and so exercise phronesis to a degree sufficient for excellence in ruling. I cannot offer a fully satisfactory treatment of this issue, but my claims earlier would not require significant modification in order to be made consistent with a view like Inglis's.

[49] Kraut 2002: 362–71 reads the references to ruling in this passage in a narrowly restricted way, applying only to "permanent rulers"; this restriction allows him to read "the person who is ruled" as a category that includes people who "will occupy minor offices, but will always be subordinate to those who are better equipped to govern" (371). My objection to this reading is essentially the same as my objection to Garsten 2013 in note 7. I offer further reasons to reject such interpretations of "being ruled" in Chapter 5.

well. Rather, they need to be guided by correct beliefs about what to do, beliefs supplied to them by the rulers: "True belief, not practical wisdom, is the virtue of someone who is being ruled" (*Pol.* 3.4.1277b28–9). These claims might lead us to suppose that, as Aristotle sees it, ruling is necessary for the possession or exercise of practical wisdom. If practical wisdom is the exclusive privilege of rulers, then surely a man must be a ruler if he is to live well, since practical wisdom is necessary for a rational agent's well-being (*EN* 6.12.1144a36, 13.1144b30–3).[50] But this conclusion misinterprets Aristotle's argument. To see why, we should take a closer look at the distinction between the virtues of rulers and ruled.

We can easily misunderstand this distinction if we begin with a rigidly hierarchical political model in mind. For a clearer view, we should begin with a relationship in which hierarchy seems less problematic to us. Consider, then, the relationship of a foreign language teacher and a beginning student. However counterintuitive it may seem, this relationship is one of Aristotelian ruler to ruled. The teacher decides what the student should do in order to learn well, and the student does what the teacher decides. A good teacher is one who is able to guide and direct a student to do what will enable her to learn the language effectively. The student, for her part, does not need to deliberate about or decide what to do to learn the language. Rather, she can learn the language well simply by following a good teacher's instructions. Of course, following those instructions well and learning the language successfully require that she possess other intellectual abilities and traits of character, such as a good memory and disciplined persistence. Moreover, to say that she may rely on her teacher's instructions is not at all to say that she may be passive; successful language learning is hardly possible for a student who is not active. What the student does not require is the intellectual ability to work out how to teach herself the language. She will no doubt find the task easier if she already has a great deal of linguistic knowledge, but what most fundamentally makes her an excellent student is that she follows a good teacher's instructions well.

The teacher-student relationship, however, although a useful illustration of ruling and being ruled, is not a good model for political rule. It more closely resembles parental rule both in the teacher's asymmetrical

---

[50] A common reading: Robinson 1962: 14–15, Vander Waerdt 1985, Kahn 1990, Adkins 1991, Newell 1991, Reeve 1998: lxii, Schofield 1999b: 104–5, 2000: 319, Frede 2005: 172–9, Collins 2006: 130. Deslauriers 2013: 135 does not make this argument, but does seem to interpret the distinction between the virtues of ruler and ruled as restricting the exercise of practical wisdom to rulers.

authority and in the goal of leading the ruled to become independently competent with no further need of a teacher. Political rule is more complex because ruler and ruled characteristically share in ruling and being ruled, and it is a failure to appreciate this point that has, in part, allowed readers to find in these passages an argument that a man can only live well when he is ruling over others. It may now be more readily apparent, however, that such interpretations misconstrue the relationship between ruling and practical wisdom. If we keep in mind that in political rule a person can rule and be ruled simultaneously or by turns, Aristotle's claim will appear in a different light. Crucially, "ruler" and "ruled" do not name mutually exclusive classes into which individual rational agents must fall. Rather, they describe agents insofar as they deliberate and direct others to act in accordance with the results of that deliberation or, conversely, are the recipients of such direction; "ruler" and "ruled" are the names of roles. The virtues of ruler and ruled are, accordingly, the dispositions and abilities required to act well in each role, and in political rule, at any rate, one can even play both roles simultaneously. By analogy, a bricklayer's excellence does not depend on any architectural expertise; it does not follow that a person who is an excellent bricklayer cannot also be an expert architect, or that the architect cannot join in the bricklaying that he directs. Unlike architectural expertise, however, the dispositions and abilities by which one exercises political rule well are the same dispositions and abilities that make someone an excellent human being. Yet from the fact that the role of ruling demands the very same virtues required for flourishing as a human being, we are not entitled to infer that one must exercise that role in order to flourish. Though a ruler may need to be practically wise in order to rule well, it does not follow that a person needs to rule in order to be practically wise or to exercise his practical wisdom.[51] Aristotle's claims about the virtues of citizens qua ruler and ruled therefore do not suggest that ruling is a necessary component of a good human life or choiceworthy for its own sake.[52]

[51] Newman 1887–1902.i: 238, whose reading of *Pol.* 3.4 is otherwise similar to my own, conflates the capacity for rule – which the good man will necessarily have if the virtue of ruling is identical to the virtue of a man – with the activity of ruling – which is not the only activity in which one exercises practical wisdom – and so makes the unwarranted inference to which I am here objecting.

[52] For similar and complementary critiques of the view that exercising practical wisdom requires ruling, see Mulgan 1990, Miller 1995: 238, and Rosler 2005: 92–5. Strictly speaking, the virtues of a ruling citizen and the virtues of a human being will coincide only in correct constitutions, and perhaps even only in the best (see my discussion of Inglis 2014 in note 48), because excellent citizenship in deviant constitutions may require citizens to act contrary to justice and other virtues. The virtue of a ruling citizen in an oligarchy is therefore not identical to, and is in fact at odds with, the virtue of a good man. If this conclusion seems counterintuitive, one might consider that we

A prima facie more promising source for that thesis is Aristotle's discussion early in *Politics* 7 about whether the "political and practical way of life" or "the contemplative way of life" is most choiceworthy. The opening chapters present a dialectical intervention in a dispute between proponents of each way of life. As so often, Aristotle does not unequivocally endorse any single side in the dispute. Consequently, it is not entirely clear how he answers the question that he poses, or even whether he supplies a positive answer at all rather than simply rejecting unsatisfactory positions. On one prominent interpretation, the argument rejects the assumption that the two alternatives are mutually exclusive and defends a mixed way of life. Since both ways of life exclude important intrinsically valuable forms of activity, the best way of life must include both.[53] Yet this reading moves too quickly. Though Aristotle evidently rejects the purely contemplative life "released from the political community" (*Pol.* 7.2.1324a16–17) and defends the political life against certain objections, it is not obvious that he defends the political life on the grounds that politics is an intrinsically valuable form of activity that we should all want to engage in for its own sake.

Any interpretation of these chapters must take account of Aristotle's explicitly limited ambitions for the argument. Before setting off to consider the merits and faults of each way of life, he denies that "political thought and contemplation" need to raise the question of the most choiceworthy way of life for every individual (7.2.1324a13–23). This claim seems odd, not least because the text seems to proceed immediately to address just this issue. By declaring the question "extraneous" (πάρεργον, 7.2.1324a22), however, Aristotle is not denying that it has any relevance whatsoever; the opening sentence of book 7 has already told us that "anyone who intends to make the appropriate inquiry regarding the best constitution must necessarily determine first of all what the most choiceworthy way of life is"

---

can easily begin to identify the traits that make someone a good thief or a good torturer, and yet acknowledge that a good human being will be neither; like "thief" and "torturer," "citizen" is the name of a *role*. For a helpful treatment of this issue, see Rosler 2005: 23–5. Against this interpretation, some have objected that being a good citizen must always be a good thing to be; e.g., Kraut 2002: 362–4, Roberts 2009, Garver 2011: 80–2. My argument here is consistent with this view, since both recognize, in Garver's words, that "just because ruler and ruled are different doesn't mean that the good person cannot be good at both." Keyt 2007 presents a careful discussion of this question, arguing, I think persuasively, that "good citizenship" in deviant constitutions can require injustice. For the (less persuasive) view that good citizenship under such conditions will still typically be rational, see Horn 2013.

[53] For this view, Irwin 1990: 80–2. The commentaries of Kraut 1997 and Simpson 1998 offer similar interpretations.

(7.1.1323a14–16). Rather, he denies that anyone engaged in this inquiry must determine whether a political way of life is most choiceworthy for absolutely every individual who is capable of choosing how to live. The inquiry into the best constitution would be unaffected by the conclusion that a thoroughly apolitical way of life would be the best for some people; all that the inquiry assumes is that "sharing in a city" is choiceworthy either for everyone or for most people (7.2.1324a17–19). If it turns out that a contemplative life entirely disengaged from politics is the absolute best but only for a few extraordinary individuals, it will make no difference to political theory. Not only will some kind of political life still be necessary for the majority of human beings, but the point of considering the best way of life as part of an inquiry into the best constitution is to determine what kind of life the constitution should promote for its citizens; for the purposes of that project, it would be irrelevant if a few exceptional people would live best with minimal or no participation in political community.[54] So the argument of book 7 does not need to determine what kind of life is the highest achievable for a human being. It is enough to show what kind of life is most choiceworthy for "more or less everybody" (7.1.1323a20).

In light of the limitations on what Aristotle intends the argument of these chapters to establish, it is less surprising that he does not quite answer the question that he poses. On the one hand, he has, in effect, already laid out an answer to the question in the *Ethics*.[55] On the other, his main aim in these chapters is to show that the different views he considers are all mistaken. The contemplativists are right to disparage the pursuit of despotic rule over others (7.2.1324a35–7, 1324b22–1325a15); ruling natural slaves has nothing grand or noble about it (7.3.1325a23–7), and ruling free people as though they were slaves is unjust (7.3.1325a34–b14). Moreover, as the contemplativists admit, a life of political action need not be unjust if

---

[54] For this way of understanding the argument, see Kraut 1997: 61–2.

[55] By "the *Ethics*" here I mean both the *Nicomachean* and the *Eudemian*, since I take them to be at least broadly consistent in defending a view of the best way of life that can be described as what Keyt 1983 calls "moderate intellectualism," giving pride of place to activities of theoretical contemplation but including practical activity in accordance with other virtues of character and intellect. My argument here, however, is compatible with a wide variety of interpretations of these texts and does not depend on any particular view about whether the *Politics*, or some portions of it, ante- or postdate the *EE*, the *EN*, both, or neither (for opposed positions on this question, compare the introduction of Keyt and Miller 1991, Simpson 1998, and Kraut 2002: 16–19). On some interpretations (e.g., Kenny 1992, Richardson Lear 2004), the *EN* and the *EE* give markedly different accounts of the best way of life. But while I draw primarily on the *EN*, I assume only that the *Politics*, the *EN*, and the *EE* can be presumed consistent until it is shown otherwise; if they are not, some adjustment of detail will be required, but I do not think these details would undermine my argument here.

one rules in a political way, ruling and being ruled in turn (7.2.1324a37–8, 3.1325a27–30). But they are mistaken to regard political activity as necessarily hindering one's own happiness and, more generally, to think that an inactive life will be better than an active one (7.3.1325a31–4). Not only do we flourish through engaging in certain kinds of activity, but the political life offers us opportunities to exercise the virtues in pursuit of noble aims. Yet the champions of the *vita activa* share the mistaken assumption that philosophic contemplation is not itself a form of action. This assumption, in turn, rests on a superficial conception of action as action undertaken for the sake of its results rather than for the sake of the activity itself. In fact, actions that include their own ends in themselves are more fully actions than those that aim at goals external to the action (7.3.1325b14–23). If we understand the nature of action, we see not only that contemplation is itself a kind of action, but that there is no fundamental incompatibility between contemplation and participation in politics.

In a sense, then, the argument of 7.2–3 does endorse a mixed life of political participation and philosophic contemplation.[56] It does not, however, do so on the grounds that political activity is intrinsically valuable. The qualified defense of the political life shows that political participation does not inherently conflict with living well and that it is possible to exercise the virtues and to achieve worthwhile ends in politics. But that claim falls short of the thesis that exercising rule in cooperative deliberation and judicial decisions is an intrinsic good. In fact, Aristotle denies that political activity has its end in itself when he contrasts it with contemplative activity, which does (7.3.1325b16–23). To find a defense of the intrinsic value of political activity in this passage, we must assume that we can exercise the virtues and pursue noble goals only when we are engaged in activities that have their ends wholly in themselves and are choiceworthy simply for their own sake. That assumption is in fact widely held on the evidence of Aristotle's own declarations about virtuous action. But it is, I think, a severely oversimplified interpretation of Aristotle's view. A more nuanced account will enable us to see how politics can be valuable as a

---

[56] Kraut 1997: 62 claims that the argument aims to show merely that neither activity is inherently flawed. But the argument considers ways of life, not specific activities, and the objections that the passage raises show that both lives, as their proponents conceive them, exclude elements of the other for bad reasons. Because the argument's aims are limited, it does not try to refute the purely contemplative view outright. On this point, I agree with Kraut, against Irwin 1990. Yet Irwin seems right to insist that the argument does not end in a stalemate, but defends a way of life that is both contemplative and politically active or "practical." My disagreement with Irwin centers on the idea that the mixed life is a good one because "political activity" is intrinsically valuable and chosen for its own sake as a component of *eudaimonia*.

medium for virtuous action despite being chosen primarily for the sake of external ends.

The *Nicomachean Ethics* emphatically affirms the intrinsic value of virtuous activity from start to finish, and it associates virtue closely with politics. As early as the fifth chapter of the first book, "the political life" is treated as a candidate for the best way of life (*EN* 1.5.1095b17–1096a3), and the climactic chapters of Book 10 declare such a life happy "in a secondary way" (10.8.1178a9). We learn early on that the goal of the political life, rightly understood, is the exercise of virtue (1.5.1095b24–1096a2), and it is part of the nature of virtuous actions that they are choiceworthy for their own sake. Virtue is among the things that we would choose "even if nothing else came about from them" (1.7.1097b2–5), and it is a necessary condition for acting virtuously – rather than simply doing what a virtuous person would do – that one choose the virtuous actions for themselves (2.4.1105a28-33). If genuine politics is devoted to virtue, and virtue is an intrinsic good, it seems plain that political activity is itself an intrinsic good.

This inference, however, is too quick. If we accept the simple view of the intrinsic value of virtuous action that some of Aristotle's claims suggest, we should be perplexed by many details of his discussion of the virtues of character. On the simple view, we can express the virtues only in the sort of activity whose primary purpose or goal is internal to the activity itself rather than lying in its external consequences. Some of the virtues readily meet this condition. For example, sharing a few drinks with some acquaintances provides a context for friendliness, temperance, and wit. These virtues are exercised in the activity of sharing drinks, and the point of sharing drinks lies in that convivial activity itself, not in its consequences. Goals that lie outside the activity will, of course, have some influence over a virtuous person's conduct in these circumstances, but such goals are not what the agent primarily aims to achieve in a friendly, temperate, witty round of drinks. Other virtues, however, are much less amenable to this sort of analysis, and none less so than the virtue that receives more attention than any other except justice: courage.

For Aristotle, the paradigmatic context for the expression of courage is warfare (3.6.1115a24–31).[57] A person acts courageously when he endures the

---

[57] Aristotle's focus on courage in battle has often been thought too narrow. I take it, however, that courage is not restricted to martial contexts, but that those contexts furnish the central or paradigmatic case of courage. For developments of this idea, see Richardson Lear 2004: 150–1 and Pakaluk 2005: 160–4.

dangers of battle as he should, when he should, for the reasons he should, and so on (3.7.1115b11–20). Though the exercise of the virtue consists chiefly in feelings of fear and confidence responding to correct reasoning, acting courageously is not simply a matter of feeling a certain way, but of feeling a certain way while deliberately choosing to do certain things – in the central case, to fight despite the imminent prospect of a painful death on the battlefield. It should be clear at once how this sort of activity differs from sharing a few drinks with some friends. Unlike a trip to the pub, facing death in battle is not the sort of thing whose fundamental purpose is achieved in the very act of doing it. A soldier does not risk his life for its own sake; he acts, rather, to protect his community or otherwise to promote its interests.[58] The simple view of the intrinsic value of virtuous activity yields the perverse conclusion that a virtuous person values risking his life in just the same way that he values learning and contemplating scientific truths, appreciating musical and poetic productions, or enjoying a meal with friends and family. These activities are worth pursuing in their own right not only in the sense that we rightly aim at them independently of any further consequences they produce; they are also the sorts of activities that are worth making opportunities in which to engage. By contrast, risking one's life in battle is worth doing only when and because the battle and the risk are the best available means to achieve worthwhile goals that lie entirely outside warfare.

If we are tempted to suppose that Aristotle embraces some sort of quasi-Homeric aristocratic warrior ethos that values the courageous display of military prowess in much the same way as more urbane aristocrats value fine wines, good company, and exquisite art, we need only read what he has to say about war: "We go to war in order to live in peace … for nobody chooses to fight a war for the sake of fighting a war, nor does anyone prepare for war [for that reason]; for a person would be thought absolutely murderous if he were to make his friends into enemies in order that there might be battles and killings" (10.7.1177b5–12, cf. *Pol.* 7.2.1325a5–10).[59] Since the activities in which we exercise courage are not choiceworthy for their own sake, courage does not fit the simple view of the intrinsic value of virtuous activity. The same is true, if less dramatically,

---

[58] Aristotle does not make this point as explicit as one might like, but Pears 1980, White 1992: 272–6, Whiting 2002, and Richardson Lear 2004: 148–54 each convincingly argue that he does recognize it.

[59] Rosler 2013: 165–6 suggests something like the quasi-Homeric idea when he maintains that Aristotle subscribes to what he calls "the ancient Greek understanding of war as *agōn*." Rosler's account of this understanding is not entirely clear, but I see no evidence that Aristotle embraces any such view.

of other virtues such as generosity, gentleness, and justice. All of these virtues primarily and essentially aim at goals that lie at least in part outside the activity that displays them; the choiceworthiness of the activity that manifests these virtues depends on the value of their external goals.

Yet Aristotle remains committed to the view that these actions, as virtuous actions, are worth choosing for their own sake and contribute to the agent's flourishing. Crucially, however, he can retain this commitment without embracing the simple view. Virtuous activities of all sorts may be good in themselves and worth choosing for their own sake even when their value depends on their orientation toward external goals, precisely because they embody the proper responsiveness to and pursuit of the whole ensemble of goods that contribute to and partially constitute human well-being. Consciously and deliberately aiming at the right goals and pursuing them at the right time, in the right way, and so on, constitute excellence in agency (εὐπραξία, *EN* 6.2.1139b3, 6.5.1140b7). This excellence is worthwhile in itself and beneficial to the agent even when circumstances prevent the achievement of the external goal, because the agent exercises his capacities for practical rational agency well by acting in the most reasonable way available to him. Nonetheless, the acts are not reasonable, and hence not worthy of choice, independently of the value of their external goals. That is why someone who courageously risks his life defending his city against foreign invasion acts virtuously and achieves some measure of the good life for himself, even though it would be irrational, and hence not virtuous, to go to war *in order to* act courageously. Rather, what makes standing firm in battle to protect one's city the virtuous thing to do is in large part that it aims at the right external goals; the value achieved in the action is the value of choosing and doing the right thing at the right time in the right way and so on.[60]

Warfare and courage help us to see that the intrinsic value of virtuous activity does not entail the intrinsic value of the activities in which the virtues are exercised. To be sure, Aristotle recognizes "the political life" of sustained and committed participation in office as a candidate for the best way of life and as a genuine context for excellent and noble action. To

---

[60] Aristotle's formulations of the relationship between intrinsically valuable activities, *eudaimonia*, and activities in accordance with virtue invite oversimplification on this point, and a fully satisfactory interpretation would require a more lengthy discussion of textual evidence and philosophical details. I largely agree with the insightful account of Curzer 2012: 32–7, which draws on Pears's distinction (Pears 1978: 273–4, 1980: 174) among internal goals, external goals, and countergoals. Similarly illuminating are the discussion of acting for the sake of the *kalon* in Richardson Lear 2004: 130–46 and the account of *eupraxia* as an internal end in Reeve 2012: 141–7.

obtain and preserve the well-being of one's political community is "more noble and more divine" than to do so for oneself alone (1.2.1094b7–10), and politics provides us with a context in which we can engage in virtuous activities of especially outstanding "nobility and grandeur" (10.7.1177b16–17). Yet these claims do not suggest that sharing in cooperative deliberation and judgment about the common affairs of the city is an intrinsically good activity any more than is going to war. On the contrary, the most explicit characterizations of political activity as such describe its fundamental aim as the flourishing of the citizens (1.2.1094a26–b7, 6.8.1141b23–7, 10.7.1177b14). Yet this flourishing is, Aristotle tells us, "different from politics, and we clearly seek it on the assumption that it is different" (10.7.1177b14–15). In this respect, politics is more like warfare than it is like theoretical contemplation: Both are chosen primarily for ends outside themselves (10.7.1177b17–18).[61]

There are, of course, disanalogies between warfare and politics. Though Aristotle is enough of a realist to recognize that the threat of warfare cannot be eliminated from human life, war is ideally to be avoided and accepted only as a necessity (*Pol.* 4.4.1291a6–10, cf. 7.2.1324b41–a10, 14.1333a30–7, 14.1333b38–1334a2).[62] Politics, by contrast, is indispensable to human well-being. Human beings can flourish only if they live in political communities, and political communities cannot function unless people cooperate in the tasks of citizenship, ruling and being ruled with a view to living well. The life devoted to politics will, accordingly, be a better and more virtuous life than one devoted strictly to military action, since it involves virtuous activity directed at the more expansive and inclusive good of the city as a whole. Yet politics does not become choiceworthy for its own sake simply by being less dispensable than warfare. Like war, politics provides an opportunity for the expression of virtues whereby human beings can flourish in at least some measure. Further, politics offers more ample scope for the expression of a broader range of virtues, and hence one might reasonably choose a political life for the sake of one's own flourishing. But it is no more sensible to engage in deliberation and

---

[61] As Dahl 2011: 80 and others note, when Aristotle writes at *EN* 10.7.1177b16–18 that virtuous actions are not chosen for themselves, he must mean that they are not chosen *solely* for themselves. If an account like the one I have given here is correct, however, the point may be the stronger one that these actions are not chosen *primarily* for their own sake, but gain the value they have in themselves from the value of the external goals at which they aim.

[62] Ostwald 2009b helpfully discusses the most important passages in Plato and Aristotle on war and its place in human life; cf. Rosler 2013, which generates problems for Aristotle's treatment of war but seems to rely on Hobbesian assumptions that Aristotle has no reason to accept.

judgment for their own sake than to go to war for its own sake. War and politics both necessarily look beyond themselves and depend for their value on goods that lie outside martial and political activities. They are, as Aristotle puts it, "unleisured" (*EN* 10.7.1177b4–18, cf. *Pol.* 7.14.1333a30–b5, 15.1334a11–40).

It is important to stress that in denying that political activity as such is choiceworthy for its own sake, we need not maintain that it is a merely instrumental means. Politics is of course often and perhaps even primarily of instrumental value, but it may also be worth choosing as a part of or as a way of engaging in activities that are themselves choiceworthy for their own sake. Crucially, however, to choose political activity in this latter way is to choose it not for its own sake, but for the sake of the activity of which it is a part, and it is this latter activity that gives its parts the value they have. Participatory citizenship may be a way of acting justly, courageously, wisely, and more generally virtuously. But it is the exercise of justice, courage, and wisdom, and not political activity as such, that is choiceworthy for its own sake.[63] Further, Aristotle explicitly acknowledges that one can act virtuously even as a private citizen (*EN* 10.8.1179a3–8), and both the *Politics* and the *Nicomachean Ethics* agree that the exercise of the practical virtues does not exhaust the content of happiness. In aiming at happiness, then, politics aims at something distinct from itself, and even when political activity is worthy of choice as a way of exercising the virtues, its value depends on the value of exercising the virtues. Politics is not an intrinsic good.

The impulse to see Aristotle as a defender of the intrinsic value of political participation no doubt owes its prevalence in part to the striking difference between his view of political community as essentially directed toward living well and the modern liberal conception of the function of the state as strictly limited and instrumental. The role that Aristotle's texts have played in communitarian and social democratic critiques of

---

[63] Edward Halper has objected to me in correspondence that in cases like these we cannot separate acting virtuously from political activity; they are not two separate actions, but one. But even if political activity were the only way to act virtuously (which I deny for reasons that I have already given), it would be a mistake to infer that they are inseparable, for we can engage in political activity without acting virtuously or even aiming to act virtuously. Moreover, even if we suppose that we should identify only one token action rather than two or more when a particular agent acts virtuously through political activity, the unity of the action is consistent with its having a plurality of parts or aspects chosen for the sake of the whole; this kind of unity is precisely the sort captured by the claim that X is chosen for the sake of Y not as an instrumental means, but as a constitutive part. The crucial point is that it is the relation of X to Y that explains why X is choiceworthy, not that X and Y are discrete token actions.

liberalism in the contractualist tradition has powerfully reinforced the dissociation of the *Politics* from anything like an "instrumentalist" view of politics.[64] Though no sensitive reader could fail to observe the gap between Aristotle's political theory and the thought of Hobbes, Locke, Kant, or Rawls, my suggestion is that the principal source of their differences is not to be located in a contrast between intrinsic and instrumental conceptions of the value of political activity. The basic disagreement between Aristotelian and modern liberal political theory is about what political activity and political community are and ought to be *for*, and a simple contrast between intrinsic and instrumental value obscures Aristotle's answer to this question. Already by insisting that a political community is formed and maintained for the sake of living well, Aristotle embraces a view of the political more expansive than the vision of government as limited to securing peace, order, or the protection of negative rights. Aristotelian political community is distinctive because it aims at the good life, not because participation in citizenship is itself a central component of that good.

5.   The Justice of Ruling and Being Ruled

If participation in the distinctively political activities of cooperative deliberation, judgment, and rule is not an intrinsic good, it might seem unclear clear why a person deprived of any share in rule would thereby be treated unjustly. For if ruling is not a good in itself that makes a crucial contribution to an individual's flourishing, then being deprived of it would seem not be a harm. Even if it is valuable as a means for engaging in virtuous activity, it hardly seems necessary for that purpose, as Aristotle acknowledges when he observes that "private people" (ἰδιῶται) who do not engage in politics are no less able to act virtuously than people in power, and perhaps even more so (*EN* 10.8.1179a3–8). Though shared rule might be the best way to ensure that the rulers do not abuse their power, rulers would not treat the ruled unjustly simply by excluding them from participation. Just and correct political rule must be exercised for the sake of the ruled, but it is unclear why that should entail allowing the ruled to share in rule.

---

[64] Strauss 1953, Arendt 1958, MacIntyre 1984, Taylor 1985, Nussbaum 1990b, Sandel 1998. For a succinct and informative overview of Aristotelian and non-Aristotelian critiques of liberalism, see Collins 2006: 6–41, though I am otherwise in deep disagreement with much of Collins's book. Aristotle's thought has also served in defenses of quite different versions of "liberalism," e.g., Salkever 1990, Rasmussen and Den Uyl 2005.

One suggestion has been that Aristotle's conception of ruling and being ruled "in turn" or "in part" (ἐν μέρει, κατὰ μέρος) would in fact apply to situations in which those who are ruled do not themselves occupy any form of office. Such citizens can be said to rule "in part," and their rulers can be said to be ruled "in part," because the interests of the ruled influence what the ruler does in exercising his rule. Thus Nichols:

> The phrase "in turn," *en merei*, also means "in part." Political rule is partial rule in that it recognizes that the ruled is a free or independent being. This means that the ruled is both similar to the ruler, unlike the slave who is defined as radically unlike his master, and also distinct from him, again unlike the slave who is an extension of the master, an article of his property. Where independence and distinction exist there are limits. The ruled has an integrity that the ruler must take into account, unlike the case of despotism. The ruled thus influences what the ruler does.[65]

On this view, I can accurately be described as ruling in part even when I do not hold any office, limited or otherwise, and even when I will not hold such an office in the future. Those who exercise rule over me, likewise, are ruled in part by me because their decisions are limited and conditioned by their recognition that I am a free and independent person whose interests they should be aiming to promote. Whatever one thinks of this proposal as a piece of political philosophy, it is inconsistent with what Aristotle says about rule.

On the one hand, the ruled citizen whom Nichols envisions would not participate in deliberation and judgment leading to the formulation of binding decisions. He would therefore not be exercising rule even in part, if the interpretation of ruling that I laid out previously is correct. On the other hand, whether or not that interpretation is correct, Nichols's reading fails to account for the distinctive character of political rule. As her appeal to the contrast between free and slave suggests, what she describes more accurately applies to the distinction between despotic rule or mastery and rule over free people. But, as Aristotle insists, rule over the free is not all of one kind. Nichols's characterization of ruling and being ruled "in part" would be more aptly taken as a characterization of ruling for the sake of the ruled; the recognition of the ruled's independence and the influence it has on the ruler's actions are already a feature of a father's rule over his children.[66] But Aristotle

---

[65] Nichols 1992: 29. Trott 2013: 152 endorses this view.
[66] This point may be obscured by Aristotle's claim that children, like slaves, are "parts" of their parents (*EN* 5.6.1134b8–12). But whether we suppose that children become "separate" at a relatively early

never describes parents and children as ruling and being ruled by turns or in part. Children do not share in rule; citizens do.

The conflation of paternal and political rule entailed by Nichols's account does, however, point in the direction of a more satisfactory answer to the question I have been addressing. Another way of formulating that question is to ask why a form of paternal rule over free adult males would be unjust. The father's rule over his children is just because his exercise of authority is necessary if both he and his children are to achieve the good for the sake of which their community exists; the child's psychological and moral development requires that he be subordinated to his father's rule without sharing in rule himself. For mature adults, however, to be under that kind of authority not only is unnecessary, but precludes the exercise of their own deliberative faculties in deciding how they will live. To be ruled without sharing in rule is for one's actions to be guided by the decisions of others and not one's own.

Exclusion from political rule would not leave the ruled without any opportunity to make their own decisions. It would, however, entail that they have no active role in shaping the decisions that are supposed to be binding on them and that determine the political conditions under which they live. But living well requires living in accordance with one's own deliberate decisions (*Pol.* 3.9.1280a31–4, *EN* 1.7.1098a16–18, 2.6.1106b36–1107a2, 2.5.1106a3–4, 3.3.1113a2–14, 6.2.1139a22–b5; cf. 3.5.1113b3–6, 5.5.1134a1–2). To be deprived of any role in determining the decisions that structure and guide one's life and actions is, in effect, to be treated as a slave: Even if others seek to decide how I will live with my own best interests in mind, I cannot actually live well if those decisions are not my own. Of course, to be subjected to despotic rule is to be ruled for the sake of the ruler rather than for one's own benefit, and so it might seem that a misguided but benevolent ruler would not be guilty of ruling despotically so long as he had what he takes to be his subjects' best interests in mind. But whatever his motivations, anyone with a conception of the human good so deficient as to omit the role of self-direction and choice could not genuinely benefit others by ruling them.

It is important to add several qualifications to the preceding account in order to avoid the misleading impression that Aristotle was a kind of protolibertarian.[67] First, for Aristotle, living in accordance with one's own

---

age or only when they reach full maturity, their potential independence makes all the difference between children and slaves.

[67] For the view that Aristotle *was* a protolibertarian of sorts, albeit inconsistently, see Keyt 1993, Long 1996.

decision is not to be identified with doing what one wants. That sort of ideal, which Aristotle associates with the "democratic" conception of freedom, is incompatible with an objective account of human well-being; living by one's own decisions is necessary, but by no means sufficient, for living well (*Pol.* 5.9.1310a28–36, 6.2.1317b11–17). Second, and crucially, living in accordance with one's own decision does not entail freedom from rule. Though a free adult male may be treated unjustly if he is deprived of any share of rule, this is not because being ruled is inherently oppressive or an obstacle to the pursuit of one's own good that requires compensation in the form of gaining a share in rule. Being ruled is an essential component of living under laws, and it is law, more than the opportunity for virtuous acts of nobility and grandeur, to which Aristotle ascribes the importance of political community for living well (1.2.1253a29–39, *EN* 10.9.1179b23–1180a24). For being ruled by laws is necessary for all but the most extraordinarily virtuous human beings to live in ways that are conducive to the common good of the communities apart from which we could not live well at all. Yet we can likewise not live well if we do not live in accordance with our own decisions.[68] Sharing in rule is a requirement of justice in politics not because it is a second best to not being ruled at all, but because it is only by cooperative sharing and interaction with others that we can achieve our personal and common good. By contrast, to subject others to my command without any regard for their own judgment and deliberation is not to cooperate with them, but to deprive them of the exercise of their freedom.

If this account of the value of sharing in rule is correct, it explains why having a share in deliberation and judgment is a necessary condition of justice in political communities even though activities such as participating in the assembly, serving on jury courts, or holding limited offices are not intrinsically valuable and worthy of choice primarily for their own sake rather than for the sake of goods external to those activities. Aristotelian citizens need not be high-minded analogues of Aristophanes' chorus of wasps, obsessed with the pleasures of cooperative deliberation

---

[68] Aristotle thus rejects a prominent modern view when he holds that living in accordance with one's own decisions not only is compatible with, but even requires, living under an expansive system of strong laws. The assumption that he seems to reject, or perhaps not to consider, is that the value of living by our own decisions depends on our freedom from coercive norms designed to direct us to choose to live a certain kind of life. One thing he does *not* think is that living according to one's own decisions is possible if we have no significant options among which to choose. But it is at least not implausible to suppose that our well-being does not depend on our liberty to choose to live in ways that are not conducive to our well-being, even if that well-being necessarily includes self-direction as a prominent component. I return to these issues in Chapter 6.

rather than with the delights of exercising power over others. Yet this reading raises a question about how expansive a share in rule needs to be in order to meet the standards of justice. If justice requires that each free adult male be permitted to participate in the institutions that exercise the highest authority in the city, then Aristotle's ideal will look like a form of democracy and his endorsement of apparently exclusionary constitutional arrangements such as kingship, aristocracy, and even polity will be incompatible with his theory of justice. If, however, sharing in rule admits of degrees ranging from issuing decisions about the most general rules in the community to formally endorsing or rejecting the proposals of others, then Aristotle's theory of political justice might be compatible with various forms of polity, aristocracy, and even kingship itself. In the next chapter, I turn to Aristotle's constitutional theory and argue that it has just these implications.

CHAPTER 5

Citizenship, Constitutions, and Political Justice

Chapter 4 argued that Aristotle's account of political community and justice requires that naturally free adult males not be ruled despotically. Furthermore, attempts to rule such people even in their own interests without according them a share in rule amount, in effect, to ruling them despotically. Since sharing in rule is what it is to be a citizen, it follows that justice requires the enfranchisement of all free adult males.

On its face, this story is obviously too simple. It is, for instance, presumably not unjust for citizenship to be withheld or rescinded from certain sorts of criminals and others who aim to subvert the common good of the city, even though they are naturally free adult males. More pressingly, justice cannot require cities to give a share in rule to their allies, to foreigners, or even to all resident aliens. Yet cases of this kind perhaps do not present counterexamples or exceptions to the rule, since it is not obvious that people in these categories must be ruled despotically by virtue of being barred from participation in rule. Metics, foreign visitors, and allies all remain free to accept or reject the city's requirements even though they have no formally recognized role in shaping the formulation and application of those requirements; if they object to the city's decisions or find their involvement with the city detrimental to their own interests, they can withdraw.[1] Permanent or native inhabitants, by contrast, cannot react to unfavorable circumstances by going back home; they *are* home. In other words, Aristotle might hold that metics and other foreigners involved with a city do not suffer injustice when that city allots them no share in rule, because metics and other foreigners are not subject to rule in the same way as permanent or native inhabitants.

Cases like these show that Aristotle's theory, as I have so far presented it, requires elaboration and qualification if it is to serve as a guide to assessing

[1] I discuss metics more fully in Section 2.

the justice of specific political arrangements. In itself, however, the need for elaboration poses no objection to the basic adequacy of the principle or to the interpretive plausibility of its claim to represent Aristotle's thought. Yet when we turn to Aristotle's discussions of specific constitutional arrangements, it may seem as though he could not possibly have intended to maintain, even with these qualifications, that justice requires all free adult males to be granted a share in rule. When he classifies generic constitutional types as "correct" and just or "deviant" and unjust, he denies that the number of people who rule supplies a criterion of correctness or deviance. Correct constitutions are those in which the rulers rule with a view to the common good (*Pol.* 3.6.1279a17–21). In some circumstances, monarchy or rule by the few could only be unjust, because those circumstances are such that those forms of rule could not promote the common good. Nonetheless, aristocracy and kingship – the "correct" counterparts to the deviant oligarchy and tyranny – are not only possible, but even in some sense "best" (3.18.1288a32–7, 4.2.1289a30–b1). Yet the principle that all free adult males should share in rule seems to entail that neither kingship nor aristocracy could conceivably be just, or at least not ideally just. Even polity, the correct version of the deviant democracy, may not extend citizenship to all free adult males (2.6.1265b26–9, 3.7.1279b2–4, 5.6.1306b6–9). The "best constitution" of book 7, whose status as a form of polity or of aristocracy has been the subject of widespread disagreement, infamously treats citizenship as incompatible with the occupations of manual labor and even of farming (7.9.1328b33–1329a2).[2] In short, there is abundant evidence that Aristotle is nothing like the egalitarian that he would have to be if he were to believe that granting a share in rule to all free adult males is even a qualified and defeasible requirement of justice.

In this chapter, I will argue that Aristotle's theory of correct and deviant constitutions is in fact consistent with, and even requires, the principle that all naturally free adult male permanent inhabitants of a city should be granted a share in rule. The principle is an application of the broader injunction against ruling free people despotically; political exclusion is unjust in a wide range of cases because it entails unjust despotic rule. This claim seems implausible when coupled with prominent interpretations of

---

[2] On the problems with identifying the best constitution of bks. 7–8 as either an aristocracy or a polity, see esp. Rowe 2000, Kraut 2002: 359–61. Schofield 1999b: 110 calls it an "ideal aristocracy" (cf. Kraut 2002: 231, note 72). Everson 1988: 90 even claims that the best constitution is a form of democracy; since this cannot be true in the sense that Aristotle uses that term, Everson's view is more charitably read as taking the best constitution to be a kind of polity.

Aristotle's account of citizenship and of the theory of correct and deviant constitutions. It is, accordingly, significant that these interpretations are widely thought to yield serious difficulties for the coherence of Aristotle's political philosophy quite independently of questions about whether he accepts the principle of justice that I have attributed to him.

On the standard reading, the theory of constitutions is taken to be inconsistent with the formal definition of citizenship in *Politics* 3.1. While the theory of constitutions makes correctness a function of the rulers' aiming at the common good of the citizens, the definition of citizenship makes the citizen body and the ruling class coextensive. The distinction between correct and mistaken constitutions is therefore inapplicable to monarchy and to rule by the few, since in either case the ruling class cannot seek its own interest at the expense of the common good of the citizens; rather, the good of the ruling class and the good of the citizen class are identical. We can resolve this problem, I argue, by recognizing that the interpretations that generate the apparent incoherence are far from compelling and that there are more plausible alternatives that do not make a mess of Aristotle's theory. This solution also shows how all three of Aristotle's generic types of correct constitution can respect the defeasible principle of justice that requires all free adult males to be permitted to share in rule.

To make good on this argument, I first present the apparent inconsistency between Aristotle's theory of constitutions and his account of citizenship as it has been most prominently formulated. I then consider some plausible and influential solutions that scholars have proposed and argue that none of these proposals is satisfactory. For all their differences, they all approach the problem by focusing on Aristotle's definition of citizenship. By contrast, the initial characterization of the theory of constitutions goes relatively unexamined. Yet the interpretation of the theory that spawns worries about its consistency with the definition of citizenship has weak textual support and counterintuitive implications that Aristotle decisively rejects. In its place, I elaborate a more satisfactory interpretation that sets the theory of constitutions squarely within Aristotle's theory of justice; this reading goes a long way toward dispelling the apparent contradiction between the theory of constitutions and the account of citizenship.

With that interpretation in place, I then turn to the account of citizenship itself. I argue that Aristotle's considered definition of citizenship lacks the troublesome implications that others have found in it. Most crucially, I show that the definition does not entail that the citizen body and the ruling class are coextensive. Aristotle's descriptions of real and hypothetical constitutions show that sharing in rule admits of degrees. The concluding portion of this chapter then shows that on this understanding of citizenship, aristocracy and monarchy can be correct constitutions without violating the principle that free adult male inhabitants should share in rule. These constitutional arrangements are not best understood as limiting citizenship to one or a few individuals, but as granting them the most authoritative positions without depriving others of a share in rule. I argue that Aristotle's treatment of justice in the distribution of political authority directly prohibits the outright exclusion of the free multitude in an aristocracy or a kingship. Though it is unclear whether his constitutional recommendations consistently meet the standards of justice that he endorses, Aristotle's theories of citizenship and of just and unjust constitutions give rise neither to the normative nor to the conceptual problems of monarchy.

1. Citizens and Constitutions: Problems and Proposed Solutions

One of the central aims of the *Politics* is to develop a descriptive and normative theory of the varieties of possible political arrangement or constitution (πολιτεία).[3] Since every city must be arranged in some way or other, political theory will have very little to say if it restricts itself to considering the city or political community in the abstract. If the inquiry is to have the practical import that Aristotle envisions for it, a theory of constitutions will be among its most crucial components. For the practical science of politics will work principally on the constitutional level rather than on the ground level of everyday political decisions (see esp. *Pol.* 4.1.1288b10–1289a25), identifying which arrangements would be best in different circumstances rather than determining whether the city should increase its grain imports, go to war with its neighbors, or find Mantitheus guilty of assault.[4] In books 4–6, Aristotle expands his treatment of

[3] One indication of the centrality of constitutions to Aristotle's concerns in the *Politics* is that all of the books, with the single exception of book 1, introduce their topics by appeal either to their relevance to the study of constitutions or to the importance of that study for an understanding of political community.

[4] Political science can, of course, offer insight into particular policy decisions, but it can no more supply wholly determinate decision procedures for first-order political deliberation than phronesis can for individuals. An Aristotelian statesman may be better able to deliberate about whether the city should increase its grain imports than someone who lacks his expertise, but there is no direct route from the general propositions of the *Politics* to particular policy decisions, which must be taken in light of a complex set of contingent particular circumstances. Discussions of phronesis rarely avert to the *Politics*, but the considerations should be largely the same. See, e.g., Wiggins 1975, Nussbaum

constitutions in order to account more fully for the actual and possible variety of arrangements. In book 3, however, the theory is more schematic and focused on general normative considerations.[5] Here the theory divides constitutions into six types on the basis of two familiar distinctions: first, the number of people who rule or have authority; second, whether or not those authoritative rulers exercise their authority with a view to the common advantage or for the sake of their own (3.6.1279a17–21, 7.1279a27–31). Constitutions in which the rulers seek the common good are "correct," while those in which they seek their own advantage are "mistaken" and are "deviations from the correct constitutions."

Thus the theory of correct and deviant constitutions rests on two relatively simple distinctions. It is easy to see that this theory provides no more than a general framework for thinking about constitutional arrangements. If nothing else, the rulers of cities may seek their own good and the common good in various proportions, and particular arrangements may unfairly privilege the ruling class to different degrees. Particular constitutions may therefore be more or less correct or deviant; the distinction does not serve as a basis for placing every particular city in one or the other mutually exclusive class. Yet even if we recognize the flexibility of the classificatory framework, a problem emerges when we ask just whose good a correct constitution is supposed to seek. The common good apparently does not include the good of all the human beings who inhabit the city's territory; it seems to exclude slaves and metics, and perhaps even free but disenfranchised laborers. In the few passages where Aristotle explicitly articulates the subject of the common good, he seems to define it as the common good of the citizens (3.7.1279a31–2, 13.1283b40–2). This limitation of the common good to the good of the citizens appears to cohere with the exclusion of both free and unfree human beings that Aristotle recognizes and endorses throughout the *Politics*. It also seems to fit well with a common understanding of Greek conceptions of citizenship as a matter of belonging to or sharing in the common life of the city broadly

1990c, Broadie 1991: ch. 4. This is so even if Garver 2011 is right to think that political science can offer more concrete guidance to would-be statesmen than to individuals; the gap between principles and actions may be less wide in politics, but the gap remains nonetheless. Frede 2013 helpfully discusses the relationship between abstract principles and concrete decisions in politics.
[5] The extent to which books 4–6 depart from or modify the account in book 3 has been exaggerated. For a survey and critique of the view that the later books are "empirical" rather than normative or "utopian," see Rowe 1991; for a different view that nonetheless finds two distinct theories of constitutions, see Hansen [1993] 2013. For reasons to think that the account in books 4–6 is a complement rather than a revision of the account in book 3, see Riesbeck 2016. Rowe 2000 is a succinct and useful introduction to the theory of constitutions in the *Politics*.

construed: To be an Athenian or a Corinthian is to take part in and con-tribute to the public cultural life of Athens or Corinth, respectively.[6]

The view that the common good that matters for Aristotle's theory of constitutions is the good shared by the citizens and only by the citizens faces a serious problem: It is apparently incompatible with Aristotle's own official definition of citizenship. By that definition, a citizen is "one who is entitled to share in deliberative and judicial rule" (3.1.1275b18–21). Many scholars have argued that this definition of citizenship renders the theory of correct and deviant constitutions incoherent because it collapses the distinction between tyranny and kingship, on the one hand, and oligarchy and aristocracy, on the other.[7] The distinction cannot apply if we read it in terms of the official definition of citizenship because that definition char-acterizes citizenship in terms of ruling. If to be a citizen is to rule, then the citizen class and the ruling class will be coextensive.[8] In a monarchy, then, the king will be the only citizen; for the king to rule in his own interest is, accordingly, for him to rule in the interest of the citizen body. Similarly, in a city ruled by the few, the small ruling class can promote the common good of the citizens solely by promoting its own good. The distinction between democracy and polity is unaffected, because when many rule it is possible for the majority to rule in its own interests at the expense of a minority. In all other cases, however, applying Aristotle's official defini-tion of citizenship to the theory of constitutions undermines the feature of that theory that is evidently intended to be of central importance. If Aristotle loses the distinction between correct and deviant constitutions, his theory is, by his own criteria, a failure.

John Cooper and David Keyt have independently developed a solution to this problem that has roots at least as far back as Newman's magisterial

---

[6] For an account of Greek citizenship along these lines drawn largely from and attributed to Aristotle, see Ostwald 1993. Whatever its merits as a description of actual Greek conceptions of what it meant to be a citizen, it is, as I will argue, to Aristotle's credit that he did not adopt it in his theory of cit-izenship, since it is too vague and indeterminate to distinguish citizens from metics, a distinction that was crucial at least to Athenian life. Did Lysias and his family fail to contribute to and share in the public life of Athens? Lysias 12 and book 1 of Plato's *Republic* suggest otherwise.

[7] Though Newman 1887–1902.i: 228–30 already identified the problem in the case of kingship, Cooper 1990 and Keyt 1993 have been the most influential recent discussions. Cooper 1990: 228 explicitly includes oligarchy and aristocracy as well as kingship and tyranny; Keyt 1993: 141 includes the former pair by implication; Morrison 1999: 144 echoes Cooper's explicitness, but elaborates the problem at greater length.

[8] Besides the works cited in the preceding note, this view of Aristotelian citizenship is taken by Miller 1995: 147–8, 212; Ober 1998: 301; Roberts 2000: 357; Kraut 2002: 285–6; Frede 2005: 170 (but cf. p. 173); Rosler 2005: 179–81; Collins 2006: 134; Garver 2011: 82.

commentary and has been adopted by other prominent scholars.[9] On the plausible assumption that Aristotle did not intend to deny the applicability of the correct/deviant distinction in cases of monarchy and rule by the few, they point to passages in which, they claim, he relies on a tacit conception of citizenship as encompassing all freeborn native inhabitants. Since in these passages Aristotle uses the term "citizen" more broadly than the official definition would warrant, it is reasonable to suppose that he uses it in this way when he characterizes correct constitutions as aiming at the common good of the citizens.[10]

So, for instance, in book 7 Aristotle claims that "a city is excellent [σπουδαία], at any rate, because the citizens who share in the constitution are excellent, and in our constitution [sc. the "best" constitution under theoretical construction in book 7] all the citizens share in the constitution" (7.13.1332a32–5). Not only does the phrase "the citizens who share in the constitution" seem to imply that there are some citizens who do not share in it; the additional observation that all of the best constitution's citizens share in it obviously supposes that the best constitution differs from others in this regard. Two other passages observe that a characteristic mark of tyranny distinguishing it from kingship is the tyrant's use of foreigners rather than citizens for his personal bodyguard (3.14.1285a24–7, 5.10.1311a7–8). Since both the king and the tyrant are the only people in their cities who meet the official definition of citizenship, the citizens whom the king employs as his guard must be citizens in some broader sense. By contrasting these citizens with foreigners, Aristotle implies that they are free native inhabitants. Furthermore, the formal definition of citizenship does not allow for female citizens unless those women share in rule, as they do in Plato's *Republic*. Yet Aristotle twice refers to female citizens without supposing that they share in rule (3.2.1275b33, 3.5.1278a28), showing that he recognizes some sense in which female citizens can be distinguished from free women who are not citizens. Donald Morrison notes another passage in which the term "citizen" appears to be used more broadly than the formal account would permit: In a description of different kinds of democracy, Aristotle observes that while some democracies require that officeholders meet a property qualification, in another kind

---

[9] Cooper 1990, Keyt 1993; both appeal to Newman 1887–1902.i: 228–30. Collins 2006 is one of the few recent works to reject any attempt to revise or extend Aristotle's official account of citizenship in response to this problem, but does not present a clear alternative solution to it.

[10] Cooper 1990 and Keyt 1993 both draw on Newman 1887–1902.i: 229, 324, 569–70 for these passages, though Keyt's list of examples is more expansive. See too Morrison 1999: 148–9.

of democracy "all the citizens who are of unimpeachable descent share, but the law rules; and another kind is where everyone shares in the offices if only he is a citizen, but the law rules" (4.4.1292a1–4). As Morrison puts it, "if to be a citizen is to have a share in the offices, citizenship cannot be used as an antecedent criterion or qualification for being granted a share in the offices. Aristotle must be using the term 'citizen' here in a broader sense."[11]

On the strength of these passages, Cooper and Keyt maintain that when Aristotle describes correct constitutions as promoting the common good of the citizens, he does so with this broader conception of citizenship in mind. On their view, the scope of the common good extends to all free native inhabitants and excludes only metics and slaves. Keyt labels all those free native inhabitants to whom Aristotle's official definition of citizenship does not apply "second-class citizens."[12] While all correct constitutions aim at the good of all the first- and second-class citizens, they differ in the number of people to whom they grant first-class citizenship: While a polity extends this status to most or all of the free adult male inhabitants, aristocracy reserves it for a few and kingship assigns it to one man only. No constitution, on this view, fails to have second-class citizens; even if all of the free adult male natives are first-class citizens, their wives are not and, in Aristotle's judgment, should not be. In every case, then, the standard of correctness for a constitutional arrangement is that the first-class citizens promote the common good of all the first- and second-class citizens together and do not subordinate the second-class citizens to their own interests. Call this *the second-class citizen solution*.

The attractions of this solution should be evident. Aristotle cannot have intended to limit the class of people whose good the rulers in a correct constitution must seek to the rulers themselves. Identifying a broader conception of citizenship that Aristotle sometimes apparently invokes explains his claim that correct constitutions aim at the common good of the citizens, and does not require us to suppose that he was blind to the obvious problem that emerges if the common good includes only those

---

[11] Morrison 1999: 149.
[12] Keyt 1993: 140. Johnson 1984 and Nichols 1992 in rather different ways defend interpretations of citizenship and of ruling and being ruled that would entail a distinction coextensive with Keyt's. Frede 2005: 173 also finds "a clear dichotomy between rulers and ordinary citizens," though this dichotomy is neither clear nor obviously consistent with her earlier claim (p. 170) that Aristotle "limits citizenship to those who *actively* participate in government" (emphasis original). I have criticized Nichols's reading in detail and noted points of disagreement with Johnson and Frede in Chapter 4; the argument that follows in the text here applies, mutatis mutandis, to these interpretations as well as to Keyt's.

who meet his official definition of citizenship. Yet this approach is not without difficulties. It is open to a variety of objections, and its ultimate consequence may not be to resolve the problem it identifies, but merely to reposition it, shifting the burden from the theory of constitutions to the theory of citizenship.

Morrison raises three forceful objections to the second-class citizen solution. First, even if Aristotle sometimes speaks of citizens in a sense broader than his official definition, the theory of constitutions laid out in book 3 comes on the heels of a lengthy argument intended to establish and defend that definition. We should, accordingly, expect him to use the term consistently with that account. Second, the passages cited as evidence of a broader conception of citizenship need not tell us anything about Aristotle's own views. Rather, Aristotle is aware that many cities operate with understandings of what it is to be a citizen that differ from his own, and in these descriptive or dialectical passages he uses the term as people in those cities would use it. Consequently, they provide no evidence that Aristotle ever adopts an alternative conception of citizenship. Finally, though the distinction between correct and deviant constitutions requires Aristotle to think of the common good as extending beyond the ruling class, we are not thereby justified in reading any precise or systematic views into the text. We should not suppose that he meant to confine the scope of the common good to the rulers, but neither should we conclude that he had some self-conscious alternative account of citizenship in mind.

Each of these objections can, with some qualification, be expanded and strengthened to cast further doubt on the adequacy of the second-class citizen solution. To take the first and third objections together, it is important to observe that the proposed solution rescues the theory of constitutions from a somewhat superficial inconsistency at the cost of rendering Aristotle's official theory of citizenship not only inadequate to his task, but inconsistent with what he allegedly believes. The account of citizenship elaborated in the first five chapters of book 3 treats sharing in rule as a necessary and sufficient condition for citizenship. Children and old men may be recognized as citizens in a qualified sense because the former will share in rule when they reach adulthood and the latter already have shared in rule but no longer do so (3.1.1275a14–19). Similar considerations apply to people who have been exiled or deprived of their citizenship (3.1.1275a20–2). In all of these cases, however, the senses in which the people in question are and are not citizens are to be explained by reference to their past or future participation in rule. Nothing of the sort is true of free native inhabitants who neither have nor are expected in the future to share in rule. If Aristotle simultaneously held a broader conception of citizenship that included such people, then his formal account would be inconsistent with his actual view. Positing the recognition of "second-class citizens," then, entails the failure of Aristotle's theory of citizenship in its own terms. It is not simply that if Aristotle had adopted the broader conception, then, as Morrison puts it, "he probably would have recognized the conflict between that definition and his earlier one, and tried to fix it."[13] More pressingly, Aristotle explicitly considers the possibility of counting people who do not share in rule as citizens, and he rejects it.

2.   Aristotle's Rejection of "Second-Class Citizens"

In *Politics* 3.5, Aristotle turns from the account of citizen virtue developed Chapter 3.4 to address a puzzle that might arise for his theory of citizenship: "Is a citizen really someone who is entitled to share in rule, or should artisans [βαναύσους] be considered citizens?" (*Pol.* 3.5.1277b34–5) This chapter has been misunderstood by scholars who have read it as principally concerned to determine whether people who engage in certain kinds of wage earning should be permitted to participate in politics.[14] The formulation of the question quoted previously makes clear, however, that "artisans" are supposed to pose some problem for the definition of a citizen as someone entitled to share in rule.[15] Yet neither a positive nor a

---

[13] Morrison 1999: 150.

[14] See especially Robinson 1962: 18, Johnson 1984, Kraut 2002: 369, Frede 2005: 176, Garsten 2013: 336. Ober 1998: 315 is closer to my reading, but still sees 3.5 as devoted to the question of whether βαναυσοι and θῆτες should be citizens. Nagle 2006: 121 concludes that "the discussion [of 3.5] ends without a resolution of the problem," presumably because he takes the problem to be whether βαναυσοι and θῆτες should be citizens; there is indeed no unequivocal answer to that question in 3.5, but that is because it is not the problem that the chapter is addressing. Keyt 1993: 141 appears to read 3.5 as a continuation of the definitional question, but concludes that βαναυσοι and θῆτες are "second-class citizens"; my argument earlier aims to show, to the contrary, that 3.5 is rejecting any such category.

[15] "Artisans" is an unsatisfactory translation of βαναυσοι, but perhaps less misleading than Reeve's "vulgar craftsmen" or Simpson's "vulgar mechanics." Both translators opt for "vulgar" to capture the connotation of the term's frequent application to forms of labor taken to be demeaning or ignoble: e.g., *Pol.* 8.2.1337b12–14: "We call the sorts of crafts that put the body in a worse condition '*banausic*,' and likewise works that earn wages." Nagle 2006: 119–20 observes that the term generally distinguishes artisans whose work was considered "such as to impede the development of both their bodies and minds"; thus βαναυσοι are often discussed together with θῆτες, who possessed insufficient land and so "had to supplement their income by seasonal work." βαναυσοι and θῆτες both devote the bulk of their time and energy to forms of work that are not choiceworthy for their own sake and the products of which principally benefit others to the detriment of the worker. βαναυσοι, however, practice some kind of craft, whereas θῆτες merely labor for others. As Nagle notes, in other contexts the term apparently describes anyone who practices a craft professionally.

negative answer to the question of whether artisans or anyone else should be granted citizenship poses any difficulty for that definition; both answers could, in fact, presuppose that definition. When Aristotle asks whether artisans should be considered citizens, the "should" does not introduce the normativity of political justice, but the normativity of concept application: "Should artisans be considered citizens?" is a question like "Should whales be considered fish?" or "Should international law be considered law?"[16] Artisans pose an apparent problem for Aristotle's definition of citizenship because at least some of them fail to meet that definition but do not clearly fall into any other category or class of persons recognized in cities. The implicit suggestion is that they should be considered citizens even though they do not share in rule, and that consequently Aristotle's account of citizenship as sharing in rule and of the virtue of a citizen as including the virtue of ruling should be revised.

The passage continues:

> Now, if even those who do not share in offices [ἀρχῶν] should be considered [citizens], then it won't be possible for this sort of virtue[17] to be [the virtue] of every citizen, since this man [the artisan] will be a citizen. But if

---

Nagle's translation of βάναυσοι as "artisans" is inconsistent with his claim that 1258b26–7 asserts the existence of βάναυσοι ἀτεχνῖται, who provide merely brute bodily labor. There seems, however, to be insufficient warrant to understand an implicit repetition of βαναύσων in this passage, especially in light of 1278a24–5, which appears to assume that βάναυσοι are craftsmen (though the logic of the argument does not require the assumption that *all* βάναυσοι are craftsmen, that seems the most natural reading).

[16] When I describe the normativity of "should" in these questions as "the normativity of concept application," I by no means intend to suggest that the questions are a priori or a matter of mere conceptual truth; it was an empirical discovery that whales are not fish. For an argument that "law" is a natural-kind concept, see Murphy 2006: 17. These questions may seem ambiguous because we can ask whether, say, someone "should be considered" a member of our group, where what we are really asking is whether we have sufficient reasons to treat her as a member. This kind of question differs from the kind I am considering here because the latter, but not the former, can be rephrased without loss of meaning into forms such as "Are whales really fish?" "Is international law really law?" "Is a citizen really someone who shares in rule?" By contrast, when we discuss whether Carol should be considered a member of our reading group, we may simply be asking whether we should invite her to future meetings, and not whether she participates often enough to count as a member.

[17] One might find the appeal to "this sort" [τοιαύτην] of virtue mysterious if it seems that no virtue of any sort has just been referred to. But, in fact, the whole of 3.4 is devoted to giving an account of the virtue of a citizen, and that is the sort of virtue to which Aristotle is referring. The bare face of that account is, of course, less than luminous; hence my attempt to shine some light on it in the previous chapter. Aristotle explicitly tells us, however, that "this is the virtue of a citizen: knowing the rule of free men in both directions" (3.4.1277b15–16). Citizen excellence includes excellence in ruling actively, the excellence required for holding office or exercising rule; thus the reference to offices immediately preceding τοιαύτην makes it even more natural to understand that expression in this way. In any case, my interpretation of 3.5 in what follows should make my understanding of this formulation of the question apparent.

none of these sorts of people is a citizen, in what class should each of them be put? For he isn't a metic, nor is he a foreigner. (3.5.1277b35–9)

The challenge that this passage sets up for Aristotle's theory of citizenship has often been misunderstood. The claim that the account of citizen virtue will not apply to artisans has been taken to rest on the view, which Aristotle endorses later in the chapter (3.5.1278a20–1), that people who engage in certain kinds of unleisured occupations are unable to develop and exercise the virtues. Read in this way, the problem that Aristotle is posing may seem to be that since laborers cannot acquire or exercise the virtues of citizenship as he has described them, permitting them to be citizens will make it impossible for all of the citizens to be good citizens. Since he goes on to say that no artisans will be citizens in the best constitution, but that they may be citizens in other constitutions, we seem to receive a solution to the problem so construed: Artisans should not be citizens if the city aims at virtue, but in the inferior constitutions that do not aim at virtue, artisans may be capable of performing their tasks as citizens well because those tasks will be less ethically demanding. This way of interpreting the chapter – call it the *normative interpretation* – errs on the level of form rather than matter, as it were; while it does not attribute to Aristotle any claims that he rejects, it misidentifies the role that those claims play in the structure of the argument and the question that they serve to answer.[18]

The conclusion that Aristotle is not here asking who should and should not be a citizen does not rest solely on the consideration that neither answer to that question would raise any problems for his definition of citizenship. The first horn of the dilemma posed in the passage quoted clearly supposes that the artisans in question do not share in rule. The definition of citizenship would thus fail to apply to them, and so too would the account of citizen virtue. The trouble is not that artisans cannot develop virtue and so are unfit for citizenship. It is, rather, that since they do not share in rule, no account of what it is to be an excellent citizen can require

---

[18] In presenting the interpretation that I oppose, I have tried to be charitable in formulating a plausible reconstruction of what might lie behind various scholarly obiter dicta about the chapter (in, e.g., Robinson 1962, Kraut 2002, Frede 2005, Nagle 2006): Because of its discussion of the status of βάναυσοι and θῆτες in the best constitution, the chapter is often assimilated to 7.9.1328b33–1329a2, and hence suffers somewhat from lack of attention to its overall structure and context. In any event, I regard the argument sketched previously as the strongest available defense of the normative interpretation (though cf. Kraut 2002: 369: "A craftsman or a farmer cannot be a good citizen of *any* city"; for reasons to reject that claim, see Rosler 2005: 23, though Rosler overstates Aristotle's interest, in 3.1–5, in determining who *ought* to be a citizen).

excellence in ruling, and hence practical wisdom, if such people are to be counted as citizens. Call this understanding of the problem that the chapter raises the *definitional interpretation*. In favor of this interpretation, the formulation of the first condition makes evident that the picture of citizen virtue in *Politics* 3.4 will be threatened only if people who do not share in rule are considered citizens. If, by contrast, Aristotle were concerned at this point with whether artisans can be good citizens, he would not present the worry in this way, since the problem would arise in the case of artisans who actually share in rule and would not be contingent on counting those who do not share in rule as citizens.

Two other considerations suffice to show that the aim of 3.5 is not to answer the normative question of inclusion and exclusion, but to defend the account of citizenship and citizen virtue against objections. First, to say that the virtue of a citizen consists in the ability both to rule and to be ruled well (3.4.1277b13–16) is not to say that everyone who is actually a citizen possesses this virtue. It is, rather, to say that this is the virtue that any citizen will exercise to the extent that he performs the tasks of citizenship well. Though this point may seem too obvious to mention, it has the important implication that a person's inability to develop and exercise these virtues has no bearing on whether he is or is not a citizen. Though such a person may not deserve to be a citizen, Aristotle has already urged his audience to distinguish between questions of justice and the definitional question that he has set out to answer (3.2.1275b36–1276a6). Thus when he says that if those who do not share in rule are citizens "it will not be possible for this sort of virtue to be [the virtue] of every citizen" (3.5.1277b35–7), he does not mean that some citizens will be unable to perform the tasks of citizenship well. He means, rather, that what he has just described as the virtue of a citizen – ruling and being ruled well – will not in fact be a true account of what it is to be a good citizen, since ruling will not be essential to citizenship.[19]

---

[19] For an analogy, compare the claims that (i) practical wisdom is a human virtue and that (ii) practical wisdom is a mammalian virtue. The second claim is false because not all mammals are rational animals, whose achievement of their good is both instrumentally and intrinsically tied up with reasoning well: The problem is not that nonrational animals cannot be virtuous because they are not rational, but that practical wisdom cannot be a virtue of a nonrational animal. It cannot be the virtue of a nonrational animal because reasoning plays no part in the "function" or "work" (ἔργον) of a nonrational animal, and a virtue is what enables anything – an animal, an instrument, a functional role such as citizenship – to perform its function well (*EN* 2.6.1106a14–21; cf. the superb treatment of this point in Lawrence 2006). Thus we should say that practical wisdom is the virtue of some mammals or of a certain kind of mammal, namely, the rational ones, but cannot be a virtue of every mammal. If people who do not share in rule are citizens, Aristotle's account of citizen virtue would be guilty of precisely this sort of mistake.

The second point in favor of reading 3.5 as a defense of the accounts of citizenship and citizen virtue rather than as a premature entry into questions of justice is that the central moves of the argument and the conclusion itself focus on whether or not artisans and others are in fact citizens, not on whether they should be. When he turns to offer a resolution to the problem, Aristotle appeals to the diversity of constitutional arrangements and their varied criteria for citizenship. The consequence of this variety is that

> in one sort of constitution it is necessary that the artisan and the hired laborer[20] be citizens, but in others it is impossible. For example, if there is a constitution which we call aristocracy and in which the honors of office [αἱ τιμαί] are assigned in accordance with virtue and merit, [then it will be impossible for the artisan and the hired laborer to be citizens], since it is not possible to engage in the pursuits of virtue while living the life of an artisan or a hired laborer. In oligarchies it is not possible for a hired laborer to be a citizen, since sharing in the offices requires large property assessments, but it is possible for an artisan to be a citizen, since many craftsmen are rich. (3.5.1278a17–25)

In other words, part of the answer to the question raised at the beginning of the chapter – should artisans be considered citizens? – is, it depends. In actual cities, the status of the artisans and the hired laborers varies: In some it is impossible for them to be citizens; in others it is possible; and in still others they will necessarily be granted citizenship. Aristotle's account of citizenship can accommodate this diversity because in each case the artisans are citizens when they are entitled in their cities to share in rule and are not citizens when they are not so entitled. Since his characterization of citizen virtue follows his account of a citizen as someone who rules and is ruled, the varied status of artisans in cities does not undermine the adequacy of his theory of citizenship.

This aspect of Aristotle's solution to the problem only takes us so far. The challenge for the definition of citizenship as sharing in rule was, in the first instance, to determine what should be said about artisans who do not share in rule: Since they do not share in rule, they will not be citizens on Aristotle's account, but they are also not metics or foreigners. The real threat to the theory as he has developed it is not that artisans are

---

[20] "Hired laborer": θής. Nagle 2006: 119 argues against the common view that θῆτες are "propertyless day-laborers," preferring to describe them as "small holders" instead. But even if all θῆτες owned some land, their status is determined primarily by their need to work for others because of the insufficiency of their land. Hence "hired laborer" seems to me a more illuminating translation, at least in this context, and even Nagle himself uses it (120 note 97).

citizens in some constitutions and not in others. It is, rather, that in at least some of those cases where they do not share in rule, they are free, permanent native inhabitants of the city. As such, it might seem that they should be considered citizens, since they plainly do not fall into any of the other categories of person regularly recognized in cities. To defend the account of citizenship that he has just developed, Aristotle must deny that such people are citizens, and this is the thesis that the rest of the chapter's claims are intended to support.

The basic argument is quite simple: There is nothing strange about denying that some artisans are citizens despite their performance of important work, since we already make this denial in other cases (3.5.1277b39–1278a3). In some instances, the work performed by artisans is in fact carried out by slaves or foreigners (3.5.1278a6–7); in other cases, these artisans are free and share in rule, while in still other cases they may share in rule if they meet the property assessment, and in still other cases they cannot possibly share in rule. The conclusion that those artisans who do not share in rule are not citizens even when they are not slaves, metics, or foreigners is no more awkward than the claim that metics are not citizens.[21] The final conclusion of the chapter thus reaffirms the definition of citizenship from 3.1: "It is clear from these things that there are many kinds of citizen, and that the one who shares in the honors of office is called a citizen most of all" (3.5.1278a34–6).[22]

As for those who do not share in rule, Aristotle revealingly says, "The man who does not share in the honors of office is like a metic" (3.5.1278a37–38). The free native inhabitants who do not share in rule are not metics, because they are permanent native inhabitants. But they are like metics because they do not share in rule despite dwelling in and contributing to the city.[23] If ever there were a place for Aristotle to

[21] Thus Nagle 2006: 121 is quite mistaken to conclude that the problem raised at the beginning of 3.5 is left unresolved.

[22] Newman 1887–1902.i: 241–2 supposes that βάναυσοι are citizens in some constitutions even without sharing in any form of rule or office. Hence he reads 3.5 as Aristotle's acknowledgment that his account of citizenship and citizen virtue does not apply universally. But what Aristotle says here is that βάναυσοι are citizens where they are citizens *because* they share in rule. I take the later claim that someone who shares in rule "is called a citizen most of all" to mean that *this* account of what a citizen is applies across different constitutions, in which more specific accounts could be relevant (cf. 3.4.1276b20–34). The alternative, that people to whom this account fails to apply are merely citizens in some mitigated way, is contradicted by what follows.

[23] The argument might seem question begging if its point is misunderstood. That point is, I take it, to show that Aristotle's account of citizenship does not generate or lack the resources to resolve the problem about how to classify laborers who neither meet its definition of citizenship nor fall into regularly recognized classes such as "metic" or "foreigner." The objection alleges that accepting Aristotle's definition leads to a dilemma that cannot be satisfactorily resolved without giving up

acknowledge a category of "second-class citizens" or a broader conception of citizenship encompassing all the free native inhabitants, this would be it. Yet so far from dubbing them citizens in some sort of secondary sense, he identifies such uses of the term as deceptive strategies for concealing political inequality: "Where this sort of thing [i.e., the meticlike status of those who do not share in rule] has been concealed, it is for the sake of deceiving the inhabitants" (3.5.1278a38–40). The second-class citizen solution, then, attributes to Aristotle a view that he rejects.[24]

This reading of 3.5 adds considerable weight to Morrison's objections to the second-class citizen solution. The theory of citizenship as sharing in rule is plainly a central thesis of the *Politics* to which Aristotle is committed. Attributing to him a broader conception of citizenship may shield his theory of correct and mistaken constitutions from consequences that he almost certainly does not intend or foresee, but it does so only by seeing it as tacitly relying on claims that are inconsistent with his overall theory and that he considers only to reject. Morrison is surely right to maintain that even if the distinction between correct and deviant constitutions presupposes a vision of the common good as including the good of people outside the ruling class, it is better to acknowledge that Aristotle failed to notice the problem than to adopt the second-class citizen solution. For that solution ascribes a self-consciousness to Aristotle's alleged alternative conception of citizenship that would make the third book of the *Politics* as a whole far more incoherent than it will seem if we allow that he misspoke and did not recognize it.[25]

---

that definition. Aristotle's response shows that the dilemma is not irresolvable in terms of the theory; it does not attempt to deflect an alleged counterexample by merely appealing to the definition that is in dispute.

[24] One reader has objected that the definitional interpretation of *Pol.* 3.5 is unprecedented. Though that objection seems hardly compelling, readers suspicious of novelty might note that the definitional interpretation evidently commended itself to Aquinas. Summarizing the problem that introduces the chapter, he writes: "But if it were to be said that none of these sorts of people is a citizen, the question will remain: In which category should artisans (*banausi*) be placed? For it cannot be said that they are foreigners, as if they were coming from elsewhere to reside in the city; nor that they are strangers, as if they were travelers who come to the city on account of some business and not for the sake of remaining. For craftsmen of this sort both have residence in the city and were born in the city, not coming from elsewhere" (*Commentary on Aristotle's Politics* 3.4, trans. mine).

[25] In fairness to Cooper, his comments on the problem could be read as suggesting not that Aristotle had some developed view of citizenship that included all free native inhabitants, but the far more plausible view – close to the one that I defend in due course – that the scope of the common good includes all free native inhabitants, and that Aristotle should never have suggested that the common good might be restricted to people who are already citizens. Keyt's more developed solution, by embracing the terminology of "second-class citizens," goes a good deal further in presenting Aristotle's actual view as incompatible with much of what the texts explicitly say.

Morrison's own preferred alternative, however, involves an even more extreme revision of Aristotle's official account of citizenship.[26] On this view, Aristotle recognizes all of the free inhabitants of a city, including metics, as citizens in a qualified sense. The formal definition of citizenship in 3.1, Morrison argues, gives an account of "full" citizenship, or what it is to be a citizen in the most complete sense, but allows that people may also count as citizens in a variety of derivative senses. Other free inhabitants, though they fall short of full citizenship because they do not share in rule, nonetheless count as citizens to various lesser degrees corresponding to the extent to which they "participate in the life of the city," understood as sharing in and contributing to the good life that is the city's purpose.[27] To be sure, Morrison does not think that Aristotle is entirely consistent on this point, that he draws on it in any systematic way, or that it fits tightly with the account of "full citizenship." Nonetheless, one virtue of Morrison's treatment of these problems is that the difficulties he finds with the theory of citizenship so interpreted are subtle and complex; it would not be surprising if even a thinker as careful as Aristotle were to fail to spot them. Because Morrison's reading does not attribute views to Aristotle that are in sharp and evident contradiction with what he says about citizenship in 3.1–5, it is more persuasive as a solution to the problem created by the apparent incompatibility of the theory of citizenship with the theory of constitutions.

Nonetheless, the argument of 3.5 discussed previously is sufficient to cast some doubt on the plausibility of the view that Aristotle sees people who do not share in rule as citizens in a lesser, qualified sense. If he held some such view, it is unlikely that he would describe cities that give the title of citizenship to people who do not share in rule as engaging in deception. Close attention to the passages that Morrison cites in favor of his conception of "degrees of citizenship" reveals little support for that interpretation. Before turning to those passages and to a different sense in which citizenship may be said to admit of degrees, however, it will be helpful to question one aspect of Morrison's approach to the problem that he shares with the scholars whose views he rejects. In each case, attempts to dissolve the tension between the theory of citizenship and the theory of constitutions focus almost exclusively on the theory of citizenship and leave the theory of constitutions relatively unexplored. Thus Morrison

---

[26] Morrison 1999: 161 makes clear that he does not take his own preferred solution to be Aristotle's consistent view, but one that the philosopher could take by further developing certain aspects of his conception of citizenship.

[27] Morrison 1999: 156–61.

examines seven potential solutions to the problem, none of which involves
any challenge to the initial characterization of correct constitutions as those
that promote the common good of the citizens. A careful consideration of
Aristotle's distinction between correct and deviant constitutions will show
that this characterization is misleading and that on the interpretation that
generates the most severe form of the problem, Aristotle does not embrace it.

3. Citizens and the Scope of the Common Good

Cooper, Keyt, and Morrison each attempt to resolve the difficulty that
follows from Aristotle's claim that correct constitutions promote the common good of the citizens if citizens are understood to be those who share
in rule. The problem, as they present it, emerges from the conjunction
of Aristotle's definition of citizenship and his distinction between correct
and deviant constitutions. Yet the idea that political justice requires the
city and its rulers to seek the common good *of the citizens* should raise
suspicions independently of either the official account of citizenship or
the division of constitutions into correct and deviant types. If Aristotle
had not sought to classify constitutional arrangements into neatly sym-
metrical pairs, it would pose no problem if a distinction between the
members of one or more of those pairs were unavailable. He might even
have chosen to forgo any talk of correct and deviant constitutional types
and maintained that a city is just to the extent that it promotes the common good and unjust to the extent that it does not. If, however, he were
then to describe the common good that the just city aims to promote
as the common good of the citizens, he would create a serious problem
for his theory of political justice. This problem would arise, moreover, on
any conception of citizenship that draws the boundary between citizens
and noncitizens more narrowly than that between a city's free permanent
inhabitants and its unfree or metic population. The problem, simply put,
is that Aristotle treats the distribution of citizenship as itself a matter of
political justice. If the demands of political justice were essentially determined by the promotion and protection of the common good of the citizens, then the scope of the citizen body would need to be determined
before questions of justice could be addressed. The inclusion or exclusion
of some of a city's free permanent inhabitants would, accordingly, admit
of no assessment in terms of political justice.[28] From the point of view of

---

[28] Ostracism and the revocation of a citizenship (ἀτιμία) are forms of exclusion that could be assessed
as just or unjust by appealing to considerations of the common good of the citizens even if the

political justice, the composition of the citizen body could be arbitrary. Yet Aristotle plainly does not think that it is.[29]

The thesis that justice requires the promotion of the common good of the citizens is therefore problematic even when considered in isolation from the details of Aristotle's theories of citizenship and of constitutions.[30] The situation only worsens when we take the theory of constitutions into account. When conjoined with the division of constitutional arrangements into correct and deviant types, the restriction of the common good to the citizens leads to a deeper difficulty than the apparent collapse of that distinction in some cases. So long as the operative sense of "citizenship" does not extend to all of the free permanent inhabitants, the claim suggests that no constitution could be deviant by virtue of whom it excludes from citizenship. Yet Aristotle's treatment of political justice in book 3 evidently supposes that a constitution can be deviant because it withholds citizenship from people to whom it ought to grant it.

To appreciate the greater severity of this problem in comparison to the purported inapplicability of the correct/deviant division, it is instructive to observe that there is no reason why that distinction should collapse

---

composition of the citizen body is antecedently determined. But precisely because both forms of exclusion represent a group's decision to expel one of its members, neither provides a satisfactory model for deciding whether to extend membership to someone who is not yet a member or for assessing the composition of the group as a whole. Aristotle considers ostracism in 3.13.1284a17–b34.

[29] One way for a theory of justice as the common good of the citizens to assess the justice of extending or withholding citizenship from some of a city's permanent free inhabitants without supposing that they are already citizens in some sense or other might run as follows: Any group of citizens, however arbitrarily its composition has been determined, may either promote or subvert its own common interests by extending membership to those who are currently excluded; if the inclusion of certain people in the citizen body would promote its common good, then it will be just; if it will hinder it, then exclusion will be just. Whatever the prospects for such a theory, it could not plausibly be ascribed to Aristotle. First, it is hard to see how the theory could sensibly describe the excluded parties as being treated justly or unjustly, since the good of the excluded party does not enter into the assessment of the justice of his exclusion. Second, it would represent groups that unjustly exclude others not as seeking their own good at the expense of the excluded, but as failing to promote their own good. Though Aristotle would agree that unjust rulers fail to promote their own real good, this is in part because being just is crucial for *eudaimonia*. If the content of justice were wholly determined by considering what promotes an agent's antecedently defined and strictly self-regarding interests, the thesis that justice is a virtue would be reduced to triviality. What both of these problems highlight is that a relation of justice must involve the distinct good of all of the parties to the relation; this aspect of justice explained why Aristotle denies that justice obtains, strictly speaking, in relations to oneself, one's property, one's slaves, and even one's children (for discussion, see Chapter 2). In view of these difficulties, I raise the possibility of a theory of this sort merely to lay it aside.

[30] Thus Newman 1887–1902.i: 216: "It must be confessed that Aristotle goes far to mar the principle when he confines the 'common advantage' which the constitution is to study to the common advantage of the citizens (3.13.1283b40), for he thus makes his requirement one which any oligarchy that chose to limit the number of the citizens might satisfy."

in the case of oligarchy and aristocracy. So long as the city is composed of a plurality of citizens, internal division remains possible. Even a few oligarchs could subordinate their common interests to their individual advantage and thereby make their rule deviant by treating one another unjustly (cf. *Pol.* 5.1.1302a8–11, 6.1305b22–39). Even on the assumption of identity between the ruling class and the citizen body, then, the distinction is applicable in all cases except monarchy. Yet monarchy, as we have seen, raises a variety of problems independent of this one. The sensible conclusion would therefore be to fault Aristotle's willingness to allow for the possibility of a just and correct form of monarchy, not to condemn his theory of constitutions or even the union of that theory with his definition of citizenship as sharing in rule. This response would, however, be inadequate, and not merely because it would leave Aristotle with a theory of political justice that fails to satisfy modern intuitions about the injustice of political exclusion. It would be inadequate, rather, because Aristotle does not judge oligarchy unjust simply because the oligarchs treat each other unjustly.

The brief discussion of 3.10 illustrates the range of concerns that Aristotle brings to his assessment of constitutions. Here he lays out a series of problems that arise for any straightforward answer to the question of "what the city's authoritative element [τὸ κύριον] should be" (3.10.1281a11). Since constitutions are distinguished in part by which group holds authority (3.7.1279a27–31, cf. 3.13.1283b5–8), this question is equivalent to asking which kind of constitution a city should have. The alternatives are limited: Either the multitude, the wealthy, the "decent" [ἐπιεικεῖς], the single best man, or a tyrant must have control. Yet each of these alternatives seems to involve difficulty. If the poor multitude has control, it may decide to seize and redistribute the property of the wealthy. Aristotle takes it as obvious that this kind of behavior would be unjust, and even "the ultimate injustice," on the grounds that it "destroys the city" and that "what is just is not destructive of a city" (3.10.1281a14–20). He then preempts the suggestion that the decision could be just because it was decreed by the city's authoritative element; the same consideration would justify the acts of a tyrant. The tyrant's coercive acts, judged by most to be paradigmatic of injustice, are backed by nothing more than his superior strength. Yet the same is true if the poor majority confiscates the property of the wealthy few (3.10.1281a21–4). This conclusion should give oligarchs no comfort, however, because giving control to the wealthy few does nothing to dispel the problem. For oligarchs, no less than democrats and tyrants, can unjustly plunder the possessions of others. If the same actions are to be just when carried out by the rich, then they must be just when carried out by the poor majority. But since the superior strength of the authoritative multitude no more justifies their coercive and destructive acts than the tyrant's power justifies his, the parallels point in the opposite direction: "It is clear that all these things are base and not just" (3.10.1281a24–8).

Aristotle's arguments in 3.10 are intended to stir up worries that the subsequent chapters aim to address rather than to establish any firm conclusions. Nonetheless, they make clear that inclusion in and exclusion from the controlling and authoritative element of the city are a central issue of political justice and that assessments of the justice of a constitutional arrangement are not limited to judgments about how well those in authority promote their own common good. Nor are Aristotle's concerns limited to the possibility that the people in authority will abuse their power in direct acts of injustice against their subjects. Rule by the "decent" or by "the one best man" might, *ex hypothesi*, evade that objection, since surely anyone who merits either of those descriptions will be at least sufficiently just to refrain from confiscating other people's possessions by force. Yet to grant such men a monopoly of authority would deprive all others of the honors that come with sharing in rule. Inclusion and exclusion are thus relevant to the assessment of a constitutional arrangement not only because the excluded may be treated unjustly as a consequence of their exclusion, but because the very fact of exclusion deprives them of the goods of inclusion.[31]

Aristotle's brief survey of some basic problems that any adequate theory of just constitutions must address is sufficient to show that he does not limit the scope of that justice to the good of the citizens, but includes the distribution of citizenship as a crucial question of justice.[32] Cooper, Keyt, and Morrison's formulation of the problem therefore misidentifies

---

[31] This is not to say that the goods of inclusion must be intrinsic goods; see Chapter 4. But while Aristotle's views about the value of the honors associated with sharing in rule and of honor more generally are somewhat obscure, his discussions of honor in the *EN* make clear that it is an intrinsic good (it is valued and chosen "for itself," *EN* 1.5.1095b22–3, 5.1096a5–9, 7.1097b2–4), though a superficial one (1.5.1095b22–30, 8.8.1159a16–27). Though its superficiality shows that a life devoted to it cannot be satisfactory, we should not conclude on those grounds that honor is unimportant.

[32] For this reason, the solution that Biondi Khan 2005 presents as an alternative to Keyt's and Morrison's is no more successful than theirs. She rightly emphasizes that Aristotle's definition of citizenship in terms of the entitlement to share in rule rather than actually ruling allows for a distinction between the ruling class and the citizen body; thus in a correct constitution the rulers will not seek merely their own common advantage, but the common advantage of themselves and everyone else who is entitled to share in rule. The trouble, however, is that this solution still leaves Aristotle unable to regard a constitution as deviant by virtue of whom it altogether excludes from citizenship. Trott 2013: 144 adopts a similar account, but confusingly says that "what follows from

the fundamental source of the apparent incoherence in Aristotle's theory of political justice as they read it. The collapse of the correct/deviant distinction would undermine Aristotle's account of monarchy, but not the theory of constitutions, and the limitation of the common good to the good of the citizens has counterintuitive implications that conflict with Aristotle's treatment of political justice quite independently of his official definition of citizenship. To be sure, the broader conception of citizenship that Cooper and Keyt find in scattered passages would resolve this difficulty in just the way that they suggest. But we have already seen reasons to reject their proposal. Morrison's alternative solution would fare better, since it allows even metics to count as citizens in the relevant sense. I will shortly argue against Morrison's interpretation of "degrees of citizenship" on independent grounds, but the fundamental issue of how we should understand the problem can be appreciated without taking a stand on the plausibility of any particular conception of citizenship. Cooper, Keyt, and Morrison all recognize that Aristotle does not in fact ignore the interests of all but the ruling class when considering the justice of constitutions. That recognition supplies their motivation for seeking a broader interpretation of citizenship. What my argument so far has aimed to show is that this very recognition should not lead, in the first instance, to a search for some idea of citizenship consistent with the claim that political justice promotes the common good of the citizens. It should, instead, lead us to reject altogether the limitation of the common good to the citizens.

This argument could hardly be successful if Aristotle were frequently explicit in describing the common good as the good shared by the citizens. It would, in that case, still be preferable to identify the restriction of the scope of the common good rather than the theories of citizenship and constitutions as the source of trouble. It would not, however, acquit Aristotle of inconsistency. Yet when we turn to the evidence offered for the view that Aristotle limits the common good in this way, it turns out to be in short supply.[33]

---

this account is that there would seem to be no members of the community who are not engaged in this activity that makes them citizens: deliberating."

[33] Biondi Khan 2005 is one of the few who have argued that the common good crucial to the distinction of correct from deviant constitutions is not only the common good of citizens. But to show that it extends beyond the citizens, she appeals only to passages that connect the common good of the city or the aim of the legislator to the virtue and well-being of noncitizens who are nonetheless members of citizen households. Yet one might suppose that these people – namely, citizen wives and children – fall within the purview of the common good because of their relationship to the citizens; the male children will become citizens themselves, and the women will play a crucial role in nourishing and educating future citizens. The sole passage Biondi Khan cites that appeals beyond

The passage that seems most clearly to limit the common good to the good of the citizens comes in the midst of a discussion in 3.13 about just grounds for rule. After noting that some people pose the question of whether "the most correct laws" aim at the advantage of better people or of the greater number, Aristotle pauses to consider how "correctness" (τὸ ὀρθόν) ought to be understood (3.13.1283b36–40). He continues:

> That which is correct in a fair and equal way [τὸ ἴσως ὀρθόν] is relative to the advantage [συμφέρον] of the whole city and to the common [advantage] of the citizens. Generally, the man who shares in ruling and being ruled is a citizen, but he differs in accordance with each constitution. But in relation to the best [constitution], the one who is able and deliberately chooses [προαιρούμενος] to be ruled and to rule with a view to the way of life that accords with virtue is a citizen. (3.13.1283b40–1284a3)

Because Aristotle maintains that a city is, in the strict sense, composed of its citizens, the expressions "the advantage of the whole city" and "the common advantage of the citizens" can be taken as equivalent.[34] Even so, the claims that immediately follow show that this description of correctness as what promotes the common good of the citizens should not be taken to exclude the composition of the citizen body from considerations of what is just and correct. As soon as he insists that correctness must be understood in relation to the common good of all of the citizens, Aristotle reminds his audience that one of the ways in which constitutions differ is in the criteria they recognize for admitting a person to citizenship. By then noting that the best constitution makes citizens of those who are able and willing to live the best kind of life, he makes it clear that a city's requirements for sharing in rule are central to its correctness and justice.[35] Thus this passage does not suggest that

---

citizen households is 3.1.1274b35–8, but this reference to "those who inhabit the city" precedes all the clarification of book 3 about what a city is and who citizens are. Hence, though I share her conclusion, I take her arguments to be insufficient, and I here aim to offer a more complete defense of our common position.

[34] The καί here at 1283b41 is reasonably read as epexegetic. For the identification of the city in the strictest sense with its citizens, see 3.1.1274b41, 7.4.1326b12–14.

[35] This characterization of the best constitution should not be understood as implying that it grants citizenship to anyone whatsoever who is willing and able to live according to its understanding of the best way of life, including foreigners, metics, and the like. Though it might be instructive to consider how the best constitution would or should respond to foreigners who petition it for membership on the grounds that they are able, willing, and eager to become its citizens, Aristotle nowhere explicitly considers the question. He may have assumed, quite plausibly, that these questions are a matter for deliberation in contingent and particular circumstances, and hence fall outside the scope of his inquiry. Similarly, the discussion of the virtues in the *EN* leaves many questions unaddressed because in Aristotle's view they admit of no informative general treatment and cannot be brought under a formulaic decision procedure. Hence Aristotle's failure to discuss these questions does not count against the view that the criteria for citizenship are essential to the justice and correctness of a constitution.

the only criterion of constitutional correctness and justice is whether a city promotes the good of those to whom it grants citizenship. On the contrary, it shows that the criteria of correctness and justice include the grounds on which the city grants people citizenship.[36]

The other prominent passage that has been cited as evidence that Aristotle restricts the scope of the common good to the citizens comes, appropriately, on the tail of his elaboration of the distinction between correct and mistaken constitutions at the opening of 3.7. Unfortunately, the passage is ambiguous, and its interpretation is complicated by the possibility that the text should be emended. I therefore begin by translating the text as emended by W. D. Ross. Immediately after a description of constitutions that aim at the common good as correct and those that aim at the advantage of their rulers as deviant, we read: "For either one should deny that those who do not share [τοὺς μὴ μετέχοντας] are citizens, or they should have a share of the benefit [κοινωνεῖν τοῦ συμφέροντος]" (3.7.1279a31–2). There are two difficulties. The first is the ambiguity of "those who do not share"; since the text does not explicitly supply an object, it is unclear whether we should understand "those who do not share in rule" or "those who do not share in the benefit." The second difficulty is that the manuscripts do not read "those who do not share," but rather "those who share"; the emendation is evidently motivated by the judgment that the reading of the manuscripts is either unintelligible or does not yield the appropriate sense.[37] Fortunately, I need not resolve

---

[36] Contrast the solution offered by Simpson 1998: 151–2 to the apparent incoherence of the correct/deviant distinction as Aristotle formulates it in 3.6–7: ruling for the advantage of all requires ruling with a view to the good life rightly understood, and rulers who have false opinions about the good life cannot be said to be ruling for the advantage of all even if the rulers believe that they are promoting the common good; when Aristotle says that deviant constitutions seek "the advantage of the rulers," he means that the rulers of a deviant constitution aim at the good as they (mis)understand it and work to exclude from rule all those who hold different opinions about the good life. But Simpson's reading requires him to equivocate on "the advantage of the rulers," implausibly shifting its sense from "what is in the interest of the rulers" to "what the rulers believe to be to the common advantage." Though we may grant that the rulers of a deviant constitution often mistakenly believe that they rule with a view to the common good, this feature of deviant rule does not require Simpson's reinterpretation of "the advantage of the rulers." We should instead interpret "the common good" and "the advantage of the rulers" *de re* rather than *de dicto*; what matters is not what the rulers think they are doing, but whether their rule promotes the common good or their own interests at the expense of the common good. This interpretation does not resolve the problem about the scope of the common good, but, as I argue presently, that problem can be addressed in other ways.

[37] Though these sorts of consideration provide the weakest kind of reason for emending a text, it should be noted that the hypothesized error admits of a straightforward explanation: τοὺς μὴ μετέχοντας becomes τοὺς μετέχοντας by haplography, one of the most common types of scribal error. Accordingly, if no acceptable sense can be given to the text as it stands, the proposed emendation is sufficiently plausible. It will become apparent that I do not believe that the manuscript

either of these issues here. Whether or not we accept the emendation, and however we construe the ambiguous phrase, the sentence is not plausibly read as restricting the scope of the common good to de facto citizens. On the contrary, it points in the opposite direction.

Suppose we accept the emendation and understand "those who do not share" as "those who do not share in rule." Aristotle's thought might then appear to be that a city's rulers should either take the nonrulers into consideration and allow them to "have a share of the benefit" or deny that they are citizens. If they do neither, but continue to call the nonrulers citizens without seeking their benefit, the constitution will be deviant; but if they choose either alternative, their rule will be just and correct. This reading would entail that the common good that matters is the good of the citizens, but it also implausibly supposes that a deviant and unjust constitution could be transformed into a correct one by a mere alteration of the rulers' linguistic practices. This reading fares no better if we substitute "the benefit" for "rule" as the object of "those who do not share." Rulers who use the label "citizens" for the disenfranchised subjects whose interests they subordinate to their own may add the injustice of deception to the injustice of oppression (cf. 3.5.1278a38–40, 2.5.1264a17–20), but there is no reason to suppose that Aristotle would think that honesty rectifies the injustice.

A more plausible interpretation of the passage sees the first alternative – that "one should deny that those who do not share are citizens" – not as one of two ways in which the rulers of a deviant constitution might straighten themselves out, as it were, but as the judgment that any reasonable person should pass on a constitution whose rulers promote their own good at the expense of the ruled: People subjected to the rulers of a deviant constitution are not even citizens, but are treated like slaves. Aristotle has, after all, already said that deviant constitutions are "despotic" because they rule free people as though they were slaves (3.6.1279a21). So understood, Aristotle is not here limiting the assessment of constitutions to their treatment of people whom they formally recognize as citizens. He is, instead, pointing to disenfranchisement as one of the signs of an unjust constitution.

Suppose, however, that we reject the emendation of "those who share" to "those who do not share," since it has no support from the manuscript tradition. The absence of an expressed object would then be

reading poses any insurmountable interpretive difficulty; hence I reject the emendation, but my argument does not depend on this point.

unproblematic, since supplying "the benefit" would undermine the evident contrast; it would make little sense to say "either one should deny that those who share in the benefit are citizens or they ought to share in the benefit." If, however, we supply "rule" as the object, the passage might appear to be affirming that it is only the common good of the citizens – those who share in rule – that matters for assessing constitutions: Since a just city seeks the common good of the citizens, those who share in rule should share in the benefit or we should deny that they are citizens. Rather than recommending a change in linguistic practice, the injunction to deny that such people are citizens would be a call to action: The city should actually disenfranchise those whom it does not intend to include within the scope of the common good. Though this interpretation is not altogether implausible on its face, its implications are obviously at odds with later chapters' treatment of justice in the distribution of citizenship. An alternative reading that avoids those implications would therefore be preferable. Fortunately, just such an alternative is available.

Admittedly, the unemended text speaks not of people who have been given no share in rule, but of people who share in rule and therefore meet the formal criterion of citizenship. Yet nothing prevents a city's rulers from treating some people who share in rule as though their welfare has no bearing on the common good. Democratic constitutions, as Aristotle depicts them in book 3, subordinate the interests of the wealthy few to the interests of the free majority (3.7.1279b9–10, 8.1279b34–1280a6). Wealthy people do not formally cease to be citizens; they may still participate in the assembly and the courts and may even exercise considerable influence.[38] But a democratic city can effectively exclude the minority from the common good by enacting policies that impose uncompensated losses on the rich for the benefit of the less wealthy citizens.[39] Citizens who are excluded from the common good in this and similar ways are not treated as citizens should be treated; hence, Aristotle suggests, one might as well deny that they are citizens in the first place. Again, this recommendation should not

---

[38] One need only think of Pericles or Alcibiades. The treatment of democracy in book 3 should not be taken as equally applicable to every democratic constitution; 4.4.1291b14–1292a37 shows that Aristotle recognizes a variety of democratic arrangements, some far more deviant than others; cf. 4.14.1297b35–1298a33 and the long discussion of 6.1–5.1317a18–1320b17.

[39] Such policies are clearly possible even if they were not characteristic of the Athenian democracy at any period. For an interesting case that the Athenian democracy satisfied Rawls's difference principle – which states that inequalities are just only if they are more advantageous to those who are most disadvantaged by them than a greater level of equality would be – within the political society composed of male Athenian citizens (as contrasted with the whole Athenian society including women, slaves, and foreigners), see Ober 1996b.

be understood as a method of rectifying the constitution, but as a call for a clear-headed identification of injustice.[40] Clinging to the fact that the city permits those whom it treats unjustly to participate in its formal institutions merely obfuscates the deviance of a constitution that subordinates the good of some to the interests of its rulers. Denying that such people are citizens would have the virtue of telling it like it is.[41] Yet so far from limiting the scope of political justice to the common good of the citizens, Aristotle's claim presupposes that this real or effective disenfranchisement would be unjust, and thus that the distribution of citizenship is among the fundamental issues that render a constitution just or unjust, deviant or correct.

The two passages that seemed to limit the sphere of political concern to people who antecedently meet Aristotle's definition of citizenship therefore not only fail to have that implication, but even deny it. This is not especially surprising, since the claim that a just city promotes the common good of its citizens does not, all by itself, suggest that the distribution of citizenship is irrelevant from the point of view of justice. To justify that conclusion, promoting the common good of the citizens would need to be sufficient for justice, and not merely necessary. Aristotle does not make this stronger claim. The few passages that might have supported it in fact indicate that he rejects it. Finally, the more general conception of justice in which his theory of political justice is embedded is inconsistent with any such arbitrary restriction on the scope of political justice. This last point deserves more attention.

4. Justice and the Principle of Nondespotic Rule

One source of the suspicion that Aristotle's theory of political justice is strictly limited to relations between people who already recognize

---

[40] That Aristotle's interest here is normative, and not merely classificatory, should be clear from the inherently normative character of the correct/deviant distinction that this passage is intended to clarify as well as from his formulation of the second alternative: "or they should [δεῖ] have a share in the benefit."

[41] cf. Simpson 1998: 154: "Either use words properly and admit that those ruled for someone else's advantage are being treated like slaves and so should not be called citizens, or exercise rule for their advantage also. To do the first is to admit despotism openly; to fail to do the second is to admit it in fact." Simpson thus supposes that the implied subject of the impersonal φατέον in 1279a31 is "the rulers"; my reading earlier, taking the subject impersonally, shows that this point is not crucial. Simpson rejects the emendation of 1279a32 and understands τοὺς μετέχοντας as "fellow citizens who, while entitled to share in rule, are effectively excluded from it." So long as "effectively excluded" does not mean that they are formally excluded from participation in the city's institutions, his reading is in essence the same as my own. Presumably, τοὺς μετέχοντας cannot refer to people who have no share in rule or who are formally excluded from political institutions.

one another as citizens may be that, as I have argued in previous chapters, Aristotle conceives of justice as internally related to community. Requirements of justice have their content and their normative authority as constraints on the successful achievement of the good at which each of the participants of a cooperative endeavor aims. The relative capacities and abilities of the parties further condition the standards of fairness and the legitimate modes of authority that they may exercise over one another. Justice is the common good, and hence it requires whatever is necessary to promote and preserve the shared and mutual benefits that supply each participant with his or her normative reasons for engaging in that cooperative activity with others.[42] Yet precisely because justice is internal to community in this way, it may seem to follow that standards of justice apply only where people are already actually cooperating in some specific form of community. Just as an adult male does not owe to every free woman what he owes to his own wife by virtue of his special relationship to her, so too adult male citizens of Corinth do not owe to the citizens of Thebes what they owe to their fellow Corinthians. But if this is so, then it might seem that a city's free but noncitizen inhabitants could not conceivably be treated unjustly by being excluded from citizenship. If citizenship is membership in the political community, and requirements of justice apply only to members of a community, then justice, it seems, cannot require that anyone not already included in the community be granted membership.

One need not challenge this conclusion immediately in order to see that it does not entail that no standards of justice apply to our relations with people who are members neither of our political community nor of any of the more limited and less comprehensive communities that the city embraces. It is at least clear that Aristotle does not suppose that the bounds of justice are coextensive with the boundaries of the political community.[43] In rejecting the view that a flourishing city is one that conquers its neighbors (*Pol.* 7.2.1324a35–b5), he says:

> It would perhaps seem exceedingly strange to those who are willing to consider the matter if the statesman's task is to be able to contemplate how he might rule over and be master of his neighbors, whether they are willing or unwilling. How, after all, could what is not even lawful be characteristic of a statesman or a lawgiver? To rule not only justly but unjustly is not lawful,

---

[42] For the distinction between normative and explanatory reasons, see Chapter 2.7.

[43] Curzer 2012: ch. 13 and Garver 2011: 82 maintain that Aristotle does not recognize justice beyond the polis. In addition to the following arguments against that view, see Miller 1995: 84–6 and Long 1996. I hope to consider this question more fully elsewhere.

and it is possible to exercise power in a way that is not just ... and it would be strange if there is not something that by nature is fit to be ruled despotically and something that is not fit to be ruled despotically, and so, if this is how it is, one should not try to rule over everyone despotically, but over those fit to be ruled in that way. (7.2.1324b22–8, 36–9)

Similarly, in a different context:

> Military training should not be taken up in order to enslave those who do not deserve it, but, first of all, in order not to be enslaved to others; second, in order to seek leadership for the benefit of those who are ruled, but not for the sake of despotism over all; and third, to rule as masters over those who deserve to be slaves. (7.14.1333b38–1334a2)

Though a modern reader's attention is most apt to fall on the thought that some people deserve to be enslaved, Aristotle's emphasis in these passages is directed to the negative claim that cities that aim to enslave or rule despotically over the naturally free inhabitants of other cities are guilty of injustice. In fact, the idea seems to be that ruling over unwilling subjects for one's own interest is simply unjust so long as those people are not natural slaves.[44] Morrison finds in these passages a "principle of just foreign policy"[45] and considers the possibility that Aristotle conceives of noncitizen residents of a city as the metaphysical equivalents of the inhabitants of a foreign city. Yet it is misleading to describe the injunction against despotic rule as a principle of "foreign policy." The principle as applied to interpolitical relations is precisely the same principle that is operative in all relations with naturally free people and that explains why slavery is unjust in every case in which the enslaved person is not a slave by nature. Moreover, a crucial component of Aristotle's case for the qualified justice of slavery is that mastery is actually beneficial to natural slaves. Human beings who lack the capacity for higher-order deliberation that enables them to enter into cooperative relationships with others as fully independent agents are, according to Aristotle, aided and benefited rather than harmed by being ruled for their masters' benefit.[46] The prohibition

---

[44] Morrison 1999: 155 rightly observes that unjust despotic rule is rule for the sake of the ruler over unwilling subjects: "Very likely Aristotle is not distinguishing between these two elements here, because he is making the plausible assumption that they typically go together. When the subjects perceive that being ruled by some person or persons is not in their interest, they normally withdraw consent and must be ruled forcibly or not at all." For more on justice and consent, see Chapter 6.

[45] Morrison 1999: 155–6

[46] On this point, see Chapter 2 and Lockwood 2007: Master and slave share "the same benefit" rather than "a common benefit," where the latter requires that the agents and the goods that benefit them are distinct from one another, while the slave is in effect a "part" of his master.

on despotic rule is therefore best understood as a prohibition on ruling other human beings at their expense; this prohibition is not violated by mastery over natural slaves precisely because natural slaves need not be ruled to their own detriment.[47] To describe this principle as a principle of just foreign policy inverts the priority of the two applications. The principle applies to foreign policy because it applies to our relations with all human beings.[48] It is a basic principle of justice.

The prohibition of ruling others at their expense can be stated more generally as an injunction to refrain from benefiting oneself by directly harming others. To say that this injunction represents a basic principle of justice is not to deny that justice is internal to community. For the principle applies not only to the relations that an agent already has, but to any relations into which an agent might enter with other human beings. Of course, not every relation is a community, because not every relation is cooperative: A relation might be one of complete mutual hostility and enmity unmediated by any communal ties. Yet the possibility of total hostility has no implications for the theory of justice because we have no reason to describe such a relation as just. The thesis that justice is internal to community maintains that justice obtains when people cooperate together for their shared and mutual benefit, not that justice is owed only to those with whom one is already cooperating. Different forms of cooperation yield different standards of justice because what it takes for a specific set of people to achieve the specific good in which they have a common stake will vary according to the character of that good and those people's relevant capacities and abilities. In every case, however, relations in which one party benefits disproportionately at the overall expense of others are unjust: Justice is the common good. In short, the claim that justice is internal to community does not allow anyone to avoid injustice merely by refusing to admit others to membership in the community.

---

[47] It is primarily on this point, and not on any empirical claims about the existence or prevalence of radically nonautonomous human beings, that Aristotle's defense of slavery seems most vulnerable to decisive objections. It is tolerably clear that there are at least some human beings who lack the capacity to be fully independent rational agents, but not at all that they would be benefited by being ruled for the sake of others.

[48] Characterizing this principle as one of "foreign policy" is also misleading in a second way, because only political communities have a "foreign policy," whereas the principle as I understand it governs the actions of individual agents in their relations to all others. To describe my relationship to a stranger I meet while traveling between cities as governed by a principle of "foreign policy" is either to obfuscate by metaphor or to say what is false.

Exclusion will be unjust to the extent that it imposes on those who are excluded losses uncompensated for by an equal or greater gain in goods.[49]

When this basic principle of justice is applied to the distribution of citizenship, exclusion will be unjust when it constitutes or leads to despotic rule over naturally free people. Thus while Aristotle does not extend the scope of political justice to natural slaves, he does, in one way, extend it to all of a city's free native inhabitants. Foreigners who are not permanent residents fall outside the bounds of specifically political justice precisely because they are citizens of other cities. Women and children, however, are not altogether excluded from consideration by being excluded from citizenship. Neither women nor children, on Aristotle's view, are ruled despotically by virtue of being denied citizenship. It is not simply that neither is fit for the tasks, though this is at least apparent in the case of children. It is, just as importantly, that neither is treated unjustly because neither is harmed.[50] Moreover, women and children are not merely included within the scope of political justice only to be excluded from it; both should also be objects of political concern. The inclusion of male children in the common good is most obvious; since they will eventually become citizens,

---

[49] If this formulation sounds too individualistic and instrumentalist to reflect Aristotle's thought accurately, it should be kept in mind that it does not say what kinds of good can compensate for what kinds of losses. In particular, it does not assume that the relation between any one person's good and those of others is merely instrumental; it therefore leaves open the possibility that the loss of, say, participation in the assembly could be compensated for by gains in the aggregate economic welfare of the whole city (an especially oligarchic thought) or that no amount of personal wealth could conceivably compensate for the good of sharing in rule as an equal with others. Proportionality of losses and gains requires only that goods be comparable, not that they be commensurable in terms of their quantitative contribution to some qualitatively single good: Nussbaum 1990c forcefully argues that Aristotle rejects the commensurability of goods, but this conclusion falls short of showing that he rejects all forms of the comparability of goods. For a similar verdict on an earlier version of Nussbaum's argument, see Price 1989: 113. Wiggins 1975 remains instructive on this point.

[50] Aristotle may assume, quite plausibly, that a person is not harmed by being denied the opportunity to engage in activities for which he does not possess some minimal but substantive competence. His treatment of the distribution of citizenship shows that this minimal competence need not be any special skill, and the summation argument suggests that the required competence should not be measured simply by considering only what an individual is capable of achieving on his own, but also what he is capable of achieving when cooperating together with others. Because he sets the bar so low, however, his exclusion of women from citizenship seems problematic even in light of the mistaken assumption that women are incapable of becoming fully independent rational agents: As the summation argument shows, independent excellence is not necessary. Schollmeier 2003 notices this problem and cites it as a reason to believe that Aristotle did not endorse the exclusion of women from politics; though this is no doubt the conclusion that Aristotle should have drawn, even the most liberal application of the principle of charity cannot license us to say that he therefore *did* draw it.

the best constitution will devote much of its attention to their education (7.13–8.7). Yet the education of women is also a concern to the good legislator; Aristotle severely criticizes the Spartans for neglecting the education of their women (2.9.1269b12–1270a11). In both cases, however, concern for the education and welfare of women and children is entirely consistent with the claim that a just city promotes the common good of the citizens: For each citizen is also the member of a household, and as such his good is closely connected to the good of his wife and children. The flourishing of the citizens does not compete for the city's attention with the flourishing of their households.

Since the principle of nondespotic rule applies to all free people, it therefore also applies, a fortiori, to all of a city's free native inhabitants. Thus Cooper and Keyt's judgment that the bounds of political justice and the common good extend to all such people is vindicated without revising or extending Aristotle's account of citizenship or attributing to him a broader conception of "second-class citizenship."[51] What is so far unclear is why any special status should attach to *native* inhabitants. As I noted previously, foreigners who do not intend to reside in a city for an extended period do not pose any problems of exclusion, since people are not ruled despotically simply because they are not permitted to join in collective deliberation and judgment with the members of a community in which they have no lasting stake or commitment. Metics, however, raise a more complex set of questions. As long-term and even permanent residents of a city, metics do seem to have a stake in and at least potentially a deep commitment to their cities of residence. It is therefore not immediately clear why they should not be included in the common good, both as potential recipients of citizenship and, more generally, as people whose welfare the city should seek to promote.

The answer to both questions, I think, is that metics need not be ruled despotically by being excluded from citizenship or from any direct

---

[51] Morrison 1999 at times argues as though being an object of political concern or included in the common good were the essence of being a citizen, thereby suggesting that Aristotle's definition of citizenship is intended to answer the question "Who deserves political concern?" In fact, however, even if Aristotle maintained that being a citizen and being an object of political concern were coextensive, his account of citizenship does not set out to determine who deserves political concern, but what it is to be a citizen; this is clear from 3.2.1275b37–1276a6, which distinguishes the question "What is a citizen?" from the question of whether someone is a citizen "justly or unjustly." Accordingly, even if political concern were extended to citizens alone, it would be one thing to ask whether someone is a citizen and another to ask whether someone *should be* a citizen, whether or not he actually is. Morrison's assumption is not idiosyncratic: Newman 1887–1902.i: 287 infers that noncitizens will be "wholly uncared for."

inclusion in the common good.[52] The principal difference between metics and noncitizen native inhabitants is that the former, but not the latter, are typically citizens of other cities who have voluntarily chosen to dwell in a foreign city. This difference is relevant to determining whether exclusion from citizenship amounts to despotic rule. A metic's decision to live in a city and to obey its laws is characteristically voluntary in a way that a native inhabitant's is not. Consequently, a metic's stake in the city is far less stable and determinate than that of any native, and he is at least in principle capable of withdrawing from a city if he judges living under its laws to be detrimental to his interests.[53] As a result, granting citizenship to metics poses distinct dangers to a city, and withholding citizenship from metics does not amount to subjecting them involuntarily to rule that is detrimental to their good. Admittedly, these conditions are not met in every case: Some metics may have lost their citizenship in their native cities, may be deeply committed to their cities of residence, or may be both. The difference between a metic and a native noncitizen may also become very difficult to draw, since some metic families live in a city for several generations. Accordingly, no simple set of criteria can license the exclusion of all metics from citizenship. Yet the basic principle of justice already

---

[52] I propose this as an "answer" in the sense that I take it to identify some assumptions about metics that Aristotle held and that explain why the principle of nondespotic rule does not require that they be given a share in rule. That is, I do not maintain only the weaker thesis that these assumptions are consistent with what Aristotle says, but the stronger thesis that they are implicit in his overall view. I readily acknowledge that the boundary between these two kinds of claim is often hopelessly vague. For some helpful reflections on attributing implicit (and even unconscious) beliefs to authors, rightly stressing the basic similarity between textual interpretation and the rational explanation of action more generally, see Bevir 1997. I am grateful to Don Morrison for pressing me to clarify my thinking on this point.

[53] One might think that citizens, no less than metics, are "free to leave" if they find a city's laws uncongenial. But this is false. In the paradigmatic case, a metic is a citizen of another community who takes up residence in a second community without giving up his citizenship in his home city. At a pragmatic level, this means that metics have somewhere to go, whereas citizens do not; at a deeper level, it means that their loyalties and commitments are likely to be more tenuous, unstable, and susceptible to conflict than those of citizens. The ownership of land – which, in Athens, was not permitted to metics – no doubt plays a role in creating and sustaining these differences, but it cannot be of fundamental importance, because cities could conceivably choose to allow metics to own land without granting them citizenship. There may be some relevant sense in which citizens are "free to leave" – one thinks of Socrates in the *Crito* – but the differences in the two cases are more striking and important than their similarities; the important point is not that citizens are not at liberty to leave the city if they have somewhere else to go, but that they are characteristically not already members of another political community. It may be helpful to remember that any political community in which citizenship involves active participation in forming and applying policy will need to withhold citizenship from at least some foreign visitors; it is more interesting, though beyond the scope of my aims here, to consider whether and why Aristotle must reject the idea of dual citizenship.

ensures that a city cannot justly treat metics in any way it pleases. The exclusion of metics poses different problems from the exclusion of native inhabitants, but metics no less than any other naturally free human beings cannot justly be subjected to despotic rule.[54]

The principle of nondespotic rule thus has diverse applications in various contexts, but is nonetheless a basic principle of justice. Moreover, it is this principle that sets the criterion for Aristotle's distinction between correct and deviant constitutions. Since the principle prohibits despotic rule over all free people, any city that rules its free inhabitants despotically will be unjust and deviant. As the case of metics shows, however, it is not immediately clear when and on what grounds exclusion from citizenship amounts to ruling the excluded despotically. So far, I have argued that Aristotle's theory of correct and deviant constitutions is not incompatible with his account of citizenship; since a constitution will be deviant if it rules any of the city's free inhabitants despotically, there is no need to revise or supplement the conception of citizenship as sharing in rule. Yet on prominent interpretations of that conception, Aristotle could not consistently hold that the principle of nondespotic rule requires a city to grant a share of rule to all of its native free adult male inhabitants. Because he recognizes correct forms of monarchy and rule by the few, he apparently denies that it is always unjust to withhold citizenship from a substantial portion of a city's free native male adults. This conclusion, however, presupposes that the definition of citizenship as sharing in rule makes the citizen body coextensive with the ruling class. In the next section, I will reject this view and argue, to the contrary, that rule and authority admit of degrees.

5. Citizenship and Degrees of Authority

The argument against the view that Aristotelian citizenship is coextensive with membership in the city's ruling body is simple: Being a citizen is a matter of being entitled to share in rule by holding some form of office, but some offices are more authoritative than others, and a person may be eligible for some offices without being eligible to occupy the most

---

[54] My treatment of this question is indebted to Keyt 1993: 146. Keyt attributes to Aristotle a much stronger thesis about the inherent injustice of coercion than I would be willing to concede. A weaker thesis, allowing that people may justifiably be coerced when their lack of consent is sufficiently unreasonable and not merely when they themselves are coercing others, is strong enough for Aristotle's purposes and consistent with this account of justice toward metics. I discuss coercion and justice at greater length in Chapter 6.

authoritative offices that constitute the city's ruling body. Otherwise put, if offices differ in their degree of authority over the city's affairs, and if some citizens may be entitled to hold less authoritative offices without thereby being entitled to hold the most authoritative ones, then some citizens will share in rule without being members of what Aristotle calls "the ruling body" (τὸ πολίτευμα).

Aristotle's two most general characterizations of a constitution acknowledge that offices can be assigned different degrees of authority and that one of the principal differences among various kinds of constitution is the way that they distribute their most authoritative offices:

> A constitution is an arrangement of a city's offices [ἀρχῶν], both of the others and especially of the one that is authoritative over all [τῆς κυρίας πάντων]. For in every case the ruling body [τὸ πολίτευμα] of the city is authoritative, and the constitution *is* the ruling body. I mean, for instance, that in democracies the demos is authoritative, and in oligarchies, by contrast, the few are. We say that there is also a constitution different from these, and we will give the same account about the others, as well. (*Pol.* 3.6.1278b8–15)

> For a constitution is the arrangement of the offices, and everyone distributes these either according to the ability of those who share or according to some equality common among them. I mean, for instance, of the needy or the well-off or something common to both. So it is necessary that there be just as many constitutions as there are arrangements that accord with the superiorities and differences of the parts. (4.3.1290a7–13)

The first passage picks out one office as most authoritative and identifies the composition of that office as a crucial determinant of a constitution's character.[55] Democratic constitutions give authority to the free citizen body as a whole by arranging the most authoritative office so that its decisions are determined by and reflect the judgment of a majority of the free. Oligarchies, by contrast, give authority to the few by restricting participation in and control of the most authoritative office to a select subset of the free (cf. 3.8.1279b34–1280a6). A satisfactory analysis of constitutional

---

[55] The argument identifies the πολίτευμα with the ἀρχή that is κυρία πάντων; the gender of the article (τῆς κυρίας πάντων) assures that this is an ἀρχή and not a more abstract "part" or "element"; without this identification, the appeal to the authoritativeness of the πολίτευμα cannot do the argumentative work that it is clearly intended to do (γὰρ, 1278b10). This is not to say, however, that the πολίτευμα is an "office" such as a generalship or even an assembly. My argument should later make the relationship between these terms clearer. I opt for "ruling body" as a translation for πολίτευμα both because it fits the context well (the city's πολίτευμα is in every case authoritative) and because it is sufficiently vague not to beg any questions. I also think the term well expresses what I argue later that the πολίτευμα is, but my argument does not depend on this translation.

types will need to be more fine-grained than the dichotomy between oligarchy and democracy allows, but the contrast between the many and the few serves well enough to illustrate the dependence of constitutional variety on the distribution of access to the city's most authoritative office.

The second passage is less clear, but it too implies the possibility of a hierarchy of offices. The argument explicitly focuses on differences among classes of the citizens – these are the "parts" – rather than the offices. Yet it describes constitutions as varying along with their different ways of distributing offices to these parts. One way to distribute offices is to grant every citizen a formally equal share of authority. But Aristotle's description also covers cases in which authority is distributed in proportion to ability or some other purportedly relevant but unequally distributed trait, such as wealth. Strictly equal distribution is only one alternative (4.3.1290a8–9); offices may also be arranged "in accord with the superiorities and differences of the parts" (4.3.1290a12–13). This is, moreover, an arrangement of offices, not a restriction on qualification for office. When read together with the previous characterization of the constitution (3.6.1278b8–15), this passage suggests that these strictly unequal distributions are distributions of more and less authoritative offices.[56] The detailed analysis of constitutional variety that follows in book 4 bears out this suggestion.

In the final chapters of book 4, Aristotle turns from a consideration of the different kinds of constitution to a more detailed analysis of their differences in terms of the three institutional "parts" of every constitution: "the deliberative part" (τὸ βουλευόμενον), "the offices" (αἱ ἀρχαί), and "the part that administers justice" (τὸ δικάζον, 4.14.1297b41–1298a3). Constitutions differ most of all in how they arrange these various parts, and one of Aristotle's aims in these chapters is to examine the ways that the parts can be divided and which alternatives are most characteristic of and conducive to specific kinds of constitution (4.14.1297b37–41). In considering the implications of this analysis for the relationship between citizenship and degrees of authority, it is important to avoid two possible misunderstandings.

---

[56] Taken on its own, this passage might seem vague enough to be read instead as pointing only to the inequality between citizens and noncitizens. But if inclusion or exclusion were the main point, it would, I think, be clumsy to describe the differences between constitutions in terms of their "arrangements of offices"; in any case, my argument does not rest on a decontextualized interpretation of the passage, but on consideration of its argument in light of its role in book 4 and the related claims in book 3.

First, it might be tempting to think of "the deliberative element" as a particular office or institutional body such as an assembly.[57] This identification could seem especially attractive in view of the apparent symmetry between book 4's distinction of "the offices" from the deliberative and judicial functions and book 3's distinction between "definite" offices and the "indefinite" offices of the assembly and the law court (3.1.1275a23–32). Yet as Aristotle notes shortly after introducing that distinction, not all constitutions must have assemblies or any form of indefinite office. Rather,

> in those other constitutions it is not the person who holds indefinite office who is an assemblyman or a juror, but a person whose office is determinate, since [in these cases] deliberation and judgment, whether about all things or about some things, has been assigned to all or some of them [i.e., of people who hold determinate offices]. (3.1.1275b13–17)

Though assemblies are, indeed, one especially common institutional embodiment of a city's deliberative function, they are neither the only possible locus of deliberation nor necessary for the existence of a constitution; the deliberative function could be distributed across various offices held by particular individuals or by small boards. Thus the distinction between the deliberative element and the offices is not a distinction between two mutually exclusive institutions.

In one way, all offices involve deliberation (4.15.1299a25–7). The identification of a special "deliberative element," however, serves to single out deliberation about the most general of the city's common affairs as an especially important function not at all on a par with the deliberation required of every official. This special focus is evident in the introductory list of issues over which the deliberative part has authority: war and peace; alliances and their dissolution; laws; penalties of death, exile, and confiscation of property; selecting and auditing officials (4.14.1298a3–7). Some of the officials mentioned in the last item on the list will be the holders of particular offices that, though they involve deliberation and judgment, are nonetheless subordinate to the authority of the deliberative element. A general, for instance, will deliberate about the best strategy to pursue in a battle; the constitution's deliberative part, by contrast, will deliberate about whether or not to go to war. The person who serves as general will be subordinate to the deliberative element in one sense because the deliberative element is responsible for appointing him to his position and can

---

[57] For instance, Robinson 1962: 116: "What Aristotle really means by 'the deliberative part' seems to be the biggest official body in the city, for instance the Assembly at Athens."

call him to account when he leaves office. The generalship itself, however, is subordinate to the deliberative element in the stronger sense that the general takes his orders from the part that deliberates about whether to go to war: The general acts on the initiative of the deliberative part (cf. *EN* 1.2.1094b2–3).[58]

The distinction between the offices and the deliberative element is clearest when the latter is embodied in an assembly, but the deliberative function could be turned over to a small group or even to a single individual: "It is necessary either for all of these judgments to be assigned to all the citizens, or all to some – for instance, to some single office or to several, or different judgments to different offices – or for some of them to be assigned to all and some others to some" (*Pol.* 4.14.1298a7–9). Thus, while the deliberative element is constituted by offices, whether determinate or indefinite, they are distinct from the offices that Aristotle treats as a second and distinct part of the constitution because the latter are subordinate to those that make up the deliberative part.

This point is related to the second potential misunderstanding, which stems from Aristotle's ambiguous use of expressions attributing authority to different people or offices. Aristotle twice describes the deliberative part as "authoritative" (κύριον, 4.14.1298a3–4, 6.1.1316b31–2); he thereby strongly suggests that the deliberative element is that most authoritative office picked out in his generic description of the constitution in book 3 (3.6.1278b8–10 earlier). Yet every office is authoritative over something, and the scope of its authority – the range of things that fall within its decision making – is one of its defining features (4.14.1298a1–3, 15.1299a5). Strictly speaking, then, authority is dispersed throughout all of a city's offices. When Aristotle describes the city's deliberative element as authoritative, however, he is making a stronger claim: The deliberative element is the most authoritative part of the city, and that is why those who control the deliberative element control the city as a whole and determine its character as democratic, oligarchic, aristocratic, or whatever.[59] When we recall the list of issues over which the deliberative element has authority, its status as the most authoritative part of the city should be unsurprising.

---

[58] Kraut 2002: 227 recognizes that any city requires a plurality of offices and that some of these will be "more important than others." His examples, however, present officials such as a general or a treasurer as "more important" than the assembly in a constitution in which "the most important decisions … are made collectively by an assembly of which all male citizens are members" (he is describing the best constitution of bks. 7–8). Thus what Kraut calls "important" cannot be equivalent to "authoritative," since the assembly in such a constitution will have higher authority than the general.

[59] Miller 1995: 166–7 helpfully elaborates this point.

Whoever has control, whether individually or collectively, over decisions about war and peace, about the appointment of less authoritative officials, about exile and the confiscation of property, and about the content of the laws themselves does not merely hold one more position of authority in the city. Rather, the deliberative part has authority over every other holder of authority. This, then, is one way in which authority comes in degrees: Some positions of authority include other positions of authority within their own scope.

This much is sufficient to establish the formal possibility that some of a city's residents might be entitled to hold lower-level offices without being eligible to participate in the most authoritative ones. By itself, however, this formal possibility does not tell against the view that Aristotle envisions citizenship as coextensive with membership in the city's ruling body. For even if Aristotle allows for the possibility that people who have no share in the city's deliberative part could nonetheless be citizens, he does not highlight this sort of case. For Aristotle, the most important cases of citizens who do not share in the ruling body are not people who merely hold lower-level offices or sit on juries without participating in the city's deliberative element. Rather, the deliberative element itself can be divided in such a way that different people have more or less authority within it, with only some citizens counting as members of the ruling body.

6. Citizenship and the Ruling Body

Aristotle's recognition of citizens who do not share in the ruling body is clearest in the cases of oligarchy and aristocracy. Along with democracy, these constitutional types represent the three general ways of distributing participation in the city's deliberative part. In democracies, all the citizens are entitled to participate in deliberation about all of the city's most important affairs; in oligarchies, the deliberative function is reserved for only a few; in aristocracies, deliberation about some issues is open to all, but in other cases limited to officials elected on the basis of their excellence (*Pol.* 4.14.1298a9–10, 35, b5–8). Each of these arrangements admits of variation. Thus in one version of the democratic arrangement, the citizens come together to deliberate as a group only on major issues concerned with establishing laws and modifying the basic features of the constitution. Otherwise the deliberative function is assigned to offices that are filled by different groups of citizens by turns (4.14.1298a11–19). This arrangement is democratic despite the absence of a vigorous assembly because access to the most authoritative offices is distributed equally throughout the body of the citizens; every citizen can, and presumably at some point will, exercise the highest authority possible in the city.[60] At the opposite extreme, the citizens of a democratic city can come together to deliberate collectively about everything, giving officials no independent authority at all and rendering all of the officials' decisions merely preliminary (4.14.1298a28–33). In each variation on the democratic arrangement, however, the constitution's democratic character is a consequence of every citizen's ability to participate in collective deliberation about the most central matters of general policy.

By the same token, oligarchy and aristocracy are not best described as constitutions in which only the few wealthy or the few excellent men are citizens. Oligarchy is the more extreme case, since even moderate oligarchies, in Aristotle's view, restrict participation in common deliberation to people who possess a significant amount of wealth. Yet Aristotle recognizes both real and hypothetical oligarchic arrangements that give some role to those who fall below the minimum property requirement. In a brief discussion following his survey of various ways to distribute participation in deliberation, he maintains that it is beneficial for oligarchies to include some people from the multitude or to set up a predeliberative body to control the agenda of deliberative assemblies, "for in that way the demos will share in deliberation and will not be able to undermine anything that concerns the constitution" (4.14.1298b30–1). Possible roles for the demos include voting for, but not against, the resolutions; offering advice to the officials but not engaging in deliberation themselves; or having a veto power without being able to pass proposals themselves (4.14.1298b32–40). Such limited rights of participation in deliberation are insufficient for membership in the city's ruling body.

If such limited participation also seems to fall short of formal citizenship, however, it is worth noting that Aristotle treats election to office by the demos as consistent with oligarchy. The second oligarchic mode of distributing deliberative privileges that he identifies is one in which the citizens who actually participate in deliberation are elected. Though they must meet the minimal property assessment in order to be eligible for office, their actual appointment is determined by vote (4.14.1298a40–b2). The ensuing contrast with the third oligarchic mode suggests that the

---

[60] In his description of this first democratic "mode" (τρόπος), Aristotle does not say that the officials are chosen by lot or by some other nonelectoral process of selection, but that seems to be implied; unlike the citizens in the second democratic mode, those in the first do not come together as a group to select officials or even to audit them; cf. 1298a19–24.

demos – the collective body of those whose wealth falls below the minimal assessment – participates in the elections; the third mode differs from
the second in part because in the third mode "those who are authoritative
over deliberation elect themselves" (4.14.1298b2–3). Moreover, Aristotle
offers empirical evidence of oligarchies in which citizens not eligible for
office nonetheless elect the officials. In his analysis of factional strife and
constitutional change, he distinguishes two ways in which oligarchies
can be "changed from within" through rivalries among members of the
oligarchy who engage in "demagoguery." One sort of oligarchic demagoguery is strictly internal, with some of the wealthy rulers appealing to
others to form factions in opposition to the rest – Aristotle's examples
are internal tensions within the Thirty and the Four Hundred at Athens
(5.6.1306a22–7). The other sort, however, occurs

> whenever those who are in the oligarchy engage in demagoguery toward the
> crowd, as the guardians of the constitution in Larissa used to do because
> the crowd elected them, and as happens in all oligarchies where the people
> who elect the offices are not the people from whom the officials are elected,
> but where the offices are based on large assessments or on [membership in]
> political clubs and the hoplites or the demos elects them, as used to happen
> in Abydus. (5.6.1305b28–33)

The existence and role of citizens who fall outside the ruling body are even
clearer in aristocracy. "The constitution is an aristocracy," Aristotle writes,
"when all [deliberate about] war and peace and auditing of officials, but
officials [ἄρχοντες] [deliberate about] the rest and are elected rather than
chosen by lot" (4.14.1298b5–8). Here too Aristotle offers a real-world
example. To illustrate his claim that aristocracies can undergo gradual
constitutional change as a result of small modifications, he tells of how
some of the generals of Thurii persuaded the city to abolish term-limits
on the generalship, "seeing that the demos would eagerly vote for them"
(5.7.1307a40–b19). Whoever the demos of Thurii were, they were able
to vote for generals but not to hold the other offices against which the
generals formed their faction.[61] Broadly speaking, then, an aristocratic
constitution is one in which many share in rule by electing and auditing officials and by having a formally recognized voice in decisions about

---

[61] 5.7.1307b8–9 suggests that the demos in this passage consists of people with property sufficient to
maintain the equipment needed for military service: The generals who took over Thurii were "well
regarded among the multitude of the garrisons." Even if the demos of Thurii excludes many who
would count as members of the demos in Athens, it clearly refers to those who did not have control
of the city's affairs; cf. 1307b9–10.

war and peace, but only the most excellent citizens have authority over other important matters.[62] Those who elect and audit officials and share in deliberation about war plainly meet Aristotle's official criteria of citizenship.[63] Yet they will not be members of the city's ruling body if they are not elected to the positions that exercise the most authority.

There is one final reason for doubting that citizens entitled to share in deliberation about only some issues fail to be members of the ruling body: If the deliberative part of the city is the most authoritative, and these citizens participate in it to some extent, then surely they participate in the ruling body, since the ruling body is the most authoritative part of the city. The preceding argument shows, however, that while the deliberative function remains the most authoritative of the three constitutional parts that Aristotle identifies, authority can be distributed unevenly within it. Electing and auditing officials are components of the deliberative part of the constitution (4.14.1298a3–7), and yet the examples of aristocracy and some kinds of oligarchy have shown that some citizens may be entitled to elect and audit officials without holding those more authoritative offices. Yet the election and auditing of officials are not subordinate to the remaining deliberative functions in the way that offices outside the deliberative part of the city are. This suggests a second way in which authority comes in degrees: Some positions of authority have a broader scope than others. In either case, then, an office's degree of authority is a function of its authority's scope, and one office can be more authoritative than another either by including that other within its scope – as the deliberative assembly does in relation to the generalship – or simply by having a broader scope. The difference is important, since it entails that a less

---

[62] The "aristocracy" that Aristotle is discussing in 4.14 may be what he elsewhere calls "so-called aristocracy," which is probably better described as a mixed constitution that gives a place to considerations of excellence but does not make it the sole qualification for office (4.7.1293b7–21; cf. Miller 1995: 164–5, Kraut 2002: 231–2). But it is worth noting that 4.14.1298b5–8 illustrates a standard of distribution that is distinct from the democratic and oligarchic methods described in the immediately preceding passages, and that this standard itself is not "mixed." The discussion of "so-called aristocracy" suggests that it differs from the pure aristocracy of the best constitution by its mixture of democratic and oligarchic principles of distribution with the aristocratic principle (4.7.1293b12–13). In any case, it is evident that the principle of distribution that Aristotle describes in 4.14 is central to his general notion of aristocracy and not applicable only to some attenuated form of it.

[63] In fact, the citizens in an Aristotelian aristocracy who are not parts of the city's ruling body nonetheless have more direct authority simply by virtue of their citizenship than a citizen of the United States, who, as such, has no role in auditing officials (since the United States does not routinely audit officials at all) or any direct role in deciding whether the country will go to war. For an attempt, by turns amusing and depressing, to construct an Aristotelian analysis of the πολιτεία of the United States, see Simpson 2007.

authoritative office need not be directly and nonreciprocally subordinate to a more authoritative one. In both cases, Aristotle's analysis of constitutions illustrates that citizens may or may not be entitled to hold the most authoritative offices: Citizenship admits of various degrees of authority.

In case this argument seems too indirect to dispel doubt, it is worth noting that there are more direct, independent reasons to deny that Aristotle conceives of citizenship as entailing membership in the ruling body. First, he distinguishes constitutional types largely by which class of citizens holds the most authority (3.6.1278b8–15, 7.1279a25–31). A constitution is an oligarchy because the wealthy few have control, an aristocracy because the few citizens who are most excellent, or who are deemed most excellent, have control. Admittedly, democracy constitutes a somewhat special case, since the nonwealthy majority's control of the constitution does not depend on any de facto exclusion of wealthy citizens from participation in the institutional bodies that exercise the most authority. Minority groups in a democracy therefore lack control over the city's affairs *as groups* without the members of those groups being any less entitled than other citizens to hold any official position. If the demos is most authoritative in a democracy, then, its control is not a consequence of exclusion or unequal distributions of authority to individuals. Instead, the demos gains control through a strictly equal distribution of access to positions of authority. Rather than showing that the nonelite citizens in an oligarchy or an aristocracy are members of the ruling body, however, democracy's example suggests that the selective composition of the ruling body does not require formal exclusion of others from institutions. A fortiori, the nonelites in constitutions that do formally exclude some citizens from positions of authority are not members of the city's ruling body.

A second consideration that tells against an identification of citizenship and membership in the ruling body is terminological. The word that I have translated as "ruling body," πολίτευμα, appears nineteen times in the *Politics*. Most of those uses provide no clear indications of the boundaries of the πολίτευμα or even whether the term is entirely synonymous with πολιτεία. At least three passages, however, strongly suggest that πολίτευμα refers to a more restricted group within the citizen body, namely, the group that has the most authority and control over the constitution. I have already appealed to two of these passages (3.6.1278b8–15, 7.1279a25–31). What I can now add to the more abstract argument that I have cited them to support is that both, after identifying the πολίτευμα as the controlling or authoritative part of the city, immediately supply subsets of the citizen body as examples of the πολιτεύματα of different constitutions: the demos, the few, the many, or one man. The foregoing analysis of Aristotle's description of constitutions has shown in the case of all but the last of these examples that the groups here picked out as constituting the πολίτευμα are not coextensive with the citizen body.

The tendency to treat πολίτευμα as strictly synonymous with πολιτεία no doubt gains much of its impetus from these passages' claims that "the πολιτεία is the πολίτευμα" (3.6.1278b11) and that "πολιτεία and πολίτευμα signify the same thing" (3.7.1279a25–6). Without embarking upon a complicated analysis of Aristotle's theory of language and his uses of the verb "to be," however, we can see that these claims are not intended to establish a strict identity between πολιτεία and πολίτευμα or the synonymy of the terms themselves. Compare, first, the claim in the *Nicomachean Ethics* that each human being *is* his intellect because the intellect is the human being's most authoritative aspect (*EN* 9.8.1168b28–1169a3). Just as this claim does not require Aristotle to forget that human beings have bodies and related faculties of perception and imagination or to treat a human being's possession of these faculties as wholly contingent, so too his claim that the πολιτεία is the πολίτευμα does not require him to insist that the πολιτεία is *nothing but* the πολίτευμα. Rather, the constitution is its ruling body in the same sense that a human being is his intellect: The ruling body and the intellect are the most authoritative or controlling elements of each, and it is their condition and relation to the other parts of their respective wholes that are most crucial for determining the condition and character of those wholes.[64]

The third passage in which the πολίτευμα seems to refer to a restricted group of citizens rather than the whole citizen body is also the least ambiguous. It is a continuation of the discussion of internal oligarchic strife cited earlier. Oligarchies can be undone from within whenever some of the oligarchs appeal to "the crowd" against other members of the oligarchy,

---

[64] The reference to *akrasia* and *enkrateia* in *EN* 9.8.1168b34–5 show that the intellect's status as most authoritative does not depend on whether it effectively exercises power (κράτος) over the others; one might speculate that, by analogy, a city's ruling body remains authoritative even if loses effective control over some other part(s) of the city. In that case, being in control and authoritative (τὸ κύριον εἶναι) would be consistent with being overpowered by others, and a city whose ruling body is being overpowered by some other segment of the city would be akin to an *akratic* individual. It seems possible for a government to "stay in power" without having significant control over its citizens, but the analogy between city and soul should perhaps not be pushed too far. My thoughts on this analogy are indebted to conversation with Don Morrison.

as the guardians of the constitution in Larissa used to do because the crowd elected them, and as happens in all oligarchies where the people who elect the offices are not the people from whom the officials are elected, but where the offices are based on large assessments or on [membership in] political clubs and the hoplites or the demos elects them, as used to happen in Abydus, and when the law courts are not filled from the ruling body [πολιτεύματος], since by engaging in demagoguery in relation to judicial decisions they bring about a change in the constitution, the very thing that happened in Heraclea Pontica. (*Pol.* 5.6.1305b29–36)

The important point here is not to determine exactly how Aristotle imagines an oligarchy being undermined and transformed into a different kind of constitution by some of its rulers' pandering to judges, but that he sees oligarchies as especially vulnerable to this kind of instability when participation in their law courts is not limited to citizens who are members of the ruling body. Like elections and audits, participation in the courts is sufficient for Aristotelian citizenship.[65] The jurors in Heraclea Pontica, therefore, were citizens but not parts of the ruling body.[66] Thus, in light of the general analysis of constitutions, this passage makes clear that Aristotle does not regard citizenship as coextensive with membership in the city's ruling body.

7. Degrees of What?

By distinguishing citizenship from membership in the ruling body, this interpretation might seem only trivially different from the second-class citizenship interpretation. In particular, the appeal to degrees of authority resembles Morrison's preferred alternative to Keyt and Cooper's proposals. Yet my account differs from Morrison's and, a fortiori, from Cooper and Keyt's in two important ways. First, for Morrison what admits of degrees is citizenship, not rule or authority. Second, and related to the first, Morrison sees sharing in rule as the highest degree of citizenship

[65] It is worth noting that Ross's text of the definition at 3.1.1275b18–21 reads καί where the manuscripts (apparently unanimously) read ἤ: If the manuscript reading is correct, then the Aristotelian citizen is one who shares in deliberative *or* judicial rule; hence a person who is entitled to sit on juries but not to participate in collective deliberation would count as a citizen (thus Miller 1995: 146 note 13). I have not insisted on the textual point, however, because it is clear that Aristotle considers judicial service a form of rule or office in the broad sense (3.1.1275a26–32) and that deliberation and judgment are common to all three of the constitutional "parts" identified in 4.14.1297b37–1298a3.

[66] Thus Miller 1995: 150 seems mistaken to identify the πολίτευμα with "the government" in a sense that includes all of the city's offices. Similarly, Nagle 2006: 115 glosses the πολίτευμα as "the politically active subgroup in the larger community." Both are too broad.

and extends lesser degrees of citizenship to people who do not share in rule. On my account, by contrast, all and only those who are entitled to share in rule are citizens, but citizens may hold varying degrees of authority. A considerable strength of my alternative is that it does not require any revision to Aristotle's theory of citizenship; it requires only that we appreciate that the theory is consistent with hierarchical degrees of rule and authority, an implication of which I take Aristotle to have been fully aware. A second advantage of my account is that it allows for a clear and unambiguous distinction between citizens and metics.

Morrison finds support for the view that metics are citizens in an incomplete way in the passage leading up to Aristotle's first stab at a definition of citizenship:

> The citizen is not a citizen by virtue of inhabiting a certain place, since even metics and slaves share in habitation; nor do those who share in judicial rights in such a way as to bring a charge or be charged in court, since this is true even for those who share in them on the basis of treaties. In fact, in many places not even metics share in these rights completely, but a patron must be appointed, and so they share in this sort of community in an incomplete sort of way. But in the same way children who have not yet been enrolled because of their age and old men who have been discharged should be said to be citizens in a way, but not in an excessively unqualified way. Rather, it must be added that some are incomplete and others are past their prime or some other such thing; for it makes no difference, since it is clear what is meant. For we are seeking the citizen without qualification, the one which admits of no complaint and is in need of no correction, since even in the cases of those who have lost their citizenship and of exiles it is possible to raise problems like these and to resolve them. (*Pol.* 3.1.1275a7–22)

The impulse to read this passage as claiming that metics are citizens in an incomplete way clearly takes its support from the comparison of children and old men to metics: Morrison sees them all, along with exiles and the disenfranchised, as people "who participate only imperfectly in the community."[67] A closer look, however, reveals that the comparison is not of two sets of people who both participate in an incomplete way in the same community, but of the incomplete participation in one kind of community to the incomplete participation in another kind of community. Metics "share in an incomplete sort of way in *this sort* of community," where "this sort" refers back to the sharing of judicial rights and

---

[67] Morrison 1999: 156, his translation of 1275a13. Price 1989: 199–200 reads the passage in much the same way.

liabilities. Aristotle's argument has already shown that having access to legal institutions is insufficient for citizenship on the grounds that foreign citizens of other cities have such access on the basis of treaties. Metics are then reintroduced into the discussion to strengthen the point; because they can only access the courts through a citizen patron, they share in judicial rights less completely even than foreigners whose access comes through treaties.[68] In fact, metics have already played an important role in the argument by serving, along with slaves, as a straightforward counter-example to the quickly dismissed proposal that a citizen is someone who inhabits a place. In each of their appearances in this passage, metics do argumentative work precisely because their noncitizen status is assumed. Metics are not citizens even in an incomplete way.

A significant advantage of the alternative I have been defending is that the noncitizen status of metics is entirely unmysterious: Metics are not citizens, even in some incomplete or qualified sense, because they do not share in rule, have not shared in rule, and are not expected to share in rule. Though metics pose some serious problems for Aristotle's political theory, they do so precisely because they are not citizens.

Recognizing that citizenship admits of degrees of authority also helps to explain several otherwise puzzling features of Aristotle's treatment of constitutions. First, though the complete disenfranchisement of certain classes is a not infrequently realized possibility, the more common and less theoretically tractable cases of constitutional variety are those in which the members of different groups are assigned unequal rights and privileges on the basis of divergent criteria and methods of selection. These cases present greater challenges of analysis precisely because a simple contrast between citizens and noncitizens is relatively unilluminating. From the perspective of an analysis of constitutional arrangements, the minimal criteria for citizenship are of secondary importance. What principally differentiates constitutions and is therefore most crucial for their analysis is how each constitution divides positions of rule and authority. Complete exclusion from any such position is the extreme or limiting case, and even a clear identification of the criteria for minimal inclusion will fail to track vast differences among constitutions. Consider, for instance, that in at least some oligarchies and aristocracies, all of the free native inhabitants might be permitted to participate in electing and auditing the officials.

---

[68] Athenian metics probably *could* access the courts without going through their patrons (Hansen 1991: 118), a useful reminder that Aristotle is not quite so Athenocentric as many of his readers suppose (for a sustained defense of this claim with regard to the household, see Nagle 2006).

If we describe these constitutions as those in which all of the free are citizens, we speak truly but fail to distinguish these constitutions from each other and from democracies. Yet Aristotle wants to analyze each of these types into further subtypes. It is hardly surprising, then, that the requirements for bare citizenship do not occupy the center of his attention.

Second, recognizing that citizenship admits of degrees of authority helps to demystify Aristotle's use of the term "citizen" in ways that have seemed incompatible with his formal account of citizenship as sharing in rule. Consider, for instance, the claim that all of the citizens of the best constitution "share in the constitution" (7.13.1332a32–5). On the assumption that sharing in the constitution just is sharing in rule, the implication that some citizens in other cities do not share in the constitution forces the conclusion that Aristotle must have been using the word "citizen" in a broader sense. As we have seen, however, Aristotle is willing to say that the constitution is its ruling body, but the ruling body is in many cases far from coextensive with the citizen body. Thus, Aristotle's claim about the best constitution is that in it, unlike in some other cities, citizenship entails membership in the ruling body.[69] Similarly, when distinguishing varieties of democracy, Aristotle says that in one type "all the citizens who are of unimpeachable descent share, but the law rules; and another kind is where everyone shares in the offices if only he is a citizen, but the law rules" (4.4.1292a1–4). This passage appears to rely on a broader conception of citizenship only on the assumption that "sharing in the offices" just is what it is to be a citizen. But "the offices" here need not refer to any and all forms of rule, but only to the most authoritative offices or to those that invest individuals or small groups with special responsibilities. Democracies need not make all citizens equally eligible for every position; some do, and those democracies would be well described as ones in which "everyone shares in the offices if only he is a citizen."[70]

---

[69] 7.9.1329a2–17 and 14.1332b32–1333a3 argue that the best constitution should divide military and deliberative roles among citizens on the basis of age: Younger men should serve in the military but not participate, at least fully, in deliberative institutions until they are older. Though some have scoffed at this arrangement (Schofield 1999b: 105, for instance, describes this account of ruling and being ruled as "Pickwickian" and "hijacked"), it does not temper the basic egalitarianism of the best constitution: Every member of the military class will, upon reaching the appropriate age, be equally eligible to participate fully in the deliberative institutions. See Long 2005.

[70] The democratic principle of justice distributes authority equally to every free adult man (3.9.1280a16–25), but not every democratic constitution embodies this principle to the fullest extent (e.g., 4.4.1291b39–41 describes a kind of democracy in which at least some, and perhaps even all, offices are filled on the basis of a property assessment). For the various applications of the democratic and oligarchic conceptions of justice, see the helpful treatment of Miller 1995: 166–72.

Finally, Aristotle's references to a plurality of citizens and officials in kingships and tyrannies (3.14.1285a24–7, 5.10.1311a7–8, 11.1315a4–8) are not inconsistent with his definition of citizenship so long as that definition is understood to allow that citizens may share in rule and authority to various degrees. In fact, tyranny provides an especially clear illustration of the need to acknowledge degrees of authority and their significance. The one sustained, extant Aristotelian analysis of a historical tyranny, the account of the Peisistratids in the *Constitution of the Athenians*, rightly recognizes that the tyrants were neither the only citizens nor the only people who occupied offices in Athens.[71] Peisistratus himself is said to have established local judges to hear cases in various parts of Attica (*AP* 16.5) and to have been willing to stand trial before the Areopagus Council (*AP* 16.8, cf. *Pol.* 5.12.1315b21–2); tellingly, he is also reported to have died in the year of the archonship of Philoneos (*AP* 17.1). In fact, the *Constitution of the Athenians* gives every indication that most of the official institutions operative in Athens before Peisistratus took power continued to function during his own and his sons' period of rule. Peisistratus "wanted to manage everything in accordance with the laws" (*AP* 16.8), and though a later chapter claims that at least some of the laws of Solon fell into disuse during the tyranny (*AP* 22.1), for the most part the text agrees with the tradition that Peisistratus himself, if not his sons, preserved the established laws, presumably including operation of the Council of 400 and the assembly.[72] Peisistratus's tyranny is far from paradigmatic – he "managed the affairs of the city moderately and more politically than tyrannically" (*AP* 16.2) – but his example shows that even a tyrant need not be a city's only citizen.

The compatibility of Aristotelian citizenship with wide divergences in degrees of authority does not provide a key to unlock the mysteries of Aristotle's analysis of constitutions. On any account, the classifications and descriptions of constitutions in the *Politics* contain many obscurities,

---

[71] The authenticity of the *Athenaiōn Politeia* as a work of Aristotle is disputed, but there is little doubt that it is a product of Aristotle's school written during his lifetime. Though it is sometimes inconsistent with the *Politics* on points of detail, it is an attempt to provide an analysis of the fourth century democratic constitution and its prehistory within a recognizably Aristotelian framework. For a balanced treatment of the authorship question and of agreements between the *AP* and the *Politics*, see Rhodes 1981: 60–4. For a defense of Aristotle's authorship, see Keaney 1992.

[72] In this respect the *AP* agrees with Hdt. 1.59 and Thucy. 6.54. Rhodes 1981: 218–19, 261 supplies comparanda and concludes, on *AP* 22.1, that "it is likely that the other texts are right and this passage is wrong, and that on the whole Solon's institutions did survive but the tyrants saw to it that they worked in such a way as to yield the desired results." On the council and the assembly, as well as other offices, see *AP* 7–8 with the commentary of Rhodes 1981. For my purposes, of course, the historical accuracy of the *AP* is less relevant than its evident comfort with the thought of offices existing in a tyranny.

ambiguities, and apparent inconsistencies.[73] My claim is not that acknowledging degrees of authority provides a neat solution to those problems, but rather that it contributes to a more satisfactory explanation of their existence. Aristotle could have improved his theory by being less ambiguous and more consistent in his application of terms like "citizen," "rule," "authority," "ruling body," and "constitution." The account that I have given does not resolve the ambiguities in his use of these terms, but it does make their presence less surprising than alternative accounts. On the view that citizenship does not admit of significant variation in degrees of authority, much that Aristotle says about citizens and constitutions would stand in flat and obvious contradiction with his theory of citizenship. On the view I have been defending, by contrast, the complexity and flexibility of the central concepts call for sharper terminological distinctions than Aristotle provides, but these ambiguities do not point to any deep and irresolvable contradictions that require him to abandon any of his major claims.

8. Justice and the Distribution of Citizenship

So far I have shown only that Aristotelian citizenship admits of degrees of authority. I have not yet shown that Aristotle regards the enfranchisement of native or permanent adult male inhabitants as a requirement of justice. Because citizenship is compatible with hierarchical distributions of authority, Aristotle's conditional endorsement of aristocracy and kingship does not commit him to excluding everyone but the aristocrats or the king from citizenship altogether. It remains to be seen, however, whether Aristotle in fact envisions these constitutions as extending citizenship beyond the ruling class that gives each its name and, if so, whether he does so on the grounds that justice requires giving free adult male inhabitants who are not metics some share in rule.

As I discussed in Chapter 1, Aristotle's approach to the distribution of political authority appeals to two general principles: an aristocratic principle of merit in assigning offices and a principle of summation in comparing the merit of individuals and groups. The principle of merit holds that claims to political office are to be assessed by the claimants' ability to contribute to the function or "work" of politics (*Pol.* 3.12.1282b23–1283a2), where the virtues of character and intellect make a greater contribution

[73] For a concise treatment of some of the most apparent puzzles, see Rowe 2000.

than freedom, wealth, or sheer power (3.12–3.13.1283a14–1283a22). The principle of summation holds that any particular person's merit-based claim to authority must also be assessed against the collective ability of different groups of people to govern the city well. Because a group of individuals who possess no special or outstanding virtues may nonetheless collectively be better at governing the city than any of the most virtuous individuals or a select group of them, this possibility must be taken seriously when assessing the justice of proposed constitutional arrangements. These principles seem likely to tell in favor of polity in many, if not most, cases. Hence, though an aristocracy or a kingship could be just if some individual or group of individuals turns out to be better able to govern the city than all the other citizens combined, Aristotle firmly rejects any general judgment that the multitude should not be in control of the constitution (3.11.1281b15–21).

Many commentators have understood the summation argument as intended to yield conclusions about the extension of citizenship and the criteria for inclusion within the citizen body. Yet because citizenship admits of degrees of authority and does not entail membership in the city's ruling body, the route to this conclusion is considerably less direct than it has often been taken to be. To be sure, when Aristotle first raises the question of "what should be the authoritative element of the city" in 3.10, the puzzles that he raises for each of the possible answers seem to presuppose that whoever is excluded from the ruling body is thereby excluded from citizenship as well (3.10.1281a11–34). When he turns to offer solutions to those puzzles, however, matters become considerably more complex.

His first invocation of the summation principle is directed at subverting the objection that it could not conceivably be better for the multitude, rather than the few best men, to be the city's authoritative or controlling element. Immediately after showing that the multitude's collective ability can yield a just claim to authority, he appeals to the principle a second time to argue that the same considerations help to resolve a closely related but distinct problem:

> Through these things one could resolve both the aforementioned puzzle and the one that is connected to it: Over what things should the free men and the multitude of the citizens have authority? These sorts are all of those who are neither wealthy nor have even a single merit-based claim of excellence [ἀξίωμα ἀρετῆς]. For it is not safe for them to share in the greatest offices, since they will necessarily commit some injustices and make other mistakes owing to their injustice and thoughtlessness. But it is a frightful

thing to give them no part and for them not to have any share,[74] since whenever many people are disenfranchised [ἄτιμοι] and poor, the city is necessarily full of people who are hostile to it. It is left, then, for them to share in deliberating and judging. That is precisely why both Solon and some of the other lawgivers appoint them to electing and auditing the officials [τῶν ἀρχόντων], but do not allow them to rule on their own. For all, when they have come together, have sufficient perception, and when they are mixed with the best men they benefit their cities ... but each separately is incompletely capable of passing judgment [ἀτελὴς περὶ τὸ κρίνειν]. (3.11.1281b21–38)

These two appeals to the summation principle give different answers to two different questions. The first lays out conditions in which the multitude of citizens should have control over the city. As its reappearance a few chapters later makes clear, this argument is intended as a defense of polity (3.13.1283b27–35). The second argument, however, applies to circumstances in which the conditions for polity are not met. This much should be clear, at any rate, from the character of the solution that the summation principle is invoked to support: The multitude elects and audits officials, but a select group of citizens occupies important positions of authority. This sort of arrangement does not amount to polity because it does not put the multitude in control of the authoritative body; we have already seen that this limited sort of participation by the multitude is consistent with and even characteristic of aristocracy and of less extreme varieties of oligarchy. The reference to Solon further distances this solution from control by the multitude. In a brief discussion of Solon in book 2, Aristotle makes clear that the constitution he established in Athens neither was nor

---

[74] τὸ δὲ μὴ μεταδιδόναι μήδε μετέχειν φοβερόν: Simpson 1997 translates "if they were given no share and had no participation in office, it would be cause for alarm"; Reeve 1998, similarly, "to give them no share and not to allow them to participate at all would be cause for alarm"; Robinson 1962, more loosely, "it is dangerous to allow them no share at all"; Lord [1984] 2013, more literally: "To give them no part and for them not to share [in the offices] is a matter for alarm" (Lord's parenthesis). It is worth noting, however, that the sentence's syntactical structure might be taken to require the reader to supply the same subject for both infinitives μεταδιδόναι and μετέχειν – and, in this context, the subject of both should be "those who are neither wealthy nor have even a single merit-based claim of excellence." In that case, we might render the sentence as "it is a frightful thing for them neither to give nor receive any share." If so, then Aristotle would here be arguing not simply that the multitude of free citizens should be given a share of rule, but that they should themselves give the more authoritative officials their superior share, which they presumably can do only if they elect and audit those officials. As a reader for the press has observed, however, the infinitives here might more naturally be read as gerunds, yielding something like the English expression "giving and taking in marriage," where of course the subjects of the giving and the taking are not identical. In light of the interpretation of Aristotle's view that I defend here, it is worth considering the alternative translation, though my interpretation does not depend on construing the infinitives this way.

was intended to become a democracy. Though later changes gradually transformed Athens into "the current democracy," those changes were no part of Solon's aim (2.12.1273b41–1274a15):

> It seems that Solon, at any rate, gave the demos the most necessary power, electing and auditing the offices, since if the demos were not authoritative over this, it would be enslaved and hostile. But he established all the offices from the well-known and well-off. (2.12.1274a15–19)

Aristotle concedes that Solon expanded the power of the demos. Not only did he grant them the authority to elect and audit officials, but he enabled them to serve as jurors in the law courts (2.12.1274a2–3). Aristotle does not explicitly reject the view, which he attributes to "some," that Solon instituted "the ancestral democracy" (2.12.1273b35–9).[75] The general tenor of his account, however, is critical of the received views that he reports, and a clear implication of his own alternative is that Solon did not put the demos in control of the constitution. Accordingly, when he later appeals to the Solonian constitution for an example of "over what things the free men and the multitude of the citizens should have authority" (3.11.1281b23–4), it is not to nominate polity as a solution to that problem. The question poses a problem, in fact, only because it presupposes that the multitude of citizens should not have control over the city in at least some circumstances. In other words, the question Aristotle raises is, when the summation principle does not justify polity as the best constitutional arrangement for a particular population, what role should be given those citizens who do not meet the standards for membership in the constitution's ruling body? His answer: at a minimum, election and auditing of officials.

The summation principle, then, has two related but distinct applications. On the one hand, it serves as a standard for assessing the kind of constitution that would be most just for any particular population: Here it applies to the distribution of the most authoritative offices and to membership in the city's ruling body. On the other hand, the summation principle also justifies the inclusion of all naturally free adult male inhabitants in the minimal degree of citizenship represented by the election and auditing of officials. In the former case, the principle functions positively: even when the multitude fails to meet the conditions that

---

[75] Aristotle is here inserting himself into Athenian debates about Solon's constitution, which had begun at least in the last decade of the fifth century and continued into Aristotle's time: Finley 1975: ch. 2.

justify polity, the summation principle supplies us with a set of considerations that guide us toward an answer to the question of how the composition of the city's ruling body should be determined. In the latter case, by contrast, the principle functions negatively: Because even those who can make no special claims to virtue are nonetheless capable of judging and deliberating competently about the selection and auditing of officials, the merit-based conception of justice does not justify excluding them from citizenship altogether. Unlike membership in the ruling body, however, minimal inclusion in citizenship is not justified solely by considerations of individual and collective ability. It is justified, more basically, by the principle of nondespotic rule.

The argument in book 3 against altogether excluding the multitude of the free from citizenship might, at first glance, seem not to rely at all on any considerations of justice. If many were disenfranchised, it would be "a frightful thing," since the city would be "necessarily full of people who are hostile to it" (3.11.1281b28–30). So, one might think, though there is nothing strictly unjust about withholding citizenship from such people, it would threaten the city's stability and thereby be dangerous for the citizens; the citizens therefore have "prudential" or self-interested reasons to extend some of the basic entitlements of citizenship to such people, but no "moral" or other-regarding reasons of justice enter into the decision.[76]

Though the attractions of this interpretation of the argument are fairly obvious, there are strong reasons to reject it. The dichotomy between "prudence" and "morality" is liable to distort a eudaimonistic conception of ethics such as Aristotle's, which identifies noninstrumental relations to others as crucial for an individual's own good and sees justice as a virtue that, like all virtues, benefits its possessor.[77] The dichotomy is especially ill suited to a conception of justice as essentially bound up with mutually beneficial cooperation. As I argued in Chapters 2 and 3, one condition for the justice of any interaction is, on Aristotle's view, that all of the parties have sufficient reason to cooperate willingly with one another. Since the instrumental or constitutive goods achieved by cooperation supply agents with those reasons, any evidence that some

---

[76] For this view of the argument, see Ober 1998: 321, Morrison 1999: 154, and Kraut 2002: 408.

[77] For a highly selective but suggestive history of the devolution of Aristotelian φρόνησις to modern "prudence" via Latin prudentia, see Den Uyl 1991. For some conceptual and historical explorations of the modern distinction between the moral and the nonmoral, where the moral excludes the prudential, see the essays in the second half of MacIntyre 1971 and, for a less historical treatment, Williams 1985. I share with Kraut 2006c the view that Aristotle does not operate with a concept of the moral as a distinct domain of practical reasons.

parties to an interaction do not have such reasons is evidence of injustice. Accordingly, when Aristotle says that the disenfranchised multitude will be hostile to the regime that disenfranchises them, he is in fact pointing to a consideration of justice. The instability and danger that he envisions as consequences of this hostility do, of course, provide the citizens with self-regarding reasons not to disenfranchise the free multitude. Yet these self-regarding reasons are neither external to considerations of justice nor entirely independent of the other-regarding reasons that are essential to those considerations. If justice is the common good of mutually beneficial cooperation, then self-regarding reasons cannot be completely incidental to its content. If, conversely, Aristotle were concerned solely with the citizens' strictly self-regarding interest in avoiding instability, he could just as well recommend that the city adopt one of the deceptive sophistries that he elsewhere castigates (2.5.1264a18–22, 3.5.1278a38–40, 4.13.1297a14–b1, 6.8.1307b40–1308a3).

Here again Solon helps to clarify Aristotle's thought. The account of the Solonian constitution in book 2 cites the same justification for minimal inclusion of the free multitude that appears in the argument in book 3. It adds, however, that the demos that is not given authority over elections and audits would not merely be hostile, but enslaved (2.12.1274a17–18). Though he does not say so explicitly in the argument from book 3, we now have reason to understand that argument as appealing to the same considerations. The argument against excluding the free multitude appeals to the injustice of that exclusion, and enslavement is Aristotle's pervasive analogy for injustice. It is easy enough to recognize that people who exercise rule over those to whom they are in no way formally accountable may be less constrained from treating their subjects unjustly than they would be if they were in fact accountable to those subjects in some way – if, that is, both groups share in ruling and being ruled. Yet, as I argued in the concluding section of the previous chapter and as this chapter has helped to confirm, Aristotle has good reasons to maintain that being altogether excluded from citizenship can itself be a form of injustice and subjection to despotic rule. Such exclusion threatens the ability of a city's permanent inhabitants to be ruled willingly and therefore to live in accordance with their own deliberate decision.

There are deep and complex problems about the extent to which Aristotle's own recommendations fully and consistently meet the standards of justice that he embraces. As I have already suggested, the implications of these standards for the treatment of metics seem far more complicated than Aristotle ever acknowledges. Moreover, he rather infamously appears at times to be complacent toward and even supportive of political arrangements that exclude the members of certain class and status groups from citizenship. On the one hand, we should not be too surprised at this attitude. Aristotle himself believes that even the generically correct constitutions, with the sole exception of the best constitution, are only imperfectly just (4.8.1293b23–8). Even those less than ideal correct constitutions have rarely existed; the great majority of constitutions that do or have existed have, in his view, been deviant in some significant way (4.7.1293a39–b1). Aristotle is thus willing to accept a great deal of imperfection in the world, and the Aristotelian statesman typically seeks to improve existing conditions through reform rather than to impose perfect form on unsuitable matter.[78] More problematically, however, the best constitution itself – the constitution that is supposed to be "what one would pray for" (7.4.1325b36, 5.1327a4, 10.1330a26, 11.1330a37, 12.1331b21, 13.1332a29; cf. 2.1.1260b28–9) – seems to violate the principles of justice that Aristotle elsewhere defends. Besides excluding farmers and even skilled laborers from citizenship (7.9.1328b33–1329a2), Aristotle's ideal has been charged with depending on the unjust economic exploitation of its metics and of embracing conventional, and not merely natural, slavery.[79] This is not the place for a detailed exploration of the problems and prospects of Aristotle's best constitution. I shall simply go on record as maintaining that although some of these problems are indeed unavoidable for Aristotle – the problems of economic exploitation and the political exclusion of laborers in particular – we have no good grounds for concluding that they are the products of any self-conscious violation or rejection of the principle of nondespotic rule on Aristotle's part.[80]

If Aristotle accepts that principle and the applications of it that this chapter has argued for, his defense of kingship and rejection of tyranny will turn out to pose no deep problems for his political philosophy as a

[78] For accounts of this aspect of Aristotle's thought, see, briefly, Kraut 2002: 196 and, more fully, Miller 2007 and Garver 2011. Ober 1998: 292–3 suggests that the emphasis in the *Politics* on "practical internal amelioration of existing regimes" can be explained by the requirement imposed at the creation of the League of Corinth in 337 forbidding constitutional changes. Though this suggestion is not implausible, it seems insufficient on its own to account for Aristotle's pervasive preference for reform over "revolution," which coheres well with his understanding of political life and action, particularly his appreciation of the dangers of faction and instability (on which see *Pol.* 5 and especially Garver 2011). Rosler 2005: 250–8 presents a less speculative and more illuminating contextual account of why Aristotle "attempted to cool off the political extremism of his time."

[79] For clear and forceful indictments of Aristotle on this score, see Charles 1988, Annas 1996, and Schofield 1999b. For an even-handed critique, see Kraut 2002: 214–20.

[80] On this point, I accept the main thrust of the persuasive response by Miller 1996 to Annas 1996. See further Long 2005: 184–9.

whole. If citizenship is important not primarily because it affords people opportunities for a unique form of intrinsically valuable activity, but because exclusion typically subjects the excluded to unjust domination, then what I have called the normative problem of monarchy will arise only if kingship entails that kind of unjust domination. If citizenship is compatible with divergent degrees of authority, then the king need not be the only citizen, and what I have called the conceptual problem of monarchy will be resolved, because a political community ruled by a king will not cease to be composed of a plurality of citizens. The conclusions of this chapter are sufficient to show that Aristotle can consistently endorse a form of kingship, and so too of other, less concentrated distributions of authority. It remains to be seen, however, whether his actual defense of kingship points to an arrangement in which the king and his fellow citizens share in ruling and being ruled or whether Aristotelian kingship compromises the standards of political justice and fails to embody a distinctively political community. In the next and final chapter, therefore, I will return to those questions. After defending some particular answers to them, I will turn to ask why Aristotle devoted so much attention to monarchy in book 3 when he elsewhere seems not to take it seriously even as a part of ideal theory.

CHAPTER 6

Kingship as Political Rule and Political Community

The arguments of the preceding chapters have aimed to show that the conceptual framework of Aristotle's political theory allows for his defense of kingship without generating what I have called the normative and the conceptual problems of monarchy. After setting out Aristotle's general understanding of community, justice, and friendship in Chapter 2, Chapter 3 maintained that Aristotle's account of political community neither presupposes nor entails the intrinsic value of political activity or the necessity of citizenship for a good human life. This conclusion runs counter to one major interpretive claim that generates the normative paradox; if citizenship is not necessary for living well, then kingship need not deprive the king's subjects of the opportunity to flourish as rational animals. Disposing of the thesis that politics is an indispensable intrinsic good is, however, insufficient for meeting the objection that underlies the normative paradox. As Chapter 3 went on to show, Aristotle treats inclusion in citizenship as a requirement of justice that admits of only a few general kinds of exception. After proposing some reasons for this judgment that do not appeal to the intrinsic value of citizenship or its necessity for living well, I moved on in Chapter 4 to explain how this demand for political inclusion could be consistent with Aristotle's endorsement of apparently exclusive political arrangements. Central to this explanation is a distinction between sharing in rule – and hence being a citizen in Aristotle's "official" sense – and the varying degrees and levels of authority possessed by citizens. This distinction allows us to see that Aristotle's classification of constitutions does not hinge on the number of citizens so much as on the number of citizens who hold positions of the highest authority and thereby compose the "ruling body" of the city. Aristotle's "correct" constitutions are less exclusive than many readers have thought, but they are more hierarchical. By allowing for levels of hierarchy among citizens, Aristotle can consistently endorse aristocracy and kingship in certain circumstances without violating or suspending the requirement that a city's adult male permanent inhabitants should be granted at least a minimal share in rule. This account of citizenship and authority also points toward a straightforward resolution of the conceptual version of the paradox of monarchy. Put simply, if the king is not the only citizen, then an Aristotelian kingship is no less a political community composed of a plurality of citizens than an Aristotelian polity would be.

The arguments of the preceding chapters therefore show that Aristotle can, in principle, recognize a correct and just form of monarchy alongside the deviance and injustice of tyranny. To show that there is conceptual space for kingship in Aristotle's theory does not, however, show that the kind of kingship he envisions occupies that space. Several features of Aristotle's defense of kingship cast doubt on that idea: His extended comparison of kingship to the rule of a household seems to commit him to a conflation of the household and the city much like the one for which he takes Plato to task; his description of the "total king" as ruling "simply and not in part" apparently denies to kingship one of the essential features of distinctively political rule and community; his characterization of the king as not subject to the rule of law evidently denies another. Even the invocation of the summation principle in defense of total kingship seems to acknowledge that kingship could not be a form of political community, since it might seem that only a superhuman demigod could meet the conditions laid down by that principle, and no such person could enter into a relationship of fundamental equality such as political community is supposed to be.

In the first part of this chapter, I take up each of these problems in turn and argue that each is misconceived. This part has five sections. The first considers the role of consent and approval by the ruled in distinguishing kingship from tyranny; making the justice of monarchy contingent on the consent and approval of the ruled ensures that they share in rule sufficiently to count as citizens. The second section examines what Aristotle means when he says that the king does not rule "in turn" (κατὰ μέρος), arguing that this phrase distinguishes alternation from continuous rule but does not describe shared rule as such; hence to deny that the king rules κατὰ μέρος is not to imply that his subjects do not in any way share in ruling as well as being ruled. In the third section, I turn to the claim that the absolute king is not subject to the rule of law; properly understood, the king does not differ in this respect from the few best men in an aristocracy or the multitude in a polity. The fourth section addresses arguments that the total king's "incomparable virtue" must differ in kind from normal human virtue and shows that neither Aristotle's technical conception of commensurability nor his various analogies and metaphors can be called upon to sustain this contention. Finally, in the fifth section I consider Aristotle's comparison of kingship to the rule of a household; contrary to what many have supposed, this comparison does not commit Aristotle to collapsing the distinction between political and household rule. Aristotle's king is not a superhuman whose presence justifies a suspension of the political, but an exceptional human being whose presence justifies extraordinary ways of doing politics.

Meeting these objections at length is important for at least two reasons. First, it shows that Aristotle's core conception of political community is consistent not simply with some form of monarchy, but with the kingship that he devotes so much space in book 3 to defending. If the two were inconsistent, that would cast doubt on the interpretation of the nature and value of political community that I have elaborated in Chapters 1–5; by contrast, their consistency lends further support to that interpretation. Second, the application of the core conception of politics to the case of monarchy illuminates aspects of the core conception that more egalitarian arrangements leave relatively obscure. Appreciating the coherence of Aristotle's defense of kingship not only enables a more accurate assessment of the *Politics* as a whole, but sheds light on fundamental features of its view of politics. The concluding sections of this chapter therefore address the theoretical aim of Aristotle's defense of kingship: Why does he defend kingship at all and at such length? I identify that aim as primarily, though not exclusively, a critical response to Plato's ideal of a philosopher-king whose status as a ruler is a function of, if not identical to, his knowledge of "the kingly art." Like Plato's ideal statesman, Aristotle's total king is a theoretically possible but practically improbable ideal who serves as a standard for critiquing existing arrangements and rejecting would-be monarchs. Unlike Plato, however, Aristotle insists even at the level of ideal theory that rulership is not simply a matter of knowledge and authoritative command. Aristotelian political rule is not most fundamentally the exercise and application of theoretical or technical expertise, but an inherently reciprocal mode of authority exercised via the nonscientific and nontechnical processes of practical deliberation and judgment. Aristotle's defense of the "total king" highlights the way in which the specifically practical nature of politics allows not only for the possibility, but especially for the excellence, of collective deliberation and judgment. Aristotelian kingship is thus not an unfortunate addendum to an otherwise coherent theory, but a crucial stage in the elaboration of Aristotle's distinctive conception of politics.

1. Kingship, Tyranny, and the Consent of the Ruled

Chapter 5 has shown that citizenship, as Aristotle conceives it, admits degrees of authority. Though every citizen shares in rule, it need not be the case that every citizen does or can occupy the offices charged with making the most general decisions of law and policy. Those who do exercise control over these decisions are members of the ruling body (πολίτευμα), but a citizen may serve on juries, elect and audit officials, and even participate in deliberation about a limited range of shared concerns without being a member of that body. In light of this distinction, it becomes easy to see how kingship could avoid restricting citizenship to the king himself: Though the king alone composes the ruling body and has control over laws and policy, other citizens hold particular positions responsible for implementing that policy and applying those laws. More fundamentally, though we do not typically imagine a king's being elected to office in the way that the best and brightest might be elected in an aristocracy, a king may in fact owe his preeminent position to the recognition and approval of those he rules, however formally or informally expressed. Thus the king's subjects may in effect elect and audit him and thereby possess the same sort of authority as ordinary citizens who are not members of a city's ruling body. Otherwise put, kingship may be a kind of aristocracy of one.

There are several indications that Aristotle envisions kingship in just this way. No monarchy could function if a single person tried to manage all of the tasks ordinarily assigned to different officials. Mere practicality therefore demands that at least some of these tasks be delegated to others. The need for "fellow rulers" even serves as the basis for objections to kingship in the dialectical treatment of the issue in book 3. Since monarchs must appoint officials and in fact make people who are well disposed to them their "fellow rulers," it may seem that kingship accepts in practice what it denies in theory: The king is not uniquely qualified to rule (*Pol.* 3.16.1287b8–11, 25–35). This objection never receives an explicit response, so it may be tempting to conclude that Aristotle tacitly accepts it as decisive.[1] More plausibly, however, the response is implicit in the final appeal to the summation principle in defense of kingship (3.15.1286a6–29). That concluding argument brushes aside much of the preceding discussion as at best indirectly relevant to the main question; what matters is

---

[1] As does Nichols 1992: 79.

whether the would-be king passes the test set by the summation principle and is in fact better able to govern the city than all the others taken together would be. The objections and difficulties posed in the foregoing discussion serve in part to supply some criteria for passing that test. But the reassertion of the summation argument in 3.17 makes clear that the conditional justice of kingship follows from the same principles of justice in the distribution of political authority that more frequently tell in favor of polity or aristocracy. Furthermore, even the formulation of the objection points toward the obvious, if unexpressed, answer: The "officials appointed by him" (3.16.1287b9), his "fellow rulers" (συνάρχους, 3.16.1287b31), are subordinate to the monarch rather than his equals in authority. Though the full complexity of constitutional arrangements emerges only in the middle books, the concluding argument of book 3 works in part by appeal to the parallel between aristocracy and kingship. The argument as a whole therefore gives us no more reason to expect the king to be the city's only citizen than we would expect aristocrats to be the only citizens in an aristocracy.

Later discussions of monarchy in the *Politics* explicitly refer to citizens, suggesting that both kingship and tyranny are perfectly compatible with the existence of a plurality of citizens (5.10.1311a7–8, 11.1314b1–13, 11.1315a6–8).[2] This is just what we should expect. Far from being citizens only in some diluted, secondary sense, such people may meet the formal definition of citizenship from 3.1 just as well as democratic citizens do.[3] A more pressing worry, however, is that citizens in these circumstances fail to share in anything like the reciprocal rule that Aristotle so often seems to make essential to politics. The king's subjects may share in rule by holding subordinate offices, serving on juries, and so on. Yet surely citizens who can implement policy but have no role in formulating or at least ratifying it would fail to share in ruling and being ruled in any robust sense. They would be ruled by a king who is not himself subject to rule. So, while the citizens of a kingship might share in *his* rule, they would not also rule in their own right; their possession and exercise of authority would be a mere matter of delegation.[4]

---

[2] None of these passages explicitly refers to παμβασιλεία, but their generality suggests that they are meant to apply to tyranny and kingship quite broadly, not merely to some limited range of types. The passages thereby show that Aristotle finds nothing strange in the idea of a monarch ruling over citizens. We should, accordingly, not suppose that the reference to citizens in the book 3 discussion of παμβασιλεία uses that term in some sort of deviant sense.

[3] For arguments against interpreting the references to citizens in these passages in terms of some attenuated sense of "citizenship," see Chapter 5.

[4] Kraut 2002: 414–15 attempts to avoid the paradox of monarchy and related problems by maintaining that the king is not the only citizen. But his account of Aristotelian citizenship makes it unclear whether he can consistently embrace this solution. The "politically active citizens" that Kraut finds

This problem seems not to have exercised Aristotle much, probably because he assumed that its guiding premise is false. In two important passages contrasting kingship and tyranny, he attributes a more fundamental role to the king's subjects than the foregoing description of them as mere delegates would allow. First:

> There is a third kind of tyranny which seems to be tyranny most of all, since it is a counterpart to total kingship. The monarchy that is unaccountable and rules over people who are all similar or better for its own advantage rather than for the advantage of the ruled is necessarily this sort of tyranny. That is why it is coercive: For nobody who is free willingly endures this sort of rule. (4.10.1295a19–23)

Again, later:

> Kingships no longer come about these days, but if monarchies do arise, they are rather tyrannies, because kingship is voluntary rule and has authority over rather great things, but there are many people who are similar and nobody is so outstanding as to measure up to the magnitude and worth of the rule. So, for this reason people do not put up with it willingly, and if someone comes to rule through deception or force, this already seems to be tyranny. (5.10.1313a3–10)

These passages set several criteria for distinguishing tyranny from kingship. The first is the familiar requirement for correct constitutions: The king promotes the common good of the ruled rather than aiming at his own interests. The second criterion is the likewise familiar application of the summation principle: The king is better than those he rules, whereas the tyrant rules over his equals or even his betters. The third and fourth criteria are less familiar. The tyrant, but not the king, rules without being accountable. Related to the king's accountability is the fact that the people he rules are ruled willingly; they not only acquiesce, as they might to the rule of a tyrant, but voluntarily embrace the king's authority. These last two features of kingship call for some consideration.[5]

---

in a kingship are those who occupy minor offices that merely implement the king's policy, and by his own account, such people do not engage in "ruling." He does not explain how people who merely implement policy over which they have no active influence can be said to share in political rule with those who do – why, in other words, the king rules over *citizens* rather than *bureaucrats*. Kraut's complex and wide-ranging view of the *Politics* no doubt has the resources to address this problem adequately. As it stands, however, his treatment of the issue is at best underdeveloped.

[5] Note that 4.10 1295a19–23 explicitly contrasts tyranny with παμβασιλεία; hence there are no grounds for supposing that Aristotle is here describing some more limited sort of kingship. Insofar as the passages in books 4 and 5 ascribe features to kingship generically, we should expect them to belong to παμβασιλεία as the paradigm of kingship.

Aristotle's word for "unaccountable" is ἀνυπεύθυνος, perhaps most literally "not subject to correction." It carries with it an unmistakable association with the Athenian democratic system of official audits (εὔθυναι) held at the end of every official's term of office. In Athens, anyone who had been formally assigned some official duty had to submit to an audit in which a special board would investigate the handling of any funds and hear accusations of any other kinds of offense. If found guilty, the official could be punished with a fine or, depending on the charge, more severe penalties. In the Athenian case, the audit was a complex formal procedure and an integral institutional component of the democracy.[6] The underlying function and purpose of the audits can, however, be appreciated in abstraction from any particular institutional embodiment of them. By making officials accountable, the system of audits aims to deter them from abusing their positions and to punish them for any such abuse. In virtue of these powers, the system also gives the auditors themselves a measure of power and authority over the officials. In effect, it makes the officials dependent on those over whom they exercise their authority and provides a counterweight to the asymmetry of power that inevitably results whenever some members of a group are granted special authority and privilege. Though Aristotle has nothing to say about the institutional structure of audits in a kingship, his appeal to accountability to distinguish it from tyranny has bite because it insists on the preservation of the reciprocity and mutuality in political rule that tyranny surreptitiously suspends when it does not openly violate. Short on institutional detail as it may be, the accountability criterion makes clear that kingship is not imposed upon the citizens from above and unconstrained in its operations, but essentially dependent on their recognition and approval.

The importance of recognition and approval is reinforced by the claim that tyranny is coercive while kingship is voluntary.[7] Though Aristotle

---

[6] For details, see Hansen 1991: 222–4, who suggests that the εὔθυναι were less important means of controlling officials than the procedure of "denunciation" (εἰσαγγελία) and the charge of proposing illegal decrees (γραφὴ παρανόμων). In support, he cites the relatively small number of convictions stemming from εὔθυναι for which we have evidence. Yet since we also know that the εὔθυναι were held every year, the infrequency of conviction might be taken as evidence for the success of the institution in deterring abuse of official privileges.

[7] The scope of "the involuntary" or the unwilling in these passages should be taken to include what EN 3.1 calls "mixed" actions. An action is "mixed" when fear of greater evils or the attraction of some noble aim leads an agent to do something willingly that he would otherwise be unwilling to do; Aristotle's examples are a shameful act compelled by the threats of a tyrant and throwing a ship's cargo overboard during a storm at sea (EN 3.1.1109b30–1110b17). By contrast, EE 2.8 describes these cases as "involuntary" or "unwilling" acts (EE 2.8.1225a2–20).

elsewhere suggests that ruling over unwilling subjects is unjust as such (7.2.1324b22–41), his explicit invocations of this criterion are largely restricted to discussions of kingship and tyranny (3.14.1285a27–8, b2–5, 4.10.1295a15–24, 5.10.1313a3–8, 11.1314a33–8). Moreover, while it is clear that the consent of the ruled will be a mark of kingship and lack of consent a mark of tyranny, there are at least two reasons for doubting that consent or its absence plays any fundamental role in making a monarchic constitution just or unjust. First, people can consent to a political arrangement in the mistaken belief that it promotes their interests; "barbarian kingship" and Greek "dictatorship" (αἰσυμνητεία), the quasi-tyrannical kingships that Aristotle identifies, are cases in point (3.14.1285a14–1285b3). People can be mistaken about both ends and means (7.13.1331b26–38), and so can be brought to agree willingly to arrangements that are not in fact beneficial to them.[8] Thus consent is insufficient for justice, which requires that the constitution promote the genuine interests of the ruled. But if consent is powerless on its own to render an arrangement just, its absence might seem equally powerless to render it unjust. It would, at any rate, seem strange to maintain that a constitution could be unjust even if its laws and policies actually promote the common good of its citizens. Yet if the consent of the ruled is necessary for justice, then fools could make their own city's constitution unjust simply by withholding their consent to it on the basis of mistaken conceptions of justice and the good. Since Aristotle does not elsewhere suggest that the justice of an arrangement could be held hostage in this way, mere consent seems neither sufficient nor necessary for justice.

This problem will not arise if Aristotle takes consent to be *evidence* of constitutional correctness rather than a *criterion* with explanatory power: Though the constitution is not just because people consent to it, consent is a regular feature of just political arrangements.[9] Because justice promotes and protects the common good, and the common good is the mutual benefit of each of the citizens, each of the citizens will have good reason to embrace a just constitutional scheme. In addition to avoiding the problematic consequences of treating consent as a criterion of justice, this view helps to explain the relative paucity of appeals to consent in

---

[8] In fact, consent to arrangements that do not promote one's own good seems to be a regular feature of politics; for a brief consideration of this familiar point in an Aristotelian context, presented as a critique of subjectivist theories of social and political well-being, see Nussbaum 1990b. What is less immediately clear is whether most or all members of a political community could consent to arrangements that either do not promote or even obstruct their own pursuit of the good.

[9] This is the view of Miller 1995: 273.

the *Politics*. It also fits well with the texts that do appeal to consent. Both of the passages cited previously claim that citizens do not accept tyranny willingly because it is deviant, and thus explain consent by appeal to correctness rather than the other way around.

There are, however, several reasons to be dissatisfied with this evidential interpretation of consent. First, it renders the appeal to consent otiose and irrelevant. If the citizens' willingness to be ruled plays no role in explaining the justice of a constitutional arrangement, then its appearance in a contrast between kingship and tyranny is out of place. Of course, if there were an independently assessable empirical correlation between kingship and consent, on the one hand, and tyranny and dissent, on the other, then the substantive justice and injustice of the respective constitutions could play a genuine explanatory role. Aristotle might then be taken to be defending his account of kingship and tyranny by showing that it issues in a successful explanation of political phenomena. But this kind of empirical explanation is not what Aristotle is up to in the passages quoted. Nor, if he were, would such an account be successful. For it is unlikely that citizens' actual willingness to be ruled under a particular regime tracks that regime's substantive justice. Not only do people frequently endorse unjust constitutions, but there are good Aristotelian reasons to believe that people will not always endorse just ones when they are available; people tend to judge badly in their own case (3.9.1280a9–16), and excellent laws and education are necessary if more than a few lucky people are to develop the virtues of character and intellect that would make their spontaneous judgments consistently correct (7.13.1332a28–b11, 8.1–2.1337a11–34, *EN* 10.9.1179b20–1180a5). In the real world, we have little reason to expect that consent or its absence is reliable empirical evidence of justice or injustice.

If Aristotle's references to the citizens' willingness to be ruled are to amount to more than a recommendation of consent to just political arrangements, consent must have a more direct role to play in explaining constitutional correctness. An alternative explanation of Aristotle's appeal to consent in light of his more fundamental requirement that correct constitutions promote the good of the ruled would be to see being ruled willingly as an aspect of the well-being at which the just constitution is supposed to aim.[10] This strategy has at least this much going for it: It is indeed, on Aristotle's view, impossible for a naturally free adult to

---

[10] This is the view adopted by Long 1996 in a friendly critique of Miller 1995; Long's reasons for dissatisfaction with Miller's treatment of what Long calls "the consent-based criterion" differ from my own.

flourish so long as he is subjected to the coercive rule of others and made to act in some significant way contrary to his own best judgment. As I discussed in the final section of Chapter 4, the Aristotelian good life is a life of rational agency lived in accordance with the agent's own deliberate decisions, and the centrality of self-directed rational activity to human well-being is one reason why exclusion from citizenship threatens to violate the principle of nondespotic rule. It does not follow, however, that anyone who lives according to his own deliberate decision thereby lives well, even if external circumstances are favorable and he succeeds in achieving all of his ends. The vicious person, no less than the virtuous, acts in accordance with his own decisions (3.2.1112a1–11, 5.8.1135b19–25, 7.3.1146b22–4, 7.4.1148a11–16, 7.7.1150a18–27, 7.8.1150b29–31, 8.1151a5–7, 7.9.1151a29–b2, 7.10.1152a19–24). The difference lies in the content of those decisions; part of what it is to be virtuous is to be disposed to choose the right means to the best ends. Accordingly, while self-direction is a feature of a good human life and is not a mere instrumental means to intrinsically valuable ends, it is not unconditionally good. Rather, insofar as it consists in an absence of interference by others, it is an external good, and like all external goods its value depends on the quality of its use, which in turn depends on the character and intelligence of the agent who puts it to use (*Pol.* 7.1.1323a21–b13, *EN* 1.8.1098b12–16, 8.1099a31–b8).[11]

The conditional value of self-direction ensures that consent will have no independent role to play in determining the justice of kingship or any other constitution. This is a welcome consequence for Aristotle, since any view that makes consent without qualification a necessary condition for justice does, in fact, leave justice hostage to the will of the governed without regard to the content or reasonableness of that will.[12] Yet

---

[11] Self-direction or, as Aristotle would put it, living in accord with one's own deliberate decision, is misleadingly described as an external good insofar as it is partially a matter of the agent's own psychology and therefore not an external thing that an agent puts to use: It can be threatened not only by externally imposed coercion, but by internal disorder such as *akrasia*, habits of excessive deference, and so on. In political contexts, however, freedom from coercion is its most important aspect, and such freedom is external. Long 1996: 787–9 argues that liberty is a constitutive part of well-being despite being an external good on the grounds that not all external goods are mere means to living well. His prime example is friendship; Aristotle explicitly says both that friends are external goods and that, in the complete form of friendship, friends value one another for each other's sake and hence not merely as instrumental means to their own flourishing. Even if we concede this claim about the relationship of external goods to well-being, both friendship and liberty/ self-direction remain external goods and share the conditional value of all external goods; moreover, they depend for their value on the same thing, i.e., the character of the agents involved and the quality of their activities and decisions.

[12] In other words, it immediately yields minimal state libertarianism if not anarchism (on which see Nozick 1974, Long and Machan 2008). Thus consent theorists eager to defend the state have frequently had recourse to various devices of hypothetical rather than actual, or implicit rather than

the conditional value of self-direction can help to explain why consent is a feature, and not merely an ideal consequence, of constitutional correctness without making unqualified consent necessary or sufficient for justice. Because self-direction – living in accordance with one's own deliberate decisions – is crucial for human flourishing, no political arrangement that thwarts self-direction by undermining people's opportunities to live according to their own judgment could be just, since what is just must promote the citizens' good. Yet because self-direction is not unconditionally valuable, not every constitution or policy that a person could intelligibly resist will be contrary to that person's good.[13] So, for instance, an old-fashioned oligarch who believes that his inherited wealth qualifies him to a larger share of political authority will not necessarily suffer injustice at the hands of a more egalitarian constitution even though he does not accept that constitution willingly. Nor, Aristotle thinks, would he suffer injustice if required to make larger financial contributions to the city than his less well-off fellow citizens (*Pol.* 3.12.1283a17–22), though complying with this law might involve acting contrary to his own will. Rather, if the oligarch got what he wanted, he would be guilty of injustice and hence acting contrary to his own good in addition to harming others. Not only do others have sufficient reason to reject his proposals; he himself has sufficient reason to reject them. The oligarch's will exerts no independent force on the justice or injustice of the arrangement. His dissent has no bearing on the justice of the case because his objections are unreasonable.

So a lack of consent can be unreasonable and thereby of no direct relevance to justice. It does not follow, however, that consent is completely incidental to justice. Though justice does not require respect for unreasonable refusal of consent, self-direction, and hence consent, remain an integral feature of the good at which just constitutions are supposed to aim. Justly exercised rule must therefore invite the rational and uncoerced consent of the ruled. This sort of account might seem susceptible to cynical manipulation: "We would of course prefer your consent," the rulers might say, "but we'll compel you to comply all the same." In fact, however,

---

explicit, consent (for a concise but helpful treatment of consent theories of political authority, see Murphy 2006). Long 1996 thinks that Aristotle's view does in fact have this implication but that he fails to recognize it or embrace it consistently.

[13] Long 1996 sensibly suggests that Aristotle connects the justice or injustice of a constitution to the citizens' consent to the constitution itself rather than to all of the particular policies and decisions enacted by the members of its ruling body. Though Aristotle surely does not see unanimous agreement to every decision as a necessary condition for justice, I do not think much rides on this distinction for my argument.

a genuine respect for the good of others requires a general commitment to interacting with them on a basis of rational persuasion and to avoiding the use of force and deception. Yet this commitment is not compromised by a willingness to use force or the threat of force against people who are decidedly unreasonable.[14] What it excludes is an authoritarian mode of interaction that treats the judgment and consent of the ruled as, at best, facilitating their obedience. To rule justly over mature rational agents is to present them with directives that they can be expected to embrace for good reasons. This, in turn, requires that the rulers treat the rational consent of the ruled as part of the good that they aim to promote and therefore that they employ coercive measures only as a last resort. As Aristotle says of punishment, "just punishments and corrections have virtue as their source, but they are necessary, and they have their nobility by virtue of necessity; for it is more choiceworthy for neither a man nor a city to have any need of such things" (7.13.1332a12–15).

The conditional value of self-direction thus allows us to see how the consent of the ruled can be a feature of a correct political arrangement rather than a mere symptom or an independently necessary condition of justice. Kingship, accordingly, will not depend for its justice on the unanimous agreement of every citizen in welcoming the king's rule. Yet it will be just, in part, because the citizens endorse and approve the king's rule. Put negatively, the rule of a single individual of outstanding excellence will not be just if he can acquire and retain his position only by force or deception: "If they are not willing he will simply not be a king; it is, rather, the tyrant who rules even over those who are not willing" (5.10.1313a14–16).[15] Rather than constituting a distinct criterion of just rule, however, the citizens' consent is an aspect of the common good that the correct constitution must promote and protect. It is, moreover, both a constitutive part of the common good and of instrumental value in promoting it; for not only is consent an element of the self-direction that is so central to well-being, but dissent in itself threatens the stability of the constitution (5.9.1309b14–18).[16] So while Aristotle does not emphasize the

---

[14] Even the view that makes actual unqualified consent necessary for justice allows that the use of force and coercion can be just. What it forbids is their *initiation*; it is not unjust to use force to defend oneself against force and coercion. Such, at least, would be the more common and less extreme view; some radical pacifists might go so far as to denounce all use of force or coercion whatsoever. For "the principle of noncoercion" and an attempt to show that Aristotle endorses it, see Keyt 1993.

[15] Reading ἀλλ'ὁ τύραννος with the mss. rather than Ross's ἀλλὰ τύραννος.

[16] Aristotle understands stability as necessary but not sufficient for justice, but also thinks that justice tends to yield stability, though it is far from guaranteeing it. The complex relationship between justice and stability is an important theme through book 5 of the *Politics* especially, and the role of

importance of consent or approval outside his treatment of monarchy in books 4 and 5, its value is best understood in terms of the general requirements of correct constitutions. As he puts it when describing the general aims of political science, "one ought to introduce a sort of arrangement that people will easily be persuaded and able to share in on the basis of existing circumstances" (4.1.1289a1–3).[17]

2.   Ruling and Being Ruled in Turn

The role of consent in distinguishing kingship from tyranny shows that even the subjects of a king can be said to share in rule. So far from mere passive subjects or fully dependent delegates, the citizens in a kingship legitimate the king's rule through their consent and continued approval. Kingship thereby retains the shared and reciprocal character of distinctively political rule. So much seems, at least, to be the upshot of Aristotle's contrast between kingship and tyranny. Though he does not make these points explicit in book 3, the later passages show that they are implicit in his conception of kingship, and indeed in his conception of correct constitutions more broadly.

There are, however, a number of puzzling passages in the book 3 defense of kingship that could cast doubt on the consistency of that defense with the account of kingship that I have teased out of the text so far. The first of these that I will consider comes at the finale of the dialectical treatment of kingship in *Politics* 3.15–17. There, after reasserting the applicability of the summation principle to the case of kingship, Aristotle concludes:

> It is doubtless not appropriate to kill or exile or ostracize such a man, nor to suppose that he deserves to be ruled in part [κατὰ μέρος]. For by nature the part does not exceed the whole, and this is what has happened to the man who has so great a superiority. So all that is left is to obey such a man and for him to have authority not in part [κατὰ μέρος] but without qualification [ἁπλῶς]. (3.17.1288a24–9)

---

consent in generating stability is one reason to think that Aristotle's appeal to it in his discussion of kingship is not an isolated phenomenon. For a general discussion of stability and justice, see Miller 1995: 267–74, 287–90, Garver 2011: ch. 5

[17] Reading κοινωνεῖν at 1289a3 with the Π² family of manuscripts against Ross's καινίζειν and the alternative κινεῖν found in some manuscripts. Ross and others have presumably rejected κοινωνεῖν on the grounds that it should take a genitive object; Newman, by contrast, was not bothered by this. It seems to offer insufficient grounds for emendation, though Ross's alternative reading would not seriously impact my point here.

At first blush, this passage seems to assert that the king should be the only one who rules while all of the others are merely ruled. It would have this sense, however, only if the phrase that I have translated "in part" indicates sharing: To rule and be ruled "in part" would be to rule along with others who share in that rule, and hence to rule not "in part" would be to rule over others who are merely ruled. Though some scholars have indeed found something like this meaning in the phrase,[18] a consideration of its use in the *Politics* shows that it serves not to describe shared rule per se, but rather a certain way in which rule can be shared, namely, *alternation*.

In one use, the phrase κατὰ μέρος refers to the differential treatment or arrangement of the various parts of a whole. So, for instance, not all of a city's streets and buildings should be laid out uniformly in the neat grid pattern reportedly devised by Hippodamus of Miletus; that sort of plan should be adopted only κατὰ μέρη καὶ τόπους, "by parts and sections" (7.11.1330b29–30). Similarly, an isolated city that does not interact with other communities need not be inactive, since it can also be active κατὰ μέρη, by parts, "since the parts of the city have many communities with one another" (7.3.1325b25–7). In the context of rule and authority, though a general commands a whole army, "there is in addition sometimes an office in charge of cavalry, of light-armed soldiers, of archers, and of sailors where they exist. They are called admirals, cavalry commanders, and regiment commanders, and under these there are, by parts [κατὰ μέρος], trireme captains, company commanders, tribal commanders, and all those subordinate to them" (6.8.1322b1–5).[19] These passages all use the phrase to divide a complex whole into parts to which different functions, activities, or characteristics are then distributed or at least attributed. Call this the *divisional* sense of the phrase.[20]

Perhaps built upon the divisional sense is a second and distinct use that specifically describes alternation among groups in holding office or playing some other role. This use most commonly appears in descriptions of political rule:

> It is clear that it is better for the same people to rule continually, if it is possible. When, however, it is not possible because all the people are equal in nature, it is then also just for all to share in rule, whether ruling is a good or a base thing. For equals to yield in turn [ἐν μέρει] and to

[18] So Nichols 1992: 29. By contrast, Mulgan 1994 rejects this view in favor of the one I take here, but does not defend it at length.

[19] My translation of this sentence has benefited from that of Simpson 1997, though he seems to undertranslate κατὰ μέρος.

[20] For other examples of the divisional use of κατὰ μέρος in the *Politics* see 1.13.1260a24–25, 3.1.1275b7–11, 4.15.1299a20–3, 4.16.1301a1–2.

be alike when they are out of office imitates this [i.e., everyone sharing in rule]. For some rule and others are ruled in turn [κατὰ μέρος], as if they were becoming different people. The same goes for when some people hold some offices and others hold others. (2.2.1261a38–b6)

Hence in the case of political offices, too, when the city has been established in accord with an equality and similarity among the citizens, they think that they should rule by turns [κατὰ μέρος]. Formerly, as was natural, they thought that each person should take turns performing services [ἐν μέρει λειτουργεῖν] and should look after the other's good just as he himself, when he was ruling, looked to that man's advantage (3.6.1279a8–13).

Since every political community is composed of rulers and ruled, what needs to be examined is this, namely whether the rulers and the ruled should be different or the same throughout life. For it is clear that it will be necessary for education, too, to follow in accordance with this division. Now, if one group were to differ from the others as much as we think that the gods and the heroes differ from human beings, having first of all a great superiority in body and then in soul, such that the preeminence of the rulers is indisputable and apparent to the ruled, it is clear that it would be better for the same people always to rule and others to be ruled once and for all. But since this is not easy to attain and it isn't as.

Skylax says it is among the Indians, with the kings surpassing the ruled to such a great extent, it is clear that for many reasons it is necessary for all to share alike in ruling and being ruled κατὰ μέρος. For equality [τὸ ἴσον] is the same thing for those who are similar, and it is difficult for the constitution that has been established contrary to justice to endure. For along with the ruled there are all those in the territory who want to bring about revolution, and for those in the ruling body to be so great in number as to be stronger than all of these is an impossible thing. Nonetheless, it is indisputable that the rulers must differ from the ruled. So, how these things shall be and how they will participate is what the lawgiver should examine. We have spoken before about this. For nature has given the choice by making that which is the same in kind both younger and older, for the former of which it is fitting to be ruled and the older to rule. Nobody gets irritated when he is ruled because of his age, nor does he think that he is superior, especially when he is going to get back his contribution when he attains the appropriate age. (7.14.1332b12–41)

In each of these passages, to rule κατὰ μέρος is not simply to share rule with others, but more specifically to alternate in positions of authority.[21]

---

[21] For other instances of this use of the phrase and the synonymous ἐν μέρει or ἀνὰ μέρος to describe alternation, see 4.4.1291a36–8, 4.14.1298a11–17, 4.15.1300a24–6, 6.4.1318b23–6, 6.5.1320b1–2, 6.8.1322a26–9, 7.3.1325b7–10, 6.2.1317b2–3, 7.14.1332b12–41.

Aristotle's use of the language of ruler and ruled might misleadingly suggest an oversimplified picture on which the only alternative to ruling and being ruled κατὰ μέρος is for some people to rule and others merely to be ruled without themselves sharing in rule to any extent. On this picture, to rule and be ruled κατὰ μέρος would be constitutive of political rule, because it would be nothing more than exercising authority over people who also exercise authority over you. The third and final passage earlier is especially likely to create this impression. The formulation of the alternative that Aristotle there rejects might lead us to imagine that if an outstanding individual did appear, then it would be just for him to have a monopoly of rule and for everyone else merely to be ruled without holding any share of rule themselves. But nothing in the passage compels us to take this view of it, and several features of the passage are hard to explain if we do.

As it stands, Aristotle's question focuses on the difference between a political arrangement in which the positions of the highest authority are always held by the same people and those in which different people alternate in holding those positions. He is not asking whether one group should simply rule and another group should simply be ruled, but whether the same group of citizens should always hold the hierarchically superior positions. To see that this is the case, consider two points. First, when some people hold positions of higher authority and others hold lower ones, it makes sense to describe those who hold the higher ones as "ruling" and those who hold the lower ones as "being ruled," even when those who are in the positions of lesser authority still have *some* kind of authority or rule. "Ruling" exhibits the same ambiguity in Aristotle's usage as "having authority": The expression is sometimes used in a precise and definite sense to apply to anyone who has authority over some specific range of common concerns or collective action, but it is at other times used in a narrower and more restricted way in which it describes only the person or group who exercises the highest level of authority over common affairs as a whole. In the narrower sense, "to have authority" applies only to the ruling body of the city – the wealthy, the demos, the few excellent men, perhaps the assembly or some other institutional body. In the broader sense, the expression applies even to particular officials charged with a rather limited range of duties, such as the overseer of the markets.[22] The same goes for "ruling."[23] One good reason to interpret this passage as

---

[22] For defense of this claim, see Chapter 5.3.

[23] The appearance of this narrower use of the expression and its ambiguity with respect to the more precise use contribute to the disagreements that scholars of the *Politics* have had about what

using the expression in the narrower sense is that the question Aristotle raises and the answer he proposes make better sense taken that way. If "rulers" here refers to all those who share in rule to any extent, then it will be coextensive with "citizens." But Aristotle is asking whether the same people should have control over the city's affairs throughout their lives, not whether the composition of the citizen body should remain unchanged.

Second, and more tellingly, Aristotle goes on just a few lines later to argue that there must be ruling and being ruled κατὰ μέρος if the arrangement is to be just and that an unjust constitution cannot expect to last for long, since "along with the ruled there are all those in the territory who want to make revolution, and for those in the ruling body to be stronger in number than all of these is an impossible thing" (7.14.1332b29–32). We can infer from this claim that "the ruled" are not merely passive subjects of the active rulers. For we hear of *three* groups: the ruled, all those in the territory who want to make revolution, and those in the ruling body.[24] If, however, "the ruled" do not share in rule in any way, then they will be indistinct from those others in the territory who want to revolt. For although the latter group may include slaves and metics, even slaves and metics are ruled, and yet they are here included in a group that is contrasted with "the ruled."[25] The most sensible conclusion is that "the ruled" here refers to "the ruled citizens." Yet, as we have seen, Aristotle explicitly rejects the idea that there could be citizens who are *merely* ruled and do not participate in rule *in any way* – sharing in rule just is what it is to be a citizen. Furthermore, the contrast between these two groups and "those in the ruling body" indicates that "the ruled" are citizens who share in rule to a minimal extent but without occupying the positions of highest authority in the city; for, as I argued in Chapter 5, "the ruling body" is not necessarily coextensive with the citizen body, but is at least potentially a subset of the citizen body, a subset composed of those

---

kind of ruling is essential to citizenship. Compare, for instance, Miller 1995, Kraut 2002, and Frede 2005.

[24] We cannot sensibly suppose that "those in the territory who want to make revolution" are merely a subset of the group that Aristotle calls "the ruled," where the remaining members of the latter group do not want to make revolution, because the scenario under discussion is one in which "the ruled" *also* want to make revolution; that is why it is a problem that "for those in the ruling body to be stronger in number than all of these is an impossible thing."

[25] The population of the territory in Aristotle's best constitution will consist entirely of citizens, their wives and children, metics, and slaves; there will be no naturally free natives who are not citizens, their wives, or their children. The current passage, however, is meant to appeal to broader considerations operative in circumstances beyond the special case of the best constitution, as is clear from the counterfactual character of the scenario in which "the ruled" are excluded from the ruling body.

who occupy the city's most authoritative positions. So "ruled" here does not mean "merely ruled without having any share in rule whatsoever." Rather, it means "not occupying the positions of highest authority within the city."

Ruling and being ruled κατὰ μέρος, therefore, are not to be contrasted simply with an arrangement in which the rulers exercise their authority over subjects who do not share in rule in any way. Rather, the alternative is for a group or a single individual to exercise the highest authority without periodically yielding that position to others. This alternative in no way entails that the ruled do not share in rule; ruling and being ruled κατὰ μέρος is just one way of ruling and being ruled. So the king does not rule κατὰ μέρος, but that is not to say that his rule is in no way shared. Nonalternation is consistent with the mutuality and reciprocity of rule that I have described in the case of kingship earlier. Alternation is therefore not necessary for political rule. The claim that the king has authority "without qualification and not κατὰ μέρος" is, accordingly, consistent with the picture of kingship that emerges from Aristotle's contrast of kingship and tyranny in light of his general account of correct and deviant constitutions.

3. Kingship and the Rule of Law

Aristotle's description of the king as holding authority without qualification is not the only feature of his defense of kingship that might cast doubt on whether any sort of monarchy could be a properly political kind of rule. Equally unsettling, at least at first glance, is the claim that the absolute or total king "rules in everything according to his own will" (*Pol.* 3.16.1287a9–10) and is not "called a king in accordance with law" (3.16.1287a3–4). Elsewhere, we are told that "where laws do not rule, there is no constitution" (4.4.1292a32) and that the most deviant constitutions are those in which "not the law, but the rulers, rule" (4.5.1292b6–7). The rule of law thus seems to be essential to political justice. It is, accordingly, hard to see how a constitution in which one man's personal judgment takes the place of law could be just. Even if we suppose that the king's outstanding excellence ensures that his decisions are just or at least as just as possible in the circumstances of his community, the absence of the rule of law might still seem to render his rule distinctly nonpolitical.[26]

---

[26] Nichols 1992: 74, Yack 1993: 83.

Yet more confusingly still, Aristotle elsewhere associates kingship with the rule of law and tyranny with its opposite:

> We distinguished two kinds of tyranny when we were enquiring into kingship, since their power crosses over in a way toward kingship as well, because both of these forms of rule are in accordance with law. For among some of the barbarians, they elect autocratic monarchs, and in the old days among the ancient Greeks certain men became monarchs in this way, whom they called dictators [αἰσυμνήτας]. They have some differences with each other, but they both were kingly because they were in accordance with law and held their monarchy over subjects who were willing, but tyrannical because they ruled despotically in accordance with their own judgment (4.10.1295a7–17)

This passage refers to the previous discussion in book 3 of the various kinds of kingship. There, we recall, Aristotle distinguished "barbarian kingship" and the Greek "dictatorship" or αἰσυμνητεία from the Spartan kingship and the "heroic kingship" exercised among the Greeks earlier in their history (3.14.1285a1–b19). The barbarian kingship and the αἰσυμνητεία differ from one another only because the latter is elected and the former is hereditary (3.14.1285a31–3). Both are a sort of mix between tyranny and kingship; they are "tyrannical" because the monarchs rule their subjects despotically, but they are "kingly" and therefore not pure tyrannies because their subjects willingly embrace their rule and because that rule is "according to law" (3.14.1285b2–3, cf. 14.1285a23–9). Unfortunately, Aristotle does not explain what he means when he says that they rule despotically or that they rule according to law. We can safely infer that they rule despotically in the sense that they do not aim at the common good.[27] It is less apparent how they can be said to rule according to law. Aristotle's brief description of the kinds of kingship suggests, however, that monarchs of these kinds rule according to law in the sense that their position and its exercise are subject to rules to which they must adhere. Like the heroic kings, these monarchs rule in "certain definite matters" (3.14.1285b22) rather than with unlimited authority, and they come to occupy their position through an orderly and prescribed process – election in the case of the αἰσυμνητεία, hereditary succession in the case of heroic and barbarian kingship. These

---

[27] Simpson 1998: 181 is right to insist on this point against Newman 1887–1902.iii: 266 and Schütrumpf 1991–2005.ii: 542: "The explanation Aristotle gives for the barbarians' putting up with such rule, that they are (natural) slaves, could only be an explanation if the rule they are putting up with is the sort of rule slaves are subject to, which is rule for the advantage of the ruler." Simpson's somewhat idiosyncratic account of what it is to rule for one's own advantage is not essential to the argument.

features, along with the consent of their subjects, prevent these mixed forms of monarchy from being pure tyrannies. Yet total kingship turns out not to be subject to law.

Perhaps surprisingly, however, the apparent suspension of the rule of law does not disqualify total kingship from the status of a constitution, as other discussions of the rule of law in the *Politics* might lead us to expect. On the contrary, Aristotle singles out total kingship for discussion on the grounds that it, more than all the others, has the character of a distinctive kind of constitution. The Spartan kingship, which is further removed from total kingship in this regard, is in effect merely a "perpetual generalship," and even a democratic constitution could have such an office (3.15.1286a2–7). Though the other forms of kingship more closely approximate a distinctive constitutional type, even heroic kingship involves certain limits on the king's powers. However closely heroic kingship resembles it, total kingship is the paradigm of kingship as a distinctive constitutional type because the king's authority is not circumscribed by other offices or even laws that limit its exercise. It is easy enough to appreciate why Aristotle would adopt this analysis and focus on total kingship in his discussion of monarchy: By emphasizing the fullest and most paradigmatic manifestation of the idea, we will be better able to understand various qualifications and approximations of it as such. Yet understanding the strategy brings us no closer to seeing how a constitution that lacks the rule of law could be, from Aristotle's own perspective, anything but a contradiction in terms.

The solution to this problem emerges largely from the dialectic that follows Aristotle's move to focus on total kingship rather than on kingship's less pure varieties. As a first step toward determining whether this sort of kingship is a genuinely correct constitution after all, Aristotle asks whether it is preferable for cities to be ruled by the best laws or by the best man (3.15.1286a7–9). What follows, examining claims and counterclaims from both sides of that dispute, amounts to the main focused discussion of the rule of law in the *Politics*. It is, then, the same extended argument that yields Aristotle's insistence on the rule of law and his endorsement of a kind of kingship in which the king's rule is not subordinate to law. The appearance of these two claims in the same argument should raise doubts that Aristotle construes them as mutually exclusive. Crucially, however, that argument shows that the sense in which the law can rule and the way in which the king's rule is not subordinate to law are not in conflict.

The first and most important argument against the rule of law that Aristotle considers points to the inherent limitations of laws as universal or unqualified prescriptions: "The laws address the universal only and do not issue commands with a view to particular circumstances" (3.15.1286a9–11). Drawing an analogy with practical arts such as medicine, the opponent of the rule of law argues that ruling in accordance to written prescriptions in politics would be just as foolish as an attempt to prescribe medical treatments in strict accordance with a set of clearly formulated rules: Just as a good doctor will take account of the particular circumstances and prescribe effective treatments without adhering to any precise general rules, so too the best ruler will not be subordinate to law but will make decisions and issue commands that respond most appropriately to particular situations (3.15.1286a11–16).

Aristotle elsewhere cites these considerations as pointing to important shortcomings of laws as such. Thus earlier in book 3 he concluded that "correctly established laws should have authority, and the ruler, whether there is one or many, should have authority only over those things about which the laws are unable to speak precisely by virtue of the difficulty of defining something universal in all cases" (3.11.1282b2–6). Elsewhere the acknowledged inadequacy of laws as general rules plays an important part in his characterization of the virtue of "equity" (ἐπιείκεια): Though laws must prescribe or prohibit actions in universal terms, it is impossible to speak both universally and correctly about some matters, and the equitable person is disposed to choose and act on the basis of his appreciation for the consequent deficiencies in universal laws (*EN* 5.10.1137a31–1138a3). Aristotle thus accepts one important premise of the argument against the rule of law. As we will see, his response is not so much to reject the argument as to qualify it.

The most important argument that Aristotle considers in favor of the rule of law is that the law, as a product of reason, is not susceptible to irrational motivations and partiality in the same way that individual human beings are: "That to which the element of passion has not been added is in general better than that to which it is natural; the law does not have this element, but every human soul necessarily has it" (*Pol.* 3.15.1286b17–20). Once again, Aristotle accepts at least a qualified form of the premise: Individual human beings are liable to be led by irrational passions to abuse their authority, and hence are less to be trusted than laws; moreover, one individual is less to be trusted to wield power correctly than many (3.15.1286a31–5). The great majority of us lacks the virtue to act well without being subject to law, and even those who have attained that level of virtue will have developed it in part through a process of moral education in which laws play an indispensable role (*EN* 10.9.1179a33–1180a24, *Pol.*

3.16.1287a25–7, 3.16.1287b25–6). As Aristotle puts it in a different but related context, "it is beneficial to be responsible to others and not to be able to do whatever one wants; for the ability to do whatever one wants is not able to guard against that which is base in every human being" (6.4.1318b38–1319a1).

Much of the dispute between the rule of law and the rule of the best man turns on the dialectical exchange between these two points: Laws are inherently limited by their generality and inflexibility, but individual human beings' judgment of particular cases tends to be distorted by partiality and irrationality. Ultimately, however, the partisans of each view must concede some important ground to the other. On the supposition that the best man is capable of deliberating correctly about matters on which the laws are deficient, he must also know what the best general rules are and should therefore prescribe them as such and rule in accordance with them so far as they are not in need of correction (3.15.1286b16–24). Total kingship stands apart from other varieties not because it does away with laws, but because the king himself has authority over them. But in this respect the king does not differ from the few virtuous rulers in an aristocracy or the multitude in a polity; in all these cases, the ruling body has the authority to make or revise laws. The defender of the rule of law must acknowledge that no set of laws could avoid the need for correction and application to particular circumstances or for possible amendment and reformulation. In having this kind of authority over the laws, the total king does not stand above them any more than the ruling body of any constitution does. In the final analysis, Aristotle's discussion of the rule of law urges us to see that the question is not whether laws or human beings should have authority: The best man will rule in accordance with laws to the extent that they are sufficient, and every set of laws will stand in need of flexible application and revision if they are to serve the ends of justice and the common good. Properly understood, the question is instead whether the task of deliberation about the application and correction of laws should be entrusted to one person or to many (3.16.1287b23–5).[28]

---

[28] My reading of 3.15–16 diverges sharply from that of Simpson 1998: 186–8, who sees the two chapters as directing arguments against two distinct conceptions of kingship, the second of which is of "a king who is not subject to law at all, not even to its general prescriptions and not even to any limitation on the scope or duration of his power." On my view, there are not two distinct conceptions of total kingship in these chapters, but a gradual refinement of the single concept via the dialectical examination of the rule of law and the rule of "the best man." Simpson is mistaken, I think, to read 3.16.1287a1–8 as indicating that the "best man" of 3.15 was merely an official subordinate to laws – a supposition that is, at any rate, difficult to square with Simpson's acknowledgment of Plato's *Statesman* as an important source for the formulation of the dispute in 3.15. Despite this

Aristotle's answer to this question is by now familiar: If a single man would be capable of better deliberation and judgment than all the other citizens taken together, then he would justly rule as a king. This reapplication of the summation principle is not mere repetition, however, because the dialectical examination of the conflicting claims of the best man and the best laws has meanwhile supplied some substantive content for the principle's application. To rule justly as a king requires the possession of a deliberative excellence whereby one's own individual deliberation and judgment surpass the combined virtues of everyone else. As if that degree of excellence were not hard enough to come by, Aristotle may have in mind – or be implicitly committed to holding – that the king should be better able to govern the city's affairs than any group would be, even a group that included him.[29] In addition to the sheer deliberative skill that this would require, the king would need to possess the moral virtues to a degree sufficient to prevent abuse of his unparalleled authority. The case for the rule of law does not tell against kingship in principle, since the king's relationship to the laws is fundamentally identical to the relationship between any constitution's ruling body and its laws: In every constitution the ruling body has authority over the laws (4.14.1298a5, 1299a1–2), and in a total kingship the king himself is this ruling body. Kingship remains, in principle, a just and genuine form of political community. The examination of the counterclaims of the rule of law serves to make plain just how austere the standards governing the justice of kingship turn out to be.

4. Incomparable Virtue

Just how severe and demanding are those standards? There seem to be two kinds of situation in which an individual could meet the criteria of the summation principle. At one extreme, people living in the more primitive conditions that Aristotle associates with the early transition from prepolitical to political communities could fail to develop the virtues to

---

disagreement, Simpson's analysis of these chapters is excellent in many of its details and superior to many other treatments.

[29] For this suggestion, see Keyt 1991b. The thought is not so odd as it may at first seem: Consider whether a small group of experienced faculty members in an academic department would be better placed to make curricular decisions than would a group including those same individuals and all of the department's graduate students and undergraduate majors deliberating and voting equally. The exclusion of students from curricular decisions could be defended on a number of grounds, but competence is surely one of them.

any notable degree. Among such people, an exceptional individual or small group of individuals might be better able to govern the community's affairs even without possessing what we would be inclined to regard as extraordinary excellence.[30] The criteria of the summation principle are *comparative*, and so the justification of kingship depends on the level of collective virtue attained by the multitude of citizens. Aristotle evidently envisions early political communities as ruled by kings in part because few people in those underdeveloped cities had yet developed any substantial virtues:

> Perhaps this is why in earlier times people used to be ruled by kings, because it was a rare thing to find men who were very outstanding in virtue, especially at that time, when people were dwelling in small cities. Furthermore, they established the kings on the basis of their beneficence, which is the work of good men. But when many people happened to become similar in virtue, they no longer submitted [to kings], but began to seek something more communal and established polity. (*Pol.* 3.15.1286b8–13)[31]

At the other extreme, people living together in more developed political communities tend to be sufficiently free from necessities to develop the virtues to some degree. Though they may not amount to much as individuals, their collective ability to deliberate well about matters of common concern will reach a higher level. The level of excellence necessary to meet the criteria of the summation principle will, correspondingly, rise. It would rise so high, in fact, that it might be difficult to believe that any human being could achieve it.

In any case, Aristotle seems to think that the likelihood of kingship outside small and fairly primitive political communities is low. Its extreme improbability is one reason why he fails to discuss it at any great length after defending it in book 3 and why most of his references to it serve primarily to illuminate tyranny by contrast.[32] Yet it is one thing for the

---

[30] Newman 1887–1902.iii: 286; contra Simpson 1998: 185. Schofield 2000: 317–18 presents kingship as "by and large a rather primitive institution, suitable for communities where virtue and intelligence are not as widely distributed as he implies they have been in Greece for some centuries."

[31] Note that the language of this passage further supports the view defended earlier in Section 1 that Aristotle envisions a king's subjects as active in the establishment and persistence of the king's rule and authority; the same verb καθίστημι is used here of kings and polity. Cf., too, my discussion of citizenship in the Solonian constitution in Chapter 5.4. I owe this observation to Joe Bullock.

[32] Aristotle also seems to endorse the claim made in 3.15.1286b3–6 that aristocracy – "rule by several who are all good men" – is more choiceworthy than kingship (cf. 1287b11–15 for a reiteration of the same point); this is one reason why the best constitution of books 7–8 is not a kingship. Cf. Kraut 2002: 400, who thinks that "Aristotle is merely rehearsing an argument against kingship rather than endorsing the superiority of aristocracy," noting that *EN* 8.10.1160a35–6 describes kingship as the best constitution. Miller 1995: 156 adds *Pol.* 4.2.1289a30–b11 and explains Aristotle's ranking as

standards of excellence to be so high that no human being is likely ever to meet them; it is quite another thing for those standards to be such that no human being possibly could meet them. The worry is that the superlative excellence that the summation principle requires could not be a properly human virtue at all; anyone who achieved it would, in effect, become a superhuman and quasi-divine being who could no longer interact with mere humans on the basis even of proportionate equality. If this is the implication of Aristotle's defense of kingship, it raises a problem deeper than the putative impossibility of transcending humanity to become quasi-divine.[33] Even if this apotheosis were possible, the relationship between the deified king and his subjects would not be one of *political* community; for the king and his subjects would no longer be even proportionately equal and would not share a genuinely common good.[34]

Difficult as it may be to reconcile such a conclusion with the central claims of the *Politics* about political community, one passage in particular makes it appear almost irresistible:

> If there is some single man or more than one (who are nonetheless not able to make up a full city) so outstanding in the preeminence of virtue that neither the virtue of all the others nor their political ability is comparable with theirs (if there are more than one) or his alone (if there is a single man), these men should no longer be regarded as a part of a city. For they will be treated unjustly if they are considered worthy of equal shares even though they are so unequal in virtue and political ability. This sort of man would reasonably be like a god among human beings. From this fact it is clear too that legislation must be concerned with people who are equal both in kind and in ability, but over men of this sort there is no law; for they themselves are law. Indeed, anyone who tried to legislate for them would be ridiculous, since they would perhaps say the same things that Antisthenes said that the lions did when the hares were delivering speeches and claiming that all should have equal shares. (3.13.1284a3–17)

appealing to the principle that "among the correct constitutions, those in which political authority is relatively more concentrated are relatively better."

[33] Does Aristotle think that human beings should seek to transcend their humanity and become divine or quasi-divine? Some have seen such implications in *EN* 10.7–8 (consider, in particular, 10.7.1177b31–4: "One should not follow those who warn us to think human thoughts since we are human and mortal thoughts since we are mortal; rather, to the extent that it is possible one should become immortal [ἀθανατίζειν] and do everything with a view to living in accordance with the best part of oneself," with Reeve 2012: 195–222, 250–78). The question is too complex and controverted to discuss here, but even if – as I am inclined to deny – these passages describe a genuine transcendence of human nature, it is difficult to see how they are relevant to the justification of kingship, since the transcendence in question is centered around a life of theoretical contemplation in contrast to active political engagement.

[34] For versions of this claim, Newell 1991: 195, Nichols 1992: 74–80, Yack 1993: 83.

What Aristotle seems to be asserting here is that people whose excellence surpasses that of all their fellow citizens together do not stand in a relation of political community to those others (they "should no longer be regarded as a part of a city") and are fundamentally unequal with them. The explicit comparison of such people to gods makes the same suggestion as the appeal to Antisthenes' fable: Just as gods and humans are not members of the same kind, neither are lions and hares. The men of outstanding virtue who deserve to be kings apparently also stand outside political community and even humanity itself. With a passage like this, it is no surprise that scholars have despaired of making coherent sense of Aristotle's defense of kingship or have been driven to the desperate measures of esoteric hermeneutics.[35]

The same basic problem can be reached via another route. When Aristotle describes the individual or group that deserves to rule without qualification rather than ruling and being ruled by turns, he says that the excellence of all the others is "not comparable" to theirs (μὴ συμβλητήν, 3.13.1284a6). So far, I have presented this claim as a straightforward application of the summation principle: The excellence of all the others together will be incomparable to the excellence of some individual or group if the latter will be better able to govern the affairs of the city than the former or even than both taken together. An alternative interpretation articulated by Keyt and, more strongly, by Richard Mulgan yields an even more demanding criterion. Both cite passages from the Aristotelian corpus that use the term συμβλητός in a precise technical sense to ascribe or deny commensurability to different things.[36] As Keyt puts it, "two things are [συμβλητά] in respect of a given attribute if, and only if, the attribute can in both cases be measured by the same standard."[37] In Mulgan's formulation, two things are comparable "if they can be compared on the

---

[35] For the esoteric approach, see, e.g., Lindsay 1991, Newell 1991 (less explicitly), Nichols 1992: 74–80, Bates 2003, Collins 2006: 144, Pangle 2013, and my critique in Chapter 1.

[36] The term itself seems to be an Aristotelian or perhaps Academic coinage; Aristotle is the earliest author to use it, and aside from one passage in Theocritus (5.92, meaning "comparable") its appearances are all either in philosophical texts or are quite late. The Suda defines συμβλητά as "things that admit of comparison" (τὰ σύγκρισιν ἐπιδεχόμενα). Because all the other uses of the verbal adjective in the Aristotelian corpus (37 instances in total, according to the TLG) seem to bear the technical sense, Keyt and Mulgan have good prima facie reason to read it that way in the *Politics* as well. Nonetheless, I argue later that there are good reasons not to read the term that way in these passages and that there is a plausible alternative that avoids the problematic implications of Keyt and Mulgan's reading.

[37] Keyt 1991b: 275, citing *GC* 2.6.333a20–7 and *EN* 5.5.1133a19–26. *Met.* 13.6–7 discuss the commensurability of numbers as part of a critique of Platonic and Pythagorean belief in numbers and Forms as immaterial substances.

same scale either as fractions of one another or at least as greater than or less than or equal to one another. The appropriate qualities of the absolute ruler must therefore be on quite a different scale from the others."[38] The justification of kingship, then, requires not simply an outstandingly virtuous individual, but a person endowed with virtue of a wholly different kind. It is not that the king is *more* virtuous than all the others combined or *better* able to govern the city's affairs; such claims presuppose that the king's virtue is in fact commensurable with the virtue of the others. To the contrary, Keyt and Mulgan argue, the king simply has a different, though superior, kind of virtue; that is the point of calling him a god among men.[39] Thus they deny that the justification of kingship is an application of the summation principle, since that principle depends on the commensurability of the citizens' individual and collective virtues.[40]

Despite their impressive appeal to the technical use of συμβλητός, Keyt and Mulgan's view raises more problems than it solves. Neither explicitly considers what traits the king could have that would give him a virtue of a wholly different and yet superior kind. The problem is not that things of different kinds cannot be compared. It is, rather, that there are no obvious candidates for virtues that are both fundamentally different in kind from those of ordinary human beings and yet still relevant to the distribution of political authority. As Keyt notes, two things that are incommensurable in a certain respect may still be compared in another, but insofar as they are incommensurable it does not even make sense to compare them. He cites Aristotle's example of the sharpness of musical notes, pens, and wine; one sort of wine may have a sharper taste than another, but no wine is sharper or less sharp than a musical note.[41] Instead of supporting Keyt's reading, however, those examples cast doubt on the claim that Aristotle is using συμβλητός in this passage in the technical sense it bears elsewhere. Musical notes, pens, and wines are all "sharp" only in an equivocal sense; indeed, the very passages that Keyt cites (*Top.* 1.15.107b13–18, *Phys.* 7.4.248b7–10) associate incommensurability with equivocation ("homonymy" in Aristotle's sense). Surely a "virtue" that differs from human virtue in the way that a wine's sharpness differs from a pen's will not entitle anyone to a greater share of political authority.[42]

---

[38] Mulgan 1974: 67–8.
[39] cf. Nussbaum 1980: 421–2 for a similar view of the comparison of the king to a god.
[40] Mulgan 1974: 68, Keyt 1991b: 275.
[41] Keyt 1991b: 275.
[42] Perhaps less severe forms of homonymy than sheer equivocation would make a better fit for the king's virtue and the collective virtue of his subjects? I cannot see that they would; whatever the relationship between the virtue of one kind of being and the virtue of another, the context of

In fact, the other passage in book 3 of the *Politics* in which Aristotle uses the term συμβλητός (*Pol.* 3.12.1283a3–4) does so in order to insist that because not all goods are commensurable, a person does not deserve a greater share of political authority simply because he surpasses everyone else in some good; the relevant superiority must "contribute to the task" (3.12.1283a1–2), and the task of politics is promoting and protecting the common good of the city (3.12.1282b14–1283a23). In other words, purported virtues are relevant to the distribution of political authority only insofar as they are commensurable with a view to the requirements of ruling well. If the king's virtue were incommensurable in this sense, it could not be the basis of a just claim to rule. So not only is it mysterious how any set of traits wholly different from human virtues could be relevant to political rule, but their very relevance would presuppose their commensurability.[43]

Furthermore, neither use of the term in book 3 demands to be read in the precise technical sense found elsewhere. Its first appearance, in 3.12, follows immediately upon the use of the verb from which the adjective is formed, which I have translated previously as "to contribute."[44] Wealth and beauty do not "contribute to the task" (εἰς τὸ ἔργον συμβάλλεσθαι) of pipe playing, and hence provide no basis for a claim to superior pipes. If, the argument continues, superiority in any good or virtue whatsoever were sufficient grounds for a claim to hold superior political office, then

---

Aristotle's argument in the *Politics* demands that the king's virtue be relevant to the distribution of political authority, and it is not apparent how an appeal to focal homonymy could resolve this problem.

[43] A reader for the press suggests that the Platonic "kingly art" of the *Euthydemus* or the *Statesman* would be obvious candidates for a virtue that differs in kind from ordinary human virtue and yet remains relevant to politics. But that virtue is not fundamentally different in kind from the practical wisdom that Aristotle regards as a central component of human excellence and identifies with political science (*EN* 6.8.1141b23–33). Rather, setting aside Aristotle's rejection of Plato's conflation of practical and technical knowledge, and hence of the possibility of the kingly art as Plato conceives it (on which see Section 7), Plato's kingly art would simply be the perfection of the same sort of practical wisdom that Aristotle regards as ordinary human virtue. To be sure, this virtue is not "ordinary" in the sense that most people possess it to a considerable degree, but that is beside the point. The point is, rather, that claims to rule are assessed by reference to practical wisdom and the virtues of character discussed in the *EN* and *EE*, and such supervirtues as the Platonic kingly art, should they be possible, would be judged superior by precisely the same standard: knowing the human good and how to achieve it for the political community. Hence they would not be incommensurable in the technical sense elaborated by Keyt and Mulgan.

[44] LSJ s.v. συμβάλλω I.7. This use is common in Aristotle: Knowledge of the soul seems to contribute greatly to truth (*DA* 1.1.402a5); sound, color, and odor contribute nothing to nourishment (*DA* 2.3.414b10–11); natural emotions contribute to natural virtues (*EE* 3.7.1234a26–8); the female contributes the matter in biological reproduction (*GA* 1.19.727b31); lengthenings, shortenings, and modifications of words contribute to clarity and unusualness of speech (*Poet.* 1458a35–b2).

every good would be συμβλητόν to everything (3.12.1283a3–4). In this context, we would reasonably expect the verbal adjective to bear the same sense as the verb in the preceding sentence, and hence to mean something like "capable of being contributed" rather than "commensurable" or even "comparable" in a looser sense.[45] The argument does indeed show that goods are not all commensurable; no amount of size – presumably height or bulk – is greater than or equal to any amount of virtue.[46] It shows this, however, by showing that not all goods contribute to every task. Likewise, the virtue of all the other citizens may not be "comparable" to the virtue of an outstanding individual in the sense that their collective excellence will not "contribute to" his (3.13.1284a6); that is, the city's affairs would not be better governed if the king were to share his authority equally than if he were to occupy the sole position of highest authority.[47] But whether we take συμβλητόν in these passages to mean literally "contributable" or simply as "comparable" in a loose sense, we must understand it in light of the surrounding arguments. These arguments not only fail to suggest

[45] "Contributable," though somewhat awkward, is the more literal translation. We might hesitate to read the adjective in this way, since there are no parallels for this usage in other texts, Aristotelian or otherwise. But this objection can hardly be conclusive, given that it is by no means unusual for a term to bear distinctive senses in one or a few passages and that the only other usage of this term that we find in Aristotle yields a seriously problematic, if not incoherent, interpretation of these passages. Furthermore, in 3.12.1283a3–4, the regular formation of the verbal adjective expressing possibility would be as readily intelligible as a novel application of the "-able" suffix in English (see Smyth 472), and so the case for reading the term as "contributable" requires no special linguistic subtlety or insight. Nonetheless, those who are not convinced by these considerations should note that "contributable" is not the only alternative to the technical interpretation of συμβλητόν; we may instead understand it to mean "comparable" in a looser sense that does not yield the incoherence of the technical interpretation, in just the same way that we might say, for instance, that Anne-Sophie Mutter is an "incomparably greater" violinist than I am not because she possesses some wholly different and incommensurable sort of excellence than I do, but simply because she is so much more excellent than I could ever hope to be that comparing us is absurd. Refusing to interpret the term with the precise technical sense that Aristotle elsewhere gives it is not arbitrary or ad hoc; Aristotle's ethical and political writings often avoid technical precision and terminology that could be intelligible only to an audience already familiar with his logical and metaphysical works and use terms loosely. For example, Whiting 1988 argues convincingly against importing the precise technical sense of ἴδιον into the "function argument" of EN 1.7.

[46] The text of this passage is plagued by difficulties; Newman, Ross, and Dreizehnter all print different texts that make for minor variations. I have, broadly speaking, followed the reconstruction and interpretation of Simpson 1997 and 1998, who follows the manuscripts most closely, but the argument about the relation between συμβάλλεσθαι and συμβλητόν is mine.

[47] The argument of 3.13.1284a3–10 of course applies to aristocracy as well as to kingship. Cf. Simpson 1998: 192: "His virtue is, ex hypothesi, incommensurable and so such as not to be capable of being increased or improved by the addition to it of the virtue of others who are not on the same scale as he." Simpson's "and so" shows that he takes the virtue of the others to be non-contributable because it is "incommensurable"; my proposal is that the noncontributable character of their virtue is just what Aristotle means to pick out in describing it as μὴ συμβλητήν. This point does not depend on exactly how we understand the meaning of συμβλητήν.

the problematic claim that the would-be king's virtue is strictly incommensurable with the virtue of the other citizens; it also supplies us with the resources to understand how one person or group's excellence could be incomparably greater than another's without differing in kind from it. Thus neither argument depends on the technical use of συμβλητός in other works for its intelligibility.[48]

This clarification of the justification of kingship helps to resolve the difficulties that arise from Aristotle's puzzling comparisons of the king to a god among humans and his claim that the king is not a "part" of the city. Aristotle cannot consistently maintain that the king has a fundamentally different kind of virtue rather than an exceptionally superior degree of the virtues of justice and practical wisdom, among others. Yet the comparison of the king to a god among human beings or to a lion among hares need not be taken to have any such implication. Whatever the details of Aristotle's considered theological views, it is tolerably clear that he does not believe in anthropomorphic gods.[49] The comparison trades on just such a conception of the divine, drawn of course from the Greek poetic and mythic tradition. This anthropomorphism, however, need not be taken any more seriously than the anthropomorphic fable of the lions and the hares. Lions and hares do not talk or reason together, let alone form political communities with one another. The fable, like any analogy, highlights some similarities while ignoring others. In this case, the different specific natures of lions and hares are no more relevant than the fact that neither animal is rational in Aristotle's sense or shares in political community with the other. Similarly, the analogy of the king to a god among humans does not imply that the king will have all of the characteristics ordinarily ascribed to gods. Indeed, to suppose otherwise would be

---

[48] The use of the preposition πρός at 1283a4 and 1284a7 does not tell against taking συμβλητόν at 1283a4 and συμβλητήν at 1284a6 in the same sense as συμβάλλεσθαι at 1283a1–2, where εἰς is used. Aristotle regularly uses πρός interchangeably with εἰς when the verb has the sense of "contribute": Envy contributes to injustice (εἰς, *EE* 3.7.1234a30); explaining why opinions contrary to one's own appear true contributes to persuasiveness (πρός *EN* 7.14.1154a22–3); the female does not contribute to reproduction in the same way as the male (πρός, *GA* 1.21.730a25–6) because the female does not contribute the seed to reproduction (εἰς, *GA* 1.20.727b31). By contrast, when Aristotle asserts that two things are commensurable or incommensurable, though he occasionally uses the preposition πρός (*Met.* 13.7.1081a4–5), he most often either applies a single adjective to both items (e.g., a straight line and a circle are οὐ συμβλητά at *Phys.* 7.4.248b6; a horse and a dog are συμβλητά in color at 249a22) or uses the dative alone (e.g., *Phys.* 7.4.248a10, *GC* 2.6.333a21, *Met.* 13.6.1080a18–21).

[49] See, e.g., *Met.* 12.8.1074b1–14. Bodéüs 2000 complicates the relationship between Aristotle and traditional Greek beliefs about the gods, but even his revisionist view stops short of making Aristotle's gods fully anthropomorphic.

to imagine that Aristotle's king is immortal and has preternatural powers perhaps including shape shifting, invisibility, the ability to incite or dissipate plagues on command or to control of the weather. The purpose of the comparison is obviously not to attribute these powers to the king. What, then, is its point?

The most coherent understanding of the analogy is also the least ambitious: Aristotle's king is like a god among human beings in the sense that his unrivaled superiority and his claim to a correspondingly superior position of authority are clear to everyone with the possible exception of the severely foolish. If this deflationary reading of the comparison seems too weak, it nonetheless has the virtue of cohering with what Aristotle actually says.[50] In *Politics* 7 he describes this unparalleled excellence as so great "that the preeminence of the rulers is indisputable and apparent to the ruled" (7.14.1332b20–1). The same passage makes clear that the gods' divinity is incidental to the comparison: The outstanding people in question must "differ from the others as much as we think that the gods and the heroes differ from human beings" (7.14.1332b16–18). Unlike anthropomorphic gods, heroes are unambiguously members of the same natural kind as ordinary human beings. They serve Aristotle's purposes just as well because the emphasis of the comparison is on the manifest superiority of gods and heroes to ordinary humans, not on immortality or transcendence of human nature. Anthropomorphic gods and mythic heroes both also serve to highlight the improbability of finding anyone with the qualifications to be king. It is not that humans cannot become gods – that is no more relevant than the lion's inability to talk – but that no human being is likely to surpass his fellow citizens so much as to merit comparison to a god among them.

The same point emerges from the fable of the lions and the hares. To the hares' proposal that everyone have an equal share, the lions are said to have responded by asking, "where are your claws and teeth?"[51] One way to understand this response is to see it as pointing to the lions' superior strength; the lions can reject equality with the hares because the hares

---

[50] Newman 1887–1902.iii: 241 notes that the expression "god among men" was proverbial as an expression for outstanding individuals, citing Theognis and the comic poet Antiphanes. Its proverbial character tells in favor of a relatively deflationary reading. Cf. *EN* 7.1.1145a27–30, where Aristotle notes that the Spartans customarily call men whom they greatly admire "divine." Vander Waerdt 1985 takes this passage (and its broader context in 1145a15–33) as evidence that Aristotle recognizes a kind of transcendent, superhuman virtue that he expects the total king to have, but this reading puts too much stock in the "divine" comparison and not enough in the references to heroes, including perhaps the most proverbially mortal hero of all, Hector.

[51] Newman 1887–1902.iii: 243.

are not powerful enough to prevent them from taking a greater share for themselves.[52] Whatever Antisthenes' story was intended to suggest, however, Aristotle cannot mean to reject political equality for outstanding men on the grounds that they have the bodily or even the intellectual capacity to overpower others. He plainly rejects the view that the successful use of force is self-justifying (1.6.1255a7–21, 7.2.1324b22–41, 3.1325a41–b10). Moreover, if the fable is to provide a useful political analogy, we must understand the lions and the hares as disputing about the distribution of some common good that they cooperate to procure and preserve. The lions' claim to a superior share is, accordingly, grounded in the incomparably greater contribution that they make to the common enterprise.[53] The hares cannot rightly insist on equality with the lions, who make such a superior contribution to the community. Likewise, ordinary citizens could not rightly demand to legislate for and share authority equally with people whose virtue surpasses the collective virtue of all the others. Such people, Aristotle says, "are themselves law" (3.13.1284a13–14). Anyone who has achieved this level of excellence would be better suited than anyone else to formulate, revise, and apply laws and would be disposed to observe them precisely because they are correct laws; his inferiors, by contrast, would be less capable of devising laws of the right sort and less inclined to act accordingly out of an understanding of their correctness and a commitment to goods that they promote and protect (cf. *EN* 10.9.1179b4–1180a23).

What, though, could Aristotle mean when he says that such an outstanding man should not be considered a part of the city? The expression could indicate that the king and his subjects would not be fellow members of a single political community.[54] Yet that claim would, as I have been arguing, be inconsistent with the treatment of kingship as a kind of constitution. It also appears to be straightforwardly false. If the king holds the position of highest authority among a group of citizens who

---

[52] So Newman 1887–1902.iii: 243 seems to read it, comparing *Pol.* 6.3.1318b4 and Plato *Gorgias* 483e. Newell 1991: 207 claims that "the 'best man' may mix his benevolent expertise with the leonine qualities of a lord and a master," perhaps giving the fable a rather more Calliclean than Aristotelian reading.

[53] Simpson 1998: 178 notes that "teeth and claws can be used to protect and guard as well as to kill," but if Newman 1887–1902.iii: 243 is correct in speculating that the lions and the hares in Antisthenes' story are cooperating in hunting, then the nondefensive contribution of their claws and teeth will be clear enough: Without the lions' claws and teeth, the hares could not possibly catch their prey. Newman and Simpson's suggestions are sufficient to show that the fable need not be read as asserting the "right" of the stronger to rule over the weaker.

[54] Thus Newman 1887–1902.i: 288–9, Newell 1991: 205, Nichols 1992: 76, Collins 2006: 144.

share in ruling and being ruled with a view to their common good, then he is a member of the political community. He cannot fail to be a member of the community by transcending the need for living in a city in order to flourish as a human being, since there is no reason to think that he does transcend that need; the claim that "he who is not self-sufficient [αὐτάρκης] and superior in all the goods is not a king" (EN 8.10.1160b3–4) presumably points to the king's ability to govern the city without sharing his authority equally with others rather than to the kind of independence and freedom from need that Aristotle elsewhere denies to human beings (1.7.1097b6–15). Nor can his rule fail to be a political kind of rule as a consequence of his superiority to the other citizens; because he rules over free adult men, if his rule is not political, then it is not just, and yet the virtue in which he is supposed to be so outstanding prominently includes justice, a "virtue concerned with community" [κοινωνικὴν ἀρετήν] necessarily accompanied by all the others (Pol. 3.13.1283a37–40). Since so much that Aristotle says makes it clear that the king is a member of the political community, it is implausible to suppose that he means to deny that claim when he says that the king should not be considered a part of the city. So what *does* he mean?

When he summarizes the justification of kingship near the end of book 3, Aristotle says that a sufficiently superior man does not deserve to rule and be ruled κατὰ μέρος, "since by nature the part [τὸ μέρος] does not exceed the whole, and this is what has happened to the man who has so great a superiority" (3.17.1288a26–8). In this context, the language of part and whole makes sense: Parts are not greater than the wholes of which they are a part, and yet an individual who could govern the affairs of his city better than all of his fellow citizens together would in fact exceed them. The appeal to part-whole language immediately follows the use of the language of parts with the expression κατὰ μέρος. We might see this argument, then, as a bit of analogical wordplay. Those who share in ruling and being ruled κατὰ μέρος alternate in occupying the most authoritative offices; someone whose excellence exceeded that of all his fellow citizens to the extent that Aristotle deems necessary to justify kingship would, however, quite rightly hold the most authoritative office permanently rather than yielding it to those who would be markedly less capable of exercising authority well. Such a man should not rule in the manner of a part alternating with other parts (κατὰ μέρος) since he is himself uniquely capable of ruling more excellently than all the other parts, and hence is not aptly compared to a mere part among parts.

On this reading, the part language may seem intolerably metaphorical, obscuring rather than clarifying the point at issue. It also seems clearly false; if the king is not a part, then surely he is the whole, and yet he is obviously not.[55] As we have seen, however, *no* interpretation of the claim that the king is not a part of the city can avoid treating it as metaphorical; Aristotle cannot seriously intend to deny that the king is a part of his city. Furthermore, Aristotle's use of the language of parts is extremely flexible throughout the *Politics*, and it is doubtful that any single conception of parthood could consistently account for all of the work that the concept does in the *Politics*.[56] We are forced, then, to depend on the context of the argument to determine just what Aristotle wants to say with the language of parts in any given passage. On the reading proposed here, he means to deny that the king is a *mere part* of the city, since his outstanding virtue makes him capable of functioning as the city's whole ruling body. Though it seems fair to say that expressing this point in terms of parthood needlessly obscures Aristotle's point, it is less confused and inconsistent than the alternative reading on which the king either fails to be a member of the political community or somehow constitutes an entire city in his own right.

5. Kingship and the Household

We have seen, then, that Aristotle's king is not a semidivine "superman"[57] who transcends political community, dispenses with laws, deprives his fellow citizens of all participation in rule, or fails to take account of their will and consent to his authority. The final obstacle to a clear view of

[55] Simpson 1997 comments on the claim of 3.13.1284a8 that the outstanding minority who surpass their fellow citizens in excellence should not be considered "parts" of the city: "Rather they are a whole city by themselves – in power and virtue, that is, though not in numbers." Though the minority's outstanding excellence seems sufficient to explain how, on Aristotle's view, such people – whether a king or a group of aristocrats – might be the whole of a city's ruling body, and hence in a sense the whole constitution, it is not so easy to see how they can be the whole *city*, unless Aristotle means to exclude everyone else from citizenship and hence membership in the city – a reading that Simpson has no more interest in defending than I do. Simpson is correct, I think, to identify this point as the substance of Aristotle's claim; he is mistaken to suggest that Aristotle can consistently maintain its truth in anything but a metaphorical sense.

[56] On parthood in the *Politics* generally, see Mayhew 1997. An especially serious source of difficulty is Aristotle's failure to distinguish clearly between *parthood* (which is a transitive relation) and *membership* (which is at least not necessarily transitive), but even this distinction may not be sufficient to cover all the ground that the *Politics* traces out with the term μέρος. I owe my appreciation of these difficulties to an unpublished paper by Dhananjay Jagannathan, "The Unity of the City in Aristotle's *Politics*."

[57] This is the language of Mulgan 1974.

Aristotelian kingship as a genuine form of political community is his frequent association of kingship with the form of rule characteristic of the household. So, for instance, when he distinguishes total kingship as a fifth variety:

> The fifth kind of kingship is when there is a single individual who holds authority over everything, just as each nation [ἔθνος] and each city does over its common affairs. [This sort of kingship is] arranged in the manner of household management; for just as household management is a sort of kingship over a household, so kingship is household management over one or more cities or nations. (*Pol.* 3.14.1285b29–33)

The comparison is doubly perplexing. In addition to conflating the monarchical rule of a city with the rule of a household, it appears to treat kingship in a city interchangeably with kingship over a so-called nation or even over several cities or nations of people. Yet the difference between these kinds of community and their corresponding modes of rule is one of the major themes of the first three books of the *Politics*. Nor is this passage the only one that associates kingship and household rule. Early in book 1 we are told that "every household is ruled by its eldest in the manner of a king [βασιλεύεται ὑπὸ τοῦ πρεσβυτάτου]" (1.2.1252b20–1). Later, we read that "household management is [a form of] monarchy, since every household is ruled monarchically, but political rule is rule over people who are free and equal" (1.7.1255b16–20). A man is said to rule his children "in a kingly way," his wife "politically" (1.12.1259b1). The comparison runs in the other direction as well, from city to household: A tyrant who hopes to make himself resemble a king should strive to seem more like a "household manager" than a tyrant (5.11.1313b29–30, 11.1315a41–b2).

This apparent assimilation of kingship to household management has suggested to some that Aristotle tacitly acknowledges the nonpolitical character of kingly rule, a suggestion that might be borne out by occasional references to royal or kingly rule alongside political rule (1.1.1252a12–13, 1.3.1253b18–20, 3.17.1287b38–9).[58] The collapse of the distinction between

---

[58] Thus Newell 1991: 195, Nichols 1992: 74–5, Yack 1993: 86. Cooper 1999b: 168 note 5 cites 1.7.1255b19–20 and 3.17.1287b38–9 for the view that although kingship is "one just and valid form of rule in a polis," Aristotle nonetheless "refuses to call it a *politikos* kind of rule" because the king "is so far above ordinary good people in his moral qualities and associated knowledge that he rules not as one among them, but as a sort of god providentially found in their company." But neither of the passages that Cooper cites contrasts kingship and politics in the way he claims. The first distinguishes political rule from the "monarchical" household management of slaves and appears in a stage in Aristotle's argument at which he has not yet clearly identified the other parts of household management, let alone the varieties of constitution. The second passage draws a contrast between the "kingly" and the "political" that is resumed at 1288a7, where "kingly" is explicitly opposed to

household management and political rule would be problematic for Aristotle not only because he so emphatically stresses that distinction elsewhere, but because it plays an important role in his critique of Plato's *Republic* in book 2. Several of Aristotle's most fundamental objections to Socrates' proposals in the *Republic* charge those proposals with failing to respect the differences between a household and a city. By attempting to make the city too much of a unity, Socrates seeks to transform it, in effect, into an extended household. This transformation is not in fact possible, but even if it were, it would be harmful because it would undermine the essential complexity and heterogeneity of political community. The city differs from the household not simply in numbers, but in the increasingly complex differentiation of roles that people play and the intersections among them. As such, the city simply cannot be unified in the way and to the extent that a household can. The city's complexity and differentiation of roles are, in turn, crucial for its attainment of self-sufficiency (2.2.1261a10–1261b16).[59] The vision of a city as an extended household also subverts the special relationships that people have with their families and with personal friends; Socratic political unity would make friendship "watery," reducing all relationships to the tenuous bonds that citizens sometimes have with one another rather than spreading the robust concern of personal friendship throughout the whole citizen body (2.3.1261b16–40).[60] Thus two related strands of Aristotle's response to Plato's political thought appeal to the difference between political community and the household: The critique of the *Republic* and its dilution of the distinctively political develops and extends the more general objection to the Platonic effacement of all essential distinctions between varieties of rule and community.

Aristotle's comparisons of kingship to household management threaten to leave his account vulnerable to the same objections that he directs against Plato. To evade those objections, there must be some sense to the analogy that nonetheless preserves the integrity of kingship as a specifically political form of rule and as an arrangement of a distinctively political community. There must, that is to say, be some respect in which the king stands to the city as the head of a household stands to his household without thereby simply attempting to treat a greater number of people in

---

"political" and "aristocratic," suggesting that "political" is being used there in its specific sense of "polity" rather than its general sense of "constitution."

[59] On self-sufficiency, its value, and its role in distinguishing political community from other varieties, see Chapter 3.

[60] On Aristotle's criticisms of the proposals of Plato's *Republic*, see Nussbaum 1980, Stalley 1991, Mayhew 1995, 1997.

272 Kingship as Political Rule and Political Community

the way that a man treats his household. Elsewhere, analogies between the household and the city illuminate the former without obscuring the difference between the two forms of community. Thus in the *Nicomachean Ethics*, the proper friendships of various members of the household are compared to the relationships characteristic of different constitutions. The friendship of brothers resembles polity because brothers tend to be more or less equal and therefore to stand on a footing of equality (*EN* 8.10.1161a3–6, 8.11.1161a25–30). The friendship of husband and wife is like aristocracy, since the hierarchy and inequality of marriage accord with differences in the merit and virtues of husband and wife, with each ruling in a fitting proportion relative to the other (8.10.1160b32–1161a3, 11.1161a22–5). The father's friendship with his children is like kingship; both father and king far exceed others in authority and in the magnitude of the benefits that they bestow on others (*EN* 8.10.1160b24–32, 8.11.1161a10–22). In each case, the salient feature of the relationship highlighted by the political analogy is the kind of equality or inequality of the parties and its consequences for the character of their friendship.

The application of these analogies in no way diminishes the distinguishing features of the household and the city or their importance; husbands and wives need not treat one another as aristocratic citizens do any more than aristocratic citizens treat one another as husbands and wives. So too, the *Politics* analogy of the king to the household manager may be no deeper than the earlier analogy of the father and the king: The king's relationship to a city's other citizens is most prominently characterized by the king's outstanding superiority and beneficence. That comparison can stand, however, without blocking our view of the important disanalogies between a king and a father: The father rules over immature people whose good he takes to be a part of his own and exercises an asymmetrical authority over them, while the king rules mature adults whose consent and approval of his rule play an important role in legitimating it. Aristotle's analogy may in fact have a simpler rationale: The king and the household manager are both single individuals who occupy the highest positions of authority; they are both monarchs in the literal sense of the term. As we have seen, on this point of comparison the king and the head of a household are alike. It hardly follows that the king's rule is a form of household management or that he treats the city as though it were an extended household.[61] If this simple point is primarily what Aristotle has

---

[61] The passages that seem to contrast monarchy and political rule most strongly (*Pol.* 1.1.1252a12–13, 1.7.1255b16–20) occur early in book 1, where Aristotle aims to distinguish political rule from other

in mind when comparing kingship and household management, it also helpfully contributes to an explanation of the otherwise mysterious inclusion of kingship over a nation and kingship over multiple cities.[62] Though neither form of rule could be a form of political rule in Aristotle's sense, both share their monarchical character with political kingship and household management. The introduction of total kingship makes the grouping especially apt, since total kingship resembles ethnic and imperial kingship more than the other forms of political kingship do in the extent of its authority.

We can, then, appreciate the point of Aristotle's analogy between kingship and household management without supposing that the mere fact of an analogy between them collapses all their nontrivial differences. The impulse to see the analogy as an acknowledgment of kingship's nonpolitical character is now more difficult to sustain in the presence of abundant evidence that Aristotle does indeed represent kingship as distinctively political. It has been the burden of this book to show that when Aristotle's accounts of political community and of kingship are properly understood, kingship turns out to be the genuinely political form of rule that Aristotle intends it to be. Supposing that my efforts to discharge that burden have been successful, it remains to consider a more fundamental question: Why should Aristotle have bothered to defend kingship in the first place?

6. Kingship's Positive and Negative Critical Functions

Though we have seen that Aristotle does not require a would-be king to transcend human nature and acquire divine attributes, it is nonetheless difficult to conclude that the emergence of a sufficiently virtuous individual is much more likely than such an apotheosis. Outside communities that are only emerging from a prepolitical stage of social development, the multitude of citizens or at least some subset of them will typically have attained a degree of collective deliberative excellence beyond that of ordinarily

varieties, and so emphasizes the focal case in which citizens rule by turns. By any estimation, genuinely political kingships – as opposed to tyrannies and kingships in nonpolitical societies – are a rare and special case, and it would be unreasonable to expect Aristotle to introduce his conception of the distinctively political in such a refined form that its application to noncentral cases would be clear from the beginning. Rather, he continues to develop and refine the idea through books 2 and 3, and part of the point of his defense of kingship is, as I argue in Section 6, to clarify certain aspects of the political.

[62] Nichols 1992: 75 takes the reference to nations (ἔθνη) as an indication that "overall kingship is not over a city as such" and thus finds yet another indication of the nonpolitical character of Aristotelian kingship.

virtuous individuals. Over citizens such as these, the only man who could justly be king would be extraordinarily virtuous. To appreciate just how extraordinary the man would have to be, consider an important constraint on the justice of kingship that operates alongside the king's relative superiority: Not only must he be more capable of managing the city than all of the other citizens combined, but those other citizens themselves must not be so vicious that they fail to see the value of being ruled by a king and therefore refuse to accept a kingship. Since a monarch will not rule justly – and hence will not be a king – if he can gain or retain his authority only by force, even a superlatively virtuous individual will refuse to be king over a body of citizens who staunchly reject his rule. The citizens must therefore be sufficiently virtuous and reasonable to recognize the king's superiority and to acknowledge the justice of his rule. In itself, this sort of recognition does not presuppose a high degree of political excellence, because it does not presuppose a high degree of practical wisdom; one need not be highly skilled at directing and inventing political policy in order to judge it competently.[63] This need for the citizens' recognition blocks easy appeals to the collective vice of the citizen body. Though the principal qualification for kingship is indeed comparative, the comparison class is composed of ordinarily functioning adults, not of people outstanding for their vices.[64] The Aristotelian king is, accordingly, an unlikely character.

If kingship is so unlikely outside the special conditions of political communities in an early stage of development, why does Aristotle devote so much space to his defense of it? Unlike the best constitution of books 7 and 8, kingship is apparently not an ideal that legislators should strive to approximate or a standard by which we can assess existing constitutions.[65] Yet nearly a quarter of book 3 is given over to the discussion of it. If the idea were simply that kingship was just and good in the early days of Greece but inappropriate for a mature civilization, the extensive attention to

---

[63] This difference tracks the distinction between practical wisdom (φρόνησις) and understanding (σύνεσις), on which see *EN* 6.10.1142b34–1143a18. I owe my appreciation of this point to an unpublished paper by Stephen White.

[64] Recall that Aristotle's defense of kingship is not supposed to apply only to primitive political communities or to nonpolitical communities. Accordingly, while kingship may be justified in primitive conditions in which most people are not, in one sense, "ordinarily functioning adults" because they have not yet had the opportunity to develop the virtues of political community, it is essential to the success of Aristotle's defense that kingship be conditionally justifiable, at least in principle, over people who have both had that opportunity and taken successful advantage of it.

[65] For a good statement of the "approximism" that structures Aristotle's view of the relationship between the best constitution and the constitutional forms at which we should aim in particular circumstances, see Miller 2007.

kingship and the belabored dialectical exchange for and against monarchic rule would be difficult to explain. After all, Aristotle lays out his basic argument for kingship at the end of 3.13, and he might have chosen to qualify that argument by briefly noting that kings are primarily a thing of the past. Instead, he gives us three detailed chapters clarifying his view and defending it against objections. Why?

One important function of those detailed arguments is a negative critical one: By illustrating just how outstanding an individual would need to be in order to merit kingship, Aristotle effectively disposes of most possible claims to monarchic entitlement. The dialectical exchange for and against rule by the "best man" contributes to this task not only by showing that this man must be extraordinary, but by further underscoring the lesson of Aristotle's earlier appeals to the summation principle. A king must be more than the "best man" in a city; he must in effect be a whole city by possessing a whole city's worth of political virtue. Since even one person who far outshines the rest of us as individuals may yet be far from surpassing our collective excellence, there is little reason to suspect that even our most outstanding individuals should rule our cities as kings. In this way, the defense of kingship is in part a critique of tyranny.

The idea that Aristotle's defense of kingship is in fact aimed at undermining the pretensions of would-be monarchs is nothing new. Some proponents of an esoteric interpretation of the *Politics* have said much the same thing. The plausibility of an esoteric interpretation is therefore diminished further by the ability of a straightforward or nonsuspicious interpretation such as mine to acknowledge the negative critical function of Aristotle's defense of kingship without supposing or concluding that he means more or less the opposite of what he says. Moreover, the negative aspect of Aristotle's defense has more bite than an esoteric rejection of kingship or even a straightforward but unqualified rejection would have. The negative implications of Aristotle's defense of kingship fit tightly with the popular Greek view of monarchy. As Plato has the Eleatic Visitor describe it in the *Statesman*, however accommodating earlier Greeks may have been to kings, people generally refuse to believe that anyone could have the virtue and knowledge that would entitle him to sole rule; anyone granted that power would be sure to abuse it (Plato, *Plt.* 301c–d). If this were Aristotle's own view, it would be difficult to see why he would resort to esoteric writing to communicate it.[66] Ironically, Aristotle's implicit critique of monarchy is more effective if his defense of kingship is

---

[66] The interpretation of Nichols 1992 seems to boil down to the view that Plato's Eleatic Visitor describes as widely held. Other esoteric readings – e.g., Lindsay 1991, Newell 1991, Collins 2006 – are more complicated, but tend in the same direction.

taken at face value. Unlike the purported esoteric teaching, the critique of monarchy is readily available to any reader who considers the implications of the defense of kingship.

Furthermore, Aristotle's implicit critique of monarchy has more force because it does not rest on a reactionary dismissal of kingship. Instead, Aristotle sets out criteria that a human being could conceivably meet but very likely will not. These criteria have one crucial advantage over the reasoning reflected in the common view reported by the Eleatic Visitor. The common view that cities should resist monarchy because every monarch will abuse his authority is especially vulnerable to apparent refutation by the presence of exceptionally just and virtuous individuals. However inevitably power may seem to corrupt when considered in the abstract, it may be more difficult to believe that the particular people whom we know to be far more virtuous even than ordinary decent human beings could really be corrupted. On Aristotle's view, by contrast, an individual's corruptibility is only secondarily relevant. The fundamental question is whether the city's common good will be better served if he rules as a king than if he rules and is ruled in turn or holds a special position of influence in a polity or an aristocracy. The answer to that question, in turn, depends on his relative capability more than his immunity from corruption. Thus even the famously incorruptible Socrates would not merit kingship as a matter of course.[67] The case for Socrates as king would turn on his possession of superior practical wisdom – a possession he claimed not to have – and on the relative capability of his fellow citizens to govern themselves well.[68] Aristotle's defense of kingship provides us with a better critique of monarchy precisely because it subordinates considerations of individual virtue and susceptibility to corruption to inherently context-sensitive considerations of relative abilities.

In addition to this negative critical function, Aristotle's defense of kingship in book 3 and his general account of it in later books do, despite appearances, play a role as a regulative ideal that existing arrangements can seek to approximate, albeit in a less programmatic or generally applicable way than the best constitution of books 7 and 8. The best

---

[67] For Socrates' incorruptibility, cf. Plato, *Ap.* 32a–e.

[68] For Socrates' disavowal of wisdom, Plato, *Ap.* 21b–23c. Though by his own account Socrates is wiser than people who suppose that they know what they do not, this wisdom falls short of Aristotelian practical wisdom, let alone the "science of measurement" discussed by Socrates in *Prot.* 356c–7c, the "kingly art" of *Euthyd.* 291b–3b, or the "science of good and evil" of *Charm.* 174b–d. This last is explicitly distinguished from "the science of science and absence of science" – i.e., knowledge of what one does and does not know – at 174d.

constitution in some sense provides a standard against which all existing constitutions can be judged, found wanting, and at least potentially reformed. Though Aristotle occasionally seems to describe aristocracy and kingship together as "best," the "constitution of our prayers" that he elaborates in books 7 and 8 is not remotely monarchic, presumably because he himself concedes the point raised against kingship: "If aristocracy should be considered the rule of many men who are all good, and kingship the rule of one, aristocracy would be more choiceworthy for cities than kingship, whether his rule is accompanied by ability or not, if it is possible to obtain a plurality of similar men" (*Pol.* 3.15.1286b3–7).[69] Aristotle's best constitution is supposed to be composed entirely of good men. Though we need not suppose that he imagines an entire city filled with perfectly virtuous human beings, it is nonetheless apparent that a city of this kind would be least suited to kingship, since the collective excellence of such a citizen body would be least capable of being surpassed by a single individual. As good as kingship may be, then, we could always hope for something better: more excellent citizens. Kingship is thus not an ideal in the same way as the best constitution. It does, however, serve an analogous function for the reform of existing monarchies: Tyrants should strive to be more like kings.

[69] Newman 1887–1902.iii: 286 reads "ability" (δύναμις) here as referring to the king's bodyguard (Simpson 1997, following Newman, even translates the word "armed guard"). Keyt 1999: 147–8, by contrast, while taking δύναμις in 3.15 as "power," rightly observes that this term is elsewhere (*Pol.* 3.13.1284a6–7, 5.9.1309a33–9, 7.3.1325b10–14) used to contrast virtue with ability, not power. But against Keyt and Newman alike, not only is there no discussion of bodyguards anywhere in the immediate context of 3.15, but the relevant preceding use of δύναμις is at 3.13.1284a9–10, where, as Keyt agrees, those who pass the test set by the summation principle are described as "unequal in virtue and political ability [τὴν πολιτικὴν δύναμιν]." The claim at 3.15.1286b3–7, then, is not the irrelevant and almost nonsensical one that aristocracy is better than kingship whether or not the king has a bodyguard; that claim might make an intelligible contribution to a different argument, but it is out of place in this context. Reading δύναμις as a reference to the outstanding political ability that was earlier presented as justifying monarchic rule, by contrast, makes clear sense of the objection: Rule by a *plurality* of good men is better than rule by *one* man *whether or not* that one man has the requisite ability to rule: obviously so if the one man lacks the ability, but even so if he has it, since more good men must be better than fewer. Newman and those who follow him no doubt supply the reference to bodyguards on the basis of 3.15.1286b27–40, where δύναμις appears as part of a problem about how the king will enforce his rule. But there too the reference to bodyguards is implicit in the use of the words ἰσχύς, "strength" or "power," and βιάζεσθαι, "to force" or "compel"; here too δύναμις simply means "ability" in a broad sense: "There is a puzzle about his ability, too, namely whether the man who is going to rule as a king should have some force of strength [ἰσχύν] about him by which he will be able [δυνήσεται] to use force against those who are not willing to obey" (3.15.1286b27–30). Admittedly, the "ability" in question in this latter passage may be a matter of social influence rather than individual skill (as at *EN* 1.8.1099b1–2 and 8.10.1161a3). But the frequent translation of δύναμις as "power" is misleading insofar as "power" tends to suggest "force."

Tyrants often gain and keep their power by amassing considerable support, usually among poor citizens who have been wrongly treated by wealthy elites (5.10.1310b12–14). Nonetheless, their characteristic injustices make them especially vulnerable to attack by citizens whose fear motivates them when the injustice itself is insufficient (5.10.1311a25–8). Aristotle runs through a list of causes leading to attempts to depose tyrants, illustrating each with particular examples: The attack on the Peisistratids was made in revenge for an insult to Harmodius's sister; Evagoras of Cyprus was attacked by a eunuch whose wife had been seduced by the tyrant's son; Dion attacked Dionysius in Syracuse out of contempt for the latter's perpetual drunkenness; Archelaus of Macedon was attacked because he had allowed Euripides to whip Decamnichus (5.10.1311b6–1312a20). The examples may be more entertaining than instructive, but the discussion as a whole makes clear that tyrannies are threatened by their own tendency to abusive behavior, which drives those who already resent being ruled to risk their lives in attacks on the tyrant (5.10.1312b17–34, 5.11.1315a24–9). Like all deviant constitutions, tyranny's injustice makes it inherently unstable.

Kingships of various sorts are susceptible to being overthrown for many of the same reasons as tyrannies; Aristotle even frames his discussion in terms of the destruction of *monarchies*. Kingships, however, are vulnerable primarily when they tend toward despotic rule. The forms of kingship that are further removed from total kingship are longer lasting by virtue of the limited scope of their authority. The Spartan kingship, for instance, owes its long preservation in part to the restrictions on its power. In general, the less expansive an individual's authority, the less despotic and more just his behavior becomes and the less ill will he inspires in others (5.11.1313a18–26). Aristotle's advice for the long-term preservation of kingships, accordingly, is that they gradually relinquish their control by sharing it more evenly. Thus the Spartan king Theopompus preserved kingship at Sparta by weakening it through the creation of the ephorate (5.11.1313a26–33). This advice reflects the realistic assumption that actual kings are unlikely to be or to deserve to be kings of the "total" variety. It also shows a concern with the intergenerational preservation of kingship, suggesting that kingships will in the long run be either abolished or transformed in the direction of the Spartan type. This is not to say that legitimate kingships must aim at their own dissolution, but that successful kingships will tend in that direction, since successfully promoting the good of the citizens increases their opportunity to cultivate virtues of character and intellect, thereby diminishing the gap between the king and his fellow citizens. Kingship may thus seem even less relevant as an ideal if its success leads to its demise.[70] The alternative, of course, is for kingships to degenerate into tyrannies. It is here that kingship's positive critical function becomes most apparent.

There are two broad strategies for preserving tyrannies. One is to employ the paradigmatically despotic methods of tyrants: killing or banishing outstanding individuals, preventing forms of association that might foster solidarity among the citizens, devising various means of surveillance, ensuring that the populace remains poor and concerned with meeting their daily needs (5.11.1313a34–b32). This strategy aims above all at preventing citizens from acquiring the ambition, mutual trust, and ability to challenge the tyrant's rule (5.11.1314a12–29). We can infer from the frequent adoption of this strategy and the remarkably short life of most tyrannies that these methods are not likely to be especially successful. The alternative is for the tyrant to act as much like a king as he possibly can without ceasing to be a tyrant: Though as a tyrant he will rule over his subjects whether or not they are unwilling, "everything else he must either do or be thought to do in a fine and noble way, acting out the part of a king" (5.11.1314a39–40).

Aristotle's willingness to offer advice for the preservation of what he himself acknowledges to be deviant and unjust regimes has surprised and worried many readers of the *Politics* who have been uncomfortable with the apparently "Machiavellian" tenor of the advice.[71] Admittedly, his suggestions for maintaining a tyranny direct the tyrant to promote his city's common good and to minimize the pursuit of his own interests at the expense of his city. The tyrant should not use common funds in ways that will lead others to resent him, and he should render an account of revenues and expenses to make clear to everyone how he has used the money. He should present himself as dignified rather than harsh and should make a point of refraining from abusing his subjects or allowing any of the assistants who share his privileges to do the same. He should

---

[70] Aristotle does not claim that kingship of any variety is characterized by planned obsolescence, as it were; though a tendency in this direction follows from his broader account, he does not emphasize it because, as I try to show in this and the next section, his interest in defending kingship largely lies elsewhere.

[71] For this problem, see Rowe 1991; Keyt 1999: 171–81 and Miller 2007 persuasively argue that there are no sinister implications in the idea that one ought to know how to preserve deviant and unjust constitutions, since it neither follows that one ought actually to preserve them or that the immediately available alternatives are not worse. Generally speaking, a relatively stable but unjust arrangement is to be preferred both to more unjust arrangements and to the breakdown of a community in civil war. For an especially acute treatment of Aristotle's aversion to faction and emphasis on stability, see Garver 2011: ch. 5.

avoid conspicuous consumption and preferably cultivate genuine moderation. He should distribute enough honor to good citizens that they do not
think of the tyrant's rule as depriving them of honor. He should strive
to make both the wealthy few and the populace well disposed to him,
especially by creating the impression that his rule protects each from the
other. Yet what has troubled some readers about these suggestions is their
apparent indifference to the accuracy with which the appearances reflect
the reality; what preserves tyranny is the appearance of moderation and
dedication to the common good, even if it is nothing more than a façade.
It may thus begin to seem as though Aristotle advocates recourse to a "veil
of mystification" designed to legitimate unjust power relations that subjects would otherwise not be inclined to accept.[72]

Against this conclusion, however, we can see, first, that in most cases
the tyrant could not seem to be ruling justly without doing what a just
ruler would do; a policy of concealment will make his rule less secure
than a policy of never doing what would need to be concealed. Second,
and more importantly, Aristotle makes clear that the tyrant's rule will in
fact be unjust; that follows from the hypothesis that he is a tyrant. What
he advocates is that the tyrant do as much as he can to rule justly. He
even holds out some hope that acting this way will improve the tyrant's
character: "He will either be well disposed for virtue or will be half-good,
not bad but half-bad" (5.11.1315b8–10). Rather than an endorsement of
deception in politics, Aristotle's advice for the preservation of tyranny is a
realistic acknowledgment that circumstances are often far from ideal and
a recommendation to approximate that ideal to whatever extent one can.
This strategy for preserving tyranny is presumably supposed to be able to
appeal to the tyrant's interest in preserving his position, as a more direct
appeal to justice would not.[73] On the supposition that a tyranny is either
unavoidable or the best available arrangement in some particular circumstances, then, the best strategy for preserving it is for the tyrant to act as

---

[72] I take the phrase "veil of mystification" from Ober 1998: 6.

[73] In this respect, the *Politics* account should be contrasted with the strategy of Xenophon's *Hiero*,
in which the poet Simonides advises Hiero to promote the common good as a way to attain his
own happiness and not simply as a way to preserve his rule. Xenophon presents Hiero as willing
but unable to give up his tyranny. He initially pursued tyranny in the belief that it would make
him happy, but is now afraid to give it up because it has made him so many enemies. For Hiero,
then, the value of tyranny is an open question and is never assumed to be more than instrumental.
Aristotle, by contrast, presents his recommendations, which are otherwise quite similar to those
of Xenophon's Simonides, in a way that should appeal to anyone who wants to retain his tyranny,
however he values it. On the Hiero generally, see Gray 2007, who includes a useful critique of the
very different but influential reading of Strauss 1963.

unlike a tyrant as possible.[74] The account of kingship as the just counter-part to tyranny serves as a model for reforming tyrannies. Thus, while the negative critical function of that account shows us that most monarchies are unjust, its positive function directs us toward the amelioration of their worst features.

7.   Aristotelian Kingship and Platonic Political Knowledge

Important as the negative and positive functions of Aristotle's defense of kingship are, neither fully accounts for the prominence and character of that defense. A more satisfactory explanation cannot neglect the relation-ship between Aristotle's *Politics* and Plato's *Statesman*.[75] Though Aristotle nowhere explicitly refers to the dialogue as he does to the *Republic* and the *Laws*, we have already seen that one of the main themes of the *Politics* as a whole – the heterogeneity of human community and forms of rule – directly contradicts a fundamental and explicit thesis of the *Statesman*. There Plato has the unnamed Eleatic Visitor, the main speaker of the dialogue, maintain that there is no essential difference among a king, a statesman or political ruler [πολιτικός], a household manager, and a slave master (Plato, *Plt.* 258e–59a). This is the thesis that Aristotle rejects at the beginning of the *Politics*, and by now it should be clear how fundamen-tal his rejection of it is. But Aristotle's engagement with the *Statesman* extends far beyond this point. His theory of constitutions also reflects his critical engagement with the dialogue. The Eleatic Visitor argues that the unconstrained rule of an expert king or statesman is the only "correct" constitution; all the other constitutions are incorrect and are not even, properly speaking, constitutions at all (*Plt.* 293e). Aristotle's alternative classificatory scheme is less severe: Though the best constitution is in one sense "most correct," less ideal arrangements can nonetheless be correct if they promote the common good rather than the interests of the rul-ing class alone.[76] Furthermore, when Aristotle turns to consider whether kingship can really be a correct constitution after all, he approaches the

---

[74] If tyranny is the worst of the deviant constitutions, it might seem impossible for it to be the best alternative in any set of circumstances. Presumably, however, tyranny can be preferable in cities where relations between factions would otherwise devolve into outright violence and civil war.

[75] Cherry 2012 is one of the few works to offer a sustained treatment of the *Politics* as a response to the *Statesman*. Though Cherry's interpretation of Plato is controversial and, to my mind, often unper-suasive, much of his analysis of the *Politics* is consistent with the views I have developed here, and my brief synopsis of the *Statesman* later covers points on which we are broadly in agreement.

[76] For Aristotle's classification of constitutions as a response to and critical correction of Plato's, see Fortenbaugh 1991.

question in terms of a dispute between proponents of the rule of law and supporters of rule by "the best man," and he takes not only these terms but also many of the arguments on both sides directly from the *Statesman*. Thus throughout the *Politics* and in the defense of kingship in particular Aristotle is responding to the dialogue implicitly and indirectly. By briefly considering the Eleatic Visitor's claims, we can see that Aristotle's defense of kingship is the culmination of a pervasive disagreement with the view of Plato's *Statesman* and the ideal of the philosopher-king that the dialogue explores.

For our purposes, the relevant theses put forth by the Eleatic Visitor can be summarized as follows. First, only an expert knowledge of politics entitles a person to rule in any community (292c–3d). This knowledge involves a systematic understanding of the human good and of the best way to realize it in a community (259c1–5, 267a8–c4, 311b7–c10). Second, anyone who has this expertise should rule without the constraints of law (293c5–7b4). For the reasons already cited in Aristotle's consideration of the rule of law, laws as such will always be imperfectly able to prescribe the correct course of action for particular circumstances. The expert king or statesman, precisely because he possesses this expertise, should not be restrained by laws but should be free to prescribe the course of action that he correctly identifies as best in each situation. The visitor evidently supposes that anyone who possesses genuine political expertise will be able to make these judgments without error (297a5–b3). Third, in the absence of such an expert, laws should rule in a strong sense: They are to be strictly obeyed and to remain unchanged (297d3–300c3). Attempts to pass judgments on a case-by-case basis or to modify and improve the laws will succeed, if at all, only by accident. They are much more likely to fail because of people's ignorance or to be directed intentionally at serving the interests of some at the expense of the common good (300c9–1a4). Though laws can be better or worse, it is better by far for a city to adhere to its laws than to be ruled by men without the knowledge that would enable them to guide the city toward justice and happiness (302c1–d3, 311b7–c10).

The *Statesman* is a remarkably complex dialogue, and it is by no means clear how the visitor's view should be understood and what sort of relationship it bears to Plato's own views or to the arguments of the *Republic* and the *Laws*.[77] Fortunately, we need not enter into those problems here.

---

[77] For a concise and helpful presentation of a more or less traditional view of the *Statesman* and its place in Plato's political philosophy, see Klosko 2006: 195–216 and cf. Barker 1959: 164–71. For a very different and revisionist view, see Bobonich 2002, which, however, does not devote much

However the dialogue may qualify or cast doubt on the visitor's central claims, Aristotle's alternative stands in stark contrast to them. In light of the *Statesman*'s insistence that expert knowledge of politics is the only thing that entitles a person to rule, the failure of the *Politics* to take any such claims seriously should be especially striking. Aristotle's silence might even suggest that he is not concerned with the arguments of the *Statesman* at all, since he does not even consider the visitor's arguments in favor of knowledge as the sole criterion of correctness in rule. Yet he also passes over the visitor's arguments for the essential unity of rulership and opts to lay out his own alternative view instead. Much the same is true of his rejection of the visitor's insistence on the primacy of political expertise, but with one key difference. With regard to the varieties of ruling and being ruled, Aristotle first announces his disagreement and then proceeds to argue for his own view over the course of most of book 1. With regard to the role of knowledge in justifying claims to rule, Aristotle first argues for his own alternative throughout much of book 3 and then illustrates its implications and supplies further defense by way of an understated contrast with the view of the *Statesman*.[78] Where Plato uses the figure of the king to lay out a series of theses about political excellence and the justification of claims to authority, Aristotle develops a complex theory of citizenship, citizen virtue, correct and deviant constitutions, and justice in the distribution of authority and then uses the figure of the king to illuminate that theory. For Aristotle's defense of kingship is, from one perspective, simply the culmination of the theory that he has developed in the rest of book 3.

The most evident and far-reaching divergence of Aristotle's theory from the conception of politics embodied in the Platonic ideal of a philosopher-king is that, for Aristotle, the distribution of authority is a matter of *relative capability* rather than *absolute knowledge*.[79] Yet it is

attention to the *Statesman* in its own right. Cherry 2012 distances Plato from the views of the Eleatic Visitor and regards those views as deliberately problematic (for a similar approach, cf. Cooper 1999b); he also sharply distinguishes "Eleatic political science" from political philosophy as practiced by Plato's Socrates. My own approach to the *Statesman* has been most influenced by Schofield 1999f and Rowe 2000.

[78] As I noted in Chapter 2, the *Statesman*'s view of the homogeneity of rulership can be found in Xenophon's Socrates, as well, and may have been a common view. Xenophon's Socrates also talks about rulership as "the kingly art" and proceeds on the assumption that the sole or main qualification for rule is knowledge (see, e.g., Xen. *Mem.* 4.2.11). Thus Aristotle may refrain from discussing the *Statesman* explicitly because his response to it is at once a response to a more widely shared view. For the programmatic role of rulership in Xenophon's works, see the introduction to Gray 2007.

[79] Some scholars see the *Statesman* as a decisive break from the theory of the *Republic* and so distance the former from the idea of a philosopher-king. Yet whatever the differences between the two

a considerable achievement on Aristotle's part that this contrast is even available; from the Platonic perspective it would seem awkward at best to propose that anyone could be relatively more capable of exercising political authority *unless* he had more knowledge. From an Aristotelian point of view, this contrast makes sense not simply because knowledge is not the only thing that enables a person to contribute to the common good of his political community, but because the intellectual virtue that contributes most to excellence in the central political activities of deliberation and judgment about common affairs is not a kind of theoretical knowledge or technical expertise, but a sort of practical wisdom.

All three of these forms of intellectual virtue are similar insofar as they are abilities to reason well. Unlike theoretical knowledge, however, practical wisdom is not an ability to demonstrate the truth of universal and necessary conclusions on the basis of first principles (*EN* 6.3.1139b15–1140a1). It is, rather, an ability to deliberate well about particular and contingent courses of action (6.5.1140a25–b5, 6.7.1141b10–23), where deliberating well involves not only a basically correct grasp of what is good for oneself and for human beings generally, but skill in identifying the best means to these ends (6.9.1142a31–b33, 6.12.1144a25–b1). Nor is it, like technical expertise, a matter of knowing how to produce a product whose existence, character, and value are independent of the activity by which it is produced (6.4.1140a1–25). Practical wisdom and deliberation are concerned, rather, with *actions* in a more restricted sense of activities chosen for their own sake as aspects of a good human life (6.5.1140b4–5). The practical as opposed to productive character of practical wisdom and deliberation connects them more closely than any strictly technical expertise to the virtues of character; while few would doubt whether an unjust man can be a skilled carpenter, it is much less apparent whether an unjust man can be a wise and happy human being.[80]

---

dialogues in metaphysics, epistemology, or moral psychology, the *Statesman* is without doubt an exploration of the claim – explicit at 258b4, 259a6–8, 293c5–d2, and throughout – that cities should be governed by political experts, and the expertise envisioned is a systematic theoretical kind. On this question, I most closely follow Rowe 2000. For a stimulating consideration of the place of the philosopher-king in the development of Plato's political thought, see Schofield 1999f. For an opposed view, Cherry 2012, esp. ch. 5.

[80] This paragraph simplifies and condenses a complex and controversial set of questions about Aristotle's conception of practical wisdom and especially about its difference from technical expertise or craft knowledge; cf. Cherry 2012: ch. 4. For a helpful discussion of the problems and an insightful interpretation of the distinctions, see Broadie 1991: 78–90, 179–265, esp. 190–8, 202–12. The relationship between τέχνη and φρόνησις continues to be the subject of lively debate, as

Aristotle's distinction of practical wisdom or excellence from theoretical and technical knowledge enables him to embrace the Platonic insistence on the rule of reason in politics while rejecting the ideal of philosopher-kings. Unlike scientific or technical expertise, deliberative excellence is plausibly attributed in *some* degree to most ordinarily functioning adult human beings.[81] Also unlike technical or theoretical knowledge, it is more readily apparent that a group of individuals deliberating together about their common practical concerns will often arrive at conclusions superior to most that those same individuals could have discovered on their own. It is not similarly evident that five people with no understanding of geometry could be better able to calculate the surface area and volume of a cone than any of them would be working on his own, much less that those same five could be better able than Euclid or could even do much to supplement or improve the geometer's performance. Nor would five novice carpenters be likely to design better tables than a single master craftsman or to improve the quality of his design. In the realm of action and deliberation, by contrast, even the wise may benefit from sharing in deliberation with others. Action is concerned not only with contingent particulars – in that respect action and production are alike – but with a more complex range of concerns than any particular craft; practical deliberation does not aim merely to discover the most effective means to a single determinate goal, but more fundamentally considers how to integrate and order a variety of intrinsically valuable ends.[82] This complexity only increases when the practical concerns are political and common and hence include the shared good and the coordinated activity of many others. Hence it is hardly surprising that

evidenced, e.g., in Angier 2010 and Reeve 2013. These debates are of the highest interest, but my argument here does not depend on any particular resolution of them.

[81] Objection: Aristotle believes that "the many" are not virtuous, serious (σπουδαῖος), or even decent (ἐπιεικής) and so would not attribute practical wisdom to them at all. Response: But Aristotle recognizes that virtues come in degrees (e.g., *Catg.* 8.10b30–11a5, *EN* 10.3.1173a17–22) and that even the vicious may have highly cultivated deliberative abilities (*EN* 6.12.1144a23–9). Furthermore, only a few are thoroughly vicious or have a thoroughly distorted conception of the good (for a defense of this claim, see Garrett 1993, who may draw excessively sharp boundaries between the varieties of character he discusses). So, while only a few are practically wise, most ordinary functioning adults have some deliberative ability, whereas many of us have no degree of technical ability whatsoever in, say, carpentry, calculus, piano playing, shorthand notation, etc.

[82] For a spirited view of Aristotelian deliberation for which I have much sympathy, see Nussbaum 1990c, though she characteristically understates both the importance of theoretical considerations in knowledge of the good and the preeminent status of theoretical activity as part of the good. For a detailed discussion that ostensibly denies that Aristotelian deliberation is of ends but nicely illustrates my point here, see Cammack 2013b.

fewer people should display wisdom in politics than in the less extensive associations of their individual lives or that collective deliberation tends to issue in judgments superior to those of individuals.

In other words, Aristotle's distinction of the practical from the theoretical and the technical opens up the conceptual space in which the principle of summation can operate to include individuals of no great distinction, and the application of that principle thus places his approach to the question of who should rule at a great distance from the path that leads to the figure of the Platonic philosopher-king.[83] The Aristotelian παμβασιλεύς rules not because he possesses a kind of absolute theoretical-cum-technical expertise that enables him to guide and direct the common life of his city in accordance with a systematic grasp of the human good, but because he is more capable than his fellow citizens taken together of deliberating well about the common good. No doubt the Aristotelian king would not refuse to deliberate unless isolated and secluded in a palace like Herodotus's Deioces, but will hear proposals and consult advisers.[84] But Aristotle is uninterested in the institutional details. Both Plato's philosopher-king and Aristotle's παμβασιλεύς are best understood as theoretical models aimed at illuminating philosophical questions rather than as practical proposals for political reform.[85] Plato's use of that model is, furthermore, more complex and nuanced than I have described here. Nonetheless, in responding to it as he did, Aristotle may not have been reading the *Statesman* uncharitably, but just as Plato intended – as a spur to constructive philosophical thought rather than an oracle to be deciphered.[86] The result is a highly

[83] Thus when Finley 1985: 15 appeals to a distinction between "technical" and "political" knowledge or skill in his objections to both ancient and modern critics of the Athenian democracy, he is more indebted to Aristotle than he may have been happy to admit. The distinction is by no means the natural and obvious one that Finley and others present, and it is especially not obvious whether the recognition that politics does not admit of the sort of expertise exhibited by carpenters, cooks, accountants, or generals should lead us to deny the applicability of concepts such as "knowledge" to the political realm altogether or, following Aristotle, to seek a distinction among different kinds of knowledge.

[84] Deioces, the first king of the Medes, began as a highly respected individual renowned for his justice in settling disputes. When he refused to hear cases any longer unless the Medes made him king, the Medes obliged. Once king, he segregated himself in a palace separated from the rest of the Medes by a series of walls and required all business to be transacted through intermediaries, never allowing himself to be seen (Hdt. 1.96–100).

[85] For the philosopher-king as this sort of model, see Schofield 1999f.

[86] I have no considered general view on the disputed question of how best to approach the interpretation of Platonic dialogues, but it is clear that Aristotle did not adopt any subtle or complex hermeneutical strategies, probably because he was less interested in the dialogues as literary artifacts than in the philosophical ideas he found in them. For Aristotle as a reader of Plato, cf. Irwin 1995: 5–7

qualified defense of kingship that follows from and illuminates both a conception of politics and a theory of justice that displace knowledge and expertise from the central position Plato had given them and set excellence in deliberation and judgment in their place.

and Kahn 1996: 79–88. For discussions of different approaches to Plato's dialogues, see, besides these works, Griswold 1988 and Rowe 2007.

Conclusion: Ruling and Being Ruled

It is sometimes easy to forget how little we know about the original purpose, audience, and composition of Aristotle's writings. A general consensus regards them as something like lecture notes intended for students at the Lyceum, but even that is largely conjecture. It is relatively clear at least that the works as we have them were not intended for publication and are not complete, polished works in the manner of Plato's dialogues. They are instead often rough, schematic, underdeveloped, elliptical, ambiguous, or just plain obscure. Consequently, interpretation is heavily underdetermined by the texts and any detailed account of Aristotle's thought is bound to be controversial. It would therefore be foolish to claim that the view of Aristotle's political philosophy that I have defended in this book is the only plausible, let alone possible, interpretation of the texts. My claim is, instead, the more modest but still quite strong one that the texts, when taken together, are *most* plausibly read as I read them here. Aristotle views political community as a special variety of cooperative human interaction distinguished by aiming at the good life as a whole for its members and by mutuality and reciprocity in the exercise of authority. Political community is peculiarly valuable in the first instance because it establishes institutions of collective deliberation and judgment that enable citizens to coordinate their efforts to live well and to support one another in that endeavor. But political rule has further value insofar as it respects and facilitates living in accordance with one's own decisions. It is the value of self-direction as an aspect of the human good that gives citizenship its distinctive value, not the inherent attractions of political participation, real as they may be. Even markedly hierarchical arrangements of political authority can accord a substantial role to the least authoritative citizens by subjecting that hierarchy to those citizens' consent and approval. Hence monarchy can in principle be a just political system in which the king rules not over powerless subjects, but over citizens who share in ruling as well as being ruled.

As an interpretation of Aristotle, these arguments will certainly not convince everybody; differences in philosophical judgment and the ambiguities of the textual evidence make disagreement inevitable. But I hope that even those least persuaded by my reading of Aristotle will nonetheless agree that the vision of politics that I find in his writings offers us an intriguing and provocative challenge to many contemporary assumptions. Few of us, whether sophisticated theorists or plain persons, would intuitively agree that if we are to live good lives, we need to be *ruled*. Further, though many affirm the intrinsic value of political participation, few locate its value in *ruling*. Aristotle unsettles our prejudices in these respects in good part because he understands ruling not as the exercise of power over others, but as deliberative contribution to the initiation and direction of common action. Ruling and being ruled are specifically political when all parties contribute to the formation of the decisions that guide their actions, even when, for some, that contribution comes only in the form of consent and approval. Being ruled is valuable even for adults of stable and decent character because living well requires participation in the complex network of cooperative interaction that is political community, and one cannot participate in it without being ruled. Ruling is valuable not because deliberation or political action is choiceworthy for its own sake, but because deliberative contribution to the decisions that shape one's action is crucial to the full exercise of human capacities for rational agency. Ruling and being ruled *politically* – giving others a role in the formation of the deliberation that shapes their actions, and being given such a role by others – is the mode of authority appropriate for the pursuit of a common good among autonomous rational adults because it is the mode that enables each member of the community to benefit from his participation rather than being made to serve the interests of others.

This conception of politics is not wholly unfamiliar, but it is not what most of our contemporaries mean when they speak of the political. It is not for the history of philosophy to determine whether Aristotelian politics is a viable and superior alternative to today's dominant models of political thought and action. Many have thought so, and they have my sympathies. But the task of this book has been to clarify what is and is not a part of Aristotle's own conception of political community. Whatever shape our first-order political thought should ultimately take, it cannot fail to be enriched by grappling with Aristotle and the implications of his thought for our efforts to negotiate the problems and prospects of living well together.

References

Ackrill, J. L. 1980. 'Aristotle on Eudaimonia', in *Rorty* 1980, 15–33.

Adkins, A. W. H. 1963. 'Friendship and Self-Sufficiency in Aristotle and Homer', *Classical Quarterly* 13, 30–45.

1991. 'The Connection between Aristotle's *Ethics* and *Politics*', in *Keyt and Miller* 1991, 75–93.

Alpern, K. D. 1983. 'Aristotle on the Friendships of Utility and Pleasure', *Journal of the History of Philosophy* 21.3, 303–15.

Anagnostopoulos, G. (ed.). 2009. *A Companion to Aristotle*. Oxford.

Angier, T. 2010. *Techne in Aristotle's Ethics: Crafting the Moral Life*. London.

Annas, J. 1996. 'Aristotle on Human Nature and Political Virtue', *Review of Metaphysics* 49, 731–54.

Anscombe, G. E. M. 1957. *Intention*. Oxford.

Arendt, H. 1958. *The Human Condition*. Chicago.

Balot, R. 2006. *Greek Political Thought*. Oxford.

(ed.). 2009. *A Companion to Greek and Roman Political Thought*. Oxford.

Barker, E. 1959. *The Political Thought of Plato and Aristotle*. New York.

Barnes, J., Schofield, M., and Sorabji, R. (eds.). 1977. *Articles on Aristotle*, 4 vols. London.

Barnes, J. 1980. 'Aristotle and the Method of Ethics', *Revue Internationale de Philosophie* 34, 490–511.

Bar On, B. A. (ed.). 1994. *Engendering Origins: Critical Feminist Readings in Plato and Aristotle*. Albany, NY.

Bates, C. A. 2003. *Aristotle's 'Best Regime': Kingship, Democracy, and the Rule of Law*. Baton Rouge.

Belfiore, E. 2001. 'Family Friendship in Aristotle's Ethics', *Ancient Philosophy* 21, 113–32.

Berent, M. 2004. 'In Search of the Greek State: Rejoinder to M. H. Hansen', *Polis* 21, 107–46.

Bevir, M. 1994. 'Are there Perennial Problems in Political Theory?', *Political Studies* 42, 662–75.

1997. 'Mind and Method in the History of Ideas', *History and Theory* 36.2, 167–89.

1999. *The Logic of the History of Ideas*. Cambridge.

2002. 'How to Be an Intentionalist', *History and Theory* 41, 209–17.

2007. 'Esotericism and Modernity: An Encounter with Leo Strauss', *Journal of the Philosophy of History* 1.2, 201–18.

Biondi Khan, C.-A. 2005. 'Aristotle, Citizenship, and the Common Advantage', *Polis* 22.1, 1–23.

Blomqvist, K. 1998. *The Tyrant in Aristotle's Politics: Theoretical Assumptions and Historical Background*. Stockholm.

Bobonich, C. 2002. *Plato's Utopia Recast*. Oxford.

2006. 'Aristotle's Ethical Treatises', in Kraut 2006, 12–36.

Bodéüs, R. 2000. *Aristotle and the Theology of the Living Immortals*. Albany, NY.

Boyd, R. 1988. 'How to be a Moral Realist', in G. Sayre-McCord (ed.), *Essays on Moral Realism*. Ithaca, NY, 181–228.

Brink, D. 1989. *Moral Realism and the Foundations of Ethics*. Cambridge.

Broadie, S. 1991. *Ethics with Aristotle*. Oxford.

Brown, E. 2013. 'Aristotle on the Choice of Lives: Two Concepts of Self-Sufficiency', in P. Destrée and M. Zingano (eds.), *THEORIA: Studies on the Status and Meaning of Contemplation in Aristotle's Ethics*. Louvain, 135–57.

Burnet, J. 1900. *The Ethics of Aristotle*. London.

Burnyeat, M. 1980. 'Aristotle on Learning to Be Good', in Rorty 1980, 69–92.

Cammack, D. 2013a. 'Aristotle on the Virtue of the Multitude', *Political Theory* 41.2, 175–202.

2013b. 'Aristotle's Denial of Deliberation about Ends', *Polis* 30.2, 228–50.

Cartledge, P. 2009. *Ancient Greek Political Thought in Practice*. Cambridge.

Chan, J. 1992. 'Does Aristotle's Political Theory Rest on a Blunder?', *History of Political Thought* 13, 189–202.

Chappell, T. 2009. '"Naturalism" in Aristotle's Political Philosophy', in Balot 2009, 382–98.

Charles, D. 1984. *Aristotle's Philosophy of Action*. London.

1988. 'Perfectionism in Aristotle's Political Theory: Reply to Martha Nussbaum', *Oxford Studies in Ancient Philosophy* 6, Supplementary Volume, 185–206.

Cherry, K. 2012. *Plato, Aristotle, and the Purpose of Politics*. Cambridge.

Cherry, K. and Goerner, E. A. 2006. 'Does Aristotle's Polis Exist "By Nature"?', *History of Political Thought* 27.4, 563–85.

Collins, S. 2006. *Aristotle and the Rediscovery of Citizenship*. Cambridge.

Cooper, J. 1977a. 'Aristotle on the Forms of Friendship', *Review of Metaphysics* 30, 619–48.

1977b. 'Friendship and the Good in Aristotle', *Philosophical Review* 86, 290–315.

1980. 'Aristotle on Friendship', in Rorty 1980, 310–40.

1990. 'Political Animals and Civic Friendship', in Patzig 1990, 356–77.

1999a. *Reason and Emotion*. Princeton, NJ.

1999b. 'Some Remarks on Aristotle's Moral Psychology', in Cooper 1999a, 237–52.

2004a. *Nature, Knowledge, and the Good*. Princeton, NJ.

2004b. 'Plato and Aristotle on "Finality" and "(Self-)Sufficiency' in Cooper 2004a, 270–308.

2010. 'Political Community and the Highest Good', in Gotthelf and Lennox 2010, 212–63.

Curzer, H. 2012. *Aristotle and the Virtues*. Oxford.

Dahl, N. O. 2011. 'Contemplation and *eudaimonia* in the *Nicomachean Ethics*', in Miller 2011, 66–91.

Dancy, J. 2004. *Ethics without Principles*. Oxford.

D'Andrea, T. D. 2006. *Tradition, Rationality, and Virtue: the Thought of Alasdair MacIntyre*. Burlington, VT.

Davidson, D. 1973. 'Radical Interpretation', *Dialectica* 27, 314–28, repr. in Davidson 2001, *Inquiries into Truth and Interpretation*, Oxford.

Den Uyl, D. J. 1991. *The Virtue of Prudence*. New York.

Denniston, J. D. 1950. *The Greek Particles*, 2nd ed., rev. by K. J. Dover. Oxford.

Depew, D. 1991. 'Politics, Music, and Contemplation in Aristotle's Ideal State', in Keyt and Miller 1991, 346–80.

1995. 'Humans and Other Political Animals in Aristotle's *History of Animals*', *Phronesis* 40.2, 158–81.

Deslauriers, M. 2003. 'The Virtues of Women and Slaves', *Oxford Studies in Ancient Philosophy* 25, 212–31.

2006. 'The Argument of Aristotle's Politics I', *Phoenix* 60.1–2, 48–69.

2013. 'Political Unity and Inequality', in Deslauriers and Destrée 2013, 117–43.

Deslauriers, M. and Destrée, P. 2013. *The Cambridge Companion to Aristotle's Politics*. Cambridge.

Destrée, P. 2000. 'Aristote et la question du droit naturel', *Phronesis* 45.3, 220–39.

Düring, I. 1957. *Aristotle in the Ancient Biographical Tradition*. Gothenburg.

Everson, S. 1988. 'Aristotle on the Foundations of the State', *Political Studies* 36, 89–101.

Ewbank, M. B. 2005. '*Politeia* as Focal Reference in Aristotle's Taxonomy of Regimes', *Review of Metaphysics* 58.4, 815–41.

Finley, M. 1970. 'Aristotle and Economic Analysis', *Past & Present* 47.1, 3–25.

1975. *The Use and Abuse of History*. New York.

1983. *Politics in the Ancient World*. Cambridge.

1985. *Democracy Ancient and Modern*, Revised Edition. New Brunswick, N. J.

Finnis, J. 1980. *Natural Law and Natural Rights*. Oxford.

Foot, P. 2001. *Natural Goodness*. Oxford.

Fortenbaugh, W. W. 1975a. 'Aristotle's Analysis of Friendship: Function, Analogy, Resemblance, and Foal Meaning', *Phronesis* 20, 51–62.

1975b. *Aristotle on Emotion*. London.

1977. 'Aristotle on Slaves and Women', in Barnes et al. 1977, ii: 135–9.

1991. 'Aristotle on Prior and Posterior, Correct and Mistaken Constitutions', in Keyt and Miller 1991, 226–37.

2006. *Aristotle's Practical Side: On His Psychology, Ethics, Politics, and Rhetoric*. Leiden.

Frank, J. 2005. *A Democracy of Distinction: Aristotle and the Work of Politics*. Chicago.

Frede, D. 2005. 'Citizenship in Aristotle's Politics', in Kraut, R. and Skultety, S. (eds.), *Aristotle's Politics: Critical Essays*. Lanham, Md, 167–84.

2013. 'The Political Character of Aristotle's Ethics', in Deslauriers and Destrée 2013, 14–37.

Frede, M. 1992. 'On Aristotle's Conception of the Soul', in Nussbaum and Rorty 1992, 93–108.

Freeland, C. (ed.). 1998. *Feminist Interpretations of Aristotle*. Philadelphia.

Gagarin, M. 1986. *Early Greek Law*. Berkeley and Los Angeles.

Garrett, J. 1993. 'The Moral Status of "the Many" in Aristotle', *Journal of the History of Philosophy* 31.2, 171–89.

Garsten, B. 2013. 'Deliberating and Acting Together', in Deslauriers and Destrée 2013, 324–49.

Garver, E. 2011. *Aristotle's Politics: Living Well and Living Together*. Chicago.

Geach, P. 1956. 'Good and Evil', *Analysis* 17, 32–42.

Gerson, L. 2007. 'The Morality of Nations: An Aristotelian Approach', in Goodman and Talisse 2007, 77–92.

Gomez-Lobo, A. 1989. 'The Ergon Inference', *Phronesis* 34.2, 170–84.

Goodman, L. E. and Talisse, R. (eds.). 2007. *Aristotle's Politics Today*. Albany, NY.

Gotthelf, A. and Lennox, J. G. (eds.). 1987. *Philosophical Issues in Aristotle's Biology*. Cambridge.

Gray, V. 2007. *Xenophon on Government*. Cambridge.

Griswold, C. (ed.). 1988. *Platonic Writings/Platonic Readings*. New York.

Greenwood, L. H. G. 1909. *Aristotle: Nicomachean Ethics Book Six*. Cambridge.

Halper, E. 2007. 'Aristotle and the Liberal State', in Goodman and Talisse 2007, 33–44.

Hammer, D. 2009. 'What Is Politics in the Ancient World?', in Balot 2009, 20–36.

Hanke, L. 1994. *All Mankind Is One: A Study of the Disputation Between Bartolomé de Las Casas and Juan Ginés de Sepúlveda in 1550 on the Intellectual and Religious Capacity of the American Indians*. DeKalb, IL.

Hansen, M. H. 1991. *The Athenian Democracy in the Age of Demosthenes*. Oxford.

1993. 'Aristotle's Alternative to the Sixfold Classification of Constitutions', in M. Pierart (ed.), *Aristote et Athène*. Freiborg, 91–101.

1996a. 'Aristotle's Two Complementary Views of the Greek Polis', in R. W. Wallace and E. Harris (eds.), *Transitions to Empire: Essays in Greek and Roman History in Honor of E. Badian*. Norman, OK, 196–210.

1996b. 'The Ancient Athenian and Modern Liberal View of Liberty as a Democratic Ideal', in Ober and Hedrik 1996, 91–104.

1999. 'Aristotle's Reference to the Arkadian Federation at *Pol.* 1261a29', in T. H. Nielsen and J. Roy (eds.), *Defining Ancient Arkadia*. Copenhagen, 80–9.

2002. 'Was the *Polis* a State or a Stateless Society?', in T. H. Nielsen (ed.), *Even More Studies in the Ancient Greek Polis*. Stuttgart, 17–48.

2006a. *Polis: An Introduction to the Ancient Greek City-State*. Oxford.

2006b. *The Shotgun Method: The Demography of the Ancient Greek City-State Culture*. Columbia, MO.

2013. *Reflections on Aristotle's Politics*. Copenhagen.

Horn, C. 2013. 'Law, Governance, and Political Obligation', in Deslauriers and Destrée 2013, 223–46.

Inglis, K. 2014. 'Philosophical Virtue: In Defense of the Grand End', in Polansky 2014a, 263–87.

Irwin, T. 1981. 'Aristotle's Method of Ethics', in O'Meara 1981, 193–223.

1985. 'Permanent Happiness: Aristotle and Solon', *Oxford Studies in Ancient Philosophy* 3, 89–124.

1988. *Aristotle's First Principles*. Oxford.

1990. 'The Good of Political Activity,' in Patzig 1990, 73–101.

1995. *Plato's Ethics*. Oxford.

1996. 'Ethics in the *Rhetoric* and in the Ethics', in Amelie Rorty (ed.), *Essays on Aristotle's Rhetoric,* Berkeley, CA, 142–74.

1999. *Aristotle: Nicomachean Ethics*, trans. with notes, 2nd ed. Indianapolis, IN.

Joachim, H. 1951. *Aristotle, the Nicomachean Ethics: A Commentary*. Oxford.

Johnson, C. 1984. 'Who Is Aristotle's Citizen?', *Phronesis* 29.1, 73–90.

Johnson, M. R. 2005. *Aristotle on Teleology*. Oxford.

Jowett, B. 1885. *The Politics of Aristotle*, 2 vols. Oxford.

Kahn, C. 1990. 'The Normative Structure of Aristotle's *Politics*', in Patzig 1990, 369–84.

1996. *Plato and the Socratic Dialogue: The Philosophical Use of a Literary Form*. Cambridge.

Keaney, J. J. 1992. *The Composition of Aristotle's Athenaion* Politeia. Oxford.

Kelsen, H. 1937. 'The Philosophy of Aristotle and the Hellenic-Macedonian Policy', *Ethics* 48, 1–64; repr. in Barnes et al. 1977, ii: 170–94.

Kenny, A. 1992. *Aristotle on the Perfect Life*. Oxford.

Keyt, D. 1983. 'Intellectualism in Aristotle', in J. P. Anton and A. Preus (eds.), *Essays in Ancient Greek Philosophy,* Vol. 2. Albany, NY, 264–87.

1991a. 'Three Basic Theorems in Aristotle's *Politics*', in Keyt and Miller 1991, 118–41.

1991b. 'Aristotle's Theory of Distributive Justice', in Keyt and Miller 1991, 94–117.

1993. 'Aristotle and Anarchism', *Reason Papers* 18, 137–57.

1996. 'Fred Miller on Aristotle's Political Naturalism', *Ancient Philosophy* 16, 425–30.

1999. *Aristotle: Politics Books V and VI*. Oxford.

2007. 'The Good Man and the Upright Citizen in Aristotle's *Ethics* and *Politics*', in Keyt and Miller 2007, 220–40.

Keyt, D. and Miller, F. D. 1991. *A Companion to Aristotle's Politics*. Oxford.

(eds.). 2007. *Freedom, Reason, and the Polis: Essays in Ancient Greek Political Philosophy.* Cambridge.

Klosko, G. 1986. 'The Straussian Interpretation of Plato's *Republic*', *History of Political Thought* 7.22, 275–94.

2006. *The Development of Plato's Political Theory*, 2nd ed. Oxford.

Knight, K. 2007. *Aristotelian Philosophy: Ethics and Politics from Aristotle to MacIntyre*. Cambridge.

Konstan, D. 1997. *Friendship in the Classical World*. Cambridge.

Korsgaard, C. 1983. 'Two Distinctions in Goodness', *Philosophical Review* 92.2, 169–95.

2008. *The Constitution of Agency.* Oxford.

2009. *Self-Constitution: Agency, Identity, and Integrity.* Oxford.

Kosman, L. A. 1980. 'Being Properly Affected: Virtues and Feelings in Aristotle's Ethics', in Rorty 1980, 103–16.

Kraut, R. 1976. 'Aristotle on Choosing Virtue for Itself', *Archiv für Geschichte der Philosophie* 58, 223–39.

1979. 'Two Conceptions of Happiness', *Philosophical Review* 88, 167–97.

1989. *Aristotle on the Human Good.* Princeton, NJ.

1996. 'Aristotle on Method and Moral Education', in Jyl Gentzler (ed.), *Method in Ancient Philosophy.* Oxford, 271–90.

1997. *Aristotle: Politics Books VII and VIII.* Oxford.

2002. *Aristotle: Political Philosophy.* Oxford.

2006a. *The Blackwell Guide to Aristotle's Nicomachean Ethics.* Oxford.

2006b. 'How to Justify Ethical Propositions: Aristotle's Method', in Kraut 2006a, 76–95.

2006c. 'Doing without Morality: Reflections on the Meaning of *Dein* in the *Nicomachean Ethics*', *Oxford Studies in Ancient Philosophy* 30, 169–200.

2013. 'Aristotle and Rawls on the Common Good', in Deslauriers and Destrée 2013, 350–74.

Kullmann, W. 1991. 'Man as a Political Animal in Aristotle', in Keyt and Miller 1991, 94–117.

Lane, M. 2013. 'Claims to Rule: The Case of the Multitude', in Deslauriers and Destrée 2013, 247–74.

Lawrence, G. 1997. 'Nonaggregatability, Inclusiveness, and the Theory of Focal Value: "*Nicomachean Ethics*" I.7.1097b16-20', *Phronesis* 42.132–76.

2001. 'The Function of the Function Argument', *Ancient Philosophy* 21.2, 445–75

2006. 'Human Good and Human Function', in Kraut 2006b, 37–75.

Lear, J. 1988. *Aristotle: the Desire to Understand.* Cambridge.

Lebar, M. 2013. *The Value of Living Well.* Oxford.

Lebar, M. and Goldberg, N. 2012. 'Psychological Eudaimonism and Radical Interpretation in Greek Ethics', *Oxford Studies in Ancient Philosophy*, supplementary volume, 287–319.

Lennox, J. G. 1987. 'Kinds, Forms of Kinds, and the More and Less in Aristotle's Biology', in Gotthelf and Lennox 1987, 339–59.

2001a. *Aristotle's Philosophy of Biology.* Cambridge.

2001b. 'Material and Formal Natures in Aristotle's *De Partibus Animalium*', in Lennox 2001a, 182–204.

2001c. 'Nature Does Nothing in Vain … ', in Lennox 2001a, 205–23.

Lennox, J. G. and Bolton, R. (eds.). 2010. *Being, Nature, and Life in Aristotle: Essays in Honor of Alan Gotthelf.* Cambridge.

Leunissen, M. 2010. *Explanation and Teleology in Aristotle's Science of Nature.* Cambridge.

(forthcoming). 'Biology and Teleology in Aristotle's Account of the City', in J. Rocca (ed.), *Teleology in the Ancient World: The Dispensation of Nature.* Cambridge.

Lindsay, T. K. 1991. 'The "God-Like Man" versus the "Best Laws": Politics and Religion in Aristotle's *Politics*', *Review of Politics* 53, 488–509.

Lockwood, T. 2003. 'Justice in Aristotle's Household and City', *Polis* 20.1–2, 1–21.

2007. 'Is Natural Slavery Beneficial?', *Journal of the History of Philosophy* 45.2, 207–21.

Long, R. T. 1996. 'Aristotle's Conception of Freedom', *Review of Metaphysics* 49.4, 775–802.

2005. 'Aristotle's Egalitarian Utopia: The *Polis Kat' Euchen*', in H. H. Hansen (ed.), *The Imaginary Polis*. Copenhagen, 164–95.

Long, R. T. and Machan, T. R. (eds.). 2008. *Anarchism/Minarchism: Is a Government Part of a Free Country?* Burlington, VT.

Lord, C. 1982. *Education and Culture in the Political Thought of Aristotle*. Ithaca, NY.

(trans.). 1984. *Aristotle: The Politics*. Chicago.

(trans.). 2013. *Aristotle: The Politics*, 2nd ed. Chicago.

Lord, C. and O'Connor, D. K., eds. 1991. *Essays on the Foundations of Aristotelian Political Science*. Berkeley, CA.

Mack, E. 1989. 'Moral Individualism: Agent-Relativity and Deontic Restraints', *Social Philosophy and Policy* 7.1, 81–111.

MacIntyre, A. 1971. *Against the Self-Images of the Age*. London.

1984. *After Virtue*, 2nd ed. South Bend, IN.

1988. *Whose Justice? Which Rationality?* South Bend, IN.

1998. *Dependent Rational Animals*. Chicago.

2006a. *Ethics and Politics: Selected Essays*, vol. 2. Cambridge.

2006b. 'Three Perspectives on Marxism: 1953, 1968, 1995', in MacIntyre 2006, 145–58.

Martin, C. 2004. 'The Fact/Value Distinction', in D. S. Oderberg and T. D. J. Chappell, *Human Values*. London, 52–69.

Matthews, G. B. 1986. 'Gender and Essence in Aristotle', in J. L. Thompson (ed.), *Women and Philosophy*. Supplement to *Australasian Journal of Philosophy* 64, 16–25.

Mayhew, R. 1995. 'Aristotle on the Self-Sufficiency of the City', *History of Political Thought* 16.4, 488–502.

1997. 'Part and Whole in Aristotle's Political Philosophy', *Journal of Ethics* 1.4, 325–40.

2004. *The Female in Aristotle's Biology*. Chicago.

2009. 'Rulers and Ruled', in Anagnostopoulos 2009, 526–39.

Meier, C. 1980. *Die Entstehung des Politischen bei den Griechen*. Frankfurt.

Meikle, S. 1995. *Aristotle's Economic Thought*. Oxford.

Meyer, S. S. 2011. 'Living for the Sake of An Ultimate End', in Miller 2011, 47–65.

Miller, J. 1998. 'Aristotle's Paradox of Monarchy and the Biographical Tradition', *History of Political Thought* 19.14, 501–16.

(ed.). 2011. *Aristotle's Nicomachean Ethics: A Critical Guide*. Cambridge.

Miller, F. D. 1995. *Nature, Justice, and Rights in Aristotle's Politics*. Oxford.

1996. 'Aristotle and the Origins of Natural Rights', *Review of Metaphysics* 49.4, 873–907.

2000. 'Naturalism', in Rowe and Schofield 2000, 321–65.

2002. 'Aristotelian Autonomy', in Tessitore 2002, 375–402.

2007. 'Aristotelian Statecraft and Modern Politics', in Goodman and Talisse 2007, 13–31.

Modrak, D. K. 1993. 'Aristotle: Women, Deliberation, and Nature', in B.-A. Bar On (ed.), *Engendering Origins: Critical Feminist Readings of Plato and Aristotle*. New York, 207–22.

Morrell, K. 2012. *Organization, Society and Politics: An Aristotelian Perspective*. New York.

Morrison, D. 1999. 'Aristotle's Definition of Citizenship: A Problem and Some Solutions', *History of Philosophy Quarterly* 16.2, 143–65.

2001. 'Politics as a Vocation According to Aristotle', *History of Political Thought* 22, 221–41.

2013. 'The common good', in Deslauriers and Destrée 2013, 176–98.

Moss, J. 2010. 'Aristotle's Non-Trivial, Non-Insane View That Everyone Always Desires Things under the Guise of the Good', in S. Tenenbaum (ed.), *Desire, Practical Reason, and the Good*, 65–81.

Mulgan, R. G. 1974. 'A Note on Aristotle's Absolute Ruler', *Phronesis* 19.1, 66–9.

1977. *Aristotle's Political Theory*. Oxford.

1990. 'Aristotle and the Value of Political Participation', *Political Theory* 18, 192–215.

1991. 'Aristotle's Analysis of Oligarchy and Democracy', in Keyt and Miller 1991, 307–22.

1994. 'Aristotle and the Political Role of Women', *History of Political Thought* 15, 179–202.

2002. 'Nature, Custom and Reason as the Explanatory and Practical Principles of Aristotelian Political Science,' *The Review of Politics* 64, 469–95.

'Nature, Custom, and Reason as the Explanatory and Practical Principles of Aristotelian Political Science', *The Review of Politics* 64, 469–95.

Murphy, J. B. 1993. *The Moral Economy of Labor: Aristotelian Themes in Economic Theory*. New Haven, CT.

Murphy, M. C. 2001. *Natural Law and Practical Rationality*. Cambridge.

2003. *Alasdair MacIntyre*. Cambridge.

2006. *Natural Law in Jurisprudence and Political Philosophy*. Cambridge.

Nagle, D. B. 2006. *The Household as Foundation of Aristotle's Polis*. Cambridge.

Nederman, C. J. 1994. 'The Puzzle of the Political Animal: Nature and Artifice in Aristotle's Political Theory', *Review of Politics* 56, 283–304.

Newell, W. R. 1991. 'Superlative Virtue: the Problem of Monarchy in Aristotle's *Politics*', in Lord and O'Connor 1991, 191–211.

Newman, W. L. 1887–1902. *The Politics of Aristotle*, text, intro., notes, critical and explanatory, 4 vols. Oxford.

Nichols, M. 1992. *Citizens and Statesmen*. Lanham, MD.

Nozick, R. 1974. *Anarchy, State, and Utopia*. New York.

Nussbaum, M. C. 1980. 'Shame, Separateness, and Political Unity', in Rorty 1980, 395–436.

1986. *The Fragility of Goodness.* Cambridge.

1990a. 'Nature, Function, and Capability: Aristotle on Political Distribution', in Patzig 1990, 153–87.

1990b. 'Aristotelian Social Democracy', in R. B. Douglas, G. M. Mara, and H. S. Richardson (eds.), *Liberalism and the Good.* London, 203–52.

1990c. 'The Discernment of Perception: an Aristotelian Conception of Private and Public Rationality', in Nussbaum 1990d, 54–105.

1990d. *Love's Knowledge: Essays on Philosophy and Literature.* Oxford.

1995a. 'Objectification', *Philosophy and Public Affairs* 24.4, 249–91.

1995b. 'Aristotle on Human Nature and the Foundations of Ethics', in J. E. J. Altham and R. Harrison (eds.), *World, Mind, and Ethics: Essays on the Ethical Philosophy of Bernard Williams.* Cambridge, 86–131.

1998. 'Aristotle, Feminism, and Needs for Functioning', in Freeland 1998, 248–59.

2000. 'Aristotle, politics, and human capabilities: A Response to Antony, Arneson, Charlesworth, and Mulgan', *Ethics* 111.1, 102–40.

2006. *Frontiers of Justice: Disability, Nationality, Species Membership.* Cambridge, MA.

Nussbaum, M. C. and Rorty, A. O. 1992. *Essays on Aristotle's De Anima.* Oxford.

Ober, J. 1989. *Mass and Elite in Democratic Athens.* Princeton, NJ.

1996a. *The Athenian Revolution.* Princeton, NJ.

1996b. 'The Polis as a Society: Aristotle, John Rawls, and the Athenian Social Contract', in Ober 1996a, 161–87.

1996c. 'The Nature of Athenian Democracy', in Ober 1996a, 107–22.

1998. *Political Dissent in Democratic Athens: Intellectual Critics of Popular Rule.* Princeton, NJ.

2010. 'Wealthy Hellas', *Transactions of the American Philological Association* 140.2, 241–86.

Ober, J. and Hedrick, C. (eds.). 1996. *Dēmokratia: A Conversation on Democracies, Ancient and Modern.* Princeton, NJ.

O'Connor, D. K. 1990. 'Two Ideals of Friendship', *History of Philosophy Quarterly* 7.2, 109–22.

1991. 'The Aetiology of Justice', in Lord and O'Connor 1991, 136–64.

O'Meara, D. J. 1981. *Studies in Aristotle.* Washington, DC.

Ostwald, M. 1969. *Nomos and the Beginnings of the Athenian Democracy.* Oxford.

1993. 'Shares and Rights: "Citizenship" Greek Style and American Style', in Ober and Hedrick 1996, 49–62.

2009a. *Language and History in Ancient Greek Culture.* Philadelphia.

2009b, 'Peace and War in Plato and Aristotle', in Ostwald 2009a, 69–84.

Owen, G. E. L. 1960. 'Logic and Metaphysics in Some Earlier Works of Aristotle', in I. During and G. E. L. Owen (eds.), *Plato and Aristotle in the Mid-fourth Century.* Gothenburg, 163–90.

1961. '*Tithenai Ta Phainomena*', in S. Mansion (ed.), *Aristote et les problemes de methode.* Louvain. Reprinted in Owen 1986.

1986. *Logic, Science, and Dialectic.* Ithaca, NY.

Pagden, A. and Lawrance, J. (eds.). 1991. *Vitoria: Political Writings.* Cambridge.

Pakaluk, M. 1998. *Aristotle: Nicomachean Ethics Books VIII and IX.* Oxford.

2005. *Aristotle's Nicomachean Ethics: An Introduction.* Cambridge.

Pangle, T. L. 2013. *Aristotle's Teaching in the Politics.* Chicago.

Pangle, T. L. and Tarcov, N. 1987. 'Epilogue: Leo Strauss and the History of Political Philosophy', in Leo Strauss and Joseph Cropsey (eds.), *History of Political Philosophy,* 3rd ed. Chicago.

Patzig, G. 1990. *Aristoteles' 'Politik': Akten des XI. Symposium Aristotelicum 1987.* Goettingen.

Pears, D. 1978. 'Aristotle's Analysis of Courage', *Midwest Studies in Philosophy* 3, 273–85.

1980. 'Courage as a Mean', in Rorty 1980, 171–88.

Pearson, G. 2012. *Aristotle on Desire.* Cambridge.

Pocock, J. G. A. 1989. *Politics, Language, and Time: Essays on Political Thought and History.* Chicago.

Polansky, R. 1991. 'Aristotle on Political Change', in Keyt and Miller 1991, 322–45.

(ed.). 2014a. *The Cambridge Companion to Aristotle's Nicomachean Ethics.* Cambridge.

2014b. 'Giving Justice Its Due', in Polansky 2014a, 151–79.

Pomeroy, S. B. 1994. *Xenophon, Oeconomicus: A Social and Historical Commentary.* Oxford.

Price, A. W. 1989. *Love and Friendship in Plato and Aristotle.* Oxford.

Quinn, W. 1993. *Morality and Action.* Cambridge.

Rasmussen, D. B. 1999. 'Human Flourishing and the Appeal to Nature', *Social Philosophy and Policy* 16.1, 1–43.

Rasmussen, D. B. and Den Uyl, D. J. 2005. *Norms of Liberty.* Philadelphia.

Raz, J. 1986. *The Morality of Freedom.* Oxford.

Reeve, C. D. C. (trans.). 1998. *Aristotle: Politics.* Indianapolis, IN.

2009. 'The Naturalness of the Polis in Aristotle', in Anagnostopoulos 2009, 512–25.

2012. *Action, Contemplation, and Happiness: An Essay on Aristotle.* Cambridge, MA.

2013. *Aristotle on Practical Wisdom: Nicomachean Ethics VI.* Cambridge, MA.

Rhodes, P. J. 1981. *A Commentary on the Aristotelian Athenaion Politeia.* Oxford.

Richardson Lear, G. 2004. *Happy Lives and the Highest Good.* Princeton, NJ.

Riesbeck, D. J. 2015. 'Aristotle on the Politics of Marriage: Marital Rule in the *Politics*', *Classical Quarterly* 65.1, 134–52.

(2016). 'The Unity of Aristotle's Theory of Constitutions', *Apeiron* 49.1, 93–125.

Roberts, J. 2000. 'Justice and the Polis', in Rowe and Schofield 2000, 344–65.

2009. 'Excellences of the Citizen and of the Individual', in Anagnostopoulos 2009, 555–65.

Robinson, R. 1962. *Aristotle: Politics Books III–IV.* Oxford.

Rorty, A. (ed.). 1980. *Essays on Aristotle's Ethics.* Berkeley, CA.

Rosler, A. 2005. *Political Authority and Obligation in Aristotle.* Oxford.

2013. 'Civic Virtue: Citizenship, Ostracism, and War', in Deslauriers and Destrée 2013, 144–75.

Rowe, C. 1971. *The Eudemian and Nicomachean Ethics: A Study in the Development of Aristotle's Thought*. Cambridge.

1991. 'Aims and Methods in Aristotle's *Politics*', in Keyt and Miller 1991, 57–74.

2000. 'Aristotelian Constitutions', in Rowe and Schofield 2000, 366–89.

2007. *Plato and the Art of Philosophical Writing*. Cambridge.

Rowe, C. and Schofield, M. (eds.) 2000. *The Cambridge History of Greek and Roman Political Thought*. Cambridge.

Salkever, S. 1990. *Finding the Mean*. Princeton, NJ.

Sandel, M. 1998. *Liberalism and the Limits of Justice,* 2nd ed. Cambridge.

Saunders, T. 1995. *Aristotle: Politics Books I and II*. Oxford.

Saxonhouse, A. 1985. *Women in the History of Political Thought*. New York.

Schofield, M. 1990. 'Ideology and Philosophy in Aristotle's Theory of Slavery', with commentary by C. H. Kahn, in Patzig 1990, 1–31.

1999a. 'Political Friendship and the Ideology of Reciprocity', in Schofield 1999d, 82–99.

1999b. 'Equality and Hierarchy in Aristotle's Political Thought', in Schofield 1999d, 100–14.

1999c. 'Sharing in the Constitution', in Schofield 1999d, 141–59.

1999d. *Saving the City; Philosopher-Kings and Other Classical Paradigms*. London.

1999e. 'Ideology and Philosophy in Aristotle's Theory of Slavery', with appendices, in Schofield 1999d, 115–40.

1999f. 'The Disappearing Philosopher King', in Schofield 1999d, 31–50.

2000. 'Aristotle: An Introduction', in Rowe and Schofield 2000, 310–20.

Schollmeier, P. 2003. 'Aristotle and Women', *Polis* 20, 26–46.

Schütrumpf, E. 1991–2005. *Aristoteles "Politik"*, 4 vols. Berlin.

Seeskin, K. 2000. *Searching for a Distant God: The Legacy of Maimonides*. Oxford.

Sher, G. 1997. *Beyond Neutrality: Perfectionism and Politics*. Cambridge.

Shields, C. 1999. *Order in Multiplicity*. Oxford.

Simpson, P. L. P. 1994. 'Liberalism, State, and Community', *Critical Review* 8.2, 159–73.

1997. *The Politics of Aristotle*. Translated, with introduction, commentary, and notes. Chapel Hill, NC.

1998. *A Philosophical Commentary on the Politics of Aristotle*. Chapel Hill, NC.

2001. 'Aristotle's Defensible Defense of Slavery', *Hypnos* 7, 228–38.

2007. 'Aristotle's *Regime of the Americans*', in Goodman and Talisse 2007, 109–28.

Skinner, Q. 2002a. *Visions of Politics, Vol. 1: Regarding Method*. Cambridge.

2002b. 'Interpretation, Rationality, and Truth', in Skinner 2002a, 27–56.

2002c. 'Motives, Intentions, and Interpretation', in Skinner 2002a, 90–102.

Smith, N. D. 1991. 'Aristotle's Theory of Natural Slavery', in Keyt and Miller 1991, 142–55.

Stalley, R. P. 1991. 'Aristotle's Criticism of Plato's *Republic*', in Keyt and Miller 1991, 275–83.

Stern-Gillet, S. 1995. *Aristotle's Philosophy of Friendship*. Albany, NY.

Stewart, J. A. 1892. *Notes on the 'Nicomachean Ethics' of Aristotle*, 2 vols. Oxford.

Strauss, L. 1952. *Persecution and the Art of Writing*. Chicago.

    1953. *Natural Right and History*. Chicago.

    1963. *On Tyranny*, rev. ed. Ithaca, NY.

    1964. *The City and Man*. Chicago.

Taylor, C. 1985. *Philosophical Papers, Vol. 2: Philosophy and the Human Sciences*. Cambridge.

    1989. *Sources of the Self*. Harvard, Cambridge, MA.

Tessitore, A. (ed.), 2002. *Aristotle and Modern Politics: The Persistence of Political Philosophy*. South Bend, IN.

Thompson, M. 2008. *Life and Action: Elementary Structures of Practice and Practical Thought*. Cambridge, MA.

Tress, D. 1997. 'Aristotle's Child: Development through *Genesis, Oikos*, and *Polis*', *Ancient Philosophy* 17, 63–84.

Trott, A. M. 2013. *Aristotle on the Nature of Community*. New York.

Vander Waerdt, P. A. 1985. 'Kingship and Philosophy in Aristotle's Best Regime', *Phronesis* 30, 249–73.

Van Staveren, I. 2001. *The Values of Economics: An Aristotelian Perspective*. New York.

Vlassopoulos, K. 2007. *Unthinking the Greek Polis: Ancient Greek History Beyond Eurocentrism*. Cambridge.

Vlastos, G. 1973a. *Platonic Studies*. Princeton, NJ.

    1973b. 'ΙΣΟΝΟΜΙΑ ΠΟΛΙΤΙΚΗ', in Vlastos 1973a, 164–203.

    1973c. 'The Individual as Object of Love in Plato', in Vlastos 1973a, 3–42.

Waldron, J. 1995. 'The Wisdom of the Multitude', *Political Theory* 23, 563–84.

Wallach, J. R. 1992. 'Contemporary Aristotelianism', *Political Theory* 20.4, 613–41.

Ward, J. K. 1995. 'Focal Reference in Aristotle's Account of Friendship, *Eudemian Ethics* vii 2', *Apeiron* 28, 183–205.

    2002. '*Ethnos* in the *Politics*: Aristotle and Race', in J. K. Ward and T. L. Lott (eds.), *Philosophers on Race: Critical Essays*. Oxford, 14–37.

    2008. *Aristotle on Homonymy: Dialectic and Science*. Cambridge.

Weber, M. 1946. 'Politics as a Vocation', in M. Weber, H. Gerth, and C. W. Mills (eds.), *From Max Weber: Essays in Sociology*. New York, 77–128.

White, S. A. 1992. *Sovereign Virtue: Aristotle on the relation between happiness and prosperity*. Stanford, CA.

Whiting, J. 1988. 'Aristotle's Function Argument: A Defense', *Ancient Philosophy* 8, 33–48.

    2002. '*Eudaimonia*, External Results, and Choosing Actions for Themselves,' *Philosophy and Phenomenological Research* 65, 270–90.

Whitlock-Blundell, M. 1989. *Helping Friends and Harming Enemies: A Study in Sophocles and Greek Ethics*. Oxford.

Wiggins, D. 1975. 'Deliberation and Practical Reason', *Proceedings of the Aristotelian Society* 76, 29–51.

Wilkes, K. V. 1980. 'The Good Man and the Good for Man in Aristotle's Ethics', in Rorty 1980, 341–58.

Williams, B. 1980. 'Justice as a Virtue', in Rorty 1980, 189–200.

1985. *Ethics and the Limits of Philosophy*. Cambridge, MA.

Witt, C. 2011. *The Metaphysics of Gender*. Oxford.

Woodruff, P. 2005. *First Democracy: The Challenge of an Ancient Idea*. Oxford.

Wood, E. M. and Wood, N. 1978. *Class Ideology and Ancient Political Theory: Socrates, Plato, and Aristotle in Social Context*. Oxford.

Wood, E. M. 1996. 'Demos versus "We, the People": Freedom and Democracy Ancient and Modern', in Ober and Hedrick 1996, 121–38.

Woods, M. 1992. *Aristotle's Eudemian Ethics: Books I, II, and VIII*. Oxford.

Yack, B. 1993. *The Problems of a Political Animal: Community, Justice, and Conflict in Aristotelian Political Thought*. Berkeley, CA.

Young, M. A. 2005. *Negotiating the Good Life: Aristotle and the Civil Society*. Burlington, VT.

Zingano, M. 2013. 'Natural, Ethical, and Political Justice', in Deslauriers and Destrée 2013, 199–222.

2015. 'The Conceptual Unity of Friendship in the *Eudemian* and the *Nicomachean Ethics*', *Apeiron* 48.2, 195–219.

Zoepffel, R. 2006. *Aristoteles Oikonomika: Schriften zu Hauswirtschaft und Finanzwesen*. Berlin.

Index

Abydus, 219, 223
Accountability, 233, 241, 242. *See also*, Audits
Action (*praxis*)
  aim of, 87–9, 126, 129, 130, 158, 159, 168–71, 284, 285
  directing one's own, *see* Self-Direction
  directing another's, 1, 12, 72, 78, 138–42, 149–51, 164, 165, 175, 176, 215, 216, 218, 247
  as essential to happiness, 36, 168, 171, 284
  just or fair, 93, 118, 134, 199, 208
  lawful, 117, 282
  obedient, 17, 140, 147, 150, 211, 256
  political, 1, 3, 36, 73, 118, 142, 159, 167, 172, 183, 234, 285, 289
  reasonable or rational, 17, 88–90, 99, 102, 109, 110, 129, 147, 161, 171, 247, 284
  shared or communal, 49, 54, 55, 59, 138, 152, 153, 251, 285, 289
  voluntary, 86, 89, 139, 211, 242, 245–7, 257
  virtuous, 84, 88, 89, 117, 165, 168–74, 209, 256, 284
  See also, Agent(s), rational
Activity, political, *see* Political participation
Adkins, Arthur W. H., 32, 36, 67, 164
Agent(s), rational, 18, 39, 61, 74, 77–9, 86–8, 109–12, 133, 143, 144, 164, 165, 170, 171, 208, 209, 245, 247, 289. *See also*, Human being, as a rational animal
Alcibiades, 204
Alliance
  community of exchange and, 56, 105, 116–18, 130
  forming and dissolving, 215
  military or political, 12, 59, 98
  as the purview of officials, 215
Alexander of Macedon, 43
Alternation, 1, 146, 147, 154, 155, 237, 249–51, 253, 268. *See also*, Rule, "in turn"
Amasis, 146
Antiphanes, 266
Antisthenes, 260, 261, 267

Approximation, 26, 94, 95, 255, 274, 276, 280
Aquinas, St. Thomas, 194
Archelaus of Macedon, 278
Arendt, Hannah, 3, 32, 141, 174
Aristocracy, 6, 7, 9, 13, 19, 23, 27, 35, 40–2, 178, 180, 182, 184, 186, 192, 198, 217–21, 228–30, 236, 237, 239, 240, 257, 259, 264, 272, 276, 277
Aristophanes, 135, 177
Armies, 83, 94, 150, 151, 207, 219, 226, 249. *See also*, Generals and generalship
Art, *see* Craft
Artisans (*banausoi*), 188–94
Assembly, 53, 119, 135–7, 150, 177, 204, 209, 213, 215–18, 220, 227, 251
Athens, 135–6, 184, 204, 211, 215, 219, 227, 230–1, 242
Athletic competition, *see* Competition
Audits, 215, 218–20, 223, 225, 230–3, 239, 242
Authoritative element (*to kurion*), 17, 198, 199, 216, 217, 221, 222, 229, 230
Authority
  constrained by law or constitution, 24, 26, 30, 119, 131, 246, 253–8, 278, 282
  degrees of, 26, 178, 182, 212–17, 220, 221, 223–31, 235, 236. *See also*, Citizenship and degrees of authority
  derivative or delegated, 149–52, 215, 216, 218, 239, 240, 251
  to direct actions of others, 142, 144, 149, 150, 215–17. *See also*, Action (*praxis*)
  distribution of, *see* Distributive justice
  hierarchy of, 46, 146, 164, 165, 178, 214–17, 220, 224, 236, 238, 251, 253, 267, 288
  heterogeneity of, 1, 97, 133, 140, 141
  kingly, 25, 26, 28–30, 39, 40, 105, 238–41, 248, 253–69, 273, 278, 283
  relation to forms of community, 1, 13, 39, 40, 46, 47, 103–5, 133, 142–4, 147–9, 152–5, 206

Authority (*cont.*)
  shared, 1, 9, 13, 147, 149, 154, 155, 199, 214,
    216, 221, 226, 230, 231, 288
  as translation of *kurion*, 17

banausoi, see Artisans
Barbarians, 24–26, 99, 115, 116, 123, 128, 243, 254
Biondi Khan, Carrie-Ann, 7, 8, 33, 41, 199–201
Broadie, Sarah, 32, 129, 143, 182–3, 284

Cammack, Daniela, ix, 20, 21, 285
Charles, David, 15, 16, 234
Cherry, Kevin M., 32, 109, 281–4
Child or children, 1, 12, 39, 40, 49, 52, 62, 76,
  77, 82, 85, 90, 94, 100–7, 133, 139, 142–5,
  148–53, 155, 161, 175, 176, 187, 197, 200,
  209, 210, 224, 252, 270, 272
Citizenship
  broad notion of, 7, 41, 185–8, 194, 195, 200,
    210, 226
  as coextensive with share in rule, 7, 13, 33, 34,
    37, 41, 156, 179–82, 184, 185, 187, 189, 194,
    198, 201, 204, 212, 217, 224, 226, 228, 236,
    237, 252
  and the common good, 20, 21, 37, 41, 56,
    183, 184, 186, 187, 194–205, 209–11, 284,
    286, 289
  and degrees of authority, 200, 212–17, 220,
    221, 223, 225, 227–30, 235, 236, 239, 240
  and justice, *see* Distributive justice
  nature of or definition of, 7, 13, 17, 37, 41, 42,
    135–7, 156, 160–2, 179, 181, 182, 184–205,
    212, 220, 223–8
  and political activity, *see* Political participation
  and the ruling body, *see* Ruling body
    (*politeuma*)
  second-class, *see* Second-class citizens
  value of, 12, 33–7, 157–60, 165, 166, 236, 288
City (*polis*)
  benefit for the, 17, 19, 23, 26, 28, 170, 193,
    201–4, 230, 267
  concept of, 31, 38, 46, 271
  goal of or aim of, 2, 12, 31, 32, 36, 37, 46,
    87, 98, 103, 107, 114, 117, 121, 122, 126,
    130–2, 157–61, 172, 174, 190, 288. *See also,*
    Happiness (*eudaimonia*)
  governing or managing the, 21, 22, 25, 26,
    29, 36, 97, 98, 229, 240, 268, 274. *See also,*
    Ruling body (*politeuma*)
  and household, 4, 12, 14, 39–42, 47, 49, 85,
    97–9, 103, 104, 109, 113, 116, 123, 210,
    237, 270–2
  just, 196, 204–6, 210
  law(s) of, 114, 117–20, 139, 211, 215, 217, 227
  "by nature", 2, 31, 109–14, 122, 123, 154

part(s) of the, 31, 32, 39, 50, 113, 161, 214–16,
  220, 249, 260, 265–9
ruling the, *see* Rule
self-sufficiency of, *see* Self-sufficiency
as translation of polis, 2
and village, 103–9, 113, 115, 116, 121, 123, 124,
  131, 132
  See also, Citizenship
  See also, Constitution
  See also, Political community
Coercion, 117, 119, 141, 177, 198, 199, 212, 241–7,
  267, 274, 277
Colonies and colonization, 43, 104
Collins, Susan D.,8, 32, 33, 43, 137, 164, 174, 184,
  185, 261, 267, 275
Commodities, 49, 53, 55, 57, 115, 120, 126
Commensurability, 55, 95, 209, 237, 238, 261–5
Common Good
  as the aim of correct constitutions, 23, 41, 42,
    131, 141, 163, 180–3, 196, 199, 201, 202, 241,
    243, 244, 246, 247, 254, 268, 276, 281
  and citizens, *see* Citizenship
  through cooperation, 1, 20, 21, 56, 80, 86–9,
    91, 97, 98, 100, 106, 131, 172, 177, 206, 208,
    233, 267, 289
  and justice, 2, 11, 23, 28, 84–90, 121, 157, 177,
    179–81, 196, 197, 201, 202, 206, 208, 210,
    233, 243, 257, 260, 267, 280
  and kingship, *see* Kingship promotes the
    common good
  in relation to law or authority, 5–6, 117, 120,
    131, 177, 246, 254, 257, 263, 282
  scope of, *see* Citizenship and the
    common good
Community (*koinōnia*)
  aim of, 87, 97–103, 105, 106, 160, 161, 176
  being part of a, 38, 49–51, 103, 160, 161
  dissolution of, 8, 9, 38, 40, 60, 86, 91
  of exchange, 49, 52–7, 82, 86–8, 90, 105,
    116–18, 130, 139, 140. *See also,* Exchange
    of goods
  and friendship, 11, 45, 46, 57–60, 65, 73–8,
    80–3, 91–3, 95, 96, 101, 140, 271, 272
  household, *see* Household
  idea of, 1, 38, 39, 45–52, 58, 281
  and justice, 11, 45, 53, 57, 58, 74, 80–93, 95,
    96, 133, 148, 205, 206, 208
  as sharing goods in common, 48–52, 55, 58,
    81–6, 91, 96, 97, 160, 161, 207, 208. *See also,*
    Common good
  See also, Political Community
Communitarianism, 3, 35, 173
Competition, 21, 86, 87, 91, 92
Consent, 25, 30, 139, 206, 207, 212, 237, 239–48,
  255, 269, 272, 274, 288, 289

Index Locorum